ROUTLEDGE LIBRARY EDITIONS: WORK & SOCIETY

Volume 11

I0093902

SALARIES IN THE PUBLIC SERVICES IN ENGLAND AND WALES

SALARIES IN
THE PUBLIC SERVICES
IN ENGLAND AND WALES

HILDA R. KAHN

Routledge
Taylor & Francis Group
LONDON AND NEW YORK

First published in 1962 by George Allen & Unwin Ltd.

This edition first published in 2024
by Routledge
4 Park Square, Milton Park, Abingdon, Oxon OX14 4RN

and by Routledge
605 Third Avenue, New York, NY 10158

Routledge is an imprint of the Taylor & Francis Group, an informa business

British Library Cataloguing in Publication Data
A catalogue record for this book is available from the British Library

ISBN: 978-1-032-80236-7 (Set)
ISBN: 978-1-032-81711-8 (Volume 11) (hbk)
ISBN: 978-1-032-81712-5 (Volume 11) (pbk)
ISBN: 978-1-003-50101-5 (Volume 11) (ebk)

DOI: 10.4324/9781003501015

Publisher's Note
The publisher has gone to great lengths to ensure the quality of this reprint but points out that some imperfections in the original copies may be apparent.

Disclaimer
The publisher has made every effort to trace copyright holders and would welcome correspondence from those they have been unable to trace.

SALARIES IN
THE PUBLIC SERVICES
IN ENGLAND AND WALES

by Hilda R. Kahn

B.Sc.(Econ.), Ph.D.
Lecturer in Social Administration, University of Hull

PREFACE BY
THE BARONESS WOOTTON
OF ABINGER

London

GEORGE ALLEN AND UNWIN LTD

FIRST PUBLISHED IN 1962

To My Parents

Preface

Some ten years ago Hilda Kahn undertook to help me by an investigation into remuneration in the public services which was peripheral to the thesis of my book on *The Social Foundations of Wage Policy*. At that time neither of us, I think, had any idea of how far her researches would lead. As often happens, the subject opened up into endless fascinating ramifications, and the final upshot is the present volume.

Although much of the material in this book relates to an earlier date, its appearance is nevertheless timely. In recent years the relationship between the rates of pay prevailing in the public services and those in industry and the professions generally has become a matter of acute controversy. In 1955 the Royal Commission on the Civil Service took the view that scales of pay in that service should be closely related to those paid for comparable work in outside industry; and they recommended the establishment of a Civil Service Pay Research Unit charged with the duty of investigating in considerable detail just what jobs should be considered comparable to those of the various categories of Civil Servants, and just what was actually paid for them. With the advent, however, in 1962 of what purported to be an official 'Incomes Policy' the tables were turned, and private employers were (quite unsuccessfully) exhorted to imitate the Government's expressed determination to keep wage and salary advances to its own employees within a prescribed limit.

Whether as leaders or as followers, however, public employees always bulk large in the picture, since directly or indirectly the Government is much the biggest employer in the country. Yet, as Dr Kahn's researches show, within the vast body of persons employed in the Civil Service, the National Health Service and the Public Corporations, no consistent standards are applied, and no coherent wage and salary policy emerges. The picture is indeed one of extreme complexity. To quote only one of Dr Kahn's examples: in the first ten years of the National Health Service the ten Whitley Councils concerned published no less than 546 formal agreements.

Professor Parkinson, it would seem, must have had a hand in devising the scales of payment whose convolutions Dr Kahn has traced in these pages in all their intricacy. The material which she has assembled is unique in its scope and comprehensiveness, and it will, without doubt, prove invaluable, both to those who have to negotiate within the present system, and to anyone who is bold enough to try to bring order out of the present chaos.

BARBARA WOOTTON

Acknowledgments

This study could not have been undertaken but for the co-operation of some eighty organizations—employer, union and joint—concerned with the settlement, or some facet, of public service salaries. They have supplied source material of divers kinds, and have dealt with innumerable queries both orally and in writing. Space alone prevents a more individual acknowledgment, but it is with a deep sense of gratitude that I here pay tribute to both the quality and the quantity of the assistance I have received.

I should like to express my appreciation to the Editor of *The Manchester School of Economic and Social Studies* for permission to make use of the material in my article 'The Element of "Accident" in the National Salary Structure', which appeared in its May 1956 issue. I similarly wish to thank the Editor of the *Scottish Journal of Political Economy* for allowing me to draw on my paper 'The Distinction between Wages and Salaries' published in its June 1956 number, a revised and up-to-date version of which constitutes Chapter 19 of the present work.

I am very greatly indebted to Professor P. Sargant Florence for his kind and valuable help. For advice on particular sections/aspects I am much obliged to Mr H. Blum, Professor A. K. Cairncross, Professor T. E. Chester, Dr R. W. Davies, Mrs C. Fulop and Professor D. J. Robertson. I am most grateful also to Mr Philip Unwin, Director, Messrs George Allen & Unwin Ltd, for his courtesy and promptness. Last, but by no means least, I would record my very special thanks to Lady (Barbara) Wootton for her generous guidance over many years.

For the contents of the following pages, including all errors of fact or judgment, no one but myself is in any way responsible.

H.R.K.
London
November 1961

Contents

List of Tables

Notes to Tables

1. The tables show national, provincial or London salaries, according to whichever was recognized as the official standard in the field concerned.

2. Where remuneration differed for men and women, the tables contain that for men only, unless the occupation is predominantly female in which case women's rates are set out. *The text, likewise, must be taken to refer to male salaries only, except where women are specifically dealt with, or where it is indicated that there was no sex differentiation.* (Staff statistics include both sexes.)

3. *Scales* of salaries are given throughout, i.e. excluding overtime and other above-scale payments. This is of particular relevance in the case of Tables 1–10, since during 1947–56 the bulk of civil servants automatically qualified for some form of overtime pay. (*cf.* p. 312 *post.*)

4. The tables show the increases introduced for the grade as such; special 'assimilation' arrangements are not set out. Where no figure appears in the column of a table, that in the preceding column continued to apply.

5. Where the final increment was smaller than that for the scale as a whole, this is not specifically indicated. Where, in order to reach the maximum, the last increment was larger than the normal, this is mentioned in a footnote.

Introduction

In 1938 the national salary bill represented 30·1 per cent of all incomes from employment in the United Kingdom, though during the war this proportion fell somewhat.[1] Since then, however, salaries have gradually increased their share, and in 1960 accounted for 33·5 per cent of total UK income from employment.[2] Putting it another way, in 1960 salaries at £5,060 million were nearly three-fifths (58·6 per cent) as large as the total wages bill of £8,630 million.[3]

The present work is concerned with salaries in the public services of post-war England and Wales. This particular field was selected in an attempt to help fill a gap in the literature, for, their respectable size notwithstanding, salaries constitute a relatively neglected corner of the labour market. The further choice of the public sector was primarily prompted by the fact that the absence of any systematic review of its salary structure seemed an especially notable omission.

For purposes of this study, both the terms 'salaries' and 'public service' have been given a wide rather than a narrow definition. Thus certain groups are dealt with even though their status as between 'wages' and 'salaries' is somewhat debatable: Policemen and firemen were, after this survey had been begun, transferred from the salaries to the wages bill in the national income accounts, but we did not feel impelled thereby to drop them from these pages. Similarly, while the precise meaning of 'public service' is capable of different interpretations, the line has been drawn generously. Academic rewards, for example, are included although the universities—as distinct from their finances—are private, autonomous institutions. Again, salaries in the nationalized industries are covered, it appearing the most sensible course to take in remuneration in all those spheres of civil employment which, by reason of some measure of public accountability, belong to the public sector of the economy. It will be clear, however, that membership of the latter does not imply any inherent identity as between its component branches.

This investigation is formally confined to England and Wales, this being the highest common denominator of the various pay patterns, though many of the latter are equally applicable to Scotland, and

[1] In 1946 i.e. the corresponding proportion was 28·7 per cent.

[2] Central Statistical Office, *National Income and Expenditure* 1956 (HMSO 1956) Table 2 and *National Income and Expenditure* 1961 (HMSO 1961) Table 2. The figures relate to income before tax; those for 1960 are subject to revision.

[3] Comparing salaries directly with wages in fact gives a more accurate idea of their size, since 'total income from employment' also includes the pay of HM Forces and employers' contributions to national insurance, etc. and to superannuation schemes, etc. In the present context, employers' contributions should be added to wages and salaries but cannot, on the published figures, be broken down between them.

some to the whole of the United Kingdom. Within England and Wales, further, only fields of national dimensions are considered. Bodies restricted to a single locality are excluded, as are the numerous public boards, councils and commissions—largely of an advisory, regulatory or supervisory character—which now grace the periphery of Britain's system of public administration.

As to the time-span covered, the present work incorporates the substance of a thesis for which the author was awarded the degree of Doctor of Philosophy by the University of London, and in its original form was concerned with the early post-war period—more particularly the years 1946–51. Here it may be disclosed that, owing to the dimensions of the public sector and the large body of data to be sifted in respect of each of its limbs, the exercise has proved a fairly formidable undertaking; moreover, in view of other heavy commitments, the manuscript has undergone lengthy spells of cold storage both in the course of its initial genesis and prior to its revision for press. Finding it impracticable to bring up to date both the entire factual base of the study and its 'superstructure', the writer has opted for the following compromise for purposes of this book: As regards Part I, its sixty odd tables and related descriptive matter continue to be confined to the early post-war period; however, subsequent happenings of special interest or importance have been freely taken into account. As for Part II, while Chapter 18 *inter alia* comprises a number of detailed analyses based on figures operative in 1951, for the rest considerable attention has been paid to recent developments.

The broad plan of the book then is that Part I presents the 'vertical' picture for seventeen of the country's public services. For each field a short outline is given of set-up and negotiating machinery, of numbers employed and salary scales for the period indicated, as well as some account of the issues figuring in its pay history. As regards the scales themselves, due to their rich profusion the treatment is not exhaustive. In the case of the Civil and National Health Services, for instance, the inclusion of every single rate would not have been a feasible assignment; hence a selection of the more typical hierarchies has been made. Again, in order to reduce the manuscript to publishable proportions, details of all (except major) allowances, fringe benefits and service conditions have been omitted.

Part II represents the comparative and analytical part of the work, though to the writer's regret it is less extensive in the event than had originally been planned. Chapter 18 is devoted to salary structure with the contents of Part I viewed 'horizontally': Matters such as the basis of classes and grades, area differentials, the size of increments and the length of scales are investigated, while certain comparisons of cash prospects in the different services are made. Chapter 19 consists of a scrutiny of the distinction between wages and salaries. In Chapter 20 some of the problems of pay determination are considered, such as the role of the 'need' factor, what might be called the question of 'fairness versus economics', the difficulties of comparing posts and some of the implications of 'publicness'. A complete examination of the rationale of reward or of the determinants of salary levels has not, however, been attempted, though a hostage to fortune has been given by appending a section on the crucial—but (autumn 1961) *sub judice*—topic of a national wages policy. In Chapter 21, finally, some of the conclusions to which the study has led are drawn together; an effort has been made to relate both strictures and suggestions to the post-war situation as a whole.

PART I

Chapter 1

THE CIVIL SERVICE

'There is nowhere any authoritative or exhaustive definition of the Civil Service' wrote the Royal (Tomlin) Commission of 1929-31 and, in accordance with precedent, they adopted the following as a working basis:

'Those servants of the Crown, other than holders of political or judicial offices, who are employed in a civil capacity, and whose remuneration is paid wholly and directly out of monies voted by Parliament.'[1]

The Civil Service is that body of employees which carries out the policy of successive Governments. It does not include the members of the Armed Forces who—though servants of the Crown—are not employed in a civil capacity, nor does it extend to High Court judges who—though serving in a civil capacity—are not paid 'out of monies voted by Parliament'.[2] It also excludes the staffs of local authorities, nationalized industries and other public corporations.

While the term 'Civil Service' does not cover the public servants of the British Dominions or of the country's overseas dependencies, it does include the Foreign Service. Here, however, we are concerned with the Home Civil Service only, divided into more than a hundred departments and sub-departments, ranging from the National Gallery to such major bodies as the Board of Trade and Treasury. A general control over the Service is exercised by the latter, which in 1920 had conferred on it the power to make regulations for controlling the conduct of His Majesty's civil establishments and providing for the classification, remuneration and other conditions of service of all persons employed therein.[3] The Treasury is responsible for the annual presentation to Parliament of the Estimates for the Civil and Revenue

[1] *Royal Commission on the Civil Service*, Cmd. 3909 (HMSO 1931), paras. 8-9.
[2] Public expenditure is met either from moneys voted by Parliament in response to annual Estimates, or (as in the case of High Court judges) charged upon the Consolidated Fund, i.e. payable out of the Exchequer under statute without further parliamentary authority.
[3] *Tomlin Report*, op. cit., paras. 19-20.

Departments; it is out of these 'monies voted by Parliament' that civil servants' salaries are paid.[1]

The kinds of work performed by civil servants vary greatly and call for the employment of large numbers of very different groups of personnel. First, there are the two broad categories of industrial and non-industrial staff, which are treated entirely separately for purposes of pay and conditions of service. Industrial civil servants are to be found in ordnance factories, aircraft works, shipbuilding yards and so on. They comprise skilled and unskilled grades who belong to ordinary trade unions, with whom the Government have set up special negotiating machinery. As wage-earners they fall outside the scope of this study.

We are left with non-industrial staff who on 1 January 1951 numbered 675,083; this compares with 397,559 on 1 April 1939[2]—an indication of the vast changes that the Service has undergone. Non-industrial personnel is commonly divided into the staff groups shown opposite.

The administrative, executive, clerical, clerical assistant and typing grades are the basic classes of the Service, constituting a complete hierarchy in the clerico-administrative sphere and providing the backbone of the Civil Service pyramid. They owe their present structure to the Reorganization Committee of the Civil Service National Whitley Council, who issued their findings in 1920.[3]

The Inspectorate[4] is very small numerically. It comprises such groups as HM inspectors of schools and the factory inspectorate, but certain others—such as inspectors in the Inland Revenue—are differently classified. Among the messengerial grades[4] are porters, paper-keepers, cleaners as well as messengers; attendants and warders in museums are also in this group. The Post Office figure covers all those engaged on non-technical work in the Post Office[5]; as the latter is a very large employer and has a salary structure quite distinct from that of the rest of the Civil Service, we deal with it in a separate chapter.

[1] The Act by virtue of which Parliament took over the responsibility for the salaries of those employed in public offices was passed in 1816 (56 Geo. III, c. 46); it has been described as the statute which created the Civil Service: cf. E. W. Cohen, *The Growth of the British Civil Service*, 1780–1939 (Allen & Unwin, 1941), p. 20.

[2] *Digest of Civil Service Staff Statistics*, 1 *January* 1949–1 *January* 1950 and 1 *January* 1950–1 *January* 1951 (issued by Civil Service Central Staff Record, HM Treasury), Table I. The figures include the Foreign Service.

[3] *Report of the Joint Committee on the Organization, etc. of the Civil Service* (HMSO 1920).

[4] This category is not further considered.

[5] The figure for Post Office staffs i.e. does not include those in the Post Office Engineering Department.

NON-INDUSTRIAL CIVIL SERVANTS

ANALYSIS BY STAFF GROUPS AS AT 1 JANUARY 1951[1]

Staff group	No.
Administrative (Home)	3,056
Administrative (Foreign)	883
General executive	41,229
Other executive	27,733
General clerical	113,978
Other clerical	31,237
Clerical assistants, etc.	72,023
Typing	30,527
Inspectorate	4,970
Messengers, porters, etc.	41,190
Post Office staffs	202,114
Professional, scientific and technical I	23,932
Scientific and technical II	42,718
Ancillary technical	39,493
	675,083

[1] *Digest of Civil Service Staff Statistics*, 1 *January* 1950–1 *January* 1951, Table VIII. All figures in this and subsequent tables of civil service staff statistics include both whole- and part-time workers, each of the latter counting as $\frac{1}{2}$.

The professional, scientific and technical, etc. groups have greatly increased in number since pre-war days. 'Professional, scientific and technical I' comprises fully-fledged professionals in the scientific, legal and medical sphere; the 'works group' (architects, surveyors, civil engineers, etc.); and numerous miscellaneous classes— among them actuaries, statisticians, accountants and psychologists. 'Scientific and technical II' covers various types of draughtsmen, experimental officers and the technical classes; these are expected to have a technical, rather than a professional, training. The 'ancillary technical' group is composed of minor grades such as machine operators and drawing office assistants.

Departmental classes: Civil Service organization distinguishes between 'general service' or 'Treasury' classes on the one hand and 'departmental' classes on the other. The former are common to all Government departments; all their members have identical terms and conditions of employment, are centrally recruited and must have prescribed qualifications—determined by the Treasury—whatever the sector of the Service in which they will ultimately find a niche. Departmental classes are confined to one department, and have their own special grade structure and rates of pay.[1] This, it may be added, was the original pattern throughout the Service; it was only very slowly that general classes emerged to replace the earlier rigid departmentalism.[2]

A 'general service' pattern has, however, always been considered unsuitable for certain of the more specialized branches of the Service; hence departmental classes remain. These include (1951) the special departmental classes of HM inspectors of taxes in the Inland Revenue, the cadet grade in the Ministry of Labour and assistant postal controllers in the Post Office. Members of these must be of university degree standard, though there are other departmental classes at executive and clerical level, as well as a number of professional departmental grades. There is a further hybrid form of organization known as the 'linked departmental' class; most of the technical grades are organized on this pattern.

Negotiating machinery: Civil servants have the benefit of a comprehensive Whitley system. The Civil Service National Whitley Council was set up in 1919, and Departmental Whitley Councils have been established in practically all Government departments since. The area of responsibility of the National Council is co-terminous with that of the non-industrial Civil Service, except that Foreign Service personnel are not covered by its agreements, while Post Office engineering and allied grades—though classified for staff record purposes as industrial—are within the National Council's purview.[3] A special court of arbitration—the Civil Service Arbitration Tribunal—has been in existence since 1936.[4]

It should be added that changes in Civil Service salaries may be the outcome either of all-Service negotiations or of individual recognized staff associations bargaining separately with the Treasury. During the war central negotiations were the rule, but the years 1946–51 witnessed a reversion to sectional bargaining. In this latter period the National Whitley Council was used for dealing with broad questions affecting all civil servants, whereas individual associations were the medium for settling matters—such as pay—more specifically

[1] Though remuneration has been increasingly assimilated to that of the general classes.

[2] The first general service class was the lower division (clerks), created by an Order in Council of 1876: see Cohen, op. cit., p. 135.

[3] cf. Royal Commission on the Civil Service (1953), *Introductory Factual Memorandum on the Civil Service*, submitted by HM Treasury (HMSO 1954), para. 8. The reader is also referred to HM Treasury, *Staff Relations in the Civil Service* (HMSO 1958).

[4] From 1925 to 1936 claims were referred to the Industrial Court, which is still the competent body for industrial civil servants.

concerning a particular class or grade. Since 1951, however, all-Service pay settlements have again assumed increasing significance.[1]

Recruitment: As a matter of national policy, all permanent civil servants are recruited by the Civil Service Commission. The usual method of entry is by means of publicly-advertised open competitions, which may consist of a written examination, an interview or both. However, there are also limited competitions reserved for defined categories of serving civil servants, while some staff are nominated for establishment by virtue of previous temporary employment. Civil servants hold their posts at the pleasure of the Crown, which in theory may dismiss them at will; in practice, established officers enjoy a very high degree of security of tenure. All permanent staff undergo a period of probation; failure to pass this means termination of appointment.

Temporary employment
The Civil Service has always employed unestablished or temporary staff; 27·6 per cent of non-industrial civil servants were in that category in April 1939.[2] During the war all normal recruitment ceased and large numbers of additional workers were taken on; in April 1945 temporary personnel constituted 71·7 per cent of the non-industrial Civil Service.[3] In view of the extended demand for manpower after the war, it became clear that many of these 'temporaries' had come to stay; accordingly, many temporary officers were given the opportunity to compete for establishment, though on 1st January 1951 they still accounted for 35·1 per cent of the non-industrial strength of the Service.[4] As regards pay, there was, in the period under review, broad equality of treatment in almost all cases, the chief exception being the clerical classes. 'Temporary' salaries, in so far as they differed from permanent scales, will be referred to again, but not set out.

The war bonus: During the emergency of 1939–45 no pay increases as such were granted to civil servants, but in the light of the rapid rise in prices and wages, agreement was reached in 1940 for the payment of a bonus to all those at the lower levels of remuneration. As the war drew on, both its amount and scope were adjusted from time to time. In November 1945, following the cessation of hostilities, the

[1] See pp. 54 and 400–1 *post.*
[2] *Digest of Civil Service Staff Statistics,* 1 *January* 1949–1 *January* 1950, op. cit., Table V.
[3] ibid.
[4] *Digest of Civil Service Staff Statistics,* 1 *January* 1950–1 *January* 1951, Table V.

bonus was put on a permanent footing; it was merged with basic pay in the shape of a 'consolidation addition', accruing to all with basic remuneration of up to £1,500 per annum.[1] It is these additions which account for the irregularity of many of the 1946 scales shown on our tables below; however, a tidying operation took place in most fields with effect from 1st January 1947. These new rates, it was expressly agreed, 'do not in any way purport to revalue any of the grades and are without prejudice to any salary claims proper, current or pending'.[2]

The Administrative Class

This—a small group—has been called the officer class of the Service. Its duties were defined in the 1920 Report of the Civil Service National Whitley Council Reorganization Committee as

'those concerned with the formation of policy, with the co-ordination and improvement of government machinery, and with the general administration and control of the Departments of the Public Service'

and this has remained the official definition.[3] Prior to 1919 there was no uniform system of grading or remuneration; the hierarchy in 1951 was as follows:

Administrative class	*Established staff as at* 1 *January* 1951[4]
Assistant principal	295
Principal	1,294
Assistant secretary	722
Principal assistant secretary[5]	12
Under secretary	213
Deputy secretary	70
Permanent secretary	33
Permanent secretary to the Treasury	1
Others	59
	2,699

[1] The additions—ranging from £78 to £120—were, however, more favourable than the then level of war bonus.

[2] See *Whitley Bulletin* (organ of the Staff Side of the Civil Service National Whitley Council) January 1947, p. 8.

[3] *Report of the Joint Committee on the Organization, etc. of the Civil Service,* op. cit., para. 43, and *Estacode* (official handbook of Civil Service staff regulations) B k 21.

[4] Data supplied by Civil Service Central Staff Record. There were an additional 357 unestablished officers, making up the total of 3,056 given for the class (Home Civil Service) on p. 27.   [5] The grade is now obsolescent.

A permanent secretary is the official head of one of the major departments—some heads of smaller departments are graded as deputy secretary—and is responsible to the Minister concerned for all its activities. In the period under review, there was only one permanent secretary to the Treasury who was the official head of the whole (Home) Civil Service; since 1956 there is a second holder of this rank, though without special responsibilities for the Service. Under secretary posts are restricted to those advising departmental heads and Ministers on major questions of policy and co-ordinating very large blocks of work, while an assistant secretary is usually in charge of a division, with a number of principals or senior executive staff working under him.

The assistant principal is essentially a trainee grade. At the time of writing regulations provided that, subject to completing his probation successfully, he was normally to be promoted to the rank of principal within seven years' service.[1] In practice, promotion has come after approximately five years—a great improvement over pre-war days. The 'career grade', i.e. that which an entrant of average ability directly recruited to the class can expect to reach, is the assistant secretary: in 1951 eight out of every nine principals were reported to be advancing this far.[2] On the whole, promotion prospects for the class seem to have given little trouble—by contrast with the position on the professional side of the Service, where this issue has been a thorny one.

Salaries for the administrative grades—they refer to men in the London area—are set out on Table 1, the first column showing the standards announced in a Government White Paper of 1945,[3] plus the appropriate consolidation additions agreed subsequently. This White Paper effected a certain measure of reorganization by abolishing the principal assistant secretary grade, with a consequent devolution of function to assistant secretaries. The latter were therefore granted a special rise over and above the consolidation addition. As far as permanent secretaries are concerned, the post-war adjustment merely restored the rate of pay granted them in 1920 and cut during the 1921 recession, while for deputy secretaries, likewise, the 1946 figure represented the first improvement since 1919. This fact will help to put in perspective the substantial increases recommended by the Committee on Higher Civil Service Remuneration—the Chorley Committee.[4]

[1] *Estacode* B k 21.

[2] cf. Civil Service Arbitration Tribunal Award No. 142 (HMSO 1951), para. 2, and Civil Service Commission, *Posts in the Civil Service for University Graduates* (HMSO 1951), p. 5.   [3] Cmd. 6680.

[4] *Report of the Committee on Higher Civil Service Remuneration*, Cmd. 7635 (HMSO 1949).

TABLE 1

CIVIL SERVICE

ADMINISTRATIVE CLASS
(Men, London)

	Salary Scale as from			
	1 *Jan.* 1946 £ *p.a.*	1 *Jan.* 1947 £ *p.a.*	1 *Jan.* 1948 £ *p.a.*	1 *Oct.* 1950* £ *p.a.*
Assistant principal	353– 715	360×25–410 ×30–720	400×25– 450[1] ×30– 750	
Principal	892–1,220	900×30–1,080 ×35–1,220	950×30–1,100 ×35–1,250	1,000×40–1,200 ×50–1,375[2]
Assistant secretary	1,320×50–1,620 ×20–1,700	1,320×50–1,700		1,500×75–1,800 ×100–2,000
Under secretary	2,000			2,500[3]
Deputy secretary	2,500			3,250[3]
Permanent secretary[4]	3,500			4,500[3]
Permanent secretary to Treasury	3,750			5,000[3]

[1] A special £50 increase was granted (except to temporary staff) after two years' service (or on completion of probation, if later).

[2] Operative from 1 August 1950.

[3] This figure represents the full Chorley increase. Those with less than three years' service on 1 October 1950 did not receive this amount in full until 1 October 1951.

[4] The figures do not refer to the heads of minor departments.

* All salaries have been further revised since; in the case of assistant secretary and ranks below, as from 1 January 1952.

That Committee had been appointed by the Government in 1948 'to advise Ministers as to the general level of remuneration of the higher posts of the Civil Service—administrative, professional, scientific and technical—and on any particular principles involved', and their proposals for enhanced pay were based on three main grounds.[1] The first was that salaries had been allowed to fall behind during the inter-war years. Secondly, say the Committee, 'it seems to us indubitable that there is ground for improvement by comparison with salaries recently established in a number of Government spon-

[1] *Report of the Committee on Higher Civil Service Remuneration*, Cmd. 7635 (HMSO 1949), paras. 1 and 21–5.

sored employments, where the nature of the employment is so similar that the difference in salary scale is difficult to justify'. These employments—citing specialists in the National Health Service and the members and staffs of the boards of the newly nationalized industries—were also of a public nature. The third main ground for recommending an increase was the higher cost of living, though the Committee also laid stress on the additional responsibilities falling on administrative staffs,

The recommendations of the Chorley Committee were accepted by the Government in February 1949, subject to a measure of deferment in view of the country's economic difficulties. The scales were to be implemented over a period starting in that year, but following the devaluation of the pound, a last-minute postponement was announced a few days before the first instalment was due. The final upshot was that the increase became operative for superannuation purposes only in October 1949, operative in full as from October 1951, while as from October 1950 an instalment accrued, depending on length of service. As a result of the Report, revised salaries were likewise authorized for comparable senior scientific and professional staffs.

Principals and assistant principals were below the level considered by the Chorley Committee, though certain adjustments of their pay had been made effective from January 1948. However, the Association of First Division Civil Servants—the staff association concerned —had regarded that settlement as 'interim' only, and following the publication of the Chorley findings, there were further protracted negotiations as well as two references to the Civil Service Arbitration Tribunal.[1] Eventually, new rates were agreed for principals operative from August 1950, but the junior grade was left in the cold, no improvement of the 1948 scale being conceded until 1952, when the great majority of civil servants qualified for a general all-Service 'pay addition'.[2] Salaries for principals were further revised by an award of the Arbitration Tribunal[3] and for the bottom grade by agreement —operative in both instances from 1 January 1953.

The Royal (Priestley) Commission of 1953–5 stated *inter alia* that there was no class in the outside world which corresponded to the administrative. However, a careful study of the level of remuneration for middle-range managerial work in industry and commerce and of that of staffs of broadly comparable status in the local authority and university world should enable an approximate estimate to be made of the range within which salaries should lie.[4] As regards the higher

[1] Civil Service Arbitration Tribunal Award No. 118 (principals and assistant principals) (HMSO 1950) and No. 142 (assistant principals) (HMSO 1951).
[2] See *post*.   [3] No. 237 (HMSO 1953).
[4] *Royal Commission on the Civil Service 1953–5*, Cmd. 9613 (HMSO 1955) para. 420.

B

Civil Service, the Commission agreed with their association and official witnesses that the current level of pay was too low and that there was a case for an increase.[1] The actual salaries (men, London) proposed ranged from £7,000 for the permanent secretary to the Treasury and £6,000 for other permanent secretaries to £575–£1,000 a year for assistant principals. The Commission also recommended the appointment of a standing advisory committee to exercise a general oversight over the pay levels of the higher Civil Service, and this novel type of body—the Coleraine Committee—has meanwhile been added to the machinery for the settlement of Civil Service remuneration.

The Executive Class
This class—the former second division clerks—is broadly inter-mediate between the administrative and clerical classes; while the former are meant to initiate policy, the executive class is to carry it out. The 1920 Reorganization Committee assigned to it

'the higher work of Supply and Accounting Departments, and of other executive or specialized branches of the Civil Service.'[2]

While before the war the executive class was mostly confined to specialized branches, it has since been agreed that its use should be extended to sectors formerly staffed exclusively on a clerico-adminis-trative basis. Executive grades continue, however, to do the main body of Government accounting, though professional accountancy qualifications are not required. The class is not organized on an identical pattern throughout the Service; in the period under review a substantial number still had a departmental set-up. We shall here deal only with the general class.

General executive class	Established staff as at 1 January 1951[3]
Executive officer	21,639
Higher executive officer	9,267
Senior executive officer	2,826
Chief executive officer	743
Senior chief executive officer	268
Principal executive officer	134
Head of major establishment	32
Others	284
	35,193

[1] *Priestley Report*, op. cit. paras. 364–7.
[2] *Report of Joint Committee on the Organization, etc. of the Civil Service*, op. cit.
[3] Data supplied by Civil Service Central Staff Record. There were a further 6,036 unestablished officers, making up the total of 41,229 shown on p. 27.

The principal executive officer is generally considered as the highest in the class; the few posts above this rank are deemed to be in a special category. The career grade, however, lies much lower down the pyramid: the senior executive officer may be regarded as such, though older promotees may be unable to advance beyond the bottom rung. Promotion prospects used to vary widely in the past, especially for basic-grade personnel; during 1951, therefore, various pooling arrangements were instituted to ensure a more equitable allocation of higher-grade vacancies. There are also various opportunities for advancement to the administrative class. We may add that there is no very clear definition of executive duties.[1]

[1] cf. *Estacode* B k 22.

TABLE 2

CIVIL SERVICE
GENERAL EXECUTIVE CLASS
(Men, London)

	Salary Scale as from		
1 Jan. 1946 £ *p.a.*	*1 Jan.* 1947 £ *p.a.*	*1 Oct.* 1947 £ *p.a.*	*1 Jan.* 1951* £ *p.a.*
Executive officer[1]			
205– 615	210×20– 625	230×20– 290 ×25– 390 ×20– 650	250×25– 475 ×20– 575 ×25– 700
Higher executive officer			
640– 740	650×25– 750	675×25– 800	715×30– 865
Senior executive officer			
790– 965	800×25– 965	850×25–1,000	900×30–990 ×40–1,075
Chief executive officer			
1,005–1,157	1,000×30–1,090 ×35–1,160	1,000×30–1,090 ×35–1,200	1,100×40–1,220 ×50–1,325[2]
Senior chief executive officer[3]			
1,157–1,320	1,160×35–1,320	1,200×35–1,350	1,325×50–1,475[2]
Principal executive officer[4]			
1,320×50–1,600		1,350×50–1,600	1,500×75–1,800 ×100–1,900[5]

[1] The minimum was linked to age 18 (until 30 September 1947: 19), with age-pay up to 25.

[2] Operative from 1 September 1950.

[3] Formerly known as assistant accountant-general, assistant director of contracts, etc.

[4] Formerly known as deputy accountant-general, deputy director of contracts, etc. There were a number of higher posts, which were not on a uniform scale.

[5] Operative from 1 October 1950.

* These scales were increased as from 1 January 1952 and have been further revised since.

Salaries for the general executive class are set out on Table 2. Here, again, the 1946 figures were merely 'tidied' as from January 1947, but in the course of that year the Society of Civil Servants— who represent the executive grades—lodged a comprehensive claim for an increase. The agreement concluded provided for improved scales as from 1 October 1947, though these fell far short of the Society's objectives.[1] Despite various attempts to secure further revisions, no change took place for several years—in part because of the delay over the implementation of the Chorley recommendations which indirectly covered the higher executive levels. Eventually, however—in the latter part of 1950 and early in 1951—it proved possible to conclude a new settlement. From January 1952 executive grades received the all-Service pay addition, further increases becoming payable at the beginning of 1953.

Among the Priestley Commission's comments about the class were that this was a field where the difficulties of making 'fair comparisons' were greatest. Although broadly comparable work was to be found, the grading structure of the class had no parallel, for even at the lowest level very few outside employers made the distinction between the clerical officer type of recruit and the direct entrant executive officer.[2] The Commission also found that the elaborate structure of the class made it difficult to provide for adequate gaps between the various executive tiers. 'We cannot help wondering whether the work of the class really demands that there should be so many rungs in this particular ladder, and whether some simplification of the executive structure might not be in the best interests of the Service.'[3]

The Clerical Class
This is by far the largest of the general service classes; it again owes its birth to the National Whitley Council Reorganization Committee of 1920. The latter had divided the administrative and clerical work of the Service into two main groups: 'In one category may be placed all such work as either is of a simple mechanical kind . . . ; in the other category, the work which is concerned with the formation of policy . . .'.[4] To the clerical class they assigned the more complex duties falling under the first group.

Again, there is no uniform basis of organization. At headquarters the clerical class usually follows a general service pattern, many of the

[1] cf. Civil Service Arbitration Tribunal Award No. 231 (HMSO 1953), para. 4.

[2] *Priestley Report*, op. cit., para. 456. Considerable account should therefore be taken of relativities with the administrative class.

[3] ibid. para. 461.

[4] *Report of the Joint Committee on the Organization, etc. of the Civil Service*, op. cit., para. 16.

pre-war departmental grades having been merged into the general class during 1945–7. In regional and local offices, however, there were, in the period under review, still a number of departmental clerical classes, the main ones being in the Inland Revenue (tax officers), Ministry of Labour and Customs and Excise. Since the war the pay of these departmental grades has, however, more or less automatically kept in line with that of the general class.

	Established staff as at 1 January 1951[1]
General clerical class	
Clerical officer	74,123
Higher clerical officer	3,297
Others	538
	77,958

[1] Data supplied by Civil Service Central Staff Record. There were a further 36,020 temporary officers.

TABLE 3

CIVIL SERVICE

GENERAL CLERICAL CLASS
(Men, London)

	Salary Scale as from			
	1 *Jan.* 1946 £ *p.a.*	1 *Jan.* 1947 £ *p.a.*	1 *July* 1947 £ *p.a.*	1 *Oct.* 1950* £ *p.a.*
Clerical officer				
Age 16	116	125	150	150
17	124	125	150	170
18	152	152	170	190
19	175	175	190	210
20	193	208	210	230
21	223	225	230	250
22	238	238	250	270
23	250	250	270	290
24	262	262	285	310
25	274	274	300	330
	×18–292	×18–292		×20–350
	×12–428[1]	×12–430[1]	×15–450[2]	×15–500[3]
Higher clerical officer	490–615	500×20–625	525×20–650[4]	570×25–700[5]

[1] There was an efficiency bar at £328.
[2] There was an efficiency bar at £360.
[3] There was an efficiency bar at £395.
[4] Operative from 1 October 1947.
[5] Operative from 1 January 1951.

* These scales were increased as from 1 January 1952 and have been further revised since.

The 1946 figures shown on Table 3 represent the pre-war salary plus the consolidation addition; here again the scales were rounded as from January 1947. A new pay agreement, operative from 1 July of that year, gave the clerical officer increases at all points as well as an improved maximum three years earlier in his career. Higher clerical staffs had their remuneration revised on 1 October 1947— at the same time as executive officers, to whom they are closely linked in status. We may add that the senior grade is confined to those whose duties are purely or mainly supervisory, others on work of comparable responsibility having been regraded as executive officers. Two other tiers in the clerical structure—staff officers and senior staff officers—have similarly been amalgamated with corresponding executive ranks.

In both June 1948 and October 1949 the Civil Service Arbitration Tribunal rejected demands for higher pay for clerical officers[1]—in the latter instance partly on account of the country's economic troubles. By the end of 1950, however, the wage-thaw had begun, and the staffs' spokesmen—the Civil Service Clerical Association—resubmitted their earlier claim. This time the Tribunal proved accommodating, granting increases—operative from October 1950— of some ten to eleven per cent.[2] From 1 January 1952 the class received the all-Service pay addition; subsequently the Arbitration Tribunal awarded a consolidated scale, effective from the beginning of 1953.[3]

The Clerical Assistant Class

This class consists simply of the established clerical assistant grade, though in the period under review much analogous work was performed by the parallel—and numerically larger—category of temporary clerk grade III. There were 19,122 of the former and 52,901 of the latter at the beginning of 1951.[4]

The grade received its present name in 1936, when certain routine functions formerly carried out by clerical officers were devolved to clerical assistants;[5] however, there is still some overlap between the two groups. Recruitment used to be confined to girls aged 15–16, but the field of intake has since been substantially extended. Thus a

[1] Civil Service Arbitration Tribunal Award Nos. 95 (HMSO 1948) and 113 (HMSO 1949).

[2] Civil Service Arbitration Tribunal Award No. 133 (HMSO 1950).

[3] Civil Service Arbitration Tribunal Award No. 222 (HMSO 1953).

[4] *Digest of Civil Service Staff Statistics*, 1 *January* 1950–1 *January* 1951, Table VIII.

[5] Until 1946, the grade was divided into I and II, grade II being confined to departments with a large volume of low-grade machine work.

large number of vacancies in recent years has been filled by the establishment of temporary clerks—men and women—so that the class is now also open to men.[1] 'Permanent' scales for them were laid down for the first time as from January 1951, though the analogous grade of temporary clerk grade III had always been open to both sexes.

TABLE 4

CIVIL SERVICE

CLERICAL ASSISTANT CLASS
(London)

	Salary Scale as from			
	1 *Jan.* 1946 *Women*	1 *Sept.* 1947 *Women*	1 *Oct.* 1950* *Women*	1 *Jan.* 1951* *Men*[1]
Age	*s. p.w.*	*s. p.w.*	*s. p.w.*	*s. p.w.*
15	—	—	52/0	—
16	47/6	50/0	55/0	55/0
17	50/6	57/0	61/0	61/0
18	57/0	63/0	69/0	69/0
19	63/6	68/0	74/0	77/0
20	68/6	71/0	79/0	86/0
21	72/0	74/0	82/0	94/0
22	75/0	77/0	85/0	99/0
23	78/0	80/0	88/0	104/0
24	81/0	83/0	91/0	109/0
25	84/0	86/0	94/0	114/0
	87/0	90/0	98/0	118/0
	90/0	94/0	102/0	122/0
	93/0	98/0	106/0	126/0
	96/0	102/0	110/0	130/0
	99/0		114/0	134/0
			116/0	138/0
				142/0
				145/0

[1] There were no men in the class until 1951; the scale as from that date was *not* linked to age.

* These scales were increased as from 1 January 1952 and have been further revised since.

Temporary clerks: Much of the clerical work of the Service used to be performed by temporary officers, the temporary clerical structure providing (1951) for clerk grades III, II and I, with the majority in the two lower grades. A temporary clerk III corresponded to the clerical assistant, while II and I covered between them the higher ranges of clerical officer work, plus some duties intermediate between those of

[1] On 1 July 1953 the class consisted of 11,138 men and 17,320 women. It is now also open to youths aged 15–20.

clerical and higher clerical officer. Temporaries had in all cases lower scales and less favourable service conditions than their permanent counterparts, a claim for 'equal pay' having been rejected by the Civil Service Arbitration Tribunal in 1949.[1] The Priestly Commission, however—subject to certain safeguards—came out in favour of 'parity'; meanwhile, a substantial number of temporary clerks have been absorbed into the permanent Civil Service.

The Typing Grades
This class consists of various levels of staff engaged exclusively on copy- and shorthand-typing; secretaries are not included. There are also a number of supervisory grades, though technically these belong to the clerical classes. A handful only of men are employed.[2]

Typing grades	*Established staff as at* 1 *January* 1951[1]
Typists	10,106
Shorthand-typists	8,211
Superintendents and above	900
Others	34
	19,251

[1] Data supplied by Civil Service Central Staff Record. In addition, there were 11,276 unestablished staff, making up the total of 30,527 (p. 27).

Grading depends primarily on speed, the standards demanded (1951) being 100 words a minute (shorthand) and 40 words per minute (typing) for qualified personnel, i.e. shorthand/copy-typists grade I. Lower standards are laid down for grade II, and there is also a handful of learner typists. The great majority are in grade I. We may add that though there are various opportunities for promotion to the clerical classes, the bulk of staff do not achieve advancement beyond the typing world.

Salaries for qualified (grade I) staff are shown on Table 5. They refer to women,[3] and are not therefore comparable with other Civil Service rates, except those for female clerical assistants on Table 4. Proficiency allowances over and above the basic scale accrue to those reaching defined higher standards of competence; there are additions, likewise, for those employed on dictating machines, varityper or

[1] Award No. 114.

[2] The number of established posts held by men on 1 July 1953 was 204.

[3] Scales for men were in existence, but are not shown in view of the small numbers employed.

The Civil Service
41

stenotyping work. However, the Government pool of verbatim short-hand writers has a separate pattern of salaries.

TABLE 5

CIVIL SERVICE
TYPING GRADES
(Women, London)

Shorthand-Typist[1] Salary Scale as from				Typist[1] Salary Scale as from		
1 Jan. 1946 s. p.w.	1 July 1947 s. p.w.	1 Oct. 1950* s. p.w.	Age	1 Jan. 1946 s. p.w.	1 July 1947 s. p.w.	1 Oct. 1950* s. p.w.
—	57/0	65/0	15	—	52/0	57/0
56/0	60/0	68/0	16	52/0	55/0	60/0
59/0	68/0	76/0	17	55/0	61/0	67/0
66/0	76/0	84/0	18	61/0	66/0	75/0
74/0	80/0	88/0	19	66/6	71/0	78/0
79/6	84/0	92/0	20	69/6	73/6	81/0
84/0	88/0	98/0	21	73/0	76/0	84/0
87/0	92/0	102/0	22	75/0	78/6	87/0
90/0	96/0	106/0	23	78/0	81/0	90/0
93/0	100/0	110/0	24	81/0	83/6	93/0
96/0	104/0	114/0	25	84/0	86/0	96/0
99/0	108/0	118/0		87/0	90/0	100/0
102/0	112/0	122/0		90/0	94/0	104/0
105/0	116/0	126/0		93/0	98/0	108/0
108/0		130/0		96/0	102/0	112/0
				99/0		115/0

[1] The scales shown are those for qualified (i.e. grade I) staff, but are exclusive of proficiency allowances.

* These scales were increased as from 1 January 1952 and have been further revised since.

Remuneration in the typing world has for many years been reviewed immediately after that of clerical officers. During and after the 1939–45 war, however, there was an acute shortage of staff, and one of the measures adopted to aid recruitment was to grant the typing grades pay increases relatively larger than those given to the clerical classes. As a result, while the clerical officer maximum had, by 1953, increased by only 64 per cent over the 1939 level, those of shorthand- and copy-typists had gone up by 100 and 122 per cent, respectively.[1]

[1] *Introductory Factual Memorandum*, op. cit., paras. 396–400. At other points of the scale the position was not as unfavourable to the clerical officer.

Professional, Scientific and Technical Classes
Until 1946 each department was a law unto itself as far as its professional, scientific and technical staff was concerned, there being a very
large number of departmental grades, with different salary scales,
standards of qualification and methods of recruitment. A thorough-
going reorganization took place at the end of the second world war,
which has been considered comparable to that of 1920 on the clerico-
administrative side. It involved the introduction of general service
and linked departmental classes over a wide area, replacing what is
freely admitted to have been pre-war departmental chaos.[1] Departmental grades as a species are not, however, extinct, nor has the process of rationalization gone equally far everywhere. We shall here be
able to deal only with the legal class, the scientific Civil Service and
the technical classes.[2]

The Legal Class
At one time the salaries of Civil Service lawyers were paid out of
lump sum allowances granted to the chief legal officer in each
department,[3] but this system was abolished after the first world war
when standard salary scales were introduced. During the second war
a Committee under the chairmanship of Sir Alan Barlow enquired
into remuneration and allied matters. The Barlow Report, issued in
March 1944, stressed the serious deficiency of capable men in the
legal Civil Service—a situation that could not, in the Committee's
opinion, be remedied under the then service conditions and rates of
pay.[4] In September 1945 a reorganization was announced, embodying
many of the Barlow recommendations.

The legal class is confined to barristers and solicitors, and is employed both in predominantly legal departments and in the legal
sections of general Government departments. In some respects their
duties involve activities similar to those in private practice—advocacy
before the courts, conveyancing and so on; in others they are peculiar

---

[1] cf. Final Report of Committee on Structure of the Post-War Civil Service,
Whitley Bulletin, June 1949.
[2] For details of other professional classes see e.g. the Reports of the Committee on the Organization, Structure and Remuneration of the Works Group
of Professional Civil Servants (HMSO 1951); the Committee on the Pay and
Organization of Civil Service Medical Staffs (HMSO 1951); and the Committee on
the Organization, Structure and Remuneration of the Professional Accountant
Class in the Civil Service (HMSO 1952). For details of the 'works group', medical
officer and draughtsmen classes see also *Priestley Report*, op. cit. Chap. XIII.
[3] cf. Civil Service Arbitration Tribunal Award No. 135 (HMSO 1950), p. 2.
[4] *Report of Committee on Legal Departments of the Civil Service* (HMSO, 1944)
para 9.

to Government service, e.g. the drafting of statutory instruments.[1] The Barlow Committee had recommended an increased use of non-professional staff for work analogous to that of managing clerks in private practice, for which purpose they proposed the creation of special quasi-legal grades. However, the Treasury did not accept this suggestion. The legal pyramid, with numbers as at 1 January 1951, is shown below:

Legal class	*Established staff as at 1 January* 1951[1]
Legal assistant	227
Senior legal assistant	227
Assistant solicitor	81
Principal assistant solicitor	10
Solicitor/legal adviser	28
Director of Public Prosecutions; Public Trustee	2
HM Procurator-General and Treasury Solicitor	1
	576

[1] Data supplied by Civil Service Central Staff Record; the number of temporary officers as at 1 January 1951 is not available. On 1 April 1954 there were 528 established and 60 temporary staff.

Legal establishments—insofar as they are organized on a general service pattern—are usually headed by a solicitor or legal adviser; the Treasury Solicitor is the head of the whole legal Civil Service and acts for those departments not having a legal adviser of their own. Again, there are departmental variants such as the different levels of parliamentary counsel, and there are also a number of senior posts—such as that of the Chief Registrar of Friendly Societies—whose salaries were not precisely assimilated to those on Table 6.

The salaries announced in 1945 became operative on 1 January 1946 and were not again revised—apart from being 'tidied'—until the end of 1950. Though an attempt had been made in 1949 to secure for senior legal assistants an increase comparable to that given to principals (administrative) in 1948,[2] this was not granted by the Treasury. The 1950 scales for the two bottom ranks were the result of a Civil

[1] Royal Commission on the Civil Service (1953), *Supplement to Introductory Factual Memorandum on the Civil Service* (Medical and Legal Staffs) (HMSO 1954), para. 3.

[2] Civil Service Arbitration Tribunal Award No. 135, op. cit. para. 8.

Service Arbitration award;[1] those for the higher grades were adjusted as a result of the Chorley recommendations. As from 1 January 1952, those on salaries not exceeding £1,500 received the all-Service pay addition.

[1] No. 135. Following a further reference to arbitration in 1953 (Award No. 219) the salary scale of legal assistants was slightly adjusted with retrospective effect from 1 January 1951.

TABLE 6

CIVIL SERVICE

LEGAL CLASS
(Men, London)

	Salary Scale as from		
	1 *January* 1946 £ *p.a.*	1 *January* 1947 £ *p.a.*	1 *October* 1950* £ *p.a.*
Legal assistant			
During probation	490 at age 26 plus £25 for each year above 26, subject to an upper limit of £690	500 at age 26 plus £25 for each year above 26, subject to an upper limit of £700	600 at age 26
On confirmation of appointment[1]	790– 955	800 × 25– 950	800 × 30–1,070[2]
Senior legal assistant	1,005–1,320	1,000 × 30–1,090 × 35–1,320	1,150 × 40–1,230 × 50–1,500
Assistant solicitor	1,420 × 50–1,620 × 20–1,700	1,420 × 50–1,700	1,625 × 75–1,850 × 100–2,000
Principal assistant solicitor	2,000		2,500[3]
Solicitor/legal adviser	2,500		3,250[3]
Director of Public Prosecutions; Public Trustee	3,000		4,000[3]
HM Procurator-General and Treasury Solicitor	3,500		4,500[3]

[1] The minimum was linked to age 30, £25 being deducted for each year below.

[2] As from 1 January 1951 the scale was £800 × 30–980, × 40–£1,070.

[3] This figure represents the full Chorley increase. Those with less than three years' service on 1 October 1950 did not receive this amount in full until 1 October 1951.

* All salaries have been further revised since; in the case of assistant solicitor and ranks below, as from 1 January 1952.

The Scientific Civil Service

The scientific classes were thoroughly overhauled after the war, being among the first of the specialist groups to undergo a comprehensive scheme of unification. The 'new deal' for the Scientific Civil Service was announced in a White Paper of September 1945[1] and was based on the recommendations of another Barlow Committee.[2] It provided for three—instead of two—classes, the scientific and experimental officer classes corresponding broadly with the administrative and executive classes—a relationship deliberately embodied in the 1946 reorganization.[3] As compared with pre-war, scientists are employed on a greatly increased scale.

The Scientific Officer Class

This has been described as 'the initiating, directing, inventive brain of the scientific research, design and development work of the Civil Service';[4] it is confined to university graduates and to be used for 'high quality' work only. Numbers on 1 January 1951 were:

Scientific officer class	Established staff as at 1 January 1951[1]
Scientific officer	669
Senior scientific officer	789
Principal scientific officer	975
Senior principal scientific officer	329
Deputy chief scientific officer	100
Chief scientific officer	30
Posts above chief scientific officer	15
	2,907

[1] Data supplied by Civil Service Central Staff Record; the number of temporary officers as at 1 January 1951 is not available. On 1 April 1955 there were 2,878½ established and 537½ temporary staff.

As regards duties, broadly speaking those of the grades above principal scientific officer include responsibility for the administration and direction of scientific work, while the lower levels concentrate on such work themselves. Senior posts may, however, be created for outstanding individual research staff,[5] a provision which has no parallel on the administrative side of the Service.

[1] Cmd. 6679.
[2] Published as annexe to Cmd. 6679.
[3] Cmd. 6679, op. cit., para. 18.
[4] *Estacode* B k 41.
[5] *Estacode* B k 41 and *Introductory Factual Memorandum*, op. cit., para. 214.

TABLE 7

CIVIL SERVICE

SCIENTIFIC OFFICER CLASS
(Men, London)

Salary Scale as from

	1 *January* 1946 £ *p.a.*	1 *January* 1947 £ *p.a.*	1 *January* 1948 £ *p.a.*	1 *October* 1950* £ *p.a.*
Scientific officer[1]	353– 590	360 × 25– 600	400 × 25– 650	400 × 25–450 × 30–650[2]
Senior scientific officer	640– 840	650 × 25– 850	700 × 25– 900	750 × 30– 950[3]
Principal scientific officer	892–1,220	900 × 30–1,080 × 35–1,220	950 × 30–1,100 × 35–1,250	1,000 × 40–1,200 × 50–1,375[3]
Senior principal scientific officer	1,320 × 50–1,520			1,500 × 75–1,750
Deputy chief scientific officer	1,600 × 50–1,800			1,850 × 100–2,125
Chief scientific officer[4]	2,000			2,500[5]
Secretary, Dept. of Scientific and Industrial Research	3,500			4,500[5]

[1] A special increase was granted on confirmation of appointment.

[2] The increase in increments was operative from 1 May 1951.

[3] Operative from 1 August 1950.

[4] There were a number of posts with pay intermediate between that of chief scientific officer and the Secretary of the Department of Scientific and Industrial Research.

[5] This figure represents the full Chorley increase. Those with less than three years' service on 1 October 1950 did not receive this amount in full until 1 October 1951.

* All salaries have been further revised since; in the case of deputy chief scientific officer and ranks below, as from 1 January 1952.

Recruitment is to either of the two bottom rungs, the majority entering as scientific officers. The normal career grade is the principal scientific officer: The 1945 White Paper stated that every recruit of proved ability should reach this far; outstanding men should do so in their early thirties.[1] The White Paper also urged that ultimate prospects in the class should be improved by increasing the number of higher posts; prospects are of course much less favourable than in the administrative world, where the assistant secretary is the 'career expectation' and where only one promotion is required to attain the rank of principal.

The Experimental Officer Class
This class was newly created in 1946: It is the main support of the scientific officer class, many of whose duties were devolved upon it.[2] Recruitment may be either to the basic grade or at experimental officer level, the minimum qualification normally required at the time of writing being the General Certificate of Education, including two mathematical or scientific subjects at Advanced level. Older candidates were, however, generally expected to hold a university pass degree or Higher National Certificate.

Experimental officer class	*Established staff as at* 1 *January* 1951[1]
Assistant experimental officer	1,755
Experimental officer	1,922
Senior experimental officer	901
	4,578

[1] Data supplied by Civil Service Central Staff Record; the number of temporary officers as at 1 January 1951 is not available. On 1 April 1955 there were 5,064 established and 966 temporary staff.

The senior experimental officer used to be the top grade in the class, but a higher tier—that of chief experimental officer—was introduced in May 1951 for certain types of post. It was not then intended that it would form part of the career normally to be expected by entrants, though the use of the grade has been extended somewhat since. There are possibilities of advancement to the scientific officer class, though the Priestley Commission pointed out that the number of promotions was in fact small.[3] As Table 8 shows, pay adjustments for the class have kept in line with those for the executive grades.

[1] Cmd. 6679, op. cit. para. 8. In a report published in 1952, the average age for promotion from senior to principal scientific officer was given as 34 years 5 months: *Tenth Report from the Select Committee on Estimates, Session* 1951–52 (HMSO, 30 July 1952), Memorandum by the Ministry of Supply, p. 139.

[2] For details see Cmd. 6679, op. cit., para. 13 and *Estacode* B k 42. For further information see also *Introductory Factual Memorandum*, op. cit. Chap. 17.

[3] *Priestley Report*, op. cit., para. 619.

TABLE 8

CIVIL SERVICE

EXPERIMENTAL OFFICER CLASS
(Men, London)

	Salary Scale as from			
	1 *Jan*. 1946 £ *p.a.*	1 *Jan*. 1947 £ *p.a.*	1 *Oct*. 1947 £ *p.a.*	1 *Jan*. 1951* £ *p.a.*
Assistant experimental officer[1]	205–428	210 × 20–430	230 × 20–290 × 25–390 × 20–490	250 × 25–475 × 20–535
Experimental officer	490–640	500 × 20–650	525 × 20–675	575 × 25–725
Senior experimental officer	690–892	700 × 25–900	735 × 25–935	780 × 30–1,000
Chief experimental officer	—	—	—	1,025 × 40–1,250[2]

[1] The minimum was linked to age 18 (until 30 September 1947: 19), with age-pay up to 25 (as from 1951/52: 26).

[2] Effective from 1 May 1951; the grade was not previously in existence.

* These scales were increased as from 1 January 1952 and have been further revised since.

The Assistant (Scientific) Class

A review of the field of work of laboratory assistants and other junior grades was undertaken in the early post-war period, and the proposal to create an assistant (scientific) class announced in March 1947;[1] in addition to laboratory assistants, it also absorbed those aiding professional staff in agriculture, medicine and veterinary science. The class has a two-tier structure, the assistant (scientific) and the senior assistant (scientific). It relies heavily on temporary officers.

Assistant (scientific) class	*Established staff as at* 1 *January* 1951[2]
Assistant (scientific)	1,757
Senior assistant (scientific)	724
	2,481

[1] EOC 27/47. The salaries applied as from 1 January 1947.

[2] Data supplied by Civil Service Central Staff Record; the number of unestablished staff as at 1 January 1951 is not available. On 1 April 1955 there were 2,612 established and 2,666 temporary officers.

Assistants are concerned with the simpler experimental tasks as well as with routine testing, cleaning of apparatus and so on, though they are not to do an excessive amount of routine work. At the time of writing, recruitment to established posts was from boys and girls mainly aged between 17½ and 26, who were normally required to have two years' experience of scientific work and hold a General Certificate of Education in four subjects at 'O' level. The academic qualification was not, however, insisted upon. Assistants are eligible for advancement to the senior grade; they can also compete for vacancies in the experimental officer class. Salaries are shown on Table 9.[1]

TABLE 9

CIVIL SERVICE
ASSISTANT (SCIENTIFIC) CLASS
(Men, London)

	Salary Scale as from		
	1 *January* 1947 £ *p.a.*	1 *February* 1951 £ *p.a.*	1 *July* 1951* £ *p.a.*
Assistant (scientific)			
Age 18	195	215	
19	210	230	
20	225	245	
21	240	260	
22	255	275	
23	270	290	
24	285	310	
25	300	330	
	×15–380	×20–350	
		×15–455	
Senior assistant (scientific)	400×20–550	475×20–625	480×20–500 ×25–650

* All scales were increased as from 1 January 1952 and have been further revised since.

The Technical Classes

The technical works, engineering and allied classes, as their full title runs, occupy a position midway between industrial grades employed on production and professional staffs—architects, engineers, surveyors—responsible for planning, development and overall direction.[2] They belong to the genus of 'linked departmental' classes.

There were some 16,000 members of the technical classes at the

[1] The minimum of the basic grade is now linked to age 16.

[2] For further details see *Estacode* B k 62, Memorandum by the Treasury to EOC 43/48, and *Introductory Factual Memorandum*, op. cit. Chap. 18.

beginning of 1951,[1] the four largest sections being clerks of works (building), quantity surveying assistants, mechanical and electrical engineering technical staffs, and the technical lands grades (e.g. assistants in estate management). The duties of these four categories vary widely, but can be divided into office work such as rate-fixing, direct labour production and inspection. Technical personnel are concerned with building and services of all kinds and deal with practically every type of equipment; however, their function is 'executive', ultimate responsibility normally resting with professional officers.

The technical pyramid, in the period under review, provided for four main tiers—I, II, III and IV—and two higher levels, known as A and B. The bulk of the staff was in III, II and I, entry being mainly to grade III. Examples of A and B posts were Royal Naval Dockyard

[1] Civil Service Arbitration Tribunal Award No. 146 (HMSO 1951). Precise statistics for 1951 are not available. At 1 April 1953 numbers were 8,369 established and 10,560 temporary staff.

TABLE 10

CIVIL SERVICE

TECHNICAL WORKS, ENGINEERING AND ALLIED CLASSES
(Men, London)

	Salary Scale as from	
	1 *January* 1946 £ *p.a.*	1 *October* 1950* £ *p.a.*
Grade IV (minimum linked to age 25)[1]	330 × 15–450	370 × 15– 500
Grade III (minimum linked to age 26)[2]	400 × 20–525	460 × 20– 575
Grade II (minimum linked to age 30)[3]	500 × 20–625	570 × 20– 675
Grade I[4]	625 × 25–750	675 × 25– 825
Grade B	750 × 25–850	830 × 25– 930
Grade A	800 × 25–950	870 × 25– 970 × 30–1,030

[1] Minus £20 for each year below. Older staff, who were qualified for the full range of duties, received £15 for each year above 25 (but not exceeding 28).

[2] Minus/plus one increment for each year below/above 26 (but not exceeding 28).

[3] Minus one increment for each year below.

[4] There was an alternative scale with a lower minimum to meet special circumstances.

* These salaries were increased as from 1 January 1952 and have been further revised since.

senior foremen or Ministry of Works chief labour supervisors. Lower down the hierarchy, a clerk of works (building) in the Ministry of Works was to be in grade III if engaged on the supervision of traditional building schemes of up to about £20,000 in value; in grade II if of the order of £20,000 and upwards; and in grade I if in charge of the more important traditional building jobs of over £100,000.[1] Grade IV personnel were employed on ancillary tasks.

Like the professional and scientific classes, the technical branch of the Civil Service was reorganized in the post-war period; prior to 1946 there were over a hundred different grades on a variety of sub-professional and technical work. The proposals for common salaries and service conditions—though not all the classes formerly designated as 'technical' were brought in—were announced in 1948–9, but applied retrospectively as from the beginning of 1946. They were revised under an award of the Civil Service Arbitration Tribunal with effect from 1 October 1950.[2] These scales, in turn, attracted the 1952 pay addition and have been further improved since.

A word now about the relationship between clerico-administrative staffs on the one hand and the various technical and professional classes on the other, following the latter's emergence from their pristine state of pre-war fragmentation. In brief, the clerico-administrative classes have served as the model with which the various technical and professional grades have tried to achieve a broad similarity of prospects and status. The extent to which, in the period under review, parity of *pay* actually existed, varied considerably. In the case of statisticians, for example, there was a complete identity of scales with the administrative class, though the highest level was that of chief statistician—equivalent to an assistant secretary—more senior staff then being eligible for transfer to the administrative hierarchy. The salaries of the scientific officer class were also, as indicated, deliberately brought into relationship with those of the administrative grades, but here it was held that an identical scale structure 'would not meet the requirements of the scientific organizations',[3] though parity has since been conceded at a number of key points. In the legal class the relativity was one degree more tenuous still, salaries here having been fixed merely 'with due regard to those . . . applicable to administrative officers',[4] and the Barlow Committee definitely frowned on grade-by-grade comparisons. These differences in the degree of assimilation to administrative class remuneration meant that

[1] Standards laid down in 1949 as per EOC 17/49.
[2] Civil Service Arbitration Tribunal Award No. 146 (HMSO 1951).
[3] Cmd. 6679, op. cit., para. 8.
[4] *Barlow Report*, op. cit., para. 36.

a statistician had his pay adjusted automatically with his administrative colleague; as regards the scientific grades, it was 'understood' that, at any rate up to principal level, they would receive a rise *pari passu*, while for legal personnel the fact of an administrative pay increase was merely a valuable bargaining weapon for claiming similar treatment. In other cases there was no explicit pronouncement on the subject and it was, as it were, by case law and precedent that relativities were established.

The pattern was repeated at a lower level: The information officer class was explicitly linked to the executive; salaries were almost identical. The scales of actuaries were 'founded upon those of the executive class',[1] though there was no precise parity. The position of the experimental officer *vis-à-vis* the executive hierarchy, likewise, has been one of equal status rather than of pay, the grades of the former having been settled 'by comparison' with those of the executive class,[2] though here again identical scales have been awarded at certain levels of the two structures. Finally, in the case of draughtsmen (engineering and architectural) and the technical grades, the relativity was very precarious and not recognized by the Treasury.[3]

At the clerical level, the grade of draughtsman (cartographic and recording)—the basic rung in the linked departmental class of that name—was considered analogous to the clerical officer,[4] but as regards the assistant (scientific) and clerical classes, the matter was a bone of contention between the Treasury and staff association.[5]

The Priestley Commission stated in this context that 'the theory of parity' was the most important general question posed for their examination.[6] The Institution of Professional Civil Servants—who represent most scientific and professional staffs—had maintained that the rates of pay and career prospects of the specialist classes were markedly inferior to those of what they regarded as corresponding non-specialist grades; they told the Commission that it was their first aim to secure parity in this matter. In their conception the latter was achieved not necessarily by an identity of form and grade structure, but by providing over the whole of a normal career something like the same total remuneration: If promotion prospects were poorer in a specialist than in the corresponding non-specialist class, higher

---

[1] See Civil Service Arbitration Tribunal Award No. 146, op. cit. (summary of Treasury evidence), p. 6.

[2] ibid.

[3] ibid. paras. 3 and 4.

[4] ibid. p. 6.

[5] cf. Civil Service Arbitration Tribunal Award Nos. 141 and 153 (HMSO 1951) and *Priestley Report*, op. cit., paras. 649–50.

[6] *Report*, op. cit., para. 527.

salaries should be paid by way of compensation. Illustrations were provided to justify a series of 'equations' between the various specialist and clerico-administrative grades.[1]

The views of the Commission's official witnesses were that it would be wholly unsound to base the rates and structure of any specialist class on that of any allegedly 'corresponding' non-specialist class. Even if educational qualifications were comparable, no civil servant should have any prescriptive right to the same total career as a member of a different class; equation of prospects was in any case not practicable. The official witnesses also did not agree with some of the Institution's 'equations', and thought that current relativities were about right.[2]

The Priestley Commission, though granting equality in a number of cases 'on merit', rejected parity—of pay or prospects—as a legitimate determinant of Civil Service remuneration.[3] The Commission emphasized that they had no wish to underrate the importance of scientific and technological development to the country's wellbeing, but felt that it would not be proper for the Civil Service to give a lead in establishing the social or economic status of scientists or any other group of workers. Their overall view was that changes in the pay and career prospects of specialist staffs should come about by a process of evolution—through the application of the principle of fair comparison in an economy increasingly dependent upon scientific and technological advance—rather than by the application of a theory of parity.[4]

A related point that has given rise to ill-feeling is that the highest posts in a department are normally the preserve of the administrative class. The only appointments of permanent secretary rank filled by a professional, in the period under review, were those of Secretary to the Department of Scientific and Industrial Research and Treasury Solicitor, though there were a few miscellaneous ones which attracted a higher salary. Thus the Chairman of the Defence Research Policy Committee, Ministry of Defence, received £4,500 at a time when permanent heads were paid £3,500, while the Chief Planning Officer, Central Economic Planning Staff (a division of the Treasury) used to have a salary of £6,500.[5] However, such posts—as also some lower-paid ones—fall outside the normal class structure of the Service.

[1] *Report*, op. cit., para 527 ff.
[2] ibid. para. 529.
[3] ibid. para. 108.
[4] cf. ibid. paras. 530, 543 and p. 200 (67).
[5] *Civil Estimates*, 1951–2, Class I, p. 23. Sir Edwin Plowden, the holder of this post, retired therefrom at the end of 1953, since when it is no longer in existence.

Postscript[1]

In the autumn of 1951 the staff side of the National Whitley Council reached the conclusion that, in a period of rapidly rising prices, wages and salaries, it would be desirable to revert to the war-time method of central pay negotiation. The official side concurred, and an agreement was reached under which the great bulk of civil servants had their salaries augmented by a 'pay addition', operative from 1 January 1952. This amounted to 10 per cent on the first £500 of basic pay, 5 per cent on the second £500, and 2½ per cent on the third £500—with a flat-rate increase of £100 for those with salaries between £1,500 and £2,000 a year.

In the autumn of 1952 the staff side claimed a fresh pay addition, but the Treasury were not then prepared to contemplate any more central awards. However, they affirmed their willingness to examine grade claims and, accordingly, a series of individual settlements was reached during 1953–4.

In November 1954 a new agreement was concluded for an all-Service 'pay supplement',[2] operative from 1 July of that year. This settlement was of an interim nature to which the Treasury had reluctantly consented—and which they considered 'a lapse from orthodoxy'[3]—as likely to produce the minimum interference with the work of the Royal (Priestley) Commission on the Civil Service who were then in session. The supplements ranged from £17 10s. to £35 per annum,[4] but following Award No. 287 of the Civil Service Arbitration Tribunal, these figures were further increased as from 1 July 1955. We may add that the 1954 and 1955 supplements did not accrue as such to those with salaries over £1,500, though separate provision was made for those immediately above this level.

The Royal Commission on the Civil Service were appointed in November 1953, under the chairmanship of Sir Raymond Priestley, to consider certain questions concerning the conditions of service of civil servants, among them 'whether any changes are desirable in the principles which should govern pay; or in the rates of pay at present in force . . .'[5]

A comprehensive Report was issued in November 1955; it must suffice here to summarize the Commission's conclusions as to the

---

[1] This postscript is merely designed to give a brief summary of the *main* developments between end-1951 and the 'Priestley era'.

[2] See EC 53/54, *Whitley Bulletin*, January 1955.

[3] cf. Treasury press statement, *Whitley Bulletin*, December 1954, p. 203; EC 53/54 loc. cit.; and *Priestley Report*, op. cit., para. 180.

[4] Grades whose pay had been adjusted on an individual basis since January 1953 were not eligible.

[5] *Priestley Report*, op. cit., p. 1. See ibid. for terms of reference in full.

overall principles which should govern the determination of salaries in the Civil Service. 'The end to be served by principles of pay in the Civil Service,' say the Commission, 'may be stated as the maintenance of a Civil Service recognized as efficient and staffed by members whose remuneration and conditions of service are thought fair both by themselves and by the community they serve. The primary principle of civil service pay should be fair comparison with the current remuneration of outside staffs employed on broadly comparable work, taking account of differences in other conditions of service.' The Commission add that internal relativities should be used to supplement 'fair comparison' in settling rates in detail, but though they may have to be the first consideration when outside comparisons cannot be made, they should never be allowed to override the primary principle.[1] The Commission also gave considerable thought to the mechanics of 'fair comparison', and in accordance with their recommendations,[2] a Civil Service Pay Research Unit—a fact-finding organization of a type hitherto unknown in this country—was established in 1956.

Apart from detailed recommendations on pay, the Commission also made far-reaching proposals about hours, leave, provincial differentiation and so on, and made clear that all these 'must be regarded as a comprehensive unity'. The Priestley findings were accepted by the Government, whereupon negotiations on the National Whitley Council followed with exemplary speed, and in June 1956— after somewhat reluctant ratification by the staff associations— details of the new arrangements were formally promulgated by the Treasury.[3] As regards pay, as the Commission's proposals related to conditions as at 1 July 1955, subsequent improvements in outside remuneration were taken into account as specifically recommended in their Report: The Priestley scales up to and including principal and equivalent i.e.—but not beyond—were improved by a further 'pay supplement'. The new standards were given effect as from 1 April 1956.

Provincial Differentiation
The distribution of established non-industrial staff on 1 January 1951 was as follows:[4]

---

[1] *Priestley Report*, p. 194 (1)–(3). See ibid. and ff. for full summary of findings.
[2] ibid. paras. 155–77.
[3] See EC 27/56 and EC 28/56, *Whitley Bulletin*, August 1956. Certain modifications of the Royal Commission proposals were agreed to in the course of the negotiations.
[4] *Digest of Civil Service Staff Statistics*, 1 *January* 1950–1 *January* 1951,op. cit., Table IX. The figures include Post Office staffs.

London	133,725
Intermediate	94,218
Provincial	205,490
Overseas	4,776
	438,209

The relative proportion in London and outside varies both as between classes and departments; while administrative grades are mostly to be found in the capital, this is not true, for example, of certain scientific staff. A larger percentage of civil servants was located in London before the war, certain headquarters offices now being permanently situated outside the metropolis.

There were three separate salary scales for each Civil Service grade until end–1946. In January 1947 the London rate became the official standard, from which deductions became payable according to whether a locality was classified as 'intermediate' or 'provincial'. 'London', in 1951, covered all offices within twelve miles of Charing Cross. 'Intermediate' areas were those beyond the twelve-mile radius but within sixteen miles of Charing Cross, as well as large towns including Bristol, Birmingham, Cardiff, Leeds, Liverpool, Manchester, Newcastle and Sheffield: the rough criterion was a population of 250,000 or more.[1] 'Provincial' rates were paid everywhere else. The deductions were graduated, the amount increasing with salary as shown:

	Deductions in	
London salary[2]	*Intermediate centres*	*Provincial centres*
£ *p.a.*	£ *p.a.*	£ *p.a.*
0– 275	5	10
312– 450	10	20
487– 750	15	30
787–1,000	20	40
1,077–1,200	30	60
1,277–1,500	40	80
1,577 and over	50	100

Two groups were not covered by these arrangements. First, weekly-paid staff where there were simple flat-rate deductions: in 1951 these amounted to 3s. per week in 'intermediate' and 6s. in

[1] For details see *Introductory Factual Memorandum*, op. cit., p. 123.

[2] The gaps in the figures are due to the elaborate 'escalator' provisions at the beginning of each salary band, designed to ease the transition to the larger deduction. For full schedule, showing the deduction at every point of the London scale, see *Introductory Factual Memorandum*, op. cit., pp. 125–6.

'provincial' centres. Secondly, there are certain classes of civil servant who are liable to frequent transfers within the country; such categories—the largest is the personnel of the Inland Revenue—are immune from provincial differentiation, having a uniform salary irrespective of locality.

The Priestley Commission found that the arguments in favour of some form of area differentiation were conclusive, though a national rate with additions for London and possibly other high-cost areas would be preferable to the existing scheme. They also urged that the amount of differentiation on salaries of up to £1,000 should be increased, and revised schedules of standard deductions were accordingly brought in as from April 1956. Since then, agreement has been reached for the introduction—by stages beginning in 1958—of a new system under which the hitherto existing 'intermediate' and 'provincial' areas will be merged. The 'intermediate' is to become the 'national rate', and as from 1 January 1962 will apply to all non-industrial civil servants[1] outside the London pay area. The latter, it may be added, has been extended to cover all offices within a radius of sixteen miles from Charing Cross, while staff working within three miles of that famous underground station receive, as from January 1961, a larger allowance than the rest of their London colleagues.[2]

Sex Differentiation

The proportion of women in the non-industrial Civil Service increased from 25·6 per cent on 1 April 1939 to 33·7 per cent on 1 January 1951.[3] Their relative strength in the different classes varies widely:

*Women as proportion of various (non-industrial) classes
as at 1 January 1951*[4]

Class	%
Administrative (Home and Foreign)	8
Executive (general and departmental)	18
Clerical (general and departmental)	37
Clerical assistants	62
Typing	99
Professional, scientific and technical (staff groups I and II) and inspectorate	7
Technical ancillary	26

[1] Except those not subject to provincial differentiation.

[2] For full details see EC 58/57, *Whitley Bulletin*, February 1958, p. 27 and ff. and *Whitley Bulletin*, February 1961, p. 24.

[3] *Digest of Civil Service Staff Statistics*, 1 *January* 1949–1 *January* 1950 and 1 *January* 1950–1 *January* 1951, op. cit., Tables IV.

[4] *Digest of Civil Service Staff Statistics*, 1 *January* 1950–1 *January* 1951, Table VIII. The percentages relate to established and temporary staff

The general principle governing sex differentiation in the Civil Service, prior to the introduction of 'equal pay',[1] was that the maximum of a woman's scale was not to be less than 80 per cent of that for men in the same grade. This was modified by the provision that the absolute differential between the two maxima should not exceed £175, and that a woman's maximum was not to be below the man's in the rung beneath. Also, in recruitment grades forming the lowest tier of a class, the two sexes' minimum was to be identical. There were two further exceptions to the rule of the 4:5 ratio: At the top of the Civil Service pyramid there were separate scales at neither permanent nor deputy secretary level, while for Whitehall doctors, dentists and medical auxiliaries there was no differentiation anywhere.

This is not the place for describing the protracted struggle to achieve equal pay. The unions and associations representing Civil Service staffs had been opposed to sex differentiation for many years, while 'equal pay' as a principle was approved—as far as the Civil Service is concerned—as far back as 1914. However, nothing concrete happened for forty years when—in May 1954—the Chancellor of the Exchequer informed a deputation of the National Whitley Council that he was willing to authorize negotiations, with the object of evolving an agreed scheme for its actual introduction. Such a scheme was duly worked out:[2] It provided for equal pay to be introduced into the non-industrial Civil Service in stages—over a period of seven years—to be fully in operation by 1 January 1961. Most other public services have followed the Treasury lead—an indication of the leading role played by the Service in the sphere of salary determination.

[1] These provisions applied to 'permanent' scales.
[2] For details see *Whitley Bulletin* (Supplement) March 1955.

Chapter 2

THE LOCAL GOVERNMENT SERVICE

Local government in this country has developed gradually from early times, though in the modern sense of the term it is the product of legislation of the nineteenth and twentieth centuries. Under the existing system the law defines six types of local authority in England and Wales: Administrative counties, county boroughs, non-county boroughs, urban districts, rural districts and parishes.[1] These units differ greatly as regards size, population, functions and resources; while the county boroughs are completely self-contained, all-purpose authorities, the non-county boroughs, urban and rural districts are constituent units of the counties.[2] Parishes are units within rural districts. On the fringe of local government are various public authorities such as drainage and catchment boards, water and harbour boards—other than national bodies—created for the specific purpose indicated by their name.

Local authorities are subordinate to Parliament; as compared with the central government, their work is administrative rather than legislative. In general they have no powers except those specifically conferred upon them, are subject to central control in many respects, and with the transfer of hospitals, public assistance, gas and electricity to national organs of administration, they have lost several major spheres of activity. Nevertheless, their functions still cover a very wide field.

Local Government Staffs
The work of local authorities is not left to leisure-time councillors; since the eighteen-thirties a local government service has begun to develop.[3] Its personnel is again of many diverse kinds; the Hadow Committee of 1934 divided it into 'officers' and 'servants', the distinction being broadly that between manual and non-manual

---

[1] Local Government Act, 1933 (4. Geo. 5, c. 51) s. 1.

[2] The administrative county of London has a distinct system of local administration.

[3] cf. L. Hill, *The Local Government Officer* (Allen & Unwin, 1938) p. 14. For much useful information see also J. H. Warren, *The Local Government Service* (Allen & Unwin, 1952).

workers.[1] Manual employees are engaged in the upkeep of roads and parks; on land drainage and sewage work; as building operatives and in trading undertakings. As in the Civil Service, they are a separate category as far as pay and the negotiation of service conditions are concerned, and fall outside the range of this study.

The salaried staff can be divided into those engaged in the *administration* of local services and those employed in their *operation*; the distinction is not a hard-and-fast one but corresponds by and large to the realities of collective bargaining. The 'operators' include such well-defined groups as teachers, police, firemen and health workers; all these have their own pattern of remuneration and negotiating machinery.[2] The Burnham Committees, for instance, fix the salaries of teachers; statutory sanction is given to these by the Minister of Education. The pay of health workers—many of whom are to be found both in the national and 'public health' (i.e. local government) field—is now determined by special Whitley Councils, set up under the National Health Service. Fire brigade personnel, probation officers and police, though employees of local authorities, have their salaries promulgated in the form of statutory regulations by the Home Secretary, though the latter acts on the recommendations of the appropriate negotiating body. We deal with these various categories in later chapters.

Administrative, Professional, Technical and Clerical Workers
Here we are concerned with those engaged in the administration of local services, the great majority of whom now come under the jurisdiction of the National Joint Council for Local Authorities' Administrative, Professional, Technical and Clerical Services. Statistics as to their precise number were not available at the time of writing;[3] an estimate relating to the end of October 1948 put the total at approximately 150,000 permanent staff.[4] In addition to clerical and administrative workers, this figure includes certain technical and professional grades such as engineers, surveyors and sanitary inspectors, but not the broad groups of salaried 'operators' men-

---

[1] Ministry of Health, *Departmental Committee on the Qualifications, Recruitment, Training and Promotion of Local Government Officers* (HMSO 1934), para. 10.

[2] For a comprehensive review of local authority joint negotiating machinery see M. Turner-Samuels, *Industrial Negotiation and Arbitration* (Solicitors' Law Stationery Society, 1951) p. 14 and ff. and Oakes & Dacey, *An Outline of Local Government and Local Finance in England and Wales* (Sweet & Maxwell, 1950) Chap. 18.

[3] cf. *Guides to Official Sources No. 3: Local Government Statistics* (HMSO 1953).

[4] National Joint Council for Local Authorities' Administrative, Professional, Technical and Clerical Services, *A Survey of the Local Government Service* (1950), p. 9.

tioned earlier. The estimate also excludes all employees of the London County Council, for whom separate negotiating machinery was in existence in the period under review.

Recruitment: The Hadow Report of 1934 spoke of the lack of uniformity in the recruitment, qualifications, training and promotion of local government officers, but since then a considerable measure of standardization has been achieved. The great majority enter the service at 15 or 16; a smaller number join at what might be termed Civil Service 'executive' level, i.e. age 18 to 19. Professional workers—such as accountants, lawyers or engineers—enter after qualifying or may train in the service; university graduates of the Civil Service 'administrative' type are not systematically recruited.

Salaries: Under sections 105(2), 106(2) and 107(2) of the Local Government Act, 1933, authorities are free, with certain exceptions, to pay 'such reasonable remuneration as they may determine'; until comparatively recently there was no uniformity in the terms of employment of local government salaried staff.[1] Up to the first world war each individual authority had complete freedom of action in the matter; in the opinion of one expert, at any rate, standards were often poor both as regards qualifications and pay.[2] After that war, though the new movement of whitleyism took root elsewhere, its success in local government proved abortive; a national scale of salaries issued by the short-lived Local Government National Whitley Council of 1920 was almost generally ignored.[3] Attempts at revival were made subsequently, but not until the early forties was the country covered by a system of provincial councils; even then fewer than one-third of authorities were affiliated.

When the National Joint Council was reconstituted in 1944, it was faced with fifteen provincial councils' differing codes of salaries; it resolved to introduce a national pattern of remuneration. After prolonged negotiations this decision bore fruit, and a national 'scheme of conditions of service'[4] was approved early in 1946. The 'Charter',

[1] Throughout the rest of this chapter 'local government salaried staff' is used in its narrow sense, i.e. excluding teachers, police, etc. It likewise excludes the employees of the LCC.

[2] J. H. Warren, *Municipal Administration* (Pitman, 1948), p. 172.

[3] cf. *Local Government Service* (organ of National Association of Local Government Officers, now National and Local Government Officers' Association) March 1951, p. 388.

[4] National Joint Council for Local Authorities' Administrative, Professional, Technical and Clerical Services, *Scheme of Conditions of Service*, 1st ed. (January 1946).

as it became known, applied to all administrative, professional, technical and clerical staffs of local authorities—other than the LCC—in England and Wales, with the exception of town clerks, certain other chief officers and all those with basic pay of more than £700 a year. After this start, things moved relatively fast: The limit of £700 has been progressively raised, while two further negotiating committees —for town and district council clerks and for chief officers—were set up in 1948. As a result, practically all local government employees are now covered by national agreements.

The national 'scheme of conditions': The purpose of the Charter—the first viable set of national salaries and service conditions in the history of British local government—was to secure an improvement of both the status and standards of the local government service. It became operative on 1 April 1946, though the new salaries were applied in stages to serving officers. The Charter originally provided for five main 'divisions': general; clerical; higher clerical; miscellaneous; and administrative, professional and technical (APT). As regards the miscellaneous and APT divisions, however, these consisted simply of a number of 'abstract' scales; they merely provided a framework to be applied to individuals and posts by the detailed process of grading.

When the Charter was first introduced, it was widely welcomed by employing authorities and trade unions alike.[1] As the latter pointed out, the new rates represented a substantial improvement on all existing provincial council scales—and these had by no means been universally adopted. At the same time it was realized that the application of the division scales would be all-important, while certain features of the Charter—such as the retention of sex differentiation at the lower levels—came in for unfavourable comment.

The new scales had not affected the cost-of-living bonus which continued to accrue in addition to basic pay, but which had been unchanged since 1945.[2] Discontent became widespread, and early in 1947 the staff side formally requested its revision. This was turned down by the employers, and eventually the dispute was submitted to the National Arbitration Tribunal. The latter's award[3]—effective from 1 January 1948—consolidated bonus and basic salary for all,

[1] See e.g. *Local Government Chronicle*, 14 February 1948, p. 153, and *Local Government Service*, Feb.-March 1946 (editorial comment, President's statement to press, etc.).
[2] At £59 16s. 0d. p.a. for men, with lesser amounts for women, juveniles and those with salaries above £1,500.
[3] National Arbitration Tribunal Award No. 1051 (HMSO 1948).

but granted increases only to the general and clerical divisions.[1] It was a great disappointment to the staff.[2]

The wage-freeze was highly effective in local government; no change in remuneration took place between 1948 and 1950. In the latter part of that year, however, the staff representatives presented a claim covering all the Charter categories, contending that they had an unassailable case[3] in view of the steep rise in the cost of living since 1946, the serious recruitment difficulties and the hardship and frustration caused among existing officers. The claim was supported by a nation-wide campaign and received much publicity. Agreement was reached in April 1951, the increases ranging from £15 to £65 a year.

In January 1952 a fresh application was submitted, together with a proposal that henceforth remuneration should be adjusted periodically in relation to the Ministry of Labour's Index of Wage Rates. The Industrial Disputes Tribunal, who had to adjudicate the dispute, awarded from £10 to £25 for the general division and £25 for all other staff.[4] The enhanced rates became operative on 1 July 1952.[5]

The General Division
This is by far the largest of the divisions and carries out all the routine work of the service, though in April 1952 a separate pattern of salaries for typing and machine operator grades was introduced. Recruits usually join straight after leaving school, and in the period under review—as shown on Table 11—were paid strictly according to age. There was no automatic advancement to the higher classes.

The Clerical and Higher Clerical Divisions
In the original Charter, the clerical division was defined simply as covering officers 'performing duties of a clerical character which, having regard to their character and responsibilities, merit those officers being classified higher than the General Division'. In practice, it was staffed almost exclusively by promotees from below. No qualifying examination was required for advancement to the higher clerical division, though the latter was very small numerically.

[1] And to women in the APT division, through the consolidation of the 'male' bonus.

[2] See editorial, *Local Government Service*, March 1948.

[3] For details see *Local Government Service*, February 1951, p. 352.

[4] Industrial Disputes Tribunal Award No. 195 (HMSO 1952). The rates for women and certain other categories were to be settled in the light of these figures.

[5] There have been several further increases since. As to the individual grade structures of the divisions, outlined in the following pages, these continued to apply until end-1954, but have been recast on several occasions since—some of the most recent adjustments in part reversing those introduced in 1955.

TABLE 11

LOCAL GOVERNMENT

GENERAL DIVISION
(Men, England and Wales)[1]

Age	1 *April* 1946[2] £ p.a.	*Salary Scale as from* 1 *January* 1948 £ p.a.	1 *April* 1951* £ p.a.
16	89 14 0	135	150
17	104 14 0	140	165
18	126 4 0	160	180
19	155 2 0	180	200
20	181 12 0	200	220
21	219 16 0	220	245
22	244 16 0	245	270
23	259 16 0	260	290
24	274 16 0	275	310
25	289 16 0	290	335
26	304 16 0	305	360
27	319 16 0	320	380
28	334 16 0	335	400
29	349 16 0	350	410
30	359 16 0	360	425
31		370	
32		385	

[1] For additional allowance payable in London see text.

[2] All figures in this column include cost-of-living bonus. Staff employed before 1 April 1946 did not receive these rates in full until 1 October 1947.

* As from 1 July 1952 all salaries were increased by amounts ranging from £10 at age 16 to £25 at 30; they have been further revised since.

TABLE 12

LOCAL GOVERNMENT

CLERICAL AND HIGHER CLERICAL DIVISIONS
(Men, England and Wales)[1]

	1 *April* 1946[2] £ p.a.	*Salary Scale as from* 1 *January* 1948 £ p.a.	1 *April* 1951* £ p.a.
Clerical division	374.16.0 × 15–419.16.0	395 × 15–440	445 × 15–490
Higher clerical division	439.16.0 × 15–484.16.0	440 × 15–485	490 × 15–535

[1] For additional allowance payable in London see text.

[2] The figures in this column include the adult male cost-of-living bonus of £59 16s. 0d.; the bonus was lower for those under 21. Staff whose pre-Charter salary was more than £40 below the new scale, did not receive the full Charter rate until 1 April 1947.

* These salaries were increased by £25 as from 1 July 1952, and have been further revised since.

The Administrative, Professional and Technical Division

The APT division roughly corresponds to the lower reaches of the administrative and professional classes of the Civil Service, but also covers various technical personnel. In 1951 it consisted of eleven rungs, ranging from £440 to £1,000 per annum. These tiers—as shown on Table 13—were very short and advancement between them was not automatic; the only exception was grade IX or where an authority had fixed 'plural grading' for any particular post—i.e. a

TABLE 13

LOCAL GOVERNMENT

ADMINISTRATIVE, PROFESSIONAL & TECHNICAL DIVISION

(Men and Women, England and Wales)[1]

	Salary Scale as from		
	1 *April* 1946[2]	1 *January* 1948	1 *April* 1951*
	£ p.a.	£ p.a.	£ p.a.
Grade I	389.16.0 × 15–434.16.0	390 × 15– 435	440 × 15– 485
Grade II	419.16.0 × 15–464.16.0	420 × 15– 465	470 × 15– 515
Grade III	449.16.0 × 15–494.16.0	450 × 15– 495	500 × 15– 545
Grade IV	479.16.0 × 15–524.16.0	480 × 15– 525	530 × 15– 575
Grade V	519.16.0 × 15–549.16.0 × 20–569.16.0	520 × 15– 550 × 20– 570	570 × 15– 600 × 20– 620
Grade V(a)[3]	549.16.0 × 20–609.16.0	550 × 20– 610	600 × 20– 660
Grade VI	594.16.0 × 20–634.16.0 × 25–659.16.0	595 × 20– 635 × 25– 660	645 × 20– 685 × 25– 710
Grade VII	634.16.0 × 25–709.16.0	635 × 25– 710	685 × 25– 760
Grade VIII	684.16.0 × 25–759.16.0	685 × 25– 760	735 × 25– 810
Grade IX[4]		750 × 50– 900	790 × 40– 910
Grade X[4]		850 × 50–1,000	870 × 40– 950 × 50–1,000

[1] For additional allowance payable in London see text.

[2] The figures in this column apply to men only (because including the adult male cost-of-living bonus of £59 16s. 0d.); the bonus for women prior to consolidation was £48 2s. 0d. and was less still for any juveniles who may have held APT posts. Staff whose pre-Charter salary was more than £40 below the new scale, did not receive the full Charter rate until 1 April 1947.

[3] Introduced on 30 June 1947, the date of application being left to the discretion of employing authorities.

[4] Added at end-April 1949, to be applied not later than 1 April 1950.

* These salaries were increased by £25 as from 1 July 1952, and have been further revised since.

C

salary extending over several APT scales. We may add that in the case of professional appointments, the Intermediate only of the relevant professional examination was essential (1951) for APT I to IV, but for promotion beyond, the Final had to be passed. Entrance requirements for other recruits varied according to type of post.

The APT division had no rise between April 1946 and April 1951; the consolidation of bonus with basic salary in 1948 merely meant an extra 4*s.* per annum. The 1951 agreement gave an additional £50 to all except the two top grades; here the increase had to be scaled down so as not to exceed the ceiling—then £1,000—of the National Joint Council's jurisdiction. On the basis of the 1951 figures, the APT I scale was £5 behind that for the clerical division, while APT III was only just ahead of the higher clerical division.

We may add that the actual number of APT scales has undergone some interesting fluctuations. Under the 1946 Charter, there were eight grades, but as the gap between V and VI caused difficulties, an intermediate level was interposed in 1947. The addition of grades IX and X in 1949–50, on the other hand, was simply a case of extending the scope of the scheme, and since then the trend has been in the direction of fewer grades. Thus the 1950 peak number of eleven tiers was replaced by seven in 1955, and has since been further reduced to five—with a corresponding lengthening of the surviving scales.

The Miscellaneous Classes

The miscellaneous division was originally part of the general Charter; it provided for two grades—as shown on Table 14—with salaries within very narrow limits. A survey in 1949 revealed that this range did not allow of the satisfactory placing of all the 'miscellaneous' classes; many had for this reason been incorrectly graded elsewhere or not classified at all,[1] while the Charter conditions of service had also proved unsuitable. The National Council therefore decided to remove the division from the main scheme and to establish a separate one, sufficiently wide to cover all the miscellaneous categories.

The new scheme came into force on 1 October 1950; it relates to those whose duties are neither wholly clerical nor wholly manual such as, for example, statutory inspectors of gas meters. Those within the purview of some other joint industrial council, or supervisors whose rate of pay is customarily fixed by reference to that of those in their charge, are also excluded. As to the salaries laid down under the scheme, these do not cover juveniles aged twenty or under,

---

[1] National Joint Council for Local Authorities' Administrative, Professional, Technical and Clerical Services, *Scheme of Conditions of Service for the Miscellaneous Classes of Officers* (June 1950), p. 1.

while grade I applies only in exceptional cases. All miscellaneous employees have 'officer' status.

TABLE 14

LOCAL GOVERNMENT
MISCELLANEOUS CLASSES[1]
(Men,[2] England and Wales)[3]

	Salary Scale as from			
	1 *April* 1946[4]	1 *Jan.* 1948	1 *Oct.* 1950	1 *April* 1951*
	£ *p.a.*	£ *p.a.*	£ *p.a.*	£ *p.a.*
Grade I	314.16.0 × 15–359.16.0	315 × 15–360	245 × 10–285	285 × 10–325
Grade II	374.16.0 × 15–419.16.0	375 × 15–420	270 × 15–330	310 × 15–370
Grade III			315 × 15–375	355 × 15–415
Grade IV			360 × 15–420	400 × 15–415 × 25–440 × 15–470
Grade V			405 × 15–465	455 × 15–515
Grade VI			450 × 15–510	500 × 15–560[5]

[1] The miscellaneous division was completely reorganized with effect from 1 October 1950. Salaries before and after this date are not comparable.

[2] Miscellaneous posts apply primarily to men, but where occupied by women, carried the same salaries except for the 'bonus' element in the 1946 figures.

[3] For additional allowance payable in London see text.

[4] The figures in this column include the adult male cost-of-living bonus of £59 16s. 0d.; the bonus was lower for women and those under 21. Staff whose pre-Charter salary was more than £40 below the new scale, did not receive the full Charter rate until 1 April 1947.

[5] Where a post merited a higher salary, authorities could submit proposals to their Provincial Council for consideration.

* As from 1 July 1952 all salaries were increased by amounts ranging from £15 to £25; they have been further revised since.

Grading

Each department of a local authority has a fixed establishment, the allocation of jobs to grades being on the usual formula of 'duties and responsibilities'. The rule is that, except where an occupation has been dealt with at national level, authorities can classify staff as they please, though this is subject to an officer's right of appeal—a provision of which ample use has been made. In the early days of the Charter, there was much criticism because the National Council had not itself determined grades for the different types of work; it was claimed that staff were simply being placed in the category that happened to cover their pre-Charter salary.[1] Since then, however, the grading of several occupations has been standardized, and it is here that a national scale in the true sense of the word exists.

According to the main grading decisions arrived at by the National Joint Council during 1949–51, the fully-qualified but as yet inexperienced officer in one of the 'higher' professions—law, accountancy, engineering, surveying—started his local government career in APT V or V(a), which meant a commencing salary (1951) of £570 or £600 (outside London). 'Lower' professionals, on the other hand—such as sanitary inspectors, librarians or mental health workers—had to be satisfied with APT I–III. The 'decisions' also showed that grading takes place at certain key points only, such as straight after, or within a few years of, passing specific examinations; only one decision had then ventured beyond APT V(a).

In these first, experimental years, at any rate, national grading proved a slow and difficult process, though it was never visualized that all occupations—or levels within these—would be dealt with. In all other instances local authorities retain complete freedom in allocating staff to the divisions. An authority which does not like a particular salary award can, in theory, downgrade its establishment; alternatively, in the face of recruitment difficulties, it could decide on an opposite course. Any downgrading would of course be strongly resisted. On the other hand—whether the danger is real or not is another matter—the whole level of local government remuneration might rise even in the absence of a formal increase, through individual authorities' upgrading their establishments on the quiet.[2]

Distribution of Local Authority Staff

Grading then is the key to the question of salaries in local government; a 'Survey of the Local Government Service', published by the National Joint Council in 1950, gave some interesting details on this topic. The Survey was compiled from replies to a questionnaire, sent out in order to obtain a broad picture of the local government administrative system and the working of the Charter. Sixty-six per cent of authorities co-operated in the enquiry, the number of permanent staff covered being some 116,000.[3] The statistics related to the

---

[1] See *Local Government Service*, June 1946, pp. 93 and 103; December 1946, p. 225; and March 1948, p. 45.

[2] The leading article in the *Local Government Service*, April 1949, claimed that many authorities were in fact upgrading on account of serious staffing difficulties. To achieve such upgrading, in place of spectacular 'all-out' offensives, was put forward as a more worth-while tactic after the unfavourable arbitration award of 1948 (ibid. March 1948, p. 45) and by the 1949 annual conference of NALGO (ibid. July–August 1949).

[3] *Survey of Local Government Service*, op. cit., pp. 8 and 10.

31 October 1948; no later figures were available at the time of writing.

Distribution of local authority administrative, professional, technical and clerical staff: 31 *October* 1948[1]

Division/grade	Proportion in grade %
General division	42·8
Miscellaneous division	7·9
Clerical division	9·9
Higher clerical division	2·3
APT division: grade I	5·5
,, ,, ,, II	5·4
,, ,, ,, III	4·9
,, ,, ,, IV	4·9
,, ,, ,, V	4·2
,, ,, ,, V(a)	·8
,, ,, ,, VI	3·3
,, ,, ,, VII	1·7
,, ,, ,, VIII	1·4
Salary £760–£1,000[2]	2·9
Salary over £1,000	2·2

[1] *Survey of Local Government Service*, op. cit., p. 11.
[2] APT IX and X did not exist at the time of the survey.

The proportions in the different grades differed drastically according to sex:

Division/grade	Proportion in grade: Males %	Females %
General division	27·4	79·0
Miscellaneous division	10·7	1·1
Clerical and higher clerical division	12·1	12·4
APT and higher	49·8	7·5
	100·0	100·0

Thus while about one-half of men were graded as APT or above, only 7·5 per cent of women were so classified, the great majority being in the general division.

As far as the different types of authority are concerned, the metropolitan boroughs were giving their staff a considerably more favourable classification than other groups of local authorities. Thus

25·8 per cent only of metropolitan borough employees were in the general division, as against proportions ranging from 40·3 to 45·5 per cent for all other types of authority. There were significant differences also *within* each of these groupings. Among county boroughs, for example (average 45·5 per cent), Birmingham had 35·6 and Oldham 32·3 per cent in the general division. Sheffield and Nottingham, on the other hand, had so classified 59·6 and 60·7 per cent of their staff.[1] County Councils had the highest proportion—7 per cent —in the '£760 and over' categories.

That there should be differences as between county councils and, say, rural district councils in the proportion of senior officers employed is not surprising; in view of the great disparities between authorities with the same legal label, variations in their grading structure are likewise to be expected. For foolproof comparisons we have to take two authorities with not merely the same legal status, but also with approximately similar populations and staff complements. The following 'pairs' meet these requirements:[2]

Authority	Population mid-1948	Number of staff: 31 Oct. 1948	Proportion in general division
			%
Monmouthshire (county council)	316,200	469	29·4
Sussex (West) (county council)	310,300	478	40·6
Sheffield (county borough)	514,400	2,593	59·6
Leeds (county borough)	501,900	2,677	51·7

In both cases, though legal status and hence statutory responsibilities are identical and population and number of staff roughly similar, the proportion allocated to the general division varied considerably. This may partly be due to the incidence of non-statutory functions undertaken by these authorities, as also to differences in their administrative set-up or office organization. All the same, where two county councils/boroughs with approximately the same populations and staff complements have graded that staff very dis-

[1] *Survey of Local Government Service*, op. cit., pp. 18–23.

[2] Source: ibid. Chap. 1. In most cases comparison is complicated because, even where legal status and population are similar, numbers employed vary widely.

similarly, there is a *prima facie* case that at least part of the reason is authorities' varying evaluation of what must be largely analogous work. The more advantageous grading in metropolitan boroughs, likewise, appears to be a case of these paying higher remuneration to their routine clerical personnel over and above the formal London 'weighting'. All this is ample illustration of the wide discretion still left to local authorities in the payment of salaries to their clerico-administrative workers—a latitude which they do not possess in remunerating, say, policemen or manual employees.

The London County Council

In the period under review, the London County Council was not represented on the National Joint Council for Local Authorities' Administrative, Professional, Technical and Clerical Services, having built up an independent salary and wage structure. The total number employed by the LCC—including manual workers, domestic staff, teachers and other salaried employees—was, in 1951, stated to be approximately 60,000; those engaged on administrative, professional and clerical duties—i.e. analogous to the 'Charter' grades—numbered about 11,000.[1] There were three main classes on the clerico-administrative side: The typing grades, the general clerical class and the major establishment; in addition, there was a small higher clerical class. Special scales were fixed for various professional categories in the Council's employ, but in the case of teachers, nurses and similar well-defined groups, the LCC invariably conformed to the national pay pattern.

Clerks and Chief Officers

Local authorities are required by statute to engage certain categories of senior staff. All county, borough and urban district councils must appoint 'fit persons' to be clerk, treasurer, medical officer of health and surveyor, respectively, and all authorities except counties must have one or more sanitary inspectors.[2] The employment of certain others—chief education officers, for instance—is obligatory under other legislation. Over and above these statutory appointments, the number of chief officer posts varies according to type of authority, non-statutory activites and departmental set-up.

The lack of negotiating machinery for dealing with the pay of these most senior personnel and the resultant 'chaotic and difficult position' led in 1948 to the establishment of two bodies, the Joint Negotiating Committee for Town Clerks and District Council Clerks and

---

[1] *Establishment Committee Report* (6 March 1951) p. 137.
[2] Local Government Act, 1933, Part IV, ss. 98–107.

the Joint Negotiating Committee for Chief Officers of Local Authorities.[1] These two Committees are less formal bodies than the National Joint Council—of which they are independent—and many authorities were reluctant to implement their proposals.[2] However, a decision of the Industrial Disputes Tribunal in November 1951 clearly established the enforceability of the Chief Officer Committee's recommendations, as did a spate of analogous awards in the course of the following year.[3]

Town and District Council Clerks

The Joint Negotiating Committee for Town Clerks and District Council Clerks was set up to deal with all clerks of local authorities other than those of county councils. The first memorandum on remuneration was sent to authorities in 1949; it was subsequently agreed that—like the Chorley increases for senior civil servants—the new salaries should become operative in stages as from 1 October 1950 and 1 October 1951.

The memorandum defined the clerk's status as that of chief executive and administrative officer of the council, responsible for co-ordinating the whole of its work. We may point out that there is no parallel in local government to the top-level 'pure administrator' of the Civil Service; usually the clerk is a solicitor. However, the question of his qualifications has given rise to some controversy, and the view has been expressed that it is from an ingrained habit of mind rather than from any positive conviction that most people regard it as proper that clerks should be legally qualified.[4]

The Joint Negotiating Committee's recommendations were not in the form of fixed scales; instead the principle of salary ranges was adopted. The Committee pointed out that clerks' responsibilities differed even where the population served was similar, and that there were local considerations—such as the fact that some clerks also acted as their authority's chief financial officer or legal adviser—which could best be dealt with by giving authorities a certain lati-

[1] cf. Joint Negotiating Committee for Town Clerks and District Council Clerks, *Memorandum of Recommendations* (8 September 1949) Preamble, para 1.

[2] By the end of 1951 about 75 per cent of boroughs had adopted the proposed salaries for town clerks, while about 59 per cent of the authorities affected had applied the scales (or not less favourable rates) laid down by the Chief Officer Committee.

[3] See Industrial Disputes Tribunal Award No. 57 (HMSO 1951) and Award Nos. 232, 233, 234, 241, 246 and 250 (HMSO 1952).

[4] See 'Legal Education', *Local Government Chronicle*, 10 June 1950. The Hadow Report (op. cit. paras. 98–100) had emphasized that administrative ability was the essential qualification.

tude in the matter. Fourteen sets of ranges, based on population groups, were accordingly laid down; each authority was free to fix the commencing salary at any point within the appropriate range, though it had no discretion as regards the number and amount of increments.

TABLE 15

LOCAL GOVERNMENT

TOWN CLERKS AND DISTRICT COUNCIL CLERKS
(England and Wales)

Salaries[1] as from 1 October 1950*

Population of Authority	Minimum Salary £ p.a.	Annual Increments	Maximum Salary £ p.a.
Under 5,000	500– 650	3 of £50	650– 800
5/10,000	700– 850	3 of £50	850–1,000
10/15,000	800–1,000	4 of £50	1,000–1,200
15/20,000	1,000–1,200	4 of £50	1,200–1,400
20/30,000	1,150–1,350	4 of £50	1,350–1,550
30/45,000	1,350–1,550	4 of £50	1,550–1,750
45/60,000	1,500–1,750	5 of £50	1,750–2,000
60/75,000	1,750–2,000	2 of £100, 1 of £50	2,000–2,250
75/100,000	2,000–2,250	2 of £100, 1 of £50	2,250–2,500
100/150,000	2,250–2,500	2 of £100, 1 of £50	2,500–2,750
150/250,000	2,500–2,750	2 of £100, 1 of £50	2,750–3,000
250/400,000	2,750–3,000	2 of £100, 1 of £50	3,000–3,250
400/600,000	3,000–3,250	2 of £100, 1 of £50	3,250–3,500
Over 600,000[2]	Not less than 3,250		At discretion

[1] Excluding all additional fees payable if acting as clerk of the peace, returning officer, registration officer, etc.
[2] And Cities of London and Westminster.

* These salaries were introduced in instalments, and in many cases not payable in full until 1 October 1951. They have been revised since.

As shown on Table 15, all authorities with populations over 600,000 were given complete liberty as regards the maximum of their clerk's pay; in view of their special position, the Cities of London and Westminster were also placed in this category. If a clerk also held the post of clerk of the peace—the principal officer of a court of quarter sessions[1]—an additional salary in respect of that office was payable to him.[2] Further, he was entitled to keep the personal fees arising from his acting as returning officer, acting returning officer and registration officer at parliamentary and local elections, nearly all town clerks having some duties in connection with these.[3] Moneys, such as those paid by articled clerks, could likewise be retained. These various extras, it should be pointed out, may have involved fairly substantial additions to the basic remuneration.

Chief Officers

The Joint Negotiating Committee for Chief Officers established in 1948 was made responsible for the pay and service conditions of certain chief officers whatever their remuneration, and for all other staff —chiefs and others—with salaries in excess of the Charter ceiling. Town etc. clerks, chief medical officers, chief constables and so on— for whom separate machinery exists—were, however, excluded from its scope, though *deputy* town clerks were placed under its jurisdiction.

The first memorandum of recommendations in this instance was issued in September 1950, the new salaries again becoming operative in instalments commencing in October of that year. The memorandum applied only to chief accountants, treasurers, engineers, surveyors, architects and chief education officers, these being the categories for whom the Negotiating Committee was made the competent body whatever their remuneration. Other chief officers, we may add, were to come under the wing of the Committee only if their pay was above the APT ceiling.

As Tables 15 and 16 show, these first experiments in national payfixing for town clerks and chief officers were based on an identical pattern; however, the general level of the chief officer salary ranges was considerably lower than the clerks'. The maximum possible remuneration for the town clerk—excluding additional fees—of an

[1] The appointment arises only in those boroughs having a separate court of quarter sessions, and in many cases is a separate appointment.

[2] *Halsbury's Statutes of England*, 2nd ed., vol. 14, p. 703.

[3] Fees and allowances for registration officers are fixed by the Treasury under s. 44 of the Representation of the People Act, 1949. Those for (acting) returning officers were laid down in the Returning Officers' Expenses (England and Wales) Regulations, 1950 (SI 1950 No. 769). The amounts vary with the constituency's population, precise duties undertaken, etc.

TABLE 16

LOCAL GOVERNMENT
CHIEF OFFICERS
(Accountants and Treasurers, Engineers and Surveyors,
Chief Education Officers, Architects)
(England and Wales)

Salaries as from 1 *October* 1950*

Population of Authority	Minimum Salary £ p.a.	Annual Increments	Maximum Salary £ p.a.
Under 5,000	450– 600	3 of £50	600– 750
5/10,000	600– 750	3 of £50	750– 900
10/15,000	600– 850	3 of £50	750–1,000
15/20,000	750–1,000	3 of £50	900–1,150
20/30,000	800–1,100	3 of £50	950–1,250
30/45,000	900–1,300	4 of £50	1,100–1,500
45/60,000	1,050–1,450	4 of £50	1,250–1,650
60/75,000	1,250–1,650	4 of £50	1,450–1,850
75/100,000	1,350–1,850	5 of £50	1,600–2,100
100/150,000	1,550–2,050	5 of £50	1,800–2,300
150/250,000	1,750–2,250	2 of £100, 1 of £50	2,000–2,500
250/400,000	2,000–2,500	2 of £100, 1 of £50	2,250–2,750
400/600,000	2,100–2,700	3 of £100	2,400–3,000
Over 600,000[1]	At discretion		At discretion

[1] And Cities of London and Westminster.

* These salaries were introduced in instalments, and in many cases not payable in full until 1 October 1951. They have been revised since.

authority with a population of 400,000–600,000, for instance, was £3,500; for chief officers it was £3,000. On the other hand, the discretion conferred on (the larger) local authorities was much greater in the case of chief officers, among other things because it was recognized that a local authority would not necessarily wish to place all chiefs on the same scale. It should be added that all salaries under the chief officer agreement were inclusive; no fees were here to be retained.

As pointed out, a number of authorities showed themselves reluctant to implement the chief officer agreement, and the question of pay for other personnel within the Committee's purview has likewise proved difficult. However, recommendations were eventually issued, operative from 1 April 1952. These provided for nine scales, ranging from £1,000 to £2,000; the latter figure could be exceeded, and it was up to each authority how to allocate staff. Remuneration here, that is, was not based on population.

Clerks of County Councils

Section 99 of the Local Government Act, 1933, stipulates that 'every county council shall pay to the clerk of the council such reasonable salary as may be determined by the council, subject to the approval of the Minister'.[1] County council clerks are thus in a special position in that their remuneration has to be endorsed from the centre, and at the time of the 1946–8 exchanges culminating in the formation of the town clerk and chief officer Committees, declared themselves unwilling to participate in similar machinery. However, since 1959 a Joint Negotiating Committee is functioning.

In 1945 the County Councils Association submitted to the Minister of Health—at the latter's request—ranges of salaries to be used for his guidance in discharging his statutory function of approving the remuneration of county council clerks. Revised recommendations were drawn up in 1951, substantially in excess of those of 1945;[2] these are set out below. We may add that these were not negotiated scales as are those for town clerks and chief officers; although the staffs were consulted, the proposals were essentially those of the employers. The schedule was again to be applied on the Chorley model, i.e. in stages beginning on 1 October 1950.

The scales were drawn up to apply to clerks who received an *additional* salary in respect of their office of clerk of the peace; where a county council clerk did not so act, his maximum in an over-600,000 authority, for instance, was 'not exceeding £5,000'. The amounts accruing to clerks of the peace vary widely; they do not necessarily depend on population, as the incidence of quarter sessions business is partly independent of the latter.[3] Fees received as acting

[1] Originally the Minister of Health, now the Minister of Housing and Local Government. The salaries of clerks appointed before 1931 are subject to the approval of the Home Secretary.

[2] Details of both sets of recommendations are contained in the Report to the Parliamentary and General Purposes Committee of the County Councils Association, *Supplement to Official Gazette*, April 1951, p. 92 and ff.

[3] cf. *Halsbury's Statutes of England*, 2nd ed., vol. 14, p. 703. Clerks appointed before 1931 receive a single salary in respect of their two offices (in their case always held jointly). Special arrangements apply in London and Middlesex.

returning officer at parliamentary elections or from articled clerks were also additional, but others—including those received as registration officer—were to be handed over to the county fund. In practice, there was a certain amount of variation in the precise terms on which salaries were paid.

Clerks of County Councils:
Recommendations of County Councils Association

Population	Minimum salary £ p.a.	Increments	Maximum salary £ p.a.
Not exceeding 60,000	1,600–1,900	5 of £50	1,850–2,150
60/ 75,000	1,900–2,200		2,150–2,450
75/100,000	2,200–2,500		2,450–2,750
100/150,000	2,450–2,750	2 of £100	2,700–3,000
150/250,000	2,700–3,000	1 of £50	2,950–3,250
250/400,000	3,000–3,300		3,250–3,550
400/600,000	3,300–3,600		3,550–3,850
Over 600,000	At discretion, but not less than £3,600		At discretion, but not exceeding £4,500

It will be seen that the remuneration recommended for county council clerks was higher than for town clerks, but while the former was inclusive of fees as registration officer, these were an additional emolument for the latter. On the other hand, clerks of county councils almost invariably act as clerk of the peace, while in the case of boroughs—insofar as the appointment arises—the two are frequently separate appointments. Comparisons are difficult in the circumstances.

Provincial Differentiation
Local government salaries apply throughout England and Wales, but in the Metropolitan Police Area an additional London allowance is paid. It accrues to all except (town, etc.) clerks and chief officers, in whose case authorities are able to weight the scale itself without making a formal addition.

The rates of London weighting introduced as from 1 April 1948 applied equally—unlike those previously in force—to all divisions and both sexes. The amounts were £10 per annum for those up to age 20, £20 for staff aged 21–25, and £30 for those 26 years or over; for many years attempts to secure more favourable additions came to nought.[1] As we saw, however, the 1948 Survey of the Local Government Service revealed that metropolitan borough employees were being more advantageously graded than their provincial colleagues, and we may add that in 1953 the National Joint Council formally authorized increased scales or superior grading for certain classes of metropolitan and Birmingham Corporation staff. To some extent, therefore, provincial differentiation in local government is effected via the medium of the salary structure itself rather than through that of the official London allowance.

Sex Differentiation

It is estimated that at end-1948 women constituted about 30 per cent of the total labour force in local government administration.[2] In the general, clerical and higher clerical divisions the ratio of women's to men's scales used to be, as in the Civil Service, approximately 4:5, though at the APT level men and women have had identical scales since the inception of the Charter.[3] The memoranda dealing with chief officers, town, and county council clerks likewise did not formally discriminate between the sexes.

Whether there has been equal pay in practice is a somewhat delicate point, as the system of grading obscures the position. As was shown earlier, only a very small proportion of women hold higher posts, and there have been complaints that female staff have been allocated to the clerical divisions, where their male colleagues on more or less identical duties have been graded as APT.[4] Among town etc. clerks and the more august of chief officers, women are in any case quite the exception, though they hold posts as chief children's officers and, to a lesser extent, chief librarians. There is also a sprinkling of female chief archivists, (deputy) medical officers of health and housing managers.[5]

In April 1955 the National Joint Council announced that, following the action taken by HM Government, it had agreed that equal pay should be introduced into the local government service by an analogously-phased scheme.

[1] In 1953, for example, the Industrial Disputes Tribunal (Award No. 354) ruled that the claim for a higher allowance had not been established. The above rates were not in fact increased until 1 May 1960.

[2] *Survey of Local Government Service*, op. cit., p. 9.

[3] However, until end-1947 women received a lower cost-of-living bonus.

[4] See *Local Government Chronicle*, 9 July 1949, p. 684.

[5] See *Municipal Year Book and Public Utilities Directory* (1951-2), sections 31 and 33.

Chapter 3

EDUCATION

There was nothing approaching a system of elementary education until the establishment of the 'charity' schools of the seventeenth and eighteenth centuries, later supplemented by the widespread setting up of Sunday schools. In the nineteenth century a more comprehensive effort by various religious bodies led to the foundation of voluntary schools; gradually these superseded the earlier institutions.[1] The State's interest in the field goes back to the inauguration of annual grants in 1833; at that time large numbers were still entirely without the means of instruction, the principle of compulsory schooling not being accepted until the 1870's. The Government's direct concern with higher education dates from the turn of the century, though numerous privately-endowed grammar and several 'public schools' had by then a long history.

The central authority now responsible for publicly-aided education in England and Wales is the Ministry of Education, though it does not provide, own or directly control any educational institution, administration being decentralized among 146 local education authorities. A far-reaching reorganization of the educational pattern was effected by the Education Act of 1944. This divided the system into three—primary, secondary and further education—and made it the duty of every local education authority 'to contribute towards the spiritual, moral, mental and physical development of the community by securing that efficient education throughout those stages shall be available . . .'[2] Primary education includes the nursery, infant, junior and 'special' school stages up to the twelfth year; secondary education covers grammar, secondary technical and secondary modern schools. Further education comprises all (other) types of provision for those over compulsory school age.

In addition to the schools directly provided by local education authorities, there are numerous voluntary agencies in the field. Many of these obtain financial assistance from local funds ('controlled', 'aided' or 'special agreement' schools) or from the central government direct ('direct-grant' schools); they are part of the grant-aided

---

[1] Throughout the period there were also a number of 'dame' schools.
[2] Education Act, 1944 (7 & 8 Geo. 6. c. 31) s. 7.

network. Others, maintained by private individuals or educational
trusts, receive no financial aid from any public source; though they
may be 'recognized as efficient' by the central authority, they are outside the statutory system. Also outside the Minister's jurisdiction are
the universities which are self-governing institutions, 'approved
schools' which are under the aegis of the Home Office, while agricultural education is the joint responsibility of the Ministries of Education and Agriculture.

Teaching Staff
Teachers are employees of local education authorities or of the
governing or managing bodies of the schools in which they work.
Numbers as at end-March 1950 were:

*Teachers in grant-aided schools and establishments
as at* 31 *March* 1950[1]

Primary and secondary schools	211,784
Special schools	3,207
Establishments for further education	7,339
Training colleges	2,503
Miscellaneous	3,646
	228,479

This total includes 5,584 staff in direct-grant schools and voluntary
training colleges, but excludes 15,016 employed in independent
schools 'recognized as efficient'. The number of teachers in other
independent establishments was not known at the time of writing,
but the smallness of the private sector can be gauged from the fact
that in 1950 92·5 per cent of the child population aged 5 and under 14
were in grant-aided institutions.[2]

The Burnham Machinery
Since 1919 salaries for teachers have been centrally determined by a
number of standing joint committees, known—after their first chairman—as the Burnham Committees. Under the Education Act of
1944 this machinery was revised, there now being three statutory
bodies. The Burnham Main Committee deals with teachers in primary
and secondary schools, the Burnham Technical Committee with those
in establishments of further education, while a third Committee considers the salaries of farm institute staffs. The duty of these bodies is
'to submit to the Minister, whenever they think fit or whenever they

[1] Ministry of Education, *Education* 1900–50, Cmd. 8244 (HMSO 1951), Table 51.
The items have been grouped. Teachers in farm institutes and approved schools
are not included in Ministry of Education statistics.
[2] ibid. Table 95.

may be required by him so to do, such scales of remuneration for teachers as they consider suitable'.[1] When Burnham decisions are so submitted, the Minister of Education must approve or reject them, section 89 being deliberately worded so as to leave him with no responsibility for either framing or amending scales.[2] If approved, they are promulgated by statutory instrument.

A fourth body settles the remuneration of the staffs of training colleges (other than training departments of universities). This Committee is not set up under section 89 of the 1944 Act, a substantial proportion of colleges being voluntary. However, though its recommendations are not given statutory sanction, they are formally endorsed by the Minister and recognized for grant purposes; hence for all practical purposes they are equally binding. Each of the four Committees consists of an authorities' panel and a teachers' panel, plus an independent chairman nominated from the centre.

Though originally Burnham scales did not possess mandatory force, they were ultimately almost always adopted. The Burnham reports now apply compulsorily to all full-time teachers in schools and colleges maintained by local education authorities, a sizeable minority being voluntary institutions. In direct-grant schools, on the other hand, payment of Burnham rates is not obligatory: the Schools Grant Regulations 1951, for example, merely provided that 'the scales of remuneration for teachers in the school shall be adequate and reasonable.'[3]

Primary and Secondary Schools
The great majority of teachers are employed in primary and secondary schools. Details of their distribution in 1950 are given below:

*Teachers in maintained primary and secondary schools
as at 31 March 1950[4]*

Primary[5] schools	130,412
Secondary modern schools	42,269
Secondary grammar schools	27,233
Secondary technical schools	3,370
Miscellaneous[6]	4,384
	207,668

[1] Education Act, 1944, s. 89.
[2] cf. 21 December 1944, HC Deb. 406, 1942.
[3] SI 1951 No. 1745, s. 41(1) and s. 50 (f).
[4] Cmd. 8244, op. cit., Table 51. The total differs from that for primary and secondary schools on p. 80 through the exclusion of direct-grant schools.
[5] Including visiting, relief and nursery school teachers.
[6] Includes 'divided service, primary and secondary schools' and 'practical instruction centres and miscellaneous'.

This total included 27,417 head teachers, the remainder being officially described as 'assistant teachers'.

Training and qualifications: Teachers are prepared for their professional life either at training colleges or by university training departments. The former, in the period under review, were mostly providing two-year courses covering both academic and professional subjects, though in June 1957 it was announced that the course would be extended to three years as from September 1960. Universities offer a one-year training for those already holding a degree.

Out of the 207,668 primary and secondary teachers at end-March 1950, 7,884 were non-qualified in the sense of being neither graduates nor college-trained. 169,197 were professionally trained, but the number with a university degree (or equivalent) was relatively small— only 33,960. The proportion varied between different types of institution ; while only 3·3 per cent of primary school teachers held degrees, the percentage in grammar schools was 77. The proportion of graduates in *all* grant-aided institutions, we may add, was then 18·2 per cent.[1]

Salaries: Teachers' remuneration at one time varied in chaotic fashion, salaries being a matter for local arrangement, with great disparity between voluntary and Board schools and the profession as a whole 'disgracefully exploited'.[2] The Burnham Committee substituted an era of peace for one of friction and bad feeling, and evolved order out of chaos by reducing more than three hundred differing local authority scales to four—subsequently three—in elementary and two in secondary schools. Nevertheless, the Burnham system maintained the historic distinction between elementary and secondary education: the two types of school were covered by entirely separate reports.[3]

The McNair Committee, reviewing the situation in 1944, were of the opinion that a revision of the whole system was necessary. They were strongly opposed to the continued differentiation in elementary and secondary teachers' pay: there should be only one grade of qualified teacher and one basic scale, to which additions should be made for special qualifications and experience. The Committee went out of their way to emphasize the tradition of cheapness which had

[1] Cmd. 8244, op. cit. Tables 53 and 51.
[2] ibid. p. 89 and Board of Education, *Report of the (McNair) Committee on the Supply, Recruitment and Training of Teachers and Youth Leaders* (HMSO 1944), para. 17. In 1900 more than half the certificated men assistants were paid less than £100 a year.
[3] *McNair Report*, op. cit., para. 134 and ff.

dogged elementary education in particular for many years, from which the country had not yet emancipated itself. The salaries of all teachers should be substantially increased, being in their view demonstrably inadequate and comparing most unfavourably with those in other professions.[1]

When the unified Burnham (Main) Committee issued its first Report,[2] applicable alike in primary, secondary modern, secondary technical and secondary grammar schools, it received a mixed reception. On the one hand, it was hailed as historic and epoch-making[3] in view of the fact that it unified the profession, bringing parity of salaries both as between grammar and elementary teachers and as between area and area. On the other hand, the four secondary associations lodged a vigorous protest against the new scales which, as far as grammar school staffs were concerned, constituted a considerable levelling process. The Report became operative as from 1 April 1945.

The new Burnham structure provided for one basic scale, to which additions were made in respect of

    (*a*) a degree or equivalent
    (*b*) full-time study or training in excess of two years
    (*c*) a headship
    (*d*) special responsibilities, qualifications, etc.
    (*e*) service in a 'special' school (i.e. for the handicapped)
    (*f*) service in the London area.

Speaking in very broad terms, this general pattern has been maintained, though there have been important changes of detail. Before dealing with these, we must briefly sketch in the outlines of Burnham history following the issue of the 1945 document. This latter ran its course of three years—the intended life-span, we may add, of most post-war Burnham reports. The 1948 agreement[4] left the basic minimum unchanged, though it added two increments at the maximum and improved the graduate allowance. However, it did not give any increase to younger non-graduate staff; this, as well as the scheme of head teacher allowances which it introduced, caused strong resentment.[5]

[1] *McNair Report*, op cit., paras. 107–130, 147 and 154.

[2] Ministry of Education, *Report of the Burnham Committee on Scales of Salaries for Teachers in Primary and Secondary Schools, England and Wales*, 1945 (HMSO 1945).

[3] cf. *Schoolmaster and Woman Teacher's Chronicle* (organ of National Union of Teachers) 16 November 1944, leading article; and ibid. 8 March 1945, 'Random Reflections'.

[4] Ministry of Education, *Report of the Burnham Committee on Scales of Salaries for Teachers in Primary and Secondary Schools, England and Wales*, 1948 (HMSO 1948).

[5] cf. *Schoolmaster*, 16 October 1947, leading article, p. 326.

TABLE 17

EDUCATION

TEACHERS: PRIMARY AND SECONDARY SCHOOLS
(Men, England and Wales)[1]

		Salary Scale as from		
		1 *April* 1945 £ *p.a.*	1 *April* 1948 £ *p.a.*	1 *April* 1951* £ *p.a.*
Qualified assistant teacher				
Without degree		300×15–525	300×15–555	375×18–630[2]
With degree[3]		315×15–555	330×15–585	435×18–690[2]
do. plus 3 years'	full-time	330×15–570	345×15–600	453×18–708[2]
do. plus 4 years' }	study or	345×15–585	360×15–615	471×18–726[2]
do. plus 5 years'	training	360×15–600	375×15–630	489×18–744[2]
Additional[4] special responsibility allowance		50–100	50–150	40–[5]

Qualified head teacher

Appropriate salary as qualified assistant teacher, plus head teacher allowance, based on school's 'unit total'[6]

Group	Unit Total			
0	1– 40	See text	55 }	55
I	41– 100			80
II	101– 200		100	110
III	201– 300	for	140	145
IV	301– 400		180	180
V	401– 500		220	220
VI	501– 600	this	260	260
VII	601– 700		300	300
VIII	701– 800		340	340
IX	801– 900	period	380	380
X	901–1,000		420	420
XI	1,001–1,100		460	460
XII	1,101–1,200		500	500
XIII	1,201–1,300		540	540
XIV	1,301–1,400		580	580
XV	1,401–1,600		620	620
XVI	1,601–1,800		660	660
XVII	1,801–2,000		700	700
XVIII	2,001–2,200		740	740
XIX	2,201–2,400		780	780
XX	2,401–2,700		820	820
XXI	2,701–3,000		860	860
XXII	3,001 or over		900	900

[1] For additional allowance payable in London see text.

[2] The final increment was £21.

[3] During the three years beginning 1 April 1948, teachers holding a first-class honours degree received an additional £15 at the minimum and £30 at the maximum.

[4] Prior to 1 April 1948, the graduate addition had to be foregone if a special allowance was received.

In July 1949 the teachers' organizations sought to have the 1948 agreement amended, but the authorities felt unable to grant this, so that the 1948 Report also remained in force for three years. The main provisions of the 1951 settlement[1] were to add £75 to the basic scale, shorten the latter by three points, raise the annual increment from £15 to £18 and increase the graduate addition. Press comment generally took the line that the rise was well-deserved, just as—some six months earlier—a large number of MPs made clear that in their view teachers' remuneration was totally inadequate.[2]

The 1951 negotiations had included a 'gentlemen's agreement' that, if warranted by trends in the cost of living, the staffs might take up the question of improving the basic scale before the Report's normal expiry; within six months of the latter's coming into force, it was the subject of representations by the teachers. The discussions proved abortive, however, and when in March 1952 both panels agreed to resort to arbitration and to make the arbitrators' decision their own recommendation to the Minister, this procedure was declared to be ruled out by section 89 of the Education Act, under which the Burnham Committee cannot commit itself in advance in this manner. It was therefore agreed to seek the *advice* of three independent persons—thus observing constitutional proprieties—which both panels of the Committee subsequently accepted. This finally culminated in a flat-rate 'special addition' of £40, payable as from 1 July 1952 to all grades of teachers[3] in all types of schools. New and improved Burnham rates became operative from 1 April 1954, the basic scale for qualified men then being raised to £450–£725 per annum.[4]

[1] Ministry of Education, *Report of the Burnham Committee on Scales of Salaries for Teachers in Primary and Secondary Schools, England and Wales*, 1951 (HMSO 1951).
[2] 4 May 1950, HC Deb. 474, 1908–2049.
[3] The reader is reminded that, in fields in which sex differentiation obtained in the period under review, *all figures—as explained on p. 21—must be taken to refer to men only*. The July 1952 'special addition' for women, for example, was only £32 p.a.
[4] Further increases have been effected since.

[5] There was no upper limit, and salaries could be further supplemented from an authority's 'area pool'.
[6] The salary could be further supplemented from an authority's 'area pool'. The 'unit total'/'area pool' system did not apply prior to 1 April 1948.

* All salary *scales* in this column were increased by £40 as from 1 July 1952. Both scales and allowances were improved as from 1 April 1954 and have been further revised since.

Graduate and training additions: 'Graduate' status for salary purposes is not confined to those holding a university degree, but applies
also to those with professional and equivalent qualifications. It was
the weighting given to the possession of a degree that caused such
resentment among grammer school staffs in 1944–5, but there has
been a considerable improvement since. Thus under the 1945 Report
a graduate was merely entitled to an extra £15 at the minimum and
£30 at the maximum of the scale, the theory being that high quality
ought in the main to be rewarded by the more discriminating system
of 'special allowances';[1] holders of these had to forego their graduate
addition. The 1948 Report fixed the latter at £30 throughout a
teacher's career, abolished the 'merger' rule (thus making it possible
to receive both a graduate and special allowance), and also made provision for a distinct payment to those with a first-class honours degree. The 1951 agreement further improved on this by raising the
graduate weighting to £60, though it did away again with the special
treatment for first-class honours men. However, an allowance in
respect of a 'good honours degree' was reintroduced in 1954, since
when both it and the general graduate addition have been considerably stepped up: As compared with 1945, therefore, there has been a
substantial widening of differentials as between graduates and non-
graduates, the combined allowance for 'good honours' men under
the 1959 Report being £165 per annum.

The study or training which give entitlement to extra remuneration
are, broadly speaking, full-time courses after age 17 at universities or
at training, technical or art colleges. The time may have been spent in
reading for a degree, a diploma or on postgraduate research; the
teacher who has devoted the usual three or four years to obtaining a
degree thus qualifies for both a graduate and a training addition. In the
period under review, the payments were one, two or three increments
throughout the scale for (respectively) three, four or five years' approved study/training. The size of the allowance has, however, since
been increased in that the 'training increments' are now slightly larger
than the annual increments, though the latter have themselves
slowly crept up since 1945. Also, a total of four increments—for six
years' study etc.—can now be earned, the maximum training addition under the 1959 Report thus being £120, as against £45 under the
1945 document.

Head Teachers
Before the 1944–5 reorganization it was only the pay of 'elementary'
heads which was fixed on a national basis, the Burnham Secondary

[1] See Statement by Minister of Education, 20 February 1945, HC Deb. 408,
710–13.

Committee merely laying down minima, leaving the rest to the discretion of individual grammar schools. And while elementary heads' scales were integrally linked to those of their junior staff, headmasters' and -mistresses' salaries bore no particular relationship to those of assistant masters and mistresses. As for the level of pre-war remuneration, the maxima for elementary heads were described as 'wholly inadequate' by the 1944 McNair Committee and those in secondary schools as at any rate 'insufficient', although here there were exceptions.[1]

The 1945 Report attempted to assimilate these two quite different systems. Taking the old elementary scheme as a basis, it divided schools into five grades according to size. The nucleus of heads' pay was that appropriate to them as assistants; on promotion they received increases of from £30 to £150, depending on the grade of their school. Heads then proceeded to maxima, ranging from £570 in grade I, to £750 in grade V, institutions.

These figures were augmented—as for assistants—by up to three 'training' increments, but a head teacher could not then draw his graduate allowance, insignificant though it was. Where a school contained at least thirty pupils who had reached the age of 15, the head received a further £50 in respect of each thirty such pupils; where the local authority still considered his salary as inadequate, it could seek the Minister's approval to a more favourable scale. These last two provisions were largely an attempt to meet the position of grammar school heads, some of whom had been enjoying a much higher income previously.

There was a considerable amount of discontent over the working of the scheme; the 1948 Report therefore introduced a new system. This brought together the various 'extras' accruing under the 1945 agreement, but in the process became itself highly elaborate: Heads still receive the salaries payable to them as assistants—including additions for training and degree—together with a new *head teacher allowance*. This latter varies with the school's 'unit total'—a figure assessed by reference to (a) the number of pupils on the school's roll, and (b) their age. Under the 1948 Report—and until 1956—each pupil under 15 counted as one unit; if aged 15 and under 16 as four; if aged 16 and under 17 as seven, while every scholar of 17 and over was worth ten units. There were, as shown on Table 17, twenty-three levels of head teacher allowances.[2] A school with a unit total of 350, for instance, was in group IV and the head received £180 over and and above his salary as assistant; if the establishment was a large one

---

[1] *McNair Report*, op. cit. paras. 25 and 142.

[2] The allowances under the 1948 and 1951 Reports were identical, except for an improvement in the position of heads of smaller schools under the latter.

with a unit total of, say, 2,500, the relevant figure was £820. The highest possible addition—under both the 1948 and 1951 agreements —was £900; however, the majority of heads being concentrated in the lower unit total groups, the smallness of the allowance in these gave rise to much dissatisfaction.

We may add that the system introduced in 1948 is still (1960) in operation, except that there are now twenty-eight levels of head teacher allowances, while the formula for calculating the unit totals has been revised to some extent in favour of heads of secondary (including modern) schools. The payments themselves for each unit total range have of course also gone up.

Allowances for Special Responsibilities[1]
The system of special additions—for duties intermediate between those of the basic-grade teacher and the head—has its historic antecedents, an official minute in 1846 already mentioning the expediency of paying small gratuities 'for the further encouragement of deserving schoolmasters'.[2] Prior to the 1944 Act there was a limited power under each of the Burnham reports to reward posts of special responsibility, but the great majority of allowances were small.

The 1945 Report provided that 'for Assistant Teachers there shall be special posts in respect of which allowances over and above the Scale Salary shall be granted for special responsibility, special work of an advanced character, special academic, professional or industrial qualifications, or other circumstances which in the opinion of the Authority justify an addition to the scale'.[3] It thus became obligatory upon authorities to grant allowances—payment had formerly been permissive—but they were not to be applied in such a manner as would amount to a general alteration in the operation of the scales. They were to be paid to 15 per cent of the full-time qualified assistant teachers in the local education authority's employ; each allowance was to be between £50 and £100 per annum, though subject to ministerial approval this could be exceeded. The 1948 Report left these provisions broadly unchanged, except that it gave authorities a somewhat greater latitude by increasing the range of the additions to £50–£150, to be payable to between $12\frac{1}{2}$ to $17\frac{1}{2}$ per cent of its assistant teacher establishment.[4]

---

[1] These allowances are payable to teachers other than heads. However, as they are computed on the same basis as head teacher allowances, we deal with them at this stage.

[2] Quoted in *Schoolmaster*, 20 September 1951, p. 321.

[3] 1945 *Report*, op. cit., para 9(a).

[4] Also, the number, value and distribution of 'special posts' was no longer to be subject to prior ministerial approval.

The 1951 Report, however, introduced significant innovations. It provided that every education authority was to allot to each school a sum of money to be spent on allowances, the total being variable within a prescribed range depending on the school's unit total.[1] For this purpose, schools were divided into 129 'unit total' groups, to each of which a range of allowance expenditure was attached.[2]

Very small schools—those with unit totals of up to 100—received no allocation for allowance expenditure;[3] those with a total of 101–200 need not, but could, grant an allowance. For all other institutions the allocations increased more than proportionately with size of school, £2,225–£3,325 being the maximum range (1951) that could be allotted to a school.[4] Burnham did not give any ruling as regards distribution to individual teachers, except that the additions were not to be less than £40 and except, again, for the somewhat ambiguous provision that they must not amount to a general alteration in the operation of the scale salaries. Otherwise, no restriction was imposed on either the size or number of payments.

Another innovation of the 1951 Report was the creation of an 'area pool'—a sum of money to be disbursed at the discretion of each authority over and above the expenditure allocated to schools for special allowances. The pool was calculated at the rate of 4s. per registered pupil in the authority's schools, and could be used to grant additional allowances to all grades of teacher or deal with cases of hardship arising from the reorganization or closure of a school.[5] Again, payment from its bounty was not to be such as would radically affect the operation of the scales.

These highly intricate provisions of the 1951 (and 1954) Report in the matter of rewarding special responsibilities resulted in wide variations in the practice of different local authorities, while the latter left a significant amount of allowance money unspent in the kitty.[6] The system was therefore amended in April 1955 and abandoned altogether as from October 1956. Since then there is a detailed pattern of allowances for deputy head teachers—analogous to that for heads; a system of standardized additions for heads of departments;

---

[1] Calculated as for head teacher allowances.
[2] For full details see 1951 *Report*, op. cit., pp. 25–6.
[3] Though they could get one from the authority's 'area pool': see *post*.
[4] Apart from additions from the authority's 'area pool'.
[5] For details see 1951 *Report*, op. cit., p. 9.
[6] Meeting representatives of the educational press in January 1954, the Minister of Education stated that in the previous year the amount spent on special allowances by local authorities was £2,450,000 out of a maximum possible total of £2,900,000. The total in 'area pools' was £1,100,000, of which authorities only spent £400,000. (Reported in *Times Educational Supplement*, 29 January 1954.)

and a scheme of 'graded posts' under which prescribed extra payments are made to a proportion of other basic-grade teachers. The
number of graded posts that can be established in any one school
again depends largely on its unit total.[1]

By way of a brief postscript it might be pointed out that, all in all,
the teaching structure is now much more highly stratified than in
1945. Thus substantial additions now accrue to deputy head teachers
and heads of departments; payments to these categories—who were
not formally recognized for salary purposes until October 1956—
were limited to a maximum of £100 per annum in 1945. The weighting for graduate status has likewise been increased much more, relatively, than has the basic scale since that date, while under the 1951
and 1954 special allowances scheme, for example, more graduates
received allowances than non-graduates—and more sizeable ones at
that. The 1956 innovation of additions for heads of departments,
similarly, is primarily designed for those doing work leading to the
'A' level of the General Certificate of Education. Further, the method
of calculating a school's unit total—the infrastructure on which the
size (and number) of several major allowances has depended since
1951—is such as to weight the scales significantly in favour of grammar school staffs: This is still the case even under the revised formula
introduced in 1956. It is grammar school staffs, again, who benefit
most from the training additions. Hence both as regards the different
levels of responsibility within a school and as between grammar and
other schools, salaries are far less 'egalitarian' than might be supposed from the existence of a single basic scale for the whole of the
profession. That such a single base has nonetheless been retained is an
interesting phenomenon.

Special Schools
Local education authorities must provide special facilities for all
physically and mentally defective children in their areas. For mild
cases this may be within the framework of ordinary primary and
secondary institutions but, for the more severely handicapped,
'special' schools must be set up. Teachers employed in these are paid
the same as those in other primary and secondary institutions, plus
an allowance which under the 1951 Report was £36 a year. If they
hold a qualification such as the diploma of the College of Teachers
of the Blind and work in an appropriate establishment, they receive a
further sum—£30 per annum in 1951. Staff in charge of 'special'
classes in ordinary schools also normally qualify for these additions.

[1] For full details see Ministry of Education, *Report of the Burnham Committee
on Scales of Salaries for Teachers in Primary and Secondary Schools, England and
Wales, 1959* (HMSO 1959).

Under the 1951 Report, 'special' teachers could be granted a further payment out of an authority's area pool.

Qualified heads in special schools receive the salaries payable to them as (special) assistants, plus a head teacher allowance. This again varies with the school's unit total, but in this instance is calculated on the basis of numbers and type of disability, instead of by reference to numbers and age. One delicate child, for example, counts as two units, while a deaf or partially deaf pupil counts as six. Under the 1951 Report, 'special' heads' allowances thus ranged from £80 for schools in unit total group I(S) to £370 for those in group VIII(S)— the highest.

Independent and 'Public' Schools

An 'independent school' has been officially defined as 'any school at which full-time education is provided for five or more pupils of compulsory school age . . . not being a school maintained by a local education authority or a school in respect of which grants are made by the Minister to the proprietor of the school'.[1] The term 'public school' cuts across the independent/grant-aided classification. The earliest such institutions are Eton, Winchester, Westminster, Charterhouse, Harrow, Rugby and Shrewsbury—the Public Schools Act of 1864 enumerates these and also St Paul's and Merchant Taylors'. Nowadays the term is no longer confined to these, but comprises all establishments—limited to 200—represented on the Headmasters' Conference.[2] The majority of direct-grant schools are in this category; quite a large proportion of public schools are thus grant-aided. Confusion arises because in popular usage the term 'public school' retains something of its old and more restricted meaning.[3]

No precise information is available as to the remuneration paid in independent schools. Those 'recognized as efficient' appear to a greater or lesser extent to be influenced by the provisions of the Burnham reports, but some at any rate of the public schools grant higher salaries. The small independent non-recognized schools, on the other hand, almost certainly pay less than the Burnham rates for qualified teachers. For one thing, these institutions are precluded from joining one of the officially-sponsored superannuation schemes, and hence have difficulty in obtaining qualified staff.

[1] Education Act, 1944, s. 114(1).

[2] They must be controlled by a governing body created by a statutory scheme or trust deed, as against 'private' schools which may be owned/controlled by a single individual. The conditions of representation relate to e.g. the degree of independence, the amount of advanced work, etc.: cf. *Public and Preparatory Schools Year Book*, 1952.

[3] cf. Board of Education, *Report of the (Fleming) Committee on the Public Schools and the General Educational System* (HMSO 1944), p. 2.

Establishments for Further Education

The salaries laid down by the Burnham Technical Committee apply to full-time teachers in establishments for further education, other than farm institutes, maintained by local education authorities. They cover technical, commercial and art colleges and institutes—both day and evening—but not the staff of secondary technical schools who come under the aegis of the Main Committee. Since 1956 the Burnham technical reports have also fixed the remuneration of those employed in colleges of advanced technology.

The 1951 grade structure in technical teaching—it was somewhat different under the 1945 and 1948 agreements—provided for assistants grade A, assistants grade B, lecturers, senior lecturers, heads of departments, vice-principals and principals. The classification of staff was left to the local education authority, but guidance in the matter was offered in the 1951 Report, which recommended the following relativity between standards of work and posts:[1]

Work of university standard	senior lecturer
Advanced work[2] and/or work of university standard	lecturer
Work of school standard and/or advanced work	assistant grade B
Work of school standard	assistant grade A

The assistant grade A was on a scale identical with that of the qualified assistant teacher in primary and secondary schools; like the latter he received an additional £60 if a graduate, and an extra one, two or three increments if he had put in the necessary years of training. The grade B assistant also qualified for these additions, but the higher staff no longer do so. The remuneration of heads of departments varies according to grade, the latter depending on factors such as the number of staff and students. The McNair Committee were of the opinion that heads' pay was the key to the technical salary hierarchy, and that that of those in charge of the most important departments should be on the professorial level.[3] Grade V heads, in 1951, in fact just managed to rub shoulders with their professorial cousins.

---

[1] Ministry of Education, *Report of the Burnham Committee on Scales of Salaries for Teachers in Establishments for Further Education, England and Wales* (HMSO 1951), Appx. VI.

[2] i.e. above the Ordinary level of the General Certificate of Education but not of university standard.

[3] *McNair Report*, op. cit., paras. 447–8.

TABLE 18

EDUCATION

TEACHING STAFFS:

ESTABLISHMENTS FOR FURTHER EDUCATION

(Men, England and Wales)[1]

		Salary Scale as from 1 *April* 1951* £ *p.a.*	
		Grade A[2]	*Grade B*
Assistant			
Without degree		375×18–630	450×25–725
With degree		435×18–690	510×25–785
do. plus 3 years'⎫ full-time		453×18–708	528×25–803
do. plus 4 years'⎬ study or		471×18–726	546×25–821
do. plus 5 years'⎭ training		489×18–744	564×25–839

Lecturer	900×25–1,000
Senior lecturer	$1,000 \times 25$–1,150[3]
Head of department	
Grade I	900×25–1,000
Grade II	$1,000 \times 25$–1,150
Grade III	$1,150 \times 25$–1,300
Grade IV	$1,300 \times 25$–1,450
Grade V	$1,450 \times 25$–1,600[3]
Vice-principal	Salary as head of department,[4] plus allowance of £50–£200.
Principal	Salary was fixed according to circumstances.

[1] For additional allowance payable in London see text.

[2] The final increment on all Grade A scales was £21.

[3] Could be exceeded in special circumstances.

[4] If vice-principal was not also the head of a department, salary was to be determined in agreement with the Minister.

* These salaries were increased by £40 as from 1 July 1952, and have been further revised since.

Remuneration for principals has not been laid down by any of the Burnham technical reports. Each of the latter asked education authorities to review and adjust salaries in agreement with the Minister in the light of 'the guidance . . . afforded by the new scales for other posts', as well as factors such as the volume of full- and part-time work and the number and type of staff for which the principal is responsible. Though the 1945 and 1948 agreements spoke of the possibility of framing standard scales, nothing has come of this. Salaries actually in force in 1951 varied from £600–£900 in small establishments to £1,800–£2,000 in large institutions; in a few exceptionally big colleges remuneration may have been up to £3,000 per annum.

On the whole, the technical reports have been trying to break away from too close a parity with the primary and secondary schools. Before the war, the remuneration of teachers in technical and commercial colleges and what are now secondary technical schools was dealt with by the same Burnham Committee, with the fundamental scales common to both. Hence there was a legacy of 'school' salaries for technical colleges, although a majority of their population is 16 or over, and many of them pursue studies of university standard. The McNair Committee were not at all concerned about preserving relativities with primary and secondary teaching; technical pay, they urged, should be related to the emoluments obtainable in industry, commerce, the Services and Government departments.[1]

The salaries shown on Table 18 were increased by £40 as from 1 July 1952, and there have been further revisions since. The grade structure in institutions other than colleges of advanced technology has remained unchanged, apart from the creation of a new tier of principal lecturer. In the colleges of advanced technology, however, the hierarchy is somewhat different.

Training Colleges

The Committee dealing with the salaries of training college staffs—sometimes referred to as the Pelham Committee—is responsible for the remuneration of the teaching personnel of training colleges other than the training departments of universities;[2] it is associated with, rather than one of, the Burnham Committees. Reports in the period under review have again been operative from 1 April 1945, 1948 and 1951;[3] however, there was no improvement in July 1952.

Salaries are set out on Table 19. The college establishment of senior lectureships was determined by the local authority (or governing body, if a voluntary college) in agreement with the Minister; as a general rule it was to be at least one-half of the full-time teaching staff. Deputy principals—whose numbers and precise terms of employment also had to be approved—received, as shown, the pay of a lecturer or senior lecturer plus an allowance. This, however, could be increased, particularly in the case of deputies of mixed colleges. Salaries for principals are again fixed on a personal basis. In 1951 they ranged from about £1,100 to £1,400 in the smaller colleges and

---

[1] *McNair Report*, op. cit., paras. 446 and 452.

[2] cf. Ministry of Education, *Report of the Committee on Scales of Salaries for the Teaching Staff of Training Colleges, England and Wales* (HMSO 1951), p. 1.

[3] And 1954, when improved rates became payable.

from £1,500 to £1,800 in the larger institutions; exceptionally, a higher rate was considered appropriate.[1]

TABLE 19

EDUCATION

TRAINING COLLEGE STAFF
(Men, England and Wales)[1]

	Salary Scale as from		
	1 *April* 1945	1 *April* 1948	1 *April* 1951*
	£ *p.a.*	£ *p.a.*	£ *p.a.*
Lecturer	400 × 20–650	450 × 20–725	550 × 25– 850
Senior lecturer	600 × 20–750	700 × 25–850	800 × 25–1,050
Deputy principal: As for lecturer/senior lecturer, plus allowance of	50–100[2]	50–150[2]	50–200[2]
Principal	Salary was fixed according to circumstances		

[1] For additional allowance payable in London see text.
[2] The figure could be exceeded subject to ministerial approval.

* These salaries were increased as from 1 April 1954 and have been further revised since.

Local Education Authority Inspectors, Organizers and Advisory Officers

The Committee on Salary Scales and Service Conditions of Inspectors, Organizers and Advisory Officers of Local Education Authorities—generally known as the Soulbury Committee—was formed in 1946. While constituted on Burnham lines, it is not an officially appointed body. An interim agreement was issued at end-1946, followed by a final Report in May 1947; this latter was in turn superseded by a fresh document in May 1951.[2] The 1951 scales became operative on 1st April—in line with Burnham; they did not apply to LCC staffs.

At the time of the 1951 Report, the Committee had considered the remuneration of inspectors of schools (other than those employed by the central government who are civil servants), inspectors and organizers of special subjects such as domestic science, of educational psychologists, organizers of school meals and of youth service

[1] Various changes in the training college salary structure have been introduced since 1956.
[2] *Report of the Committee on Salary Scales and Service Conditions of Inspectors, Organizers and Advisory Officers of Local Education Authorities*, 1951 (Councils and Education Press). Further reports have been issued since. Statistics of staff covered are not available.

officers. Its recommendations were intended as minima only. In the case of inspectors and organizers, authorities were to decide on the appropriate grade on the basis of the duties, etc. of the officer concerned 'and appropriate also to the salary structure of the Departments of the Local Authority . . .'; there was here an explicit link i.e. with the general pattern of local government remuneration. As regards educational psychologists, grade III, for example, applied to those advising the authority on psychological matters generally, including problems connected with the schooling of the maladjusted, child guidance and vocational guidance. Youth service officers, we may point out, are those entrusted with the organization of the youth service, not club leaders; salaries here were not fixed until 1951.

TABLE 20

INSPECTORS, ORGANIZERS AND ADVISORY OFFICERS OF
LOCAL EDUCATION AUTHORITIES
(Men, England and Wales)

	Salary Scale[1] *as from*	
	1 *April* 1947	1 *April* 1951*
	£ *p.a.*	£ *p.a.*
Inspector, organizer, educational psychologist		
Grade I	$550 \times 25 - 700$	$700 \times 25 - 850$
Grade II	$650 \times 25 - 850$	$850 \times 25 - 1,050$
Grade III	$800 \times 25 - 1,000$	$1,050 \times 25 - 1,250$[2]
Youth service officer		
Grade I		$525 \times 25 - 675$
Grade II		$700 \times 25 - 850$
Grade III		$850 \times 25 - 1,050$
Grade IV		$1,050 \times 25 - 1,250$

[1] The standards shown were intended as minima.

[2] In the case of inspectors and organizers, the maximum could be exceeded.

* These salaries were increased as from 1 April 1954 and have been further revised since.

Provincial Differentiation

The pre-war pay pattern provided for a system of two-tier differentiation in secondary schools, but a three- (originally four-) tier structure in elementary schools; in the latter the difference between urban and rural salaries was substantial.[1] Since 1945 there is one national scale, except that teachers in the 'London area' receive an addition which, in the period under review, was £36 per annum—increased after 16

[1] The maximum of a certificated teacher in London was then £408 and in a rural school £330 (excluding war-time additions).

years' full-time service or on attaining age 37 to £48.[1] The allowance is payable in all types of schools and colleges with the exception of those covered by the farm institute reports.

The question of the London weighting has been a vexed one. Under the 1945, 1948 and 1951 Burnham Reports, the 'London area' was smaller than the Metropolitan Police District;[2] while the teachers wanted it to be made co-terminous with the latter, the authorities were opposed to the addition altogether. In view of the deadlock, the Burnham Committee agreed to set up an independent tribunal to make recommendations in the matter; as a result, the London addition is, since 1 September 1953, payable in the whole of the Metropolitan Police District and City of London. However, the demand for allowances in other large towns has not been conceded.

Sex Differentiation

The total of 228,479 teachers in all grant-aided schools and establishments at end-March 1950 was composed of 138,366 women and 90,113 men. The proportion of the two sexes varies greatly in the different types of school, women having for a long time predominated in the education of the younger age-groups. At the secondary level, on the other hand, there is a preponderance of men, while the latter greatly exceed their female colleagues in establishments of further education. As far as status is concerned, a smaller proportion of women reach headships: 15·9 per cent of men teachers in maintained primary and secondary schools, but only 11·6 per cent of women, were heads in 1950.[3]

From their inception, the Burnham Committees' recommendations embodied differentiation between the pay of men and women teachers. The differential was not quite uniform: In theory, women received 80 per cent of the corresponding male salary; in practice, the figure was somewhere between 80 and 90 per cent. Under the 1951 Primary and Secondary Report, for instance, a qualified woman teacher had a basic minimum of £338 per annum—nine-tenths of her male colleague's £375—and she proceeded by annual increments of £15 (man: £18), so that slowly the gap widened. Her maximum was £504 against the male £630, this 4:5 ratio being achieved by giving men a 14-year scale, while a woman's occupational ladder only had 11 rungs. The graduate, training and head teacher allowances were

[1] The allowance remained unchanged until 1959, when the figures were raised to £38 and £51 respectively.

[2] For areas deemed to constitute the 'London area' until 1953 see 1951 *Primary and Secondary Report*, op. cit., Section O. The matter was debated in the Commons on 29 April 1949, when attention was drawn to the anomalies arising from its then constitution. (HC Deb. 464, 577 and ff.)

[3] cf. Cmd. 8244, op. cit., Tables 6, 51 and 53.

D

likewise lower, though the London weighting was the same for the two sexes.

Under the 1951 Burnham Technical Report, women grade A and B assistants again had a scale which was 90 per cent at the minimum and 80 per cent at the maximum of that of their male opposite num-bers, but at all higher levels a strict 4:5 ratio was maintained. In training colleges, on the other hand, the position was more favour-able to the fair sex, a differential smaller than that in the general run of schools already being a feature of pre-war days. However, follow-ing the adoption by the Government of equal pay for the Civil Ser-vice, the Burnham and Training College Salaries Committees evolved a similar seven-stage scheme, designed to bring women teachers' scales up to the level of male salaries by 1 April 1961.

Chapter 4

THE UNIVERSITIES

The universities of Great Britain vary widely as to age and tradition, constitution and size. They comprise the ancient foundations of Oxford and Cambridge; the University of London with more than one-fifth of the total student population; the civic (provincial) universities—whose number is being considerably stepped up; the Scottish foundations; and the University of Wales with its constituent institutions. Also part of the academic world are the Manchester College of Science and Technology and the Royal College of Science and Technology, Glasgow. The colleges of advanced technology, however, do not 'belong'.

The universities are autonomous, self-governing institutions; as previously indicated, they do not come under the control of the Ministry of Education. However, they now receive substantial government grants, made on the advice of the University Grants Committee—a body appointed by the Treasury and the official link between the State and the universities. The Committee co-ordinate and advise on matters of policy, over which they now exercise a considerable measure of influence.

Academic Staffs
The universities have greatly expanded since before the war, as is

Full-time academic staff, Gt Britain: 1951–2[1]

Demonstrators and assistant lecturers	1,537
Lecturers and senior lecturers	4,481
Independent lecturers, readers and assistant professors	640
Professors	1,290
Others	1,004
	8,952

[1] University Grants Committee, *University Development: Report on the Years 1947–52*, Cmd. 8875 (HMSO 1953), Appx. VII. Lecturers, assistant lecturers and demonstrators at Oxford and Cambridge are excluded.

shown by the growth of the student population from 50,246 in the session 1938–9 to 83,458 in 1951–2—with a further substantial increase since. The relative rise in the number of academic staff has been even larger, the 1951–2 total representing a 124 per cent increase over the pre-war figure of 3,994.[1]

The basic rungs in the academic structure are the assistant lecturer, lecturer, senior lecturer/reader and professor, but there is no rigid hierarchy. Thus some institutions employ assistants as a tier below that of assistant lecturer, while in the medical world appointments are not normally made below the lecturer grade. Again, some departments comprise both senior lecturers and readers; others engage one or the other. As for promotion prospects, the average entrant into academic service cannot be certain of advancement beyond the lecturer level, which must be considered the career grade for the majority. Even this far the path is not equally smooth, some assistant lectureships being temporary appointments.

Salaries

In contradistinction to practically all other services reviewed in this study, there is no system of collective bargaining for the settlement of academic salaries.[2] These are in effect laid down by the Treasury acting on the advice of the University Grants Committee, though since 1955 the Association of University Teachers, like the Committee of Vice-Chancellors and Principals, have the right to make representations to the Grants Committee.[3]

In their Report on the period 1935–47, the Grants Committee state that in the nineteen-thirties academic remuneration was generally inadequate—even by their own modest standards. The Committee refer to the improvement in this respect at the end of the war, but point out that any substantial change in the value of money or in the incomes of comparable professions would produce a new situation.[4] Such a 'new situation' in fact arose in 1948 as a result of the Government's acceptance of the Spens Report,[5] which recommended pay levels for National Health Service specialists substantially above those in university medical schools: 'To have allowed this disparity

[1] University Grants Committee, *University Development: Report on the Years* 1947–52, Cmd. 8875 (HMSO 1953), paras. 21 and 58.

[2] The only other field similarly without a system of joint negotiation *at any level* is the judiciary. Individual grades—such as top-level staff in certain services—are of course in the same position.

[3] cf. 20 July 1955, HC Deb. 544, *58*.

[4] Report of the University Grants Committee, *University Development from* 1935 *to* 1947 (HMSO 1948), pp. 45–6.

[5] *Report of the Inter-Departmental Committee on the Remuneration of Consultants and Specialists*, Cmd. 7420 (HMSO 1948).

to continue would have meant in time the depopulation of the schools'. Further, the salaries of clinical teachers were already above those of other dons; if this gap had been allowed to widen, it would have produced 'a state of almost intolerable tension throughout the universities'.[1] Hence the Grants Committee agreed that an increase in academic remuneration was unavoidable, and in March 1949 the Chancellor of the Exchequer announced that new salaries were to be introduced as from the beginning of the next session. There thus took place a substantial upward revision of university pay—non-medical as well as clinical—though these 1949 standards remained in operation until 1 October 1954.[2]

[1] Cmd. 8875, op. cit., para. 67.

[2] The 1954 figures (non-medical, outside London) were: Assistant lecturers: £550–£650; lecturers: £650–£1,350; senior lecturers/readers: a maximum of up to £1,850; professors: £1,900 (minimum), plus supplementation allowing for actual salaries of up to £2,850. For further developments see University Grants Committee, *University Development* 1952–57, Cmnd. 534 (HMSO 1958), p. 31 and ff. and Appx. VI.

TABLE 21

THE UNIVERSITIES

ACADEMIC STAFF
(Men and Women, Great Britain)[1]

	Salaries as from 1 *October* 1949*
Non-medical posts:	£ *p.a.*
Assistant lecturer	400– 500[2]
Lecturer	500–1,100
Senior lecturer/reader	–1,600 ⎫ see text
Professor	1,600– ⎭
Pre-clinical posts:	
Lecturer	600–1,200/1,800
Reader	1,200–1,800
Professor	2,000–2,500
Clinical posts:[3]	
Lecturer	600–1,500/2,000[4]
Reader	1,500–2,000[4]
Professor	2,250–2,750[5]

[1] Non-medical salaries in London were generally £50 higher.

[2] An increase to £550 was sanctioned in 1952.

[3] The salaries for clinical staffs became operative from 1 April 1949.

[4] For posts of special responsibility (e.g. headship of an independent department), the maximum could be up to £2,500.

[5] A distinction award may have been payable in addition.

* All salaries were increased as from 1 October 1954 and have been further revised since.

In pre-war days, academic remuneration varied considerably between institutions; the Grants Committee did not attempt to lay down any common standards. However, as the 1949 increases were only made possible by Exchequer assistance, it became necessary to ensure that the universities observed a certain measure of consistency; the additional grants were therefore made conditional on salaries not exceeding various specified limits. All subsequent adjustments of academic pay have been made on the same basis, though there is no strict uniformity even now; for example, individual authorities can make appointments above the minimum of the relevant scale and they retain considerable latitude in fixing the rewards of senior staff. In a special category also are the Universities of Oxford and Cambridge where the University only, but not the individual colleges,[1] are grant-aided; here the general level of remuneration is altogether higher.

Assistant Lecturers

Assistant lectureships are tenable for three or four years. Scales actually in force between 1949 and 1954 included £400 × £50–£500 (Reading, Exeter, Southampton); £450 × £25–£500 (Leeds, Nottingham); £450 × £25–£550 (Liverpool Sheffield) and £450 × £50–£500 (University of Wales, Leicester). In London the University did not itself prescribe rates for lower academic staff, though the Collegiate Council made certain recommendations which were fairly strictly adhered to by the individual colleges; the scale so recommended as from October 1949 was £450 × £50–£550. In Cambridge the assistant lecturer then started at not less than £600 per annum. An increase of £50 a year 'on account' of any subsequent revision of pay was granted by a number of universities in 1952, when the Grants Committee sanctioned the raising of the assistant lecturer maximum to £550.

No ranges have been laid down for demonstrators or research assistants either in 1949 or since; presumably the market is here imposing its own terms. Their status and pay may be assimilated to that of assistant lecturers, though it is frequently below. University scientific departments also employ technicians and laboratory assistants, but these do not form part of the academic hierarchy. The average salary of assistant lecturers and demonstrators for the whole country other than Oxford and Cambridge was £313 in 1938–9, £439 in 1946–7 and £533 for the session 1951–2.[2]

---

[1] With one or two exceptions.
[2] Cmd. 8875, op. cit., p. 87. The corresponding figure for 1956–7 was £600.

Lecturers, Senior Lecturers and Readers[1]

Lecturer scales in the period 1949–54 mostly started at £550—i.e. at £50 above the Chancellor's minimum; in London and Sheffield the figure was £600; in Cambridge at least £750. Annual increments were £50. In some cases there were efficiency bars at £800 or £900, while in others the scale was formally subdivided. As regards senior lecturers and readers, the Chancellor of the Exchequer merely prescribed 'a range of salaries with varying maxima up to (1949–54) £1,600 per annum', nor was this any more closely defined by the Grants Committee. Actual scales for these two grades overlap: in London, for instance, most senior lecturers then received £1,000 × £50–£1,250 and readers £1,050 × £50–£1,450 (£1,650 in special cases).[2] On the whole, there is more variation and fluidity here than lower down the hierarchy.

The average salary of senior lecturers and lecturers[3] was £477 in 1938–9 and £688 in 1946–7. By 1951–2 this had gone up to £955: £863 for lecturers and £1,380 for senior lecturers. For the category 'readers, assistant professors and independent lecturers' the pre-war average was £671 a year; by 1946–7 this had risen to £982 and by 1951–2 stood at £1,468 per annum.[4]

Professors[5]

Professorial pay used to vary both as between universities and as between chairs in the same institution. On the whole, remuneration was higher where income from endowments was greater, while a number of universities differentiated in favour of chairs in scientific and engineering subjects.[6] At the time of the first post-war revision, the University Grants Committee felt compelled to give some indication of the salaries they could take into account in determining their grants; faced with the problem of, on the one hand, accepting existing inequalities as a basis of grant policy or, on the other, securing uniformity of remuneration, they decided on a middle course. They agreed to recognize a basic rate of professorial pay of £1,350 per annum for university colleges, £1,450 for universities and £1,500 in London; in addition, they assessed for each institution a

[1] Excluding medical and pre-clinical staffs.

[2] There was a bar at £1,250.

[3] Lecturers at Oxford and Cambridge are excluded, but medical and pre-clinical staffs are included in the averages.

[4] Cmd. 8875, op. cit., p. 87. Average salaries in 1956–7 were £1,061 for lecturers, £1,653 for senior lecturers, and £1,760 for 'readers, assistant professors and independent lecturers'.

[5] Excluding medical and pre-clinical.

[6] *University Development* 1935–47, op. cit., p. 46.

sum to be expended in raising the salaries of some professors above the standard rate. In fixing the amount of this 'supplementation', the Grants Committee take into account, amongst other things, the number of chairs, the proportion in scientific and technological subjects and the size of the student population; they do not determine or suggest what the remuneration of a particular individual should be. It is left to each institution whether to pay a special prize to its most eminent professors or those in danger of being snatched away by an avaricious labour market, or whether, on the other hand, to embark on no differentiation or at any rate only in relation to seniority or departmental responsibilities. As a result, there is still much diversity of practice as between one university and another.

The professorial minimum was raised to £1,600 per annum in 1949 for both university colleges and universities; for London the figure became £1,650. Increased provision was also made for supplementation, in effect allowing for salaries of up to £2,500 a year. Average remuneration for professors was £1,115 in 1938–9, £1,534 in 1946–7 and £2,041 in 1951–2.[1]

Clinical and Pre-Clinical Posts

Clinical posts in university medical and dental schools are considerably more favourably remunerated than their equivalent in non-medical faculties. In 1949 a clinical professor was given a scale coterminous with (the upper half of) that of a hospital consultant; like the latter, he became eligible for an additional distinction award, payable from National Health Service funds.[2] While medical academics have always been better paid than their non-medical colleagues, the difference was not excessive; it was the acceptance in 1948 of the Spens recommendations which led, in 1949, to a rather drastic widening of the gap. In their Report on the 1947–52 quinquennium the University Grants Committee referred to—and sympathized with—the unpopularity of this salary differentiation, but felt bound to recognize it as an unavoidable necessity.[3]

The Spens Report was likewise responsible for the even less popular differentiation, introduced in 1949, in favour of medical schools' pre-clinical staffs. These posts are almost invariably filled by medically qualified personnel, but while under pre-Spens conditions pay was at about the same level as that in university scientific departments, this was felt to be no longer possible when clinical salaries were raised to the Spens level. However, the pre-clinical differential was substantially reduced in 1957.

---

[1] cf. Cmd. 8875, op. cit., p. 87. The figures include medical, etc. professors. The average salary for the session 1956–7 was £2,303.

[2] cf. Chap. 5, pp. 113 and 115 *post*.   [3] Cmd. 8875, op. cit., para. 70.

Provincial Differentiation
In the period under review, the salaries of non-medical staffs of London University were, generally speaking, £50 above those of their colleagues outside the metropolis. In the case of professors, the addition was only payable within the maximum of the range, while all clinical and pre-clinical rates were undifferentiated—as is the rule in the medical world. We may add that the London weighting for non-medical dons was increased in 1957 and is now also graduated according to rank.

Sex Differentiation
In contrast to all other forms of teaching, the universities practised 'equal pay' at all levels before the Treasury gave a lead in that direction.

It might here be mentioned that the universities are almost unique in having a system of family allowances. These are at the rate of £50 per child per annum, and accrue for as long as full-time education is received.

Chapter 5

THE NATIONAL HEALTH SERVICE[1]

The National Health Service Act was passed in 1946 and became fully operative on the 'appointed day'—5 July 1948. Under it, it is the duty of the Minister of Health

'to promote the establishment in England and Wales of a comprehensive health service designed to secure improvement in the physical and mental health of the people of England and Wales and the prevention, diagnosis and treatment of illness . . . '[2]

The range of the Health Service covers everything from the treatment of rare diseases to the surgery of the brain, from the care of the mentally ill to the provision of artificial limbs. Included also is all that goes with medical care, such as the services of a midwife and the supply of drugs. The Service falls into three main sections:

1. Hospital and specialist services
2. General medical, etc. services
3. Local health authority services

For the administration of hospital and specialist services England and Wales were originally divided into fourteen regions, for each of which a Regional Hospital Board has been set up; the number has since been increased to fifteen. These boards, in turn, have appointed a number of Hospital Management Committees to be responsible for individual, or groups of, hospitals. In addition, thirty-six institutions have been designated as teaching hospitals, which are in the charge of Boards of Governors; the regional boards have no 'say' over these.

The general medical, etc. sector includes general practitioner, dental, supplementary ophthalmic and pharmaceutical services. The administrative organ here is the Local Executive Council, of which there are 138—broadly speaking, one for each county and county borough area. For the provision of the various services, executive

---

[1] For much useful information on early Health Service history see Hill and Woodcock, *The National Health Service* (Christopher Johnson, 1949) and J. S. Ross, *The National Health Service in Great Britain* (Oxford University Press, 1952). See also H. A. Clegg and T. E. Chester, *Wages Policy and the Health Service* (Blackwell, 1957).

[2] National Health Service Act, 1946 (9 & 10 Geo. 6. c. 81), s. 1.

councils enter into contracts with general practitioners, dentists, opticians and chemists.

The third branch of the Health Service is unified under the major local authorities, which have been designated as 'local health authorities' for purposes of the Act. Each of these is obliged to make arrangements for, *inter alia*, maternity, child welfare and home nursing services, health visiting and vaccination. In addition to these and other statutory functions, health authorities are empowered to organize home help and care and after-care services; for the provision of some of these, they may call in aid the facilities of voluntary organizations.

*Persons engaged in the National Health Service
as at* 31 *December* 1951[1]

Hospital and specialist services	Whole-time	Part-time
Medical and dental	10,245	23,281
Nursing and midwifery	136,210	25,756
Other professional and technical	16,631[2]	7,382
Blood transfusion centre and mass radiography staff	1,956	
Administrative and clerical	27,285	
Regional Hospital Board HQ staff	1,736	
Maintenance and transport workers, craftsmen, etc.	22,125	
Domestic grades	105,416	33,630
Family practitioner services		
General practitioners	18,000[3]	
General dental practitioners	9,694	
Ophthalmic medical practitioners and opticians	7,975	
Local health authority services[4]		
Domiciliary midwives	7,386	
Home nurses	3,721	4,979[5]
Health visitors, etc.	1,637	4,518
Nursery nurses[6]	6,411	101
'Home helps'	3,610	21,841

[1] Source: *Report of the Ministry of Health, Period* 1 *April* 1950 *to* 31 *December* 1951, Part 1, Cmd. 8655 (HMSO 1952). As the figures are not complete—local executive councils' administrative staff e.g. are not included—no totals are given.

[2] Excluding students.

[3] Principals only; the figure is approximate.

[4] The numbers include certain staffs employed by voluntary organizations under arrangements made with local authorities.

[5] The majority were also employed in domiciliary midwifery and/or health visiting.

[6] Day nurseries only; excluding students and domestic staff.

The National Health Service does not monopolize the purveying of health, though all but a very small proportion of the population of Britain is taking advantage of it. Similarly, the great majority of general practitioners and chemists and the bulk of dentists and specialists are associated with the Service, though by no means all on a full-time basis. The Armed Forces, however, retain their own medical organization, while a limited number of doctors and nurses are engaged by private concerns in what might be termed 'industrial medicine'.

National Health Service Staffs

The personnel in the Service comprises many widely varying groups, including medical, nursing, other professional, clerico-administrative and ancillary (domestic, etc.) grades. Complete statistics were not available at the time of writing, but the table on the preceding page gives a breakdown of the main categories for end-1951.

Negotiating machinery: Prior to 1948, there already existed in the various sections of public health a number of joint committees and councils for purposes of collective bargaining; however, these were not linked with one another and difficulties had arisen from the resulting lack of co-ordination. The Whitley machinery, which has since been evolved, covers practically all NHS employees and applies to Scotland as well as England and Wales. It consists of a general and nine functional councils,[1] the former dealing with matters affecting grades in more than one occupational group. The functional councils fix the remuneration of the particular staffs within their purview; while their decisions do not need to be endorsed by the General Council, they require the approval of the Minister.[2] Under section 13 of the National Health Service Amendment Act, 1949, any dispute in matters of remuneration or service conditions is within the scope of the 1896 Conciliation Act and the 1919 Industrial Courts Act; resort to the Industrial Court has in fact been frequent.

The nine functional councils are:

(a) Administrative and Clerical Staffs Council
(b) Ancillary Staffs Council
(c) Dental Whitley Council
(d) Medical Whitley Council
(e) Nurses and Midwives Whitley Council

[1] As well as a Scottish Advisory Committee and a network of joint consultative and regional appeals committees.

[2] In October 1957 ministerial consent was withheld from a Whitley agreement concluded by the Administrative and Clerical Staffs Council; this was the first time such action had been taken since the inception of the Service.

(*f*) Optical Whitley Council
(*g*) Pharmaceutical Whitley Council
(*h*) Professional and Technical Council 'A'
(*i*) Professional and Technical Council 'B'.

The local government and National Health Service employ many grades common to the two fields; in order to avoid anomalies as well as too great a multiplicity of negotiating bodies, it was agreed that the new councils should cover such occupations in both spheres. However, local health authority administrative and clerical workers, domestic staffs (other than in residential institutions) and employees of voluntary organizations with whom health authorities have made agency arrangements have been excluded from NHS Whitley machinery.

The 1946 National Health Service Act itself had little to say on the subject of pay. Section 66 provided that

'Regulations may make provision with respect to the qualifications, remuneration, and conditions of service of any officers employed by any body constituted under this Act . . . and no officer to whom the regulations apply shall be employed otherwise than in accordance with the regulations.'

In 1951 the National Health Service (Remuneration and Conditions of Service) Regulations were made, which stipulated that the pay of any officer, belonging to a class whose remuneration has been the subject of negotiation and approved by the Minister, shall—unless otherwise authorized by the latter—'be neither more nor less than the remuneration so approved . . .'.[1] The purpose of the regulations was to give a more solid legal foundation to national rates of wages and salaries and other service conditions. The ruling that pay shall be 'neither more'—an unusual statutory provision—had become necessary because a number of hospitals had been rewarding their staffs at levels in excess of the relevant Whitley scale, and had declined to toe the line even when officially requested to do so.[2]

We shall not, in this chapter, be able to deal with the remuneration of all the numerous grades and occupations in the National Health Service. Even in the first few years of the latter, the number of settlements concluded was substantial; it may be of interest to add that by the end of 1958 the ten Councils between them had published no fewer than 546 formal agreements, though of course not all of these

[1] SI 1951 No. 1373, ss. 3(1) and 3(3).
[2] cf. *Summarized Accounts of Regional Hospital Boards, etc. for year ended 31 March* 1950, HC 158 (HMSO 1951), para. 6.

were concerned with major issues.[1] We shall here largely confine ourselves to (salaried) doctors, various professional grades and the
different branches of the nursing hierarchy.

Hospital Doctors before the Appointed Day
Before the passing of the 1946 Act, hospitals were either 'voluntary'
or under the control of local authorities. As far as consultants and
specialists were concerned, those in voluntary institutions held
honorary part-time appointments, from which a successful private
practice normally accrued. Specialists in municipal hospitals were
paid, though here also the great bulk occupied part-time posts, being
remunerated on a sessinal basis. Some salaries for hospital doctors
were, however, laid down after certain hospitals passed into municipal ownership, following the Local Government Act of 1929. These
scales are contained in what is known as the Askwith Memorandum,
which covered both medical officers in institutions then transferred to
local auspices, as well as those engaged in the administration of
municipal health. The Askwith rates did not apply to the voluntary
hospitals—nor to consultants and specialists anywhere.

The original Askwith standards—agreed to in 1929—remained unchanged throughout the 1930s, though subsequently augmented by a
war/cost-of-living bonus. In addition, there have been two revisions,
operative from April 1946 and July 1947, the 1947 rates remaining in
force until the 'appointed day'. For resident medical officers—those
employed in hospitals, sanatoria or other institutions but without
responsibility for other medical staff—the salary, as from 1 July
1947, was £532 10s. 0d. × £25–£632 10s. 0d. Full residential emoluments were supplied in addition. This scale did not apply to very
junior personnel—those without previous experience or holding one-
year appointments. Assistant medical officers in mental hospitals
received the same, but could qualify for an extra £50 a year if
possessing a diploma in psychological medicine.

The only other institutional category provided for in the Askwith
memorandum were 'medical superintendents of institutions, other
than mental hospitals', defined as those in charge of a hospital, sana-
torium, etc. with over 100 beds. Remuneration in this case was inclusive of residential emoluments; the minima operative in the last pre-
NHS year ranged from £1,035 per annum in institutions with not
more than 150, to £1,435 in those with above 750, beds. An increment
of £50 was payable every two years—up to a maximum 25 per cent
above the commencing salary, except for the highest range where
remuneration was a flat rate.

[1] cf. *Report of the Ministry of Health for the year ended* 31 *December* 1958,
Part I, Cmnd. 806 (HMSO 1959), p. 224.

On the whole, the Askwith scheme left considerable freedom of manoeuvre to local authorities. The document contained certain discretionary clauses; as a result, actual salaries paid were not necessarily in conformity with the formal scales, nor necessarily uniform as between one authority and another. Further, Askwith stipulated that within four to five years of an officer reaching his maximum, the employing authority was to consider whether a further improvement was warranted. Finally, the memorandum only laid down rates for fairly junior hospital doctors on the one hand, and the most senior on the other, these being the main grades in existence when the Askwith pattern took shape; the intermediate levels were 'at discretion' from the start. We may add that, before 1948, medical salaries in municipal hospitals tended to be closely related to those of the local authority's public health appointments—an interesting point because hospital remuneration now is entirely independent of that attaching to public health posts.

Hospital Medical and Dental Staff since the Appointed Day

Hospital medical and dental staff as at 31 *December* 1951[1]

	Whole-time	Part-time[2]
House officers	2,783	56
Senior house officers	1,329	46
Registrars	1,683	275
Senior registrars	1,327	345
Consultants	1,605	14,032
Junior hospital medical officers	500	—
Senior hospital medical and dental officers	840	2,450
Medical and deputy medical superintendents	115	51
General practitioners (medical and dental)	—	5,202
Other medical/dental staff	63	824
	10,245	23,281

[1] *Report of Ministry of Health*, 1 April 1950–31 December 1951, op. cit., p. 121. The figures relate to *paid* appointments only; there were 64 whole- and 782 part-time staff serving in an honorary capacity.

[2] The number of appointments—not persons—is shown, many part-timers holding more than one post.

Pay: An inter-departmental Committee, under the chairmanship of Sir Will Spens, had been appointed in 1947 to advise on the range of professional remuneration appropriate for consultants and specialists in a publicly organized hospital and specialist service. They were to consider the matter 'with due regard to the financial expectations of consultant and specialist practice in the past, to the financial expectations in other branches of medical practice, to the necessary post-graduate training and qualifications required and to the desirability of maintaining the proper social and economic status of specialist practice and its power to attract a suitable type of recruit'.[1] The Committee submitted their Report in May 1948 and acceptance by HM Government was announced in the following month. Proposals based on the Spens recommendations were published—after protracted discussions—in March 1949, and with modifications formed the basis of permanent contracts offered later that year. They were applied retrospectively as from 5 July 1948.

The National Health Service provided for the first time for a paid consultant and specialist service; there were no previous salary scales on which the Spens Committee could base their deliberations. However, they had before them details of average incomes, prepared on behalf of the Royal Colleges and the British Medical Association; these revealed that while 42·7 per cent of consultants—all specialties and all areas of Great Britain—had net earnings of £1,000 or less in 1938–9, 10·1 per cent were netting £4,000 and over.[2] The figures showed likewise that there were considerable variations as between the different branches of medicine: Thus in the age group 50–54, 47·4 per cent of all gynaecologists had net incomes of £4,000 and plus, as against only 3·8 per cent among ear, nose and throat specialists—to cite an extreme case.[3]

The Spens Committee felt that it would be a mistake to base future salaries on the differences disclosed by the statistical enquiry, and favoured equality of status between the various branches of specialist practice,[4] as also between teaching and non-teaching hospitals. The pay proposed for trainee specialists was likewise a break with the past, when remuneration at that level was in the nature merely of a training grant. As a corollary, i.e. as the new standards would re-

[1] *Report of the Inter-Departmental Committee on the Remuneration of Consultants and Specialists*, Cmd. 7420 (HMSO 1948), p. 3.

[2] ibid. Table 6. Spens estimated that slightly less than three-quarters of those in practice in 1938–9 and surviving in 1947 co-operated in the enquiry, and that the average net income of the proportion making the return might, in the age groups under 60, be at the most 10–15 per cent too high. For the older age groups the figures were considered of doubtful value.

[3] ibid. Table 4. The differences were much less pronounced for the lower age groups.

[4] However, though the highest remuneration would be open to all types of specialists, 'the proportion attaining that remuneration might be less in some fields than in others and might vary with the increasing importance of this or that branch of Medicine' (*Report*, para. 7).

move the hardships formerly experienced at the trainee stage, that earnings would be maintained at a consistent level until retirement, and that throughout his career the specialist would enjoy financial security in marked contrast with the uncertainties of private practice, 'some reduction was justifiable not only in the ceiling figure of the incomes attainable in the past, but also in the proportion of consultants attaining to the highest levels of remuneration'.[1]

Spens thus envisaged a spread different from that obtaining formerly, including some curtailment of both the size of, and the numbers earning, the most glittering prizes. At the same time, 'there must remain for a significant minority the opportunity to earn incomes comparable with the highest which can be earned in other professions'.[2] The Committee therefore proposed a system of 'distinction awards': 34 per cent of consultants—including those working in universities—should be eligible for these, in recognition of special contributions to medicine, exceptional ability or outstanding professional work. These recommendations found their way *in toto* into the new 'Terms'.[3]

Table 22 sets out the first set of National Health salaries, the antecedents of whose birth we have just outlined. The six-month house officer jobs are normally held immediately after passing the (university, etc.) qualifying examination; since 1953 all would-be medicos—including those planning a career in general practice—must spend one year in an approved hospital in this way prior to full registration by the General Medical Council.[4] From house officer the hierarchy—for those intending to become specialists—is to senior house officer, registrar and senior registrar; the latter is the grade from which the majority of consultants are recruited. It should be added that, in the period under review, most appointments below consultant rank were of varying, but *limited*, tenure. The main exception to this were the senior and (in part) the junior hospital medical officer grades, but these do not form part of the ideal ladder of ascent to the summit of the profession.

This limitation on the tenure of fairly senior posts—unknown in other public services—has caused some acute problems. For although the number of consultants has increased each year since the inception of the Health Service, and in spite of the fact that they have constituted throughout the most populous grade in the hospital medical

[1] *Report*, p. 10.

[2] ibid.

[3] National Health Service, *Terms and Conditions of Service of Hospital Medical and Dental Staff* (*England and Wales*), 7 June 1949. 'Terms' used subsequently refers to this document.

[4] There is no such provision in the case of dentists.

TABLE 22

NATIONAL HEALTH SERVICE

HOSPITAL MEDICAL AND DENTAL STAFF
(Men and Women, Great Britain)

Salaries as from 5 July 1948*

Trainee consultant and consultant grades:	£ *p.a.*
House officer[1]	
First post (tenable for six months)	350
Second post do.	400
Third and any subsequent post do.	450
Senior house officer	670
Registrar	
First year	775
Second and any subsequent year	890
Senior registrar	1,000 ×100–1,300
Consultant[2]	1,700[3] ×125–2,075
	×150–2,375
	×125–2,750
Other hospital grades:	
Junior hospital medical officer	700 × 50–1,000[4]
Senior hospital medical/dental officer	1,300[5]× 50–1,750

[1] £100 p.a. was deducted from the figures for board and lodging. In exceptional circumstances, salaries up to £50 higher than the standard rates could be paid.

[2] Special distinction awards of £500, £1,500 or £2,500 p.a. were payable in addition to a proportion of consultants: see text.

[3] The minimum was payable at age 32; at 31 the salary was £1,550; at any lower age it was £1,400. Consultants appointed after age 32 could be paid above the minimum, the highest commencing salary being £2,225 at 36 or over.

[4] Payable if appointed not less than two years after registration as a medical practitioner.

[5] The minimum was linked to age 32 and the position on the scale determined by age.

* These salaries were increased as from 1 April 1954 and have been further revised since.

hierarchy,[1] many senior registrars have been unable to gain advancement to it. While in all other fields it is readily accepted that only a small proportion will reach the zenith of the profession, in this instance what are in effect highly favourable prospects have gone hand in hand with much frustration and controversy, owing to the built-in expectation of certain promotion implicit in the system. However,

[1] See *Royal Commission on Doctors' and Dentists' Remuneration* 1957–60 (Chairman: Sir Harry Pilkington). Cmnd. 939 (HMSO 1960), Table 15, p. 56.

recently steps have been taken at any rate allowing senior registrars to remain in their posts until the final move up has been secured; also, a Joint Working Party was set up in 1958 to study the principles on which the hospital medical structure should be organized.[1]

The basic salary scale for full-time consultants under the 1949 Terms was £1,700 to £2,750 per annum, the maximum being attained at age 40 at the earliest. No formal definition of 'consultant' was laid down; according to professional opinion it is almost impossible to define him. In pre-NHS days such status was won as a result of having the requisite training, academic degrees and experience, but the fact of recognition was the crux of the matter. However, the implementation of the Spens Report made it necessary to come to definite decisions in this respect; small professional committees were therefore appointed for the purpose of grading hospital staff.[2]

As for the special distinction awards payable over and above the basic salary, these were accepted exactly as recommended by Spens. A Standing Advisory Committee—its precise doings have been shrouded in a certain amount of secrecy—was set up in 1949 to advise the Minister of Health which consultants should benefit, on the basis that 4 per cent were to receive the 'A' award (£2,500 per annum for whole-time staff), 10 per cent the 'B' award (£1,500 a year), and 20 per cent the 'C' award (£500 per annum). The size of these payments, we may add, remained unchanged until 1960, though the number of award-holders has of course risen *pari passu* with the expansion of the grade.[3] Full-time consultants can also supplement their salaries through, for example, fees for examinations required by employers or life insurance companies,[4] but until November 1955 they did not receive payment for domiciliary consultations. They are not entitled to undertake private practice.

Part-time consultants: Since the inception of the Health Service, the majority of consultants have continued to hold part-time appointments; for purposes of pay the position under the 1949 Terms was as follows: The average time required for each post was assessed by the employing board, travelling—up to one hour per each half-day of 3½ hours—ranking as 'work'. The part-time officer received x/11ths

---

[1] *Report of Ministry of Health for* 1958, op. cit., pp. 58–9.

[2] cf. 'The National Health Service Act in Great Britain—a Review of the First Year's Working', *The Practitioner*, Autumn 1949, pp. 6–8.

[3] The 1960 Royal Commission *inter alia* proposed an increase in the size of the payments, as well as the creation of 100 'A Plus' awards, each of £4,000 per annum: For details see Cmnd. 939, op. cit., paras. 231–4.

[4] i.e. fees may be charged for services not provided under the National Health Service.

of total remuneration—it was assumed that the full-time salary was earned in eleven half-days—plus a special weighting of from 6 to 25 per cent of 'x/11ths'; any fraction of a half-day put in, we may add, was first rounded up in the consultant's favour. Maximum pay was $9\frac{1}{2}$/11ths of the whole-time rate,[1] and there was eligibility for additional distinction awards on a *pro rata* basis. Part-time staff, further —unlike their full-time colleagues—qualified from the start for separate fees for domiciliary consultations; they also received what must have been unique in the whole field of paid employment namely travelling allowances in respect of their daily journey to work. Insofar as they belonged to 'Schedule D' rather than to 'Schedule E' for income tax purposes, part-time consultants shared the privileges generally reserved for the former category; finally, they had the right to engage in private practice from which their whole-time opposite numbers were precluded.

Part-time consultants were thus placed in a highly advantageous position, and the survey conducted by the 1957–60 Royal Commission on Doctors' and Dentists' Remuneration showed that their earnings from all sources were considerably above those of their full-time colleagues,[2] though in part this is also because a larger proportion of the former receive distinction awards.[3] An interesting point is that it is in fact largely left to the individual whether to opt for whole- or most-of-the-time service; further, the Royal Commission found that rather more than 70 per cent of part-time consultants were employed in the NHS for the equivalent of four days or more.[4] In other words, though for the great majority of consultants the Health Service constitutes the greater part of their work, most have chosen to serve under a part-time contract, for which the pattern of remuneration has indeed provided every possible encouragement. The Royal Commission has, however, proposed two changes in the system—which otherwise remains as outlined above—i.e. that, apart from those already enjoying or about to enjoy these privileges, payment for part-timers should henceforth be related to the amount of work actually put in without any additional 'weighting', while the cost of the journey to work should cease to be a charge on public funds.[5]

---

[1] In special circumstances a board could offer more, subject to the Minister's consent.

[2] In 1955/6 the average income (men, Great Britain, medical only) of whole-time consultants was £3,009; that of part-timers from all sources was £3,603: *Report*, op. cit., Table 19, p. 62.

[3] ibid. Table 28, p. 79. For example, in mid-1958 4 per cent of part-timers received the £2,500 award as against 0·5 per cent of whole-timers.

[4] ibid. para. 210.

[5] ibid. paras. 208 and 210.

For a number of reasons the Spens Committee had framed their recommendations in terms of the 1939 value of money, leaving to others the problem of adjustment to post-war conditions. They strongly emphasized that such adjustment should have regard not only to estimates of the change in the value of the currency, but to the increases in incomes which had taken place since pre-war in the medical and other professions.[1] Little can the Committee have foreseen the acute controversies to which these and the analogous recommendations in the parallel GP and dental Spens Reports[2] were to give rise, or the fierce battles which were to be fought over their interpretation. Here it must suffice to say that the 1948 standards finally agreed for hospital staffs constituted a 'betterment factor' over and above the Spens '1939' proposals of 20 per cent only, and that these levels were not revised until 1 April 1954.[3] There were further increases in 1957 and 1959: these were of an interim nature, for in February 1957 the Prime Minister announced the appointment of the Royal (Pilkington) Commission to look into the whole question of medical and dental remuneration.[4]

A brief word may be added about the position of specialists *vis-à-vis* that of general practitioners in the Health Service. Before the latter was launched, another Spens Committee—as just indicated— had surveyed what GPs had been earning in 1939, and had made proposals as to the desirable range of future incomes. But while the GP Report made a case for reducing the gap between the two classes, the aim of the Consultant Committee was to maintain the *status quo*, i.e. the greatly superior financial attractions of specialist practice. And the Government accepted both sets of recommendations. The rates initially introduced weighted the scales heavily in favour of consultants; the latter's maximum of £2,750—quite apart from any additional distinction award—was then beyond the reach of all but a small fraction of GPs. Then in 1952 came the very generous

[1] Cmd. 7420, op. cit., para 2.

[2] *Report of the Inter-Departmental Committee on the Remuneration of General Practitioners*, Cmd. 6810 (HMSO 1946) and *Report of the Inter-Departmental Committee on the Remuneration of General Dental Practitioners*, Cmd. 7402 (HMSO 1948).

[3] The basic salary for consultants was then raised by £400 at the minimum and £350 at the maximum, though those holding B and A distinction awards had the scale abated by £200 and £300 p.a. respectively. House and senior house officers, junior hospital medical officers and registrars received £75; for senior registrars the increase was £100 and for senior hospital medical officers £200 p.a.

[4] For the Commission's general findings the reader is referred to their comprehensive Report (Cmnd. 939, HMSO 1960), which includes a wealth of material, including data on the earnings of the medical and several other professions.

Danckwerts award for general practitioners;[1] this meant a swing of the pendulum in the opposite direction. However, the era of consultants chasing general practitioners and *vice versa* has since come to an end—the 1954 adjustment of specialists' pay is considered to have restored the balance—and early in 1956 the profession announced that its two principal branches were jointly to approach the Government for an increase in remuneration.[2] It was the ensuing deadlock which ultimately led to the appointment of the Royal Commission; the latter, we may add, concluded that the overall relationship in earnings between the hospital service and general practice 'should be broadly maintained unchanged'.[3] The Royal Commission, incidentally, can also be regarded as having finally presided over the decent burial of the Spens Reports,[4] which can hardly be said to have proved the happiest of guides in an admittedly complex and novel situation.

Public Health Medical Officers

At the time of writing, there were about 2,000 medical officers employed by local authorities in what is generally known as the 'public health service'. Their training is similar to that of other doctors; in addition, the great majority obtain the Diploma of Public Health— obligatory for those aiming at senior appointments. The salary structure for this sector of the profession had its origin in the 1929 Askwith memorandum, but remuneration was not uniform throughout the country owing to the wide discretion allowed by that agreement. The competent negotiating body now is Committee C of the Medical Whitley Council.

The lowest grade is that of assistant medical officer; a typical example is the school doctor. Candidates for such posts must have at least three years' previous experience. Next comes the senior medical officer; his work is both clinical and administrative. There are a small number of divisional or area medical officers and deputy medical officers, and finally there is the MOH himself, who is responsible for the general administration of the public health of a district.

A substantial difference over pay had to be referred to arbitration in October 1950. On behalf of the staff representatives it was contended that salaries should reflect parity of status with the two other

[1] For details of award and much of the evidence submitted see *Supplement to British Medical Journal*, 29 March 1952. For a briefer account see Royal Commission on Doctors' and Dentists' Remuneration, *Factual Memorandum by the Ministry of Health and the Department of Health for Scotland*, Written evidence, vol. 1 (HMSO 1957), pp. 40–3.

[2] See *British Medical Journal* (leading article), 11 February 1956.

[3] *Report*, op. cit., para. 169(d).

[4] cf. ibid. para. 166.

TABLE 23

NATIONAL HEALTH SERVICE

PUBLIC HEALTH MEDICAL OFFICERS
EMPLOYED BY LOCAL AUTHORITIES
(Men and Women, Great Britain)

	Salaries as from	
	1 *July* 1947	1 *October* 1950*
	£ *p.a.*	£ *p.a.*
Assistant medical officer	735 × 25–935[1]	850 × 50–1,150
Senior medical officer in	1,035/1,435 × 50–	
charge of service/department	1,222/1,435[2]	1,250 × 50–1,650
Deputy medical officers of	60% of mini- at discretion	66¾% of increments
health	mum of	minimum as for
	MOH[3]	of MOH MOH
Medical officer of health	1,100/2,310[4] at discretion	*see below*

MEDICAL OFFICERS OF HEALTH
Salaries as from 1 *October* 1950

Population of Authority	Minimum Salary	Annual Increments	Maximum Salary
Not exceeding	£ *p.a.*		£ *p.a.*
75,000	1,450–1,650	4 of £50	1,650–1,850
100,000	1,550–1,850	5 of £50	1,800–2,100
150,000	1,750–2,050	5 of £50	2,000–2,300
250,000	1,950–2,250	2 of £100 / 1 of £50	2,200–2,500
400,000	2,200–2,500	2 of £100 / 1 of £50	2,450–2,750
600,000	2,300–2,700	3 of £100	2,600–3,000
Over 600,000	at discretion	at discretion	at discretion

[1] After 4 and not more than 5 years on maximum, employing authority to consider whether this to be exceeded.

[2] Precise salary within range at authority's discretion. Maximum could be exceeded as for asst. medical officer. Increments were biennial.

[3] If performing the duties of an assistant medical officer, his scale applied if more favourable.

[4] Depending on population and type of authority.

* The salary of assistant medical officers was increased as from 1 June 1953, and that of all medical officers as from 1 January 1955. Further revisions have taken place since.

branches of the profession, i.e. general practitioners and hospital doctors. Preventive medicine was 'at least as important'; the staff side's claim was therefore based on the remuneration paid in the curative sectors of medicine.[1] The management side, on their part, maintained that public health was a 'wholly distinctive service . . . which hitherto had quite properly been integrated with the rest of the

[1] Industrial Court Award No. 2285 (HMSO 1950), paras. 12–15.

Local Authority Service'. Thus the work of a general practitioner—
with whom the staffs had claimed 'parity' though not 'equal pay'—
was far more arduous than that of the assistant medical officer, nor
was there any real comparability between consultants and medical
officers of health.[1] The Court's award, insofar as the main grades are
concerned, is shown on Table 23—i.e. the salaries operative from
1 October 1950.[2]

The remuneration of assistant medical officers was further improved by the Industrial Court in May 1953;[3] that of other public
health staff not until 1955. In the course of the 1955 claim the same
question of principle was raised, but the Court's award[4] amounted to
a full concession—as it was, in essence, in 1950—of the management's
case, namely that any increases should be analogous to those then
granted to other local authority chief officers rather than to salary
movements in the medical world.

We may add that, as regards the few hundred medical staff employed in the Civil Service,[5] there has been a similar tug-of-war as to
what should be the major criterion for determining remuneration.
Civil Service doctors, again, have their sights fixed on the pay levels
enjoyed by their professional colleagues in the National Health Service, while the Treasury—in the early days of the latter—showed
some reluctance to take account of these standards. Thus in 1949 the
Civil Service Medical Officers' Joint Committee asked for salaries designed to secure parity with NHS doctors, but the demand was
rejected by the Chancellor of the Exchequer who, while not disputing
that there was a case for a review, stated that the claim could not be
dealt with other than on the basis of general Civil Service policy.[6]
That policy then being one of extreme stringency, the Chancellor felt
bound to regard Civil Service doctors primarily as civil servants,
whereas for the doctors it was a case—here as elsewhere—of keeping
up with their medical Joneses, and there was much indignation at
the Treasury's seeming indifference to professional relativities.[7]

---

[1] Industrial Court Award No. 2285 (HMSO 1950), paras. 17–19.

[2] As regards deputy medical officers and certain other grades, their salaries
were referred back to the parties for further negotiation but had ultimately also to
be settled by the Court.

[3] Award No. 2452.

[4] Industrial Court Award No. 2565 (HMSO 1955).

[5] Numbers on 1 April 1954 were 363 established and 143 temporary officers;
they are employed on a wide range of duties, including the supervision of the
NHS.

[6] cf. *Whitley Bulletin*, June 1950, p. 87.

[7] Indignation was such that the BMA, for some two years, refused to accept
advertisements for Civil Service posts.

Public Health Dental Officers

Public health dental officers are those employed by local health and education authorities in the care of expectant and nursing mothers and of children of school age and under.[1] The majority are in fact engaged in the school health service. Their salaries were first determined on a national scale in 1951, the rates applying as from October 1950. For the basic grade of dental officer these were £800 × £50–£1,250, the maximum being £100 higher than for the analogous assistant medical officer. This was because dental personnel have not the same promotion opportunities. For chief dental officers the minimum then fixed was £1,250, rising to maxima depending on the authority's population; where this was between 400,000 and 600,000, for example, the figure was £1,550 per annum. In larger authorities the whole of the scale was 'at discretion', as was the remuneration of any intermediate-level staff that might be employed.[2]

Standards of pay for school dental officers have always been comparatively low, but against this a steady income was assured as well as a pension on retirement. Since July 1948 both these advantages have been extended to the general dental practitioner and, during the early stages of the Health Service, the school dental service virtually broke down, local authorities being unable to offer salaries even remotely comparable to the bumper earnings available in general practice.

Professional and Technical Staffs

There were some 24,000 professional and technical staffs—other than doctors and nurses—employed in the National Health Service at end-1951. They are a variegated lot, many of the professions concerned being of very recent growth; their expansion may be said to reflect that enormous stride forward in the field of medical science characteristic of the twentieth century.[3] The most concise way of describing them is to give the numbers in the different categories shown overleaf.

One broad group within this whole field is that of the medical auxiliary professions; we shall look at them first as they constitute some kind of a unity for purposes of pay negotiation. A report, published in 1951, defined them as

'Persons who assist medical practitioners otherwise than as nurses in the investigation and treatment of disease by virtue of some special skill acquired through a recognized course of training'.[4]

[1] At the beginning of 1954 the total number of staff (Great Britain) was 1,051.

[2] These rates were revised under Award 2496 of the Industrial Court, operative from 1 January 1954.

[3] cf. Ministry of Health, *Reports of the Committees on Medical Auxiliaries* (Chairman: Sir Zachary Cope) Cmd. 8188 (HMSO 1951), para. 26.

[4] *Cope Report*, op. cit., p. 1. Nurses are excluded purely for convenience.

Professional and technical staff other than medical, dental or nursing as at 31 *December* 1951[1]

	Whole-time	Part-time
Psychiatric social workers	240	40
Almoners	884	66
Radiographers	2,450	195
Physiotherapists	3,055	879
Occupational therapists	929	194
Speech therapists	19	131
Remedial gymnasts	169	19
Dietitians	181	6
Chiropodists	36	412
Orthoptists	116	139
Psychologists	64	57
Biochemists	133	6
Physicists	118	8
Pharmacists	1,165	134
Assistants in dispensing	610	98
Laboratory technicians	1,840	41
Dark room technicians	385	20
Hearing aid technicians	118	9
Cardiographers	85	59
Electro-encephalographers	43	1
Dental technicians	154	2
Surgical technicians	70	3
Engineers	1,360	8
Opticians	59	88
Clinical photographers	88	18
Catering officers	508	—
Chaplains	111	4,209
Others	1,641	540
	16,631	7,382

[1] Cmd. 8655, op. cit., p. 122. Some items have been grouped. In addition, there were 4,483 students.

This definition is none too illuminating, but the following are generally agreed to 'belong':[1] almoners, chiropodists, therapeutic

[1] The groups listed are either referred to as 'medical auxiliaries' in Whitley circulars or were covered by the Cope Committee. (Medical laboratory technicians—though reviewed by the latter—are, however, here excluded.)

dietitians, occupational therapists, physiotherapists, radiographers, speech therapists, orthoptists, remedial gymnasts and psychiatric social workers. Most entrants to these services hold a General Certificate of Education in prescribed subjects (or equivalent), followed by two or three years' professional training. Almoners and psychiatric social workers normally take a university social science course as part of the latter.

In May 1949 a series of eight committees, under the chairmanship of Sir Zachary Cope, was set up to consider the supply and demand, training and qualifications of various medical auxiliary groups in the National Health Service. The Committees found that the supply in practically every instance would be insufficient to meet the need—i.e. optimum requirement—of a fully-developed health service, but that because of financial, economic and other considerations, it would suffice to meet the demand, except in the case of almoners and dietitians. Remuneration was not specifically mentioned in their terms of reference, and they expressed themselves on that subject in the broadest of terms only.[1] However, the Committee recommended a system of statutory registration in order to ensure that auxiliaries are properly qualified. Such qualifications were accordingly prescribed by the National Health Service (Medical Auxiliaries) Regulations, 1954,[2] while the Professions Supplementary to Medicine Act, 1960[3] provides for the statutory registration of several of the professions.

Most of the medical auxiliaries are the province of Professional and Technical Whitley Council 'A', which took over—unamended—the agreements of the pre-NHS Joint Negotiating Committee (Hospital Staffs). The latter had been voluntarily established in 1945 and, as far as salaries are concerned, its recommendations were generally applied by the hospitals. Most professional and technical[4] workers outside the medical auxiliary sphere, we may add, had no nationwide rates prior to the 'appointed day'.

In the spring of 1949 the staff side of Professional and Technical Council 'A' made formal application for a pay rise for all the medical auxiliaries within the Council's purview; deadlock ensued and the matter was referred to arbitration.[5] The Industrial Court, who heard the parties in June 1951, noted that the then salaries had been in

---

[1] *Report*, op. cit., paras. 107 and 10.
[2] SI 1954 No. 55.
[3] 8 & 9 Eliz. 2 c. 66.
[4] Throughout this section 'professional and technical' should be taken to exclude medical, dental and nursing staffs.
[5] Industrial Court Award No. 2328 (HMSO 1951).

operation since 1948—in some cases since 1946—and that, though for different reasons, both sides agreed that the existing pay structures needed adjustment. As such a revision would involve a considerable lapse of time, the Court awarded an interim increase of £50, with effect from 1 April 1951.

This promised review took place; it involved, among other things, a certain measure of regrading of some of the staff structures. Agreement was reached on the pay increases to be granted, but the operative date proved a bone of contention, and had again to be referred to arbitration. The Industrial Court ruled that the new scales should apply as from 1 May 1952,[1] and for most of the categories concerned there was no further improvement until December 1954.[2]

Psychiatric Social Workers

Only a small number of fully qualified psychiatric social workers hold appointments in this country, though there are many in the field —untrained or with varying practical and theoretical qualifications. Some of these are engaged in hospital psychiatric departments and local authority clinics—on work analogous to that of fully qualified PSWs—but are paid on special rates laid down by Professional and Technical Council 'A'; others are employed by local authorities on other mental health duties and graded under the local government APT scheme. The salaries on Table 24 only relate to those who were fully qualified, i.e. who held the Mental Health Certificate of the London School of Economics or the analogous diploma of the Universities of Manchester and Edinburgh.

In a Report published in 1951, the Committee on Social Workers in the Mental Health Services—parallel to the Cope Committees on the other medical auxiliaries—drew attention to the acute shortage of trained personnel, following the much enlarged scope of these services.[3] They again considered the details of salaries as outside their terms of reference, but urged that psychiatric social work posts should be made financially more attractive. 'Indeed, the view is very strongly held by members of this Committee that the present salary position . . . is the most important single factor in the dearth of really suitable candidates . . .'[4]

---

[1] Industrial Court Award No. 2416 (HMSO 1952).

[2] There have been further revisions since as well as further modifications of individual grade patterns.

[3] Ministry of Health, *Report of the Committee on Social Workers in the Mental Health Services*, Cmd. 8260 (HMSO 1951), para. 3.

[4] ibid. para. 141.

TABLE 24

NATIONAL HEALTH SERVICE

PSYCHIATRIC SOCIAL WORKERS
(Men and Women, Great Britain)[1]

	Salary Scale as from	
	1 *October* 1946	1 *April* 1951
	£ *p.a.*	£ *p.a.*
Psychiatric social worker	370 × 20–530	420 × 20–580
Psychiatric social worker in post of responsibility[2]	370/445 × 20–530/605	420/495 × 20–580/655

	1 *May* 1952*
	£ *p.a.*
Psychiatric social worker	470[3] × 15–560
Psychiatric social worker in sole charge[4]	
Senior psychiatric social worker I, in charge of clinic/dept. with 1 other PSW	500 × 20–640
Senior psychiatric social worker II, in charge of clinic/dept. with 2 other PSWs	560 × 20–660
Senior psychiatric social worker III, in charge of clinic/dept. with 3 or more other PSWs	625 × 20–725
Teacher (supervisor)	560 × 20–680
Senior teacher	625 × 20–725

[1] The 1946 scales applied to England and Wales only. For additional London allowance, payable as from 1 May 1952, see text.

[2] In exceptional circumstances a higher scale could be granted.

[3] Linked to age 27, with an abatement of £15 for each year below.

[4] All grades except the basic were to have two years' experience after qualification. The minimum was lower if, exceptionally, PSWs with less experience were appointed.

* These scales were increased by £25 as from 1 December 1954, and have been further revised since.

Almoners

The gradings and salaries shown on Table 25 cover almoners who were registered with the Institute of Almoners, including those on the supplementary register of the Institute.

TABLE 25

NATIONAL HEALTH SERVICE

ALMONERS

(Men and Women, Great Britain)[1]

	Salary Scale as from	
	1 October 1946	1 April 1951
	£ p.a.	£ p.a.
Almoner	330 × 12½–380	380 × 12½–430
Senior/single-handed almoner[2]	380 × 12½–455	430 × 12½–505
Head almoner		
(i) with 2 or more assistants	450/500 × 25–600/650	500/550 × 25–650/700
(ii) in teaching hospital or where substantial number of almoners[2]	450/550 × 25–600/700	500/600 × 25–650/750

	1 May 1952*
	£ p.a.
Almoner	410 × 15–485
Senior almoner[3]	465[4] × 15–525
Almoner-in-sole charge	465[4] × 15–555
Deputy head almoner	490 × 15–550
Head almoner I: in charge of 1 almoner	465[4] × 15–555
Head almoner II: „ „ 2-5 almoners	560 × 20–660
Head almoner III: „ „ 6 or more almoners	625 × 20–725

[1] The 1946 scales applied to England and Wales only. For additional London allowance, payable as from 1 May 1952, see text.

[2] In exceptional circumstances the maximum could be exceeded.

[3] All grades except the basic were to have at least three years' experience after qualification.

[4] If, exceptionally, almoners without three years' experience were appointed, the minimum was lower.

* These scales were increased by £25 as from 1 December 1954, and have been further revised since.

Radiographers

Salaries here relate to those who were registered with and held the diploma of membership of the Society of Radiographers, and for persons registered with the Society as radiotherapy technicians. No distinction in grading or pay is made between those engaged in diagnostic, and those employed on therapeutic, work. The great majority are in the former category.

TABLE 26

NATIONAL HEALTH SERVICE
RADIOGRAPHERS[1]
(Men and Women, Great Britain)[2]

	Salary Scale as from		
	1 *October* 1946	1 *October* 1950	1*October*1951*
	£ p.a.	£ p.a.	£ p.a.
Radiographer (working under supervision)	310 × 12½–360	335 × 12½–385	355 × 15–415
Single-handed radiographer	As for radiographer/senior radiographer[3]	375 × 10–385 × 15–460	400 × 15–490
Senior radiographer (4 years' experience and in charge of 1-2 assistants, or deputy to a superintendent)	360 × 15–435	385 × 15–445[4]	415 × 15–490
Superintendent radiographer (5 years' experience and in charge of 3 or more assistants, or of mass radiography unit)	450 × 25–600[5]	475 × 25–625	500 × 25–650
Tutor in training school (to have 5 years' experience)[6]	450 × 25–600[7]	475 × 25–625	500 × 25–650

[1] The definition of the grades is that introduced in October 1950.

[2] The 1946 scales applied to England and Wales only. For additional London allowance, payable as from 1 October 1951, see text.

[3] If less than three years' experience, pay was as for basic grade.

[4] The final increment was £20.

[5] In exceptional circumstances the maximum could be exceeded.

[6] Salary could be increased where also performing full duties of a superintendent radiographer.

[7] Last increment granted after ten years' meritorious service in grade.

* All salaries were increased as from 1 February 1954, and have been further revised since.

Physiotherapists

Physiotherapy implies the use of physical means in the treatment of injury and disease. The curative value of some of these, we are told, was already known to the ancient Greeks,[1] though in this country physiotherapy has only become an organized profession within the last sixty years. Since then its scope has greatly increased. Physiotherapists are the largest single professional group—outside the medical, dental and nursing fields—employed in the Health Service.

[1] cf. *The Physiotherapist* (HMSO 1954), p. 3.

TABLE 27

PHYSIOTHERAPISTS
(Men and Women, Great Britain)[1]

	Salary Scale as from	
	1 *October* 1946	1 *April* 1951
	£ *p.a.*	£ *p.a.*
Physiotherapist	340 × 12½–400[2]	390 × 12½–450
Physiotherapist in sole charge	350 × 15 –410	400 × 15 –460
Superintendent physiotherapist with		
1-3 assistants	370 × 15 –430	420 × 15 –480
,, ,, 4-8 ,,	400 × 15 –490	450 × 15 –540
,, ,, 9 or more ,,	470 × 15 –560[3]	520 × 15 - 610[3]

	1 *May* 1952*
	£ *p.a.*
Physiotherapist	400 × 15–475
Senior physiotherapist[4]	455 × 15–515
Assistant superintendent physiotherapist	
in department with 6-13 physiotherapists	460 × 15–520
,, ,, 14 or more ,,	470 × 15–530
Superintendent physiotherapist I: in charge of 2-3 physiotherapists	470 × 15–530
Superintendent physiotherapist II: in charge of 4-8 physiotherapists	500 × 15–590
Superintendent physiotherapist III: in charge of 9-13 physiotherapists	550 × 20–650
Superintendent physiotherapist IV: in charge of 14 or more physiotherapists	590 × 20–690

[1] The 1946 scales applied to England and Wales only. For additional London allowance, payable as from 1 May 1952, see text.

[2] Operative from 1 June 1947. The scale from 1 October 1946 to 31 May 1947 was £320 × £12 10s. 0d.–£395.

[3] In exceptional circumstances the maximum could be exceeded.

[4] All grades except the basic were to have at least three years' experience after qualification.

* These scales were increased by £25 as from 1 December 1954, and have been further revised since.

Salaries are shown on Table 27. An additional allowance is paid to those who are state registered nurses or hold certain other diplomas —such as that of a physical training college—where such qualification is required for the post in question. There are separate scales for physiotherapy teachers. For a grade II principal, for instance— the head of a training school with an average annual intake of at least 25 students—the salary operative from 1 May 1952 was £620–£800.[1] This was the highest that could then be earned in the profession.

[1] Increased as from 1 December 1954.

Space prevents our setting out the salaries of the other medical auxiliary categories; in general, the position is that there has been no attempt precisely to equalize the pay accruing to the various groups. As regards relativities between them, the agreements concluded in the period under review show that psychiatric social workers were considerably ahead of all other medical auxiliaries, while chiropodists had the lowest remuneration. It remains to be added that Professional and Technical Council 'A' also deals with several occupations outside the medical auxiliary sphere—among them clinical psychologists, biochemists, physicists and bacteriologists.

Pharmacists

Pharmacy constitutes what is one of the older professions. Its members have various statutory responsibilities and they must also, under statute, have certain qualifications, though the latter, as we have seen, is now also true of some of the medical auxiliaries. Pharmacists have their own special Whitley body—Committee C of the Pharmaceutical Whitley Council—its agreements relating to those registered in accordance with legislative requirements and employed in hospitals or local authority health centres. Revised salaries (and conditions of service)—following prolonged negotiations culminating in arbitration[1]—took effect from 5 July 1949; they superseded the rather different grading arrangements and pay schedules of the pre-NHS Negotiating Committee (Hospital Staffs).[2] The 1949 scales, in turn, were increased as from the beginning of 1952.[3]

The pay of a chief pharmacist depends on the category of his employing hospital; in the period under review this was arrived at by a somewhat complicated formula, based on the average number of occupied beds as well as—except in mental and certain other types of hospital—out-patient attendances. The scheme was devised so as to give TB sanatoria and fever hospital pharmacists a less advantageous catgeory and mental, chronic, orthopaedic and accident hospital staffs a still less favourable one. For chief pharmacists in these two groups, category III was the highest possible. We may add that, while in the case of senior medical auxiliaries, salaries are frequently based on the number of personnel supervised, the management side of the Pharmaceutical Whitley Council does not consider this a satisfactory criterion for determining chief pharmacists' remunera-

[1] Industrial Court Award No. 2231 (HMSO 1949).

[2] The pay of the basic grade (assistant pharmacist) from October 1946 to July 1949 was £370–£450. That of a chief pharmacist with five assistants was £600–£700; if he had over five assistants, salary was 'at discretion'.

[3] Further improvements were granted as from 1 April 1955 and since.

E

tion,[1] for the reason that the latter have more say over the appointment of juniors, and could therefore, by expanding their departments, raise their income. Before 1949, however, number of staff supervised was made use of in devising scales.

TABLE 28

NATIONAL HEALTH SERVICE
PHARMACISTS
(Men and Women, Great Britain)[1]

	Salary Scale as from	
	5 *July* 1949	1 *January* 1952*
	£ *p.a.*	£ *p.a.*
Pharmacist[2]	425 × 25–525	450 × 25–575
Senior pharmacist[3]	475 × 25–575	525 × 25–625
Deputy chief pharmacist[3]		
Category IV hospital	} 525 × 25–625	575 × 25–675
,, V ,,		625 × 25–725
Chief pharmacist		
Category I hospital	525 × 25–625	575 × 25–675
,, II ,,	575 × 25–675	625 × 25–725
,, III ,,	625 × 25–725	680 × 25–780
,, IV ,,	675 × 25–825	735 × 25–885
,, V ,,	—	785 × 25–935

[1] For additional London allowance, payable as from 1 January 1952, see text.

[2] The minimum of the scale was linked to age 23, with an abatement of £25 for each year below. The commencing salary could be increased by up to two increments for relevant experience.

[3] The senior pharmacist grade was permissible only in category III, IV or V hospitals, and the deputy chief pharmacist in category IV or V institutions. (Category V hospitals did not exist prior to 1 January 1952.)

* These salaries were increased as from 1 April 1955 and have been further revised since.

All grades of pharmacist holding a qualification higher than the normal—such as the degree of B.Pharm—received, in the period under review, an extra £25 per annum, while chief pharmacists in certain teaching hospitals were eligible for special additions of from £100 to £200 a year over and above the salary appropriate to their hospital category. A sub-committee has been set up to nominate such hospitals and to determine the amount of the allowance; the arrangement is of course modelled on that for the distribution of distinction awards to consultants. Both these weightings are new features of the NHS pay pattern for pharmacists.

[1] cf. Industrial Court Award No. 2231, op. cit., p. 3.

The Central Health Services Council—who had been asked to review the matter—stated in their Report for 1953[1] that hospitals varied widely in the standards and conditions of their pharmaceutical services. Numbers employed were not nearly enough and there was a lamentable shortage of recruits. One of the main reasons for this appeared to be that initial salaries were low in comparison with those paid to newly-qualified staff in retail pharmacy, while maximum remuneration was poor compared with that of senior posts in industry. Also, there were many anomalies in hospital pharmacy salaries: Hospital classifications should be re-examined, so as to take into account the quality as well as the quantity of the pharmacist's work.[2] We may add that chemists providing the public with pharmaceutical services outside the hospitals—i.e. in retail establishments—are remunerated by local executive councils on the basis of prescriptions supplied, plus certain other payments such as dispensing fees. 'Item of service' i.e. is here—as in the case of general dental practitioners —the basis of reward.

Medical Laboratory Technicians

Medical laboratory technicians carry out, under direction, the practical tests required to provide information for the diagnosis, prevention or treatment of disease; they are far and away the largest group of technician in the Health Service. They fall within the purview of Professional and Technical Council 'B' of the Whitley constellation, and Table 29 overleaf sets out the salaries applicable in the early days of the National Health Service. Those in the first column are, however, practically identical with the standards current in the final pre-NHS year, which had been laid down by the now defunct Joint Negotiating Committee (Medical Laboratory Technicians).

Professional and Technical Council 'B' is also responsible for various grades of engineer, clerks of work, architects, quantity surveyors and draughtsmen; it likewise looks after certain other technical categories, including dark room, hearing aid, cardiological and dental technicians. As regards the latter, it should be noted that, while the great majority of dentists are practitioners in the National Health Service, the bulk of dental technicians are employed by them or in private laboratories, but as such are not members of the Health Service. Their remuneration is settled by the National Joint Council for the Craft of Dental Technicians, and it is of interest that, in the course of an arbitration claim in 1952, reference was made by the staffs to both the salaries and service conditions of the small group of technicians in the NHS.[3]

[1] HC 190 (HMSO 1954), para. 49.   [2] ibid. paras. 53–4.
[3] Industrial Disputes Tribunal Award No. 91 (HMSO 1952), para. 4.

TABLE 29

NATIONAL HEALTH SERVICE

MEDICAL LABORATORY TECHNICIANS
(Men and Women, Great Britain)[1]

	Salary Scale as from	
	1 *April* 1949	1 *May* 1951*
	£ *p.a.*	£ *p.a.*
Student technician[2]		
Age 16	110 0 0	125
17	125 0 0	140
18	145 0 0	160
19	165 0 0	180
20	195 0 0	210
21	225 0 0	240
22	240 10 0	260
23	260 0 0	280
24	279 10 0	300
25 and over	299 0 0	320
30 and over	312 0 0	333
Junior technician	as for student technician plus £13	as for student technician plus £13
Technician[3]	370 × 15–435	410 × 15–475
Senior technician	450 × 20–530	495 × 20–580[4]
Chief technician	530 × 20–650	580 × 20–700

[1] For additional allowance payable in London, see *post.*

[2] On passing the Intermediate Examination of the Institute of Medical Laboratory Technology (or equivalent), the student becomes a junior technician; on passing the Final, he becomes a technician.

[3] On gaining the Fellowship of the Institute of Medical Laboratory Technology (or equivalent), the salary was increased by £15. The final increment on the scales was £20.

[4] The final increment was £25.

* These scales were increased as from 18 June 1953 and have been further revised since.

Nursing and Midwifery

The total number of nursing and midwifery personnel in Great Britain at the end of 1951 was 185,900 full- and 34,000 part-time staff.[1] The majority of these were in hospitals under the National Health Service, with the bulk of the remainder engaged in the public health field on district work, health visiting and nursery nursing. The

[1] *Annual Report of the Ministry of Labour and National Service for* 1951, Cmd. 8640 (HMSO 1952), p. 39.

total in NHS hospitals in England and Wales on 31 December 1951 was :[1]

	Whole-time	Part-time
Student nurses	49,280	—
Trained nurses	45,052	7,877
Pupil assistant nurses	2,577	—
Enrolled assistant nurses	11,240	5,187
Other nursing staff	19,223	11,636
Pupil midwives	3,466	—
State certified midwives	5,372	1,056
	136,210	25,756

Of the above 136,210 full-time staff, 76,168 were in general and 19,415 in mental hospitals. A further 9,930 were in institutions for the chronic sick.

Candidates for the nursing service must normally be 18 years old and have a good general education. The main qualification to be obtained is that of admission to the general part of the State Register (SRN); in addition, there are parts for those specializing in sick children's nursing, fever, mental and mental deficiency nursing. With the exception of fever nursing—which requires a two-year training period—that for other parts of the Register takes three years.[2] A recent development has been the approval given by the General Nursing Council to various experimental schemes, providing a combined course of instruction for two parts of the Register.

There has been a spate of grand inquests into the state of the nursing profession, including the comprehensive Report of the Working Party on the Recruitment and Training of Nurses, published in 1947.[3] Among the latter's conclusions were that a new procedure for selecting both entrants and the occupants of senior posts was required; that full student status should be given to trainee nurses; and that the key problem was wastage during training: 'Out of every hundred student nurses . . . not more than fifty remain at the

[1] Cmd. 8655, op. cit., pp. 126–7. In addition, there were 3,550 full- and 332 part-time staff in non-NHS civilian hospitals.

[2] Less, if a nurse already has a basic qualification.

[3] *Report of the Working Party on the Recruitment and Training of Nurses* (Chairman: Sir Robert Wood) (HMSO 1947). See Appendix I for details of official and other reports.

end of the training period, and in many hospitals not more than about thirty . . .'[1] We may add that it was the acute shortage of all types of nursing personnel that has focused attention on the profession, though, as far as *general* hospitals are concerned, the supply position has improved considerably since the inception of the Health Service.

Pay: Salaries in the nursing world used to vary considerably; according to the 1938 Athlone Committee, the profession was badly underpaid even when the value of emoluments was taken into account. They recommended that remuneration should be on a national basis, and that 'salaries committees' should be established analogous to the Burnham machinery for teachers.[2] Accordingly, a Nurses Salaries Committee was set up in 1941, followed in 1942 by a Midwives Salaries Committee, each with Lord Rushcliffe as chairman; a special sub-committee was formed for mental nurses. The Committees presented two reports and a number of supplementary recommendations; the intial date of application was 1 April 1943. These codes represented the first set of nation-wide pay scales for nurses and midwives, and although they had no statutory authority were—with the exception of some voluntary hospitals—widely adopted throughout the country. Improved rates for all grades were secured in 1946, and many salaries were further increased in 1947. The work of the Rushcliffe Committees came to an end on the 'appointed day', when the Nurses and Midwives Whitley Council took over. The latter, we may point out, covers the whole of Great Britain and is responsible for the largest single sector of NHS staff.

Towards the end of 1948 the new Council embarked on a detailed examination of the service conditions of all nursing personnel—both in the hospital and public health field. This review extended over several years, but all settlements were applied retrospectively as from 1 February 1949. In the course of this 'overhaul', the basis of pay was reconstructed: The old system of cash remuneration, plus free residential emoluments in kind, was abandoned in favour of an inclusive rate. The (female) staff nurse, for example, who had previously drawn a cash sum of £140–£200, plus free board and lodging valued at £100, was given an all-inclusive scale of £315–£415; male nurses, we may add, had always been paid on that system. Out of this inclusive salary, the nurse—if resident—now pays for her board and lodging; the deductions for this purpose are fixed centrally and vary

[1] *Report of the Working Party on the Recruitment and Training of Nurses*, p. 35.

[2] See *First Report of the Nurses Salaries Committee*, Cmd. 6424 (HMSO 1943), Section B, para. 9.

according to rank.[1] Since the days of Rushcliffe, however, there has been a significant trend towards 'living out'.

Towards the end of 1951 the staff representatives decided that the demand for a general enhancement of standards should not be postponed; a formal claim was submitted in February 1952. Though agreement on the extent of the improvement was eventually reached, the date from which the increases should operate had to be referred to the Industrial Court; the latter's ruling was that the date should be 1 June 1952.[2] The rise amounted to £25 in the allowances for student nurses, £45 in the salaries of staff nurses and midwives, and £60 in the remuneration of matrons. These rates remained in force until 1954.[3]

The pay structure in the nursing world is highly complicated; in 1953 it was officially stated to consist of some two hundred and fifty separate salary scales.[4] We shall confine ourselves to the main categories.

Student nurses: Student nurses' salaries—rechristened in 1948 and since officially known as 'training allowances'—are shown on Table 30. The figures do not include the dependants' allowances likewise instituted in 1948 to help those with family responsibilities, and they did not apply to what are known as post-registration student nurses, such as SRNs taking a fever or children's training. For these, higher rates were in existence.

Qualified staff in general hospitals: The enrolled assistant nurse was created by the Nurses Act of 1943, primarily to give status to those who had rendered service during the war but had no formal qualification. Training, since 1949, takes one year, followed by a further twelve months' practical experience after which enrolment takes place. The role of this grade in the Health Service has been one of some controversy, though a report published in 1954[5] expressed the view that there was room for it in considerably greater numbers.

---

[1] The charges payable as from 1 June 1952 e.g. ranged from £108 p.a. for student nurses to £245 for the highest-paid matron. Non-resident staff pay for meals taken and (except matrons who receive an allowance for the purpose) the supply of uniform.

[2] Industrial Court Award No. 2427 (HMSO 1953), para. 4. Higher charges for board, lodging, etc., were introduced at the same time.

[3] i.e. they were increased as from 1 December 1954 in the case of general nursing and midwifery staff, and as from 1 April 1954 in the case of (most) mental nurses: See Industrial Court Award Nos. 2560 (HMSO 1955) and 2504 (HMSO 1954).

[4] Industrial Court Award No. 2427, op. cit., p. 4.

[5] *Report by the Standing Nursing Advisory Committee on the Position of the Enrolled Assistant Nurse within the National Health Service* (HMSO 1954).

TABLE 30

NATIONAL HEALTH SERVICE

STUDENT NURSES, PUPIL ASSISTANT NURSES AND PUPIL MIDWIVES

(Men and Women, Great Britain)[1]

	Training Allowance[2] as from			
	1 *Jan.* 1946	5 *July* 1948	1 *Sept* 1948	1 *June* 1952*
	£ *p.a.*	£ *p.a.*	£ *p.a.*	£ *p.a.*
Student nurse[3]				
1st year	130	145	200	225
2nd ,,	140	155	210	235
3rd ,, [4]	150	165	225	250
Pupil or probationer assistant nurse[5]				
1st year	130	145	200	225
2nd ,,	140	155	210	235
Pupil midwife				
(a) if SRN or RSCN	160	175	230	255
(b) if not SRN/RSCN				
1st year	135	150	205	230
2nd ,,	140	155	210	235
During second period of training	155	170	225	250
Student mental nurse				
1st year	150	175[6]	230	255
2nd ,,	155	175[6]	240	265
3rd ,,	160	180[6]	255	280

The following *proficiency allowances* were payable in addition to student *mental* nurses:

(a) £20 on completion of 2nd year of training or passing of preliminary examination.

(b) £30 on completion of 3rd year of training or passing of final examination.

(c) Prior to 1 October 1947, an allowance of £10 was also payable at end of 1st year of training.

[1] The 1946 figures applied to England and Wales only. Male student nurses (other than mental) received an additional London allowance throughout period.

[2] Including responsibility allowance. Dependants' allowances (where applicable) were payable in addition. The figures prior to 1 September 1948 include value of emoluments received in kind.

[3] A payment of £5 was made on passing preliminary state examination.

[4] On passing examination for state registration, student nurse immediately to be paid as staff nurse (since 1 September 1948).

[5] A payment of £5 was made on completion of training and passing test for enrolment.

[6] Applicable from 1 October 1947.

* These rates were increased as from 1 December 1954 (student mental nurses: as from 1 April 1954), and have been further revised since.

TABLE 31

NATIONAL HEALTH SERVICE
NURSING STAFF IN GENERAL HOSPITALS
(Women, Great Britain)[1]

	Salary Scale as from		
	1 *Oct.* 1947	1 *Feb.* 1949	1 *June* 1952*
	£ *p.a.*[2]	£ *p.a.*	£ *p.a.*
Enrolled assistant nurse	220 –270[3]	285 × 12½–385	325 × 12½–425
Staff nurse	240 –300[4]	315 × 12½–415	360 × 12½–460
Ward sister, housekeeping sister, night sister	300 –380[5]	375 × 15–500[6]	425 × 15–550[6]
Departmental sister[7]	300 –420	405 × 15–530[6]	455 × 15–580[6]
Night sister in sole charge	325 –405[8]	400 × 15–525[6]	450 × 15–575[6]
Night superintendent[9]	340 –420	415 × 15–540[6]	465 × 15–590[6]
Sister tutor[10]	380 × 15–440	500 × 15–600	560 × 15–660
Sister tutor in sole charge	440 × 20–500	525 × 20–625	585 × 20–685
Principal sister tutor	480 × 20–580	575 × 20–700[11]	635 × 20–760[11]

[1] The 1947 scales applied to England and Wales only.

[2] The figures in this column include value of residential emoluments.

[3] Cash salary was £120 × £10–£160; after 5 years, × £10–£170.

[4] Cash salary was £140 × £10–£180; after 5 years, × £10–£190; after 5 years, × £10–£200.

[5] Cash salary was £180 × £10–£220; after 5 years, × £20–£240; after 5 years, × £20–£260.

[6] The final increment was £20.

[7] Salary of departmental sister on administrative work, before 1 February 1949, was that of ward sister plus allowance of £10–£20 p.a. If on active clinical duties, rate was that of ward sister plus £0–£40. Salary subsequently standardized at £30 above ward sister's; in observation wards this could be increased up to £60.

[8] Cash salary as for ward sister, plus £25.

[9] Prior to 1 February 1949, cash salary as for ward sister plus £40. Scale as from 1 February 1949 was increased by £10, if number of beds supervised 750 or over.

[10] The designation of tutors was slightly different prior to 1 February 1949.

[11] The last increment was £25.

* All salaries were increased as from 1 December 1954 and have been further revised since.

The basic rung in the fully qualified hierarchy is the staff nurse, the usual ladder of promotion from that grade being to ward sister and thence to departmental sister, assistant matron and matron. The ward sister is responsible not only for the care of patients but also for the training of juniors; she is said to occupy a strategic position in the hospital. Departmental sisters are normally in charge of a special section such as the out-patients department or operating theatre; housekeeping sisters look after domestic arrangements. The key to the higher nursing salary structure, in the period under review, was the remuneration of the ward sister; grades like the home, departmental or night sister were in effect paid as ward sisters plus an allowance.[1]

[1] On Table 31 the allowance has, for convenience, been added to basic salary.

TABLE 32

NATIONAL HEALTH SERVICE
MATRONS
(Great Britain)[1]

	Salary Scale as from		
	1 *April* 1947 £ p.a.[2]	1 *February* 1949 £ p.a.	1 *June* 1952* £ p.a.
I. Hospitals approved for complete training[3] for state registration in general or sick children's nursing:			
Assistant matron			
Under 300 beds	400×15–460	465×15–555	525×15–615
300–399 ,,	435×15–495	500×15–590	560×15–650
400–499 ,,	460×15–520	530×15–620	590×15–680
500 beds and over	480×15–620[4]	555×15–645	615×15–705
Deputy matron			
500 beds or over	([5])	615×15–725[6]	675×15–785[6]
Matron			
Under 200 beds	450×25–575	575×25–710	635×25–770
200–299 ,,	530×25–680	600×25–770	660×25–830
300–399 ,,	580×30–760	655×30–850	715×30–910
400–499 ,,	630×30–810	710×30–900	770×30–960
500–599 ,,		755×30–935	815×30–995
600–699 ,,	675×30–925[4]	790×30–970	850×30–1,030
700–999 ,,		825×30–1,005	885×30–1,065
1,000–1,499 ,,	750×30–1,000[4]	910×30–1,090	970×30–1,150
1,500 beds and over		930×30–1,110	990×30–1,170
II. Non-training hospitals (*except sanatoria, fever and and mental hospitals*):			
Assistant matron[7]			
Under 300 beds	390×15–450	460×15–550	515×15–605
300–399 ,,	415×15–475	480×15–570	540×15–630
400–499 ,,	430×15–490	500×15–590	560×15–650
500 beds and over	460×15–520	520×15–610	580×15–670
Matron			
Under 30 beds	320 –420[8]	520×20–600	580×20–660
30–49 ,,	410×20–470		
50–99 ,,	420×20–500	540×20–625	600×20–685
100–199 ,,	440×20–540	555×20–670	615×20–730
200–299 ,,	460×25–585	575×25–715	635×25–775
300–399 ,,	525×25–675	600×25–760	660×25–820
400–499 ,,	540×25–690	620×25–775	680×25–835
500–599 ,,		650×25–810	710×25–870
600–699 ,,	580×25–755[4]	670×25–825	730×25–885
700 beds and over		690×25–840	750×25–900

Matrons: Table 32 covers matrons of hospitals approved for complete training for state registration, as well as those in non-training
institutions. A third category is employed in training schools for
enrolled assistant nurses where, in the period under review, salaries
were intermediate between those of 'full training' and 'non-training'
matrons.[1] As the table shows, the 1949 settlement introduced certain
innovations in the method of remuneration; the pre-NHS salary
ranges for those in the larger hospitals were superseded by fixed
scales, strictly linked to the number of beds in the institution. A welcome recent development has been the 1959 Whitley agreement providing for some reduction in the number of beddage groups, as well
as for the elimination altogether of the differential between matrons
in the two types of training school. Lower down the nursing ladder,
on the other hand, there has been an elaboration of certain grades.

In addition to the categories dealt with, mention should be made of
nursing auxiliaries,[2] who have no formal qualification whatever,
working in (non-mental) hospitals where they relieve trained staff
of routine tasks. Their place in the hierarchy lies between that of enrolled assistant nurse and ward orderly, the latter being a domestic
grade within the purview of the Ancillary Staffs Council. Nursing
auxiliaries are the only group for whom no national standards were
laid down at the inception of the Health Service; in the absence of
such scales the great majority were paid at ward orderly rates. However, the question of regularizing their position came to a head in
1953 and was eventually settled by the Industrial Court.[3]

---

[1] The highest an assistant nurse training school matron could reach, as from
1 June 1952, was £1,060 per annum—as against £900 in a non-training and
£1,170 in a full training school.
[2] Numbers in England and Wales at 31 December 1953 were 15,558 whole-
time and 5,831 part-time auxiliaries.
[3] Award No. 2535 (HMSO 1954).

---

[1] The 1947 scales applied to England and Wales only.
[2] The figures in this column include value of residential emoluments.
[3] Salaries were the same in 'affiliated' and 'associated' training hospitals, except
in those with under 100 beds where pay was lower.
[4] Range, not scale. Starting pay at employer's discretion, with prescribed
number of increments.
[5] This grade did not exist prior to 1 February 1949.
[6] The final increment was £20.
[7] Where two assistant matrons were employed in a hospital with under 500
beds, the second received scale salary less £20.
[8] Cash salary was £200 × £10–£260; after 5 years, × 20–£280; after 5 years,
× £20–£300.

* All salaries were increased as from 1 December 1954 and have been further
revised since.

It must be emphasized that the salaries outlined above did not apply—or did so with modifications—to nurses engaged in special institutions such as TB sanatoria or certain types of fever hospital. Similarly, the standards shown were augmented by small allowances in the case of those required to have additional qualifications—say, in the care of cripples or sick children's nursing—or of staff regularly employed on VD work. Conversely, the scales were somewhat lower for those who were only on a supplementary part of the State Register.

Mental Nursing

In formulating their recommendations in 1944, the Mental Nurses' Sub-Committee found it convenient to work from the salaries proposed for the general field; their conclusion was that at the less senior levels somewhat higher scales than for comparable 'general' grades were both justifiable and desirable.[1] This differential between general and mental nurses' pay is known as the mental 'lead'. It has fluctuated somewhat, but in the early days of the Health Service was standardized at £30 per annum for student nurses, and at £20 for all others except the most senior staffs.[2] Student mental nurses, further, are eligible for additional proficiency allowances, whereas student general nurses receive only a small cash payment on passing the preliminary state examination. As regards higher posts, the position on the 'appointed day' was that many of these attracted lower salaries in the mental than in the general field, but this has since been rectified: Thus in 1948 the top figure attainable by a matron (training and non-training) was £100 less in mental than in general hospitals; it is now the same and there has been a similar levelling up in the case of deputy matrons. However, while senior mental staffs have achieved 'parity', they do not enjoy a 'lead'. The latter, we may add, has meanwhile been more than doubled for the lower grades—in an effort no doubt to overcome the particularly serious shortage of personnel which has persisted in this sphere.

Table 33 is not exhaustive, though it more or less shows each rung of the 'mental' ladder. The latter is not identical with that in general institutions. Nursing assistants, for instance, and the intermediate level of deputy ward sister have no counterpart in the general field; on the other hand, there is no such thing as a mental enrolled assistant nurse. The set-up for deputy and assistant matrons likewise differs in the two hierarchies, while the mental structure—unlike the general

---

[1] *Report of the Mental Nurses Sub-Committee*, Cmd. 6542 (HMSO 1944), paras. 9–10.

[2] The nomenclature differs in the two hierarchies. The highest grade to enjoy the £20 lead in the period under review was the (mental) assistant matron, comparable to a (general) departmental sister.

—has catered throughout for senior male staff, men being employed here to a much greater extent, relatively, than in general hospitals. There are also important differences in the two groups' conditions of service.

TABLE 33

NATIONAL HEALTH SERVICE

NURSING STAFF IN MENTAL HOSPITALS AND MENTAL DEFICIENCY INSTITUTIONS
(Women, Great Britain)

	Salary Scale as from		
	1 *Oct.* 1947	1 *Feb.* 1949	1 *June* 1952*
	£ *p.a.*[2]	£ *p.a.*	£ *p.a.*
Nursing assistant			
Class II	165×5–175	225×10 –245	250×10 –270
„ I	210×5–280[3]	$275 \times 12\frac{1}{2}$–385	$315 \times 12\frac{1}{2}$–425
Staff nurse	260×10^{4}–310[5]	$335 \times 12\frac{1}{2}$–435	$380 \times 12\frac{1}{2}$–480
Deputy ward sister	280×10^{4}–330[5]	$375 \times 12\frac{1}{2}$–475	$420 \times 12\frac{1}{2}$–520
Ward sister	300–400[5,6]	395×15 –520[7]	445×15 –570[7]
Assistant matron	340–440[8]	425×15 –550[7]	475×15 –600[7]
Deputy matron			
(training school)			
Under 300 beds		470×15–560	525×15–615
300–399 „		500×15–590	560×15–650
400–499 „		530×15–620	590×15–680
500–599 „	([9])	555×15–645	615×15–705
600–699 „		575×15–665	635×15–725
700–999 „		595×15–685	655×15–745
1,000–1,499 „		615×15–705	675×15–765
1,500 beds and over		635×15–725	695×15–785
Matron (training school)	([9])	as in general hospital	as in general hospital

[1] The 1947 scales applied to England and Wales only.
[2] The figures in this column include value of residential emoluments.
[3] Cash salary was £110 × £5–£140, × £5 every two years to £180.
[4] Last increment payable after five years on previous point.
[5] If SRN in addition to being qualified mental nurse, salary was £10 higher.
[6] Cash salary was £180 × £10–£260; after five years, × £20–£280.
[7] The final increment was £20.
[8] Salary as for ward sister, plus allowance of £40.
[9] Salaries not set out, as basis of classification differed.

* All scales have been further revised since; in the case of the lower grades, as from 1 April 1954.

Broadmoor, etc.: On the fringe of the mental health world are the nursing staffs of what have hitherto been known as the three 'state institutions'[1]—Rampton and Moss Side Hospitals and Broadmoor. Rampton and Moss Side were set up under the Mental Deficiency Act, 1913—for mental defectives of dangerous or violent propensities; on 1 July 1947 both establishments vested in the Minister of Health. Broadmoor Criminal Lunatic Asylum was under the Home Office until April 1949 when, under the Criminal Justice Act, 1948, it also vested in the Minister; its name was changed to Broadmoor Institution. The three establishments thus now form part of the National Health Service; the nursing staff, however, continue to have the status of civil servants and, though covered by Ministry of Health Whitley machinery, maintain a considerable measure of independence.[2] Yet by training they are mental nurses in the ordinary way, and their grading and service conditions have followed those of the Health Service. Similarly with remuneration: Since 1944 and throughout the period under review the institutions' staffs were paid salaries which were £40 in excess of those nationally agreed for corresponding ordinary mental hospital personnel. There was thus an additional lead of £40 —sometimes less elegantly referred to as 'danger money'—over the rates of the general run of mental nurses.[3]

The Broadmoor Inquiry Committee, appointed in 1952 under the chairmanship of Mr Scott Henderson, QC, to review the adequacy of the security arrangements at Broadmoor, dealt among other things with staffing problems. The Committee urged that the relative financial attraction that Broadmoor offered before the war should be restored; the 'lead' of £40 was no longer effective. The special conditions prevailing at Broadmoor lent force to the argument that the pay of its nursing staff should be determined independently, and should not be automatically linked with that of the National Health Service.[4] In the light of the Report, the 'lead' of state institution salaries was raised from £40 to £90 per annum—and it has been further increased since.

Midwifery

Notwithstanding its close relation to nursing, midwifery is a distinct profession. Legislation during the present century has placed it on a sound basis; the title of 'midwife' is protected by law and applicable

[1] In accordance with Part VII of the Mental Health Act, 1959, the three institutions are in future to be known as 'special hospitals'.

[2] Disputes are still referred to the Civil Service Arbitration Tribunal and the staff continue to be represented by the Prison Officers' Association.

[3] cf. Industrial Court Award No. 2504, op. cit., p. 3; Civil Service Arbitration Tribunal Award No. 209 (HMSO 1953), paras. 17–19; and *Report of the Broadmoor Inquiry Committee*, Cmd. 8594 (HMSO 1952), paras. 4–5.

[4] ibid. paras. 22–23.

only to a woman who has gained a certificate (SCM), entitling her to admission to the official Roll of Midwives. The length of training varies: for state registered nurses, for example, it is one year; for those without any basic nursing qualification, it is two. The great majority of recruits are in fact trained nurses.

A Working Party on Midwives was set up in 1947 to investigate the shortage of staff which had then reached almost alarming proportions. It found that practising midwives were seriously overworked, and drew attention to unsatisfactory features in the course of training, the high rate of examination failures and the arduous working conditions.[1] The Working Party stated that there was no doubt that the profession was acutely dissatisfied with its remuneration; it foresaw that the whole level of medico-social salaries might be scaled up in the near future 'and in that scaling up the midwife must certainly share.' The Working Party was also concerned with the question of status, and urged that doctors should accept the midwife as their fellow practitioner.[2]

Both the Working Party and the Midwives' Salaries (Rushcliffe) Committee in their Report of 1943[3] pointed out that the prospects of the would-be midwife compared unfavourably with those of the woman who chose nursing. There was less scope for advancement—maternity hospitals were never as large as the bigger general or specialized hospitals—and the matron's responsibility and remuneration were correspondingly smaller. The Rushcliffe Committee bore this in mind in framing their recommendations. Rushcliffe also stated that it was an advantage for a midwife to have both a nursing and a midwifery qualification, but the 1949 Working Party concluded that there was no inherent reason—except in certain fields such as the Colonial Service—why a midwife should also be a SRN. While, therefore, there used to be some pay differentiation for those having the double qualification, this was abolished under the NHS.

Table 34 does not show all the scales provided for in the Whitley agreements; there is, for example, a whole complex of rates for senior staff in non-training institutions. It will be seen that both in 1949 and 1952 the bulk of midwives—i.e. the three bottom ranks—were given a scale which was £20 higher than that for the corresponding 'general' nursing category. Midwifery tutors, on the other hand, including those in sole charge, received the same as their opposite number in the general field, while a principal midwifery tutor then had a lower salary than her 'general' colleague. These differentials have since

---

[1] *Report of the Working Party on Midwives* (Chairman: Mrs M. D. Stocks) (HMSO 1949). For a summary of findings see p. 72 and ff.

[2] ibid. paras. 190–1 and 101.

[3] *Report of Midwives' Salaries Committee*, Cmd. 6460 (HMSO 1943).

TABLE 34

NATIONAL HEALTH SERVICE

MIDWIFERY STAFF

(Women, Great Britain)[1]

	Salary Scale[2] as from		
	1 *October* 1947 £ *p.a.*[3]	1 *Feb.* 1949 £ *p.a.*	1 *June* 1952* £ *p.a.*
Staff midwife	260×10–310[4]	$335 \times 12\frac{1}{2}$–435	$380 \times 12\frac{1}{2}$–480
Midwifery sister	320×10–400[5]	395×15–520[6]	445×15–570[6]
Departmental mid- wifery sister	$330/370 \times 10$–380/450[7]	425×15–550[6]	475×15–600[6]
Deputy superinten- dent midwife	([8])	445×15–570[6]	500×15–625[6]
Superintendent midwife[9] (train- ing institution)			
25–49 beds	420×20–495	485×20–625	545×20–685
50–99 ,,	440×20–575[10]	510×20–680	570×20–740
100 beds & over	470×25–650[10]	540×25–760	600×25–820
Assistant matron (training institution)			
Under 50 beds	$320/360 \times 10$–400/440[11]	460×15–585[6]	515×15–640[6]
50 beds & over	420×20–495	490×20–610	550×20–670
Matron[9] (training institution)			
10–19 beds	420×20–505	550×20–675	610×20–735
20–49 ,,	465×20–575	565×20–700	625×20–760
50–99 ,,	490×25–625	590×25–740	650×25–800
100–199 ,,	550 –750[10]	625×30–845	685×30–905
200 beds & over	600 –825[10]	650×30–890	710×30–950

[1] The 1947 scales applied to England and Wales only.

[2] *Excluding* the midwifery 'service allowance' of £20 p.a. (see text).

[3] The figures in this column include value of residential emoluments.

[4] Cash salary was $£160 \times £10$–£200; after 5 years, $\times £10$–£210. If midwife was SCM only, salary was £20 lower at minimum and £10 at maximum.

[5] Cash salary was $£200 \times £10$–£260; after 5 years, $\times £20$–£280. If SCM only and appointed on/after 1 April 1938, scale was £20 lower.

[6] The final increment was £20.

[7] Range, not scale. Range was £330/350–£380/430 in non-training, and £350/370–£400/450 in training, institutions. Starting pay at employer's discretion. Five annual increments to be paid, with discretion to grant a further three.

[8] There was no scale for this grade prior to February 1949.

[9] The bed ranges were slightly different for period prior to 1 February 1949.

[10] Range, not scale. Starting pay at employer's discretion, with prescribed number of increments.

[11] Cash salary was $£200 \times £10$–£260; after 5 years, $\times £20$–£280, plus allowance of not more than £40.

* All salaries were increased as from 1 December 1954 and have been further revised since.

been somewhat modified: principal tutors in the two spheres now get the same remuneration, for example, while staff midwives enjoy a rather larger lead over the parallel general hospital grade.

In order to counterbalance the drift into other branches of nursing, the Rushcliffe Committee had instituted a service allowance of £20 per annum, payable since January 1946 to all grades of full-time (qualified) midwives after the completion of a year's continuous employment. This 'bonus' proved the source of considerable dissatisfaction; the Whitley Council therefore decided that no further allowances should be paid after March 1952.[1] We may add that though the number of hospital midwives has increased considerably since 1949, there is still a serious shortage of trained personnel in some areas, accentuated by a continued rise in the number of hospital confinements. The problem, moreover, is not due to any dearth of trainees, but to the reluctance of newly qualified staff to practise their profession.[2]

Public Health Nursing
While the majority of nurses are employed in hospitals, a sizeable minority is engaged in district work, domiciliary midwifery, health visiting and nursery nursing. National standards for this sector of the profession were again first laid down by the Rushcliffe Committee, the original (1943) figures being revised in 1946. The rates introduced as from February 1949—representing the first settlement under the Health Service—were fixed in the light of an award of the Industrial Court, the staffs having appealed to the latter to maintain the relationship of public health salaries to those of the institutional grades on which they were based.[3] We may add that the public health pay structure is again very elaborate; apart from those shown on Table 35, there are scales for a rich variety of senior domiciliary personnel.

A separate pattern of salaries is in existence for nursery nurses working in local authority day and residential nurseries and in nursery schools and classes. Another task of the Nurses and Midwives Whitley Council is to lay down standards for all manner of part-time staff, the employment of which—originally a war-time expedient—has been significantly expanded in recent years. As for industrial nurses, on the other hand, these are not employees of the Health Service, remuneration here being settled independently by agreement between the parties.

---

[1] For new entrants the allowance ceased as from 3 August 1951. However, midwives have continued to receive an additional £20 p.a. if engaged on maternity work complicated by VD.

[2] cf. *Report of Ministry of Health for* 1958, op. cit., p. 64.

[3] Industrial Court Award No. 2256 (HMSO 1950) p. 1.

TABLE 35

NATIONAL HEALTH SERVICE

PUBLIC HEALTH AND DOMICILIARY NURSING AND MIDWIFERY STAFF
(Women, Great Britain)[1]

	Salary Scale[2] as from		
	1 *Jan.* 1946 £ p.a.	1 *Feb.* 1949 £ p.a.[3]	1 *June* 1952* £ p.a.[3]
District nurse (SRN with 'district' training)[4]	300 × 15–405	340 × 15–465	385 × 15–510
District midwife (SCM and SRN/RSCN)[5]	330 × 15–435	370 × 15–495	420 × 15–545
District nurse midwife[6] (SRN and SCM with 'district' training)[4]	320 × 15–425	360 × 15–485	410 × 15–535
Health visitor	330 × 15–435	370 × 15–495	420 × 15–545
TB visitor[7]	330 × 15–435	370 × 15–495	420 × 15–545
School nurse[7]	330 × 15–435	370 × 15–495	420 × 15–545
Senior health visitor, Senior school nurse, Senior TB visitor[7]	350 × 15–455	400 × 15–525	450 × 15–575

[1] The 1946 scales applied to England and Wales only. For additional London allowance see text.

[2] Prior to 1 February 1949 there were separate scales for those living in district homes. All rates on this table refer to *non*-resident grades.

[3] The final increment on all scales in this column was £20.

[4] If without district training, scale was £10 lower. If on health visiting duties and holding HV certificate, it was £10 higher.

[5] If SCM only, a lower scale applied.

[6] i.e. undertaking both nursing and midwifery, the average number of maternity cases being under 30.

[7] With HV certificate or equivalent. The scale was lower for those with an inferior qualification.

* All salaries were increased as from 1 December 1954 and have been further revised since.

Provincial Differentiation

Medical salaries are not differentiated by area; no London weighting accrues to those working in the metropolis. In the case of professional and technical staffs, London allowances were conceded after protracted negotiations, including several references to arbitration.[1] All the categories whose remuneration we have reviewed now qualify for a London addition, though in most instances this did not become payable until 1952. The rates then introduced were £10 a year for persons under 21, £20 if aged 21–25, and £30 for those 26 years old and over. Where, as in the case of pharmacists, the scales

[1] cf. Industrial Court Award No. 2254 (HMSO 1950) and No. 2328 (HMSO 1951).

reached sufficiently high, the allowance was £40 per annum on pay between £801 and £1,000–or £50 if over £1,000 a year.

As regards nursing, the position is that male staff (other than mental nurses)—but not female hospital grades—were paid a London addition under the Rushcliffe reports, but this was discontinued from February 1949 for all except students. Public health and domiciliary nursing and midwifery personnel—other than those living in district homes—likewise received a London weighting in pre-NHS days, and in this instance this continued to accrue after 1949 at the rate of £25 per annum if inside the LCC area, and £15 if within the Metropolitan Police District outside the LCC. When, under the National Health Service, the all-inclusive cash salary became universal, the staff felt that all nursing grades should now have identical treatment in the matter, and in this they were upheld by the Industrial Court in 1954.[1] Since 1 November 1954, therefore, all non-resident nurses and midwives in the Metropolitan Police Area—i.e. male and female and whether hospital or public health—receive a London weighting, the rates then introduced being the same as those quoted above for professional and technical workers.

Sex Differentiation

As far as doctors are concerned, the 1929 Askwith memorandum already provided that there was to be no difference in pay on grounds of sex; the Health Service continued the tradition, so that from the start men and women doctors and dentists in all sectors of the Service have enjoyed the same standards. Most professional and technical workers, likewise, were already entitled to equal pay at the inception of the Health Service. In the only instances where this was not the case—juniors in regional hospital board works organizations and dark room technicians—arrangements have since been made for its introduction on the usual formula. We may add that while only few women act as pharmacists, they predominate in most of the medical auxiliary professions.

Nursing, similarly, is primarily a woman's occupation, mental hospitals being the only field in which men are employed in any numbers. The Rushcliffe Committee had felt obliged to conform to the then widely accepted practice of superior pay for male staff, though the differential became smaller in the higher reaches of the nursing world, while men and women tutors were on identical rates.[2] The sex differential was further narrowed by the Nurses and Midwives Whitley Council; the June 1952 scale for a male 'general' staff

[1] Industrial Court Award No. 2539 (HMSO 1954).
[2] Salaries for men and women under Rushcliffe were not *strictly* comparable, however, in view of the different bases of remuneration.

nurse, for instance, was merely £10 above that for a woman. For ward and departmental sisters, men—though they had a higher minimum—had the same maximum as their female opposite numbers, and one is tempted to suggest that these trivial differences were retained largely so as not to embarrass the Treasury. Meanwhile, following the latter's lead, an analogous seven-year plan was agreed upon in 1955, providing for identical salaries for all men and women nurses as from January 1961.

Chapter 6

THE ADMINISTRATION OF JUSTICE

The administration of justice has not always been a public service; jurisdiction run privately for profit, we are told, did not shock the Norman conscience.[1] However, owing to the fact that it was both better and more popular, it was royal justice that prevailed.

The legal system in England is not a unified service; there is no hierarchical structure with a single figure at its head. Thus some of the highest judicial posts are filled on the recommendation of the Prime Minister, the Home Secretary has considerable powers in the sphere of the criminal law, and the Lord Chief Justice in the Queen's Bench Division. The nearest approach to a Minister of Justice is the Lord Chancellor; yet there are departments over which he has no control. Again, where the Roman tradition holds, the judiciary is part of the machinery of government and is a profession separate from that of the lawyer. Here, the judiciary stands apart from the Civil Service and is closely linked with the bar; it is through private practice—if he is successful enough—that a barrister may in middle or old age attain to the judiciary.[2]

For the administration of justice law is divided into civil and criminal. Lesser civil matters are dealt with by county courts; others by the High Court with appeal to the Court of Appeal and the House of Lords. Criminal justice is administered in courts of summary jurisdiction, courts of quarter sessions or the High Court; there is also a Court of Criminal Appeal.[3] The High Court has thus both civil and criminal jurisdiction; its personnel, as that of the Court of Appeal and the House of Lords, is sometimes referred to as the 'superior' judges.

County Courts
Though their jurisdiction is limited, county courts handle the great bulk of civil litigation. The maximum number of *county court judges*

[1] R. M. Jackson, *The Machinery of Justice in England* (Cambridge University Press, 1940), p. 2.
[2] ibid. pp. 19–20 and G. R. Y. Radcliffe and G. Cross, *The English Legal System* (Butterworth, 1946), pp. 385–8.
[3] Only the major courts have been mentioned.

that can be appointed is laid down by Parliament; under the High Court and County Court Judges Act, 1950, the relevant figure was sixty-five. The judges, who serve full-time, must be barristers of at least seven years' standing.

The Statutory Salaries Act, 1937[1] fixed the remuneration of county court judges at £2,000 per annum. No alteration in this figure was made until 1951, but in 1947 certain additions became payable in respect of the judges' then new duties as special divorce commissioners. These payments were on a basis appropriate to High Court judges, but varied widely from over £1,000 to under £50 a year, depending on the volume of divorce work.[2] The Judicial Offices (Salaries, &c.) Act, 1952[3] 'compounded' this extra divorce pay at £300, consolidated it with basic remuneration, and laid down a new inclusive salary of £2,800 a year. This figure applied retrospectively from 1 July 1951, though it has since been revised.

Courts of Summary Jurisdiction

Justices of the Peace: There are about one thousand courts of summary jurisdiction or magistrates' courts, which are mainly concerned with the adjudication of less serious offences. They do the great bulk of the country's criminal work, and are mostly staffed by lay, unpaid magistrates or Justices of the Peace. At the time of writing, there were approximately 21,000 JPs in England and Wales (including 6,000 on the supplemental list). Under legislation passed in the reign of Richard II they received 'Wages by the Day for the Time of their Sessions', but an 1855 'Act for diminishing Expense and Delay in the Administration of Criminal Justice . . .' considered it expedient that such payments be discontinued.[4] Their services are therefore entirely free—except for the refund of expenses—an interesting exception to the general movement from voluntary to paid service.

Metropolitan and stipendiary magistrates: Courts of summary jurisdiction are also held before metropolitan police and stipendiary magistrates, who are full-time, salaried officers, chosen from barristers of at least seven years' standing. They act in place of, or in addition to, local JPs; whether a locality has a stipendiary magistrate or relies entirely upon lay justices is largely a matter of history.[5]

[1] 1 Edw. 8. and 1 Geo. 6. c. 35.
[2] See 14 February 1951, 170 H. L. Deb. 333; and 3 December 1951, 494 HC Deb. 2151.
[3] 15 & 16 Geo. 6. and 1 Eliz. 2. c. 12, s. 1(1).
[4] 18 & 19 Vict. c. 126, s. XXI.
[5] cf. *Report of Royal Commission on Justices of the Peace*, 1946–8, Cmd. 7463 (HMSO 1948), para. 223.

In 1951 there were only seventeen stipendiaries[1] in the whole of England and Wales outside London; in the latter much of petty sessions work then devolved on up to twenty-seven metropolitan police magistrates.

The institution of paid magistrates in London arose from the deficiencies of the lay justices in the late eighteenth century.[2] Their remuneration was fixed at £2,000 a year by the 1937 Statutory Salaries Act—with £2,300 for the chief magistrate who sits at Bow Street Police Court. The Judicial Offices (Salaries, &c.) Act, 1952 raised these amounts to £2,500 and £2,800, respectively.[3] Metropolitan magistrates, therefore, although in receipt of the same figure as county court judges since 1875,[4] were now given £300 less as a result of the consolidation of county court judges' 'divorce' pay; the less glamorous brand of matrimonial jurisdiction of magistrates—affiliation, separation and so on—does not rank for extra remuneration. Though the Attorney General emphasized, in a statement to the House of Commons, that no change in the relative status of county court judges and magistrates was involved, the new differential was vigorously opposed by Members.[5]

The remuneration of provincial stipendiaries, under section 32(1) of the Justices of the Peace Act, 1949, is 'such amount as the Secretary of State may from time to time direct after consultation with the authority or authorities liable to pay the salary': Previously, the local authority had the last word.[6] It follows that the pay of stipendiaries varies: Immediately before the 1952 Judicial Offices Act, salaries were between £1,400 and £2,000; following the passing of that statute, consultations were to take place to increase these amounts to from £2,000 to £2,500.[7] However, concession of the demand for a uniform rate—equal to that of metropolitan magistrates—was not then being contemplated.

Quarter Sessions
Quarter sessions are normally held four times a year for each county and such of the larger boroughs as have their own court. County

[1] *Law List*, 1951, p. 93. There was one vacancy.
[2] Cmd. 7463, op. cit., para. 285.
[3] With effect from 1 July 1951.
[4] The salary of county court judges was fixed at £1,500 in 1865 (28 & 29 Vict. c. 99), and that of metropolitan police magistrates at a similar amount in 1875, with £1,800 for the chief magistrate (38 & 39 Vict. c. 3).
[5] 3 and 5 December 1951, 494 HC Deb. 2154 and ff.
[6] cf. Cmd. 7463, op. cit., para. 234. The salary must not exceed that of a metropolitan magistrate.
[7] ibid. para. 235 and 3 December 1951, 494 HC Deb. 2156. See also Judicial Offices (Salaries, &c.) Act, 1952, s. 4.

quarter sessions formally consist of all the JPs for the county, though
the number sitting at any one time is now limited. At the time of
writing it was not essential—though there was a growing practice—
that the chairman and his deputy should be legally qualified; if so, he
could receive a salary, though the Royal Commission on Justices of
the Peace urged that every effort should be made to obtain chairmen
who would give voluntary service.[1] At the beginning of 1952, the
majority were certainly still 'honorary',[2] and with the exception of
the chairman and deputy of London quarter sessions—the former
had to be salaried—all served part-time.

In borough quarter sessions the position is rather different. Instead
of the justices there is a sole judge known as *recorder*, who must be a
barrister of at least five years' standing. There were some 120
recorders in England and Wales in 1951,[3] all, except in the City of
London, serving part-time. They were remunerated in all cases, their
paymaster being the local authority. Although all increases in their
salaries were subject to approval by the Lord Chancellor, no
national set of scales was in existence.

Coroners
The office of coroner is a very old one; it was originally designed for
protecting the fiscal rights of the Crown, though in the course of
time the holding of inquests on sudden deaths has become its main
function.[4] Coroners are appointed by county and borough councils
as the case may be, and must be barristers, solicitors or legally qualified medical practitioners of not less than five years' standing. In 1951
there were about three hundred coronerships in England and Wales,
the great majority being part-time appointments. The amount of
work and remuneration varied in different localities, and the salary
was fixed by the Secretary of State only in default of agreement
between the parties. It should be added, however, that the Home
Secretary has since urged a reduction in part-time coronerships—and
a corresponding enlargement of remaining jurisdictions.

The Superior Judges
The Supreme Court of Judicature Act, 1873, established the Supreme
Court of Judicature, divided into the High Court of Justice and the
Court of Appeal. The High Court consists of the Chancery, Queen's
Bench and Probate, Divorce and Admiralty Divisions and the Assize

[1] *Report*, op. cit., para. 259.
[2] In February 1952 there were 23 salaried and 43 unpaid chairmen, and 20
salaried and 91 unpaid deputy chairmen.
[3] *Law List*, 1951, pp. 95-6.
[4] cf. Jackson, op. cit., p. 96.

Courts; its judges are the Lord Chancellor, the Lord Chief Justice, the President of the Probate, Divorce and Admiralty Division and the 'Justices of the High Court' or puisne judges.

The *Lord Chancellor* occupies a semi-political, semi-judicial position. For some purposes he is the head of the judiciary: For example, he presides over the judicial sittings of the House of Lords, is President of the Supreme Court and is responsible for the county court system. At the same time, he is a member of the government of the day, and his tenure of office depends on the political fortunes of his party. His remuneration until 1954 was £10,000—i.e. £6,000 in respect of his presidency of the Supreme Court and Chancery Division and £4,000 as Speaker of the House of Lords; he is also provided with rent-free accommodation. His salary was raised to £12,000 by the Judges' Remuneration Act, 1954.[1]

The *Lord Chief Justice* is President of the Queen's Bench Division and, in the Lord Chancellor's absence, of the High Court. His salary was fixed at £10,000 in 1825 but reduced *de facto* to £8,000 in 1830, at which figure it was formally confirmed in 1851.[2] Apart from a temporary reduction under the National Economy (Statutory Salaries) Order, 1931[3]—to which all judicial incomes were subject—it remained at £8,000 until 1954 when it was increased to £10,000.

The *puisne judges* are selected from barristers of at least ten years' standing: they are attached to one or other of the High Court Divisions. They also go on circuit as commissioners of assize, proceedings before them outside London being equally deemed proceedings before the High Court. When on circuit, allowances are paid to cover expenses. As to salary, this was fixed at £5,000 a year in 1832,[4] at which figure it remained—apart from the temporary 1931 cut—until 1954. In that year it was raised to £8,000 per annum. The President of the Probate, Divorce and Admiralty Division receives the same remuneration.

The Court of Appeal—concerned solely with appeals in civil cases—consists of the Lord Justices of Appeal, the Master of the Rolls and a number of other *ex officio* members. *Lord Justices of Appeal* are chosen from barristers of not less than 15 years' standing or from amongst High Court judges; however, their salary is the same as for the latter, except for the *Master of the Rolls* whose pay is £1,000 higher.

Criminal cases—in so far as they are not heard by an inferior court —are normally dealt with by assizes, including the Central Criminal

---

[1] 2 & 3 Eliz. 2. c. 27. All subsequent references to increases in 1954 were effected by that Act.
[2] 14 & 15 Vict. c. 41.   [3] S.R. & O. 1931 No. 810.
[4] 2 & 3 William IV. c. 116.

Court (the 'Old Bailey'), which is the assize court for the London area. In practice, the work of the latter is assigned to the Recorder, Common Serjeant and one of the judges of the Mayor's and City of London Court, whilst Queen's Bench Division judges try the more serious cases. The latter also undertake criminal work at assizes outside London. The Court of Criminal Appeal, unlike its opposite number on the civil side, is staffed by personnel normally engaged in original hearings: the Lord Chief Justice and Queen's Bench Division judges.

The final appeal court for both civil and criminal cases is the House of Lords,[1] composed, at the time of writing, of ten *Lords of Appeal in Ordinary*—the Law Lords—who are paid professional judges with life peerages. They must have held high judicial office for at least two, or have been practising barristers for fifteen, years. Their salary was fixed at £6,000 per annum in 1876;[2] it was raised from that level to £9,000 in 1954.

The information about salaries of the major holders of judicial office is summarized on Table 36.

[1] Appeal to the House of Lords in criminal cases is restricted.
[2] Appellate Jurisdiction Act, 1876, s. 6.

TABLE 36

THE JUDICIARY
(England and Wales)

	Salaries: end-1951* £ p.a.
County Courts:	
Judge	2,800
Metropolitan Police Courts:	
Magistrate	2,500
Chief magistrate	2,800
Supreme Court of Judicature:	
High Court of Justice	
Puisne judge	5,000
Lord Chief Justice of England	8,000
Court of Appeal	
Lord Justice of Appeal	5,000
Master of the Rolls	6,000
House of Lords	
Lord of Appeal in Ordinary	6,000
Lord Chancellor	10,000[1]

[1] £6,000 as President of Supreme Court and Chancery Division, £4,000 as Speaker of House of Lords; also receives rent-free accommodation.

* These salaries have since been increased; in the case of judges of the House of Lords and the Supreme Court of Judicature, by the Judges' Remuneration Act, 1954

There is no recognized practice of promoting judges. A county court judge must expect to remain in that office; movement to the High Court is extremely rare, though of those appointed to the latter, many have held recorderships.[1] Among the superior judiciary there may be advancement from the High Court to the Court of Appeal, or from either of these to the House of Lords, but apart from the question of prestige, there is little financial gain except in the case of promotion to Lord Chief Justice or Lord Chancellor. As indicated, there is no difference in remuneration between the High Court and Court of Appeal, though statute accords the personnel of the latter precedence of rank.[2]

Other Courts and Tribunals

We may conclude this brief review by pointing out that there are various other types of judicial personnel; for example, there are those serving on certain special courts such as the Palatine courts, courts martial or ecclesiastical courts.[3] More important, perhaps, there is what has been called the 'veritable maze of adjudicating bodies of all kinds'[4]—the numerous tribunals that have sprung up in the twentieth century and which, to a greater or lesser extent, fulfil judicial functions. Examples are the rent tribunals, the National Insurance and Industrial Injuries tribunals, the various industrial tribunals or the Special Commissioners for Income Tax.[5] These bodies, though variously classified, do not in any way form a system, there being a great diversity of structure and function.[6] Hence they are staffed in a variety of ways—on an *ad hoc* or permanent basis, by High Court judges, civil servants, lawyers or other 'experts'. The President of the Patents Appeal Tribunal, for instance, is a High Court judge; the Special Commissioners for Income Tax are civil servants. If any generalization about the 'administrative judiciary' is possible, it is that its members do not normally serve full-time—civil servants are the main exception—and that they tend to be remunerated by fee on a sessional basis rather than by fixed salary.

[1] cf. Jackson, op. cit., p. 210.

[2] Supreme Court of Judicature (Consolidation) Act, 1925, s. 16(4).

[3] For details see *Halsbury's Laws of England*, 2nd ed., vol. 8, p. 517 and ff. The proceedings of some of these courts are included in the official *Civil Judicial Statistics*, published annually by HMSO.

[4] Wm. A. Robson, *Justice and Administrative Law*, 3rd ed. (Stevens, 1951), p. 314.

[5] For full details see ibid. Chap. 3.

[6] ibid. p. 587 and ff.

Chapter 7

THE PROBATION SERVICE

The probation service is concerned with the social aspects of the administration of justice, and emerged as a combination of binding over an offender with provision for his supervision. In the last quarter of the nineteenth century some religious bodies began to appoint 'police court missionaries', but it was only under the Probation of Offenders Act, 1907, that probation received the official blessing of statute—turning it from a voluntary into a public service—and that courts were empowered to employ paid staff. The central authority for the administration of the system in England and Wales is the Home Secretary. Locally, responsibility rests on probation committees, one of which exists for each probation area in England and Wales.[1]

The law now requires that at least one man and one woman officer should be available in every petty sessional division and for every superior criminal court, it being their function 'to supervise the probationers and other persons placed under their supervision, and to advise, assist and befriend them'.[2] In addition, probation officers act as conciliators in matrimonial disputes, supervise young persons in need of care and protection, and help in the after-care of those leaving approved schools, borstals and prisons. They also carry out investigations into the home background and general environment of persons brought before court.

Though the probation service has been much expanded since pre-war days, it is still of small dimensions. Numbers at the end of February 1952 were:[3]

Probation officers	1,010
Senior probation officers	113
Deputy and assistant principal probation officers	13
Principal probation officers	39
	1,175

[1] There were 122 such areas in England and Wales in the period under review; in the Metropolitan Magistrates Courts area the Home Secretary takes the place of the probation committee. Detailed supervision over probation officers is exercised by case committees.

[2] Criminal Justice Act, 1948 (11 & 12 Geo. 6. c. 58) 5th sched. s. 3(5).

[3] Figures made available by courtesy of Home Office. The numbers include 15 temporary and 99 part-time staff.

Salaries: Every probation committee must 'pay to the probation officers appointed for their area such remuneration, allowances and expenses as may be prescribed'.[1] The prescribing is the job of the Home Secretary and, as in the case of the police and fire services, takes the form of promulgation by statutory instrument of all matters governing pay and service conditions. Since its establishment in 1950, however, the Home Secretary acts on the advice of the Joint Negotiating Committee for the Probation Service in England and Wales.

TABLE 37

PROBATION SERVICE

PROBATION OFFICERS
(Men, England and Wales)[1]

	Salary Scale as from	
	1 *December* 1946	1 *January* 1951*
	£ *p.a.*	£ *p.a.*
Probation officer		
Age 23	305	327.10.0
24	315	337.10.0
25	325	350. 0.0
26	340	365. 0.0
27	355	380. 0.0
28	370	395. 0.0
29	385	410. 0.0
30 and over	400 × 15–460	425 × 15–485
	× 20–570	× 20–590[2]
Senior probation officer	As for probation officer, plus allowance of up to £50[3].	
Higher grades	see text	

[1] For additional allowance payable in London see text.
[2] The final increment was £25.
[3] Increased as from 1 March 1952.

* All salaries were increased as from 1 January 1952 and 16 September 1952, and have been further revised since.

Salaries are shown on Table 37. Throughout the war, remuneration consisted of a basic scale plus bonus; authority to grant the latter was permissive but it was in fact paid all over the country. The bonus was merged with the base rate as from December 1946, when a modest increase was given and a London allowance instituted. The new commencing salary was linked to age 23—the latter is a minimum requirement for entry to the service—with 'weight for age' up to 30. Older recruits could not start beyond that point of the scale.

There was no change in remuneration until 1951. New standards

[1] Criminal Justice Act, 1948, s. 3(1)(b).

had been laid down in the Probation Rules, 1950,[1] but these were partly in the nature of a post-dated cheque, only one-half of the proposed rise becoming payable in 1951. The 1950 rates applied in full as from 1 January 1952, when the salary for a male officer (basic grade) became £350 at age 23, with a maximum of £610. A further increase of £65 per annum accrued as from 16 September 1952.[2]

As shown on Table 37, senior probation officers received the same salary as the bottom grade, plus an allowance of up to £50. As from March 1952 this was raised to £75 or, in a probation area with a population of at least 175,000 and no principal officer, £100 a year. Principal probation officers, in the period under review, were employed only in the larger localities where there was a substantial staff to be supervised. There used to be no power on the part of the central authority to prescribe remuneration for them; the Home Office merely recommended figures, though local committees almost invariably adopted these. The pay of most principal officers during the period 1st December 1946 to 31st December 1950 was £625 × £20 to £725. There were also a series of higher rates, the top scale (including London allowance) being £930 × £30 to £1,155 for the principal probation officer in the metropolis.

During 1950 power was given for principal officers' pay to be formally prescribed by the Home Secretary, and under a scheme introduced in March 1952—during 1951 salaries continued to be determined *ad hoc*—all principal posts were allocated to one of six groups. These were largely based on population, though other factors such as the incidence of crime were taken into account.

Provincial Differentiation
As mentioned, a London allowance of £30 per annum was instituted with effect from 1 December 1946. It is payable to all staff working in the City of London and Metropolitan Police District.

Sex Differentiation
The total of 1,175 probation officers at end-February 1952 included 456 women, of whom all but 20 were in the basic grade. Until they reached their maximum, those in that grade used to receive a salary which was a uniform £15 below that of their male opposite number, but the men's scale was considerably longer, with a resultant widening of the differential higher up. Thus the January 1952 maximum of a woman was £500 or 82 per cent of the £610 then accruing to her male colleague; her starting rate of £335, however, was almost 96 per cent of the comparable male figure. Meanwhile, equal pay has been introduced as in other sectors of the public service.

[1] SI 1950 No. 2136.   [2] There have been further revisions since.

Chapter 8

THE POLICE

There are 125 separate police forces in England and Wales, the first in the field being the Metropolitan Police, set up in 1829. Boroughs have been required to have a paid and permanent establishment since 1835, though counties not until some twenty years later. The present number of police areas is the result of the Police Act, 1946, under which all non-county borough forces—with the exception of Cambridge—were abolished. However, establishments still vary greatly in size.

The police authority in counties is the standing joint committee, in a county borough it is the watch committee, and in the City of London the Common Council. The Metropolitan Police is in a special position, the Home Secretary—through the Commissioner of Police for the Metropolis—having direct responsibility for it. The metropolitan force acts within a radius of about fifteen miles from Charing Cross, except for the square mile or so constituting the City of London; besides watching over the capital, it has certain national functions. A large measure of control over the police system vests in the Home Secretary, in part exercised via the power of the purse and in part derived from specific legislation—in particular the Police Act of 1919.

Numbers and Ranks

On 30 September 1951 the 'regular police' in England and Wales numbered 62,629, the total authorized establishment being 73,406.[1] These figures do not include civilian employees who perform much of headquarters ancillary work, nor the few hundred odd First Police Reserve—men who, in return for an annual retaining fee, hold themselves ready to serve in time of war. Also excluded is the Special Constabulary, maintained as a second line of reserve, though special constables may be appointed 'notwithstanding that a tumult, riot, or felony has not taken place or is not immediately apprehended'.[2] In September 1951 they numbered 67,137, of whom about one-third

[1] *Report of HM Inspectors of Constabulary for the year ended* 30 *September* 1951 (HMSO 1952), pp. 32–3.
[2] SR & O 1923 No. 905, s. 1.

were regularly doing spare-time duty.[1] Special constables, it should be emphasized, are unpaid volunteers; while they may be reimbursed for out-of-pocket expenses and loss of earnings, they are not entitled to any remuneration.

Certain police establishments are altogether outside the scope of the 1919 statute: There are a number of dock police forces such as those of the Port of London Authority; the Admiralty, Air Ministry and War Office each have their own constabulary; so has the British Transport Commission. All these (and a few others) are quite independent, the one service condition they share with the regulars being eligibility for the Police Long Service and Good Conduct Medal.[2] Here we shall deal exclusively with the regular police, whose rank structure and numbers—authorized establishment, not strength —at end-September 1951 were as follows:

Police:
Authorized establishment as at 30 *September* 1951[1]

Constables	58,745
Sergeants	10,231
Inspectors	2,847
Chief inspectors	665
Superintendents	614
Chief superintendents	109
Assistant chief constables	51
Chief constables	144
	73,406

[1] *Report of HM Inspectors*, op. cit., pp. 32–3. The figure for constables includes 33 acting sergeants; that for chief constables, analogous ranks in the City of London and metropolitan forces.

Constables, sergeants, inspectors, superintendents and chief constables are the basic grades; the others—as also one or two additional ranks—may be adopted where necessary. The head of each provincial force is the chief constable; under him it is usually organized into divisions under superintendents, sub-divisions under inspectors, and sections under sergeants. The metropolitan force is controlled by the Commissioner of Police of the Metropolis; the hierarchy here differs in various respects from that in the provinces.

[1] *Report of HM Inspectors*, op. cit., para 24 and p. 33.
[2] See Cmd. 8270 (HMSO 1951). The question of 'parity' of the British Transport Police with the regular police was raised in the Commons on 21 April 1952 (HC Deb. 499, 177 and ff.).

Recruitment and Promotion

The recruitment of regular policemen ceased during the war; by the
end of 1945 forces in England and Wales were over 15,000 short of
their pre-war complement.[1] In January 1946 the ban on resignations
was lifted, resulting in the exodus of both auxiliaries and regulars,
while the needs of the service made larger establishments necessary.
Since then, though the intake of 'new blood' has actually been considerably stepped up, both the 'forties and the 'fifties have witnessed
serious losses of manpower due to the premature resignation of
serving officers. It is this problem of recruitment and wastage which
has bedevilled the police service throughout the post-war period; we
shall certainly have to refer to it again when reviewing the history of
police remuneration.

Would-be policemen must be of good character and satisfy certain
requirements as to height, fitness, nationality and age; they must also
pass an educational test. To be eligible for promotion, a constable
must normally have completed five years' service, including two on
outside duty; he must not, in the immediate past, have had a punishment for a disciplinary offence—other than a reprimand or caution
—and, finally, he has to pass certain examinations. The last two
conditions apply equally before a sergeant qualifies for a move; in
addition, he must have served as such for at least two years—one of
them again 'outside'. Success in the qualifying test does not, however, automatically lead to advancement, which depends on vacancies
and actual selection.[2] Promotion beyond inspector is solely by the
latter method, though all appointments are made from amongst those
who have risen in the ranks: There is no 'officer entry' in the police
service.

The Oaksey Committee, in the course of an exhaustive examination
of police conditions of service in 1948–9, dealt *inter alia* with rates of
promotion; their findings—to a few of which only we shall refer[3]—
are of great interest. Their enquiry revealed, for example, that of
entrants joining the police in 1919–21 who were still in the service
after 24½ years, 33 per cent had been promoted to sergeant or higher,
14 per cent to inspector or above and 2·1 per cent to superintendent.
As pointed out, however, the possibility of advancement depends on
passing the qualifying examinations: The Committee found that,
after 24½ years, 51 per cent had passed the tests rendering them
eligible for holding sergeant rank; of these, 65 per cent had been

[1] *Report of the Committee on Police Conditions of Service* (Chairman: Lord
Oaksey) Part I, Cmd. 7674 (HMSO 1949), para. 7.
[2] There was one exception to this at the time of writing—i.e. the Metropolitan
Police where competitive examinations were reintroduced in 1947.
[3] For full details see *Oaksey Report* I, op. cit., Appx. II.

F

actually promoted. Similarly, three in every five qualified sergeants had become inspectors within the 24½-year period.

The survey also showed that, while a small number of the 1919–21 entrants were promoted to sergeant after six or seven years' service, others had to wait 20 or longer, the average time spent as constable before advancement being 13·2 years. The rank of inspector was generally reached after 15 to 20 years' employment. The analysis also brought to light significant variations in promotion rates as between different types of forces, as also in the proportion of men qualifying. Another interesting result was that prospects in the Metropolitan CID were substantially better than in its uniform branch: 94 per cent of CID men who joined in 1928–31 and completed 16½ years' service had, at the end of that time, risen to sergeant, compared with 40 per cent for the uniform branch and CID combined. The Oaksey Committee summed up their enquiry as showing that—for men who make the police their career—there were no grounds for the assertion that opportunities were poor, though it was doubtful whether the best men were promoted at an early enough stage.[1]

Negotiating Machinery
Section 4(1) of the Police Act, 1919, provides that 'it shall be lawful for the Secretary of State to make regulations as to the government, mutual aid, pay, allowances, clothing, expenses and conditions of service of the members of all police forces within England and Wales, and every police authority shall comply with the regulations so made'. The question of negotiating machinery has been a difficult one. The position is that under the 1919 statute membership of an outside trade union is precluded; instead, a Police Federation is provided for, to which all those below the rank of superintendent automatically belong. Further, before issuing regulations, the Home Secretary is required to submit a draft to a council, consisting of representatives of the Federation, chief officers and police authorities, and to consider any representations that body may wish to make. The Police Council has no executive power.

The whole question—also raised in Parliament on numerous occasions—was investigated by the Oaksey Committee who made a number of detailed recommendations on the subject. While some of their findings attracted criticism, their main proposal was—after a considerable amount of further heart-searching[2]—finally implemented

[1] *Report of the Committee on Police Conditions of Service*, Part II, Cmd. 7831 (HMSO 1949), para. 395 (xi).

[2] The Oaksey proposals were first remitted to a committee for further examination: see *Report of the Committee of the Police Council on Police Representative Organizations and Negotiating Machinery* (HMSO 1952).

in 1953, when the formation of a Whitley-type body was announced. The latter, known as the Police Council for Great Britain, consists of an independent chairman, an official and a staff side; it has appointed three panels to deal with (a) those above chief superintendent, (b) the two superintendent grades, and (c) the 'federated' ranks (inspectors, sergeants and constables). If approved by the Secretaries of State, agreements are given effect by statutory instrument.[1] There is also provision for the appointment of arbitrators.

Salaries

Until 1919 each police authority was a law unto itself insofar as the remuneration and conditions of service of policemen were concerned. In that year, however, a Committee under the chairmanship of Lord Desborough issued their findings,[2] an event which has recently been described as having ushered in the modern police era.[3] One of the cardinal features of the Desborough Report was that the pay of constables and sergeants should be the same in all forces, standardized scales being accordingly introduced in 1919.

Throughout the inter-war years policemen were in a highly advantageous position as regards both salaries and service conditions, but the war of 1939–45 began to make serious inroads.[4] For though a war supplement—equivalent to the Civil Service war bonus—and a small war duty allowance were paid during this period, these were in no way commensurate with the rise in the cost of living or the increases granted to the generality of industrial workers. In April 1945 revised (and consolidated) scales were introduced, but the representatives of the Police Federation were not satisfied and maintained a steady pressure for higher remuneration. Eventually, this led to a much improved settlement operative from 6 November 1946, which at the same time included an undertaking by the central authority to appoint an independent committee to review the whole field of police conditions before the end of 1949. The Police Federation, on their part, agreed that the new standards should remain in force until 1 January 1950.[5]

[1] Formally, proposals have first to be laid before the *statutory* Police Councils (for England and Wales and for Scotland) which remain distinct from the negotiating body.

[2] Cd. 253 (HMSO 1919).

[3] *Royal Commission on the Police* 1960, *Interim Report*, Cmnd. 1222 (HMSO 1960) para. 19.

[4] For further details see *Home Office Memorandum of Evidence to the Committee on Police Conditions of Service* (HMSO 1949), para. 50 and ff. and Cmnd. 1222, op. cit., Chap. III.

[5] *Home Office Memorandum*, op. cit., para. 55 and 6 November 1946, HC Deb. 428, 1395.

Things worked out differently, however, and in March 1948—in deference to views strongly expressed in the Police Council and both Houses of Parliament[1]—the Home Secretary announced that the proposed review would be undertaken at once instead of in a year's time. The Oaksey Committee were thus appointed

'to consider in the light of the need for the recruitment and retention of an adequate number of suitable men and women for the police forces of England, Wales and Scotland, and to report on pay, emoluments, allowances, pensions, promotion, methods of representation and negotiation and other conditions of service'.[2]

and they presented their Report—which is in two parts—in April and October 1949.

The facts revealed were not very inspiring. As regards the key problem of manpower, the Oaksey Committee found that by the end of 1948 the overall deficiency in police strength in England and Wales was 17·4 per cent. Even this figure was not a full measure of the seriousness of the problem, for it masked wide variations in different parts of the country. Thus in the metropolitan force the deficiency was 21·6 per cent, in Birmingham 28·5, while Coventry was fully 45·1 per cent under establishment. On the other hand, Leeds had merely a 7·5 per cent shortage, Cardiff one of 4·9 per cent, while in Scotland, similarly, the extent of undermanning was 5 per cent only. The Committee pointed out that the rate of recruitment itself had been satisfactory since 1946; it was the loss by resignation and retirement—particularly in the middle years of service—that had caused the shortage to persist.[3]

In commenting upon police duties, the Oaksey Committee quoted from the Desborough Report. That Committee had been 'satisfied that a policeman has responsibilities and obligations which are peculiar to his calling and distinguish him from other public servants and municipal employés'; they considered the police 'entitled thereby to special consideration in regard to their rate of pay and pensions'. The Desborough Committee had stated that 'the burden of individual discretion and responsibility placed upon a constable is much greater than that of any other public servant of subordinate rank'; further, 'the special temptations to which a constable is exposed are obvious, and, as any lapse must be severely dealt with, it is only just that his remuneration should be such as will not add to his temptations the difficulties and anxieties incidental to an inadequate

[1] See e.g. debate on 22 March 1948, HC Deb. 448, 2591 and ff.
[2] *Oaksey Report* I, op. cit., p. 1.
[3] ibid. paras. 12–13.

rate of pay'. Oaksey agreed with these observations: The policeman's responsibilities were essentially unchanged, though in fact more exacting because extending over a wider field.[1] The Royal Commission on the Police, in their Interim Report issued in 1960, similarly pointed out that though police duties and responsibilities had not altered in their essentials, they had increased in range and variety during the last two decades and were now exercised in increasingly difficult circumstances.[2]

The Oaksey Committee did not find it easy to discover the cumulative value of all the various factors in police remuneration. The men's representatives were inclined to base their claims upon pay alone and, in Oaksey's view, to underestimate the value of the subsidiary benefits. The police authorities and central departments, on the other hand, impressed upon them the importance of the 'concealed' emoluments—such as free accommodation and a generous pension scheme —though they differed as to the precise value to be placed on these.[3] Though Oaksey rejected pay as the only criterion bearing on the manpower problem, they were of the opinion that comparison with occupations in which conditions were in any way similar indicated that the police were underpaid. The Committee therefore proposed what they regarded as substantial increases for all ranks, which were duly accepted by the Government and became operative from 1 July 1949.[4]

There was a spurt in recruiting as a result of the Oaksey improvements, but by the middle of 1951 most gains had been lost again: The deficiency in the country as a whole was over 11,000. Meanwhile, a claim for revised pay had been submitted but had resulted in deadlock. Accordingly, third-party intervention was necessary, and in July 1951 the Home Secretary appointed Sir Malcolm Trustram Eve and two assessors to settle the dispute.

In his Report[5] Sir Malcolm stated that wastage was once again more serious than the recruitment position, that it was still essential to man up the country's constabularies, and that only an increase in salary would attract the necessary labour. Moreover, 'the mere maintenance of the "former relativity" between other occupations and industries and the Police Forces will not achieve the desired result'.

---

[1] ibid. paras. 18–19.

[2] Cmnd. 1222, op. cit., paras. 52–62.

[3] *Oaksey Report* I, op. cit., para. 20. The 1960 Royal Commission were faced with similar problems, though in this instance the Commission were themselves inclined to play down the value of emoluments: See *Report*, op. cit., Chap. VI.

[4] See *Statement on Pay and Conditions of Service of Police*, Cmd. 7707 (HMSO 1949).

[5] Not published, but made available by courtesy of Home Office.

In hard cash the Trustram Eve proposals were that the constable's minimum should be raised by £70—i.e. by £30 more than the figure to which he was entitled on 'relativity' grounds; his maximum should go up by £85. For a sergeant the rise at the maximum was £100, for an inspector £115, and for a chief inspector £130, consequential improvements being granted to the higher grades. The revised rates became operative on 3 August 1951 and remained in force until mid-January 1954.

The history of pay movements since 1954, in the words of the Royal Commission on the Police, 1960, is that awards have done no more than match increases in the cost of living and have tended to lag behind advances in industrial earnings.[1] Ministry of Labour figures for April 1960, say the Commission, suggest that the constable at his maximum had at that date fallen to 5 per cent below average industrial earnings, whereas in 1935—the 'golden age' of the police—he enjoyed a lead of not less than 55 per cent. At his minimum, similarly, the constable was (April 1960) 30 per cent behind the industrial earnings average, as against 16 per cent ahead in 1935.[2] As these figures have been widely quoted—and were indeed cited by the Commission themselves as summing up the then state of police remuneration[3]—it might perhaps be emphasized that while they provide an index of the *relative* worsening of the constable's position in the hierarchy of earned incomes, they are quite misleading as a measure of the *absolute* differential between policemen and industrial workers. Thus evidence submitted to the Commission by the Home Office showed that about 40 per cent of constables were receiving payments of from 26*s*. 8*d*. to 36*s*. 4*d*. a week for working on the additional rest day.[4] Similarly, the constable's scale relates, since 1955, to a standard week of 44 hours, but average hours worked by men in industry are long than this: The relevant figure for April 1960—to which the earnings average refers—was 48 hours.[5] Some police constables, at any rate, were then being paid for overtime apart from that put in on the additional rest-day, while all detective constables qualified for special detective duty allowances. In addition, *all* policemen received free quarters or a tax-free rent allowance, free uniform or a tax-free 'plain clothes' allowance, as well as a small 'boot' allowance. All these items are of course ignored in a comparison of points on the constable's *scale* with average industrial *earnings*. If data on police earnings had been available to the Com-

[1] Cmnd. 1222, op. cit. para. 30.
[2] ibid. para. 31.
[3] ibid.
[4] ibid. p. 73.
[5] *Ministry of Labour Gazette*, August 1960, p. 314.

mission, so that like could have been measured against like, the contrast between constable and industrial worker would have presented a rather different picture.

Such data would not, however, have altered the most crucial of the Commission's findings, namely that there was a deficiency in the police strength of Great Britain amounting to some 14 per cent—with a shortfall in the Metropolitan Police of at least 26 per cent. Further, that the ratio of recruitment to wastage had been declining, while during the first eight months of 1960 the latter had actually exceeded recruitment.[1] In the light of these and other factors, the Commission concluded that police pay was inadequate, and they recommended a scale for the constable rising to £910 after 9, and to £970 after 22, years—as against the then maximum of £695 per annum. These are certainly imaginative proposals—notwithstanding the somewhat peculiar formula on which they are based and one or two other misgivings which this writer has about particular features of the Report.[2] The new scale at any rate provides an interesting contrast to earlier attempts to cure the problems of the police service.

Turning to Table 38, before mid-1949 remuneration for the lower ranks was expressed in terms of a weekly wage, but the Oaksey Committee felt that 'it would be more in keeping with the status of the police as a profession, and with sums of these dimensions (i.e. their recommendations), for constables and sergeants to be paid an annual salary . . .'[3] The pre-Oaksey scale for constables was £5.5.0 a week, rising by 3s. to £6.12.0, with two 'additional increments' of 4s. at any time after 17 and 22 years' employment. These long-service payments were first instituted in order that the large number of constables unable to earn promotion should retain their keenness. Nominally, they were payable at the chief constable's discretion; in practice, they were nearly always granted—and at the earliest permissible stage.

The Oaksey recommendations shortened the first part of the constable's scale, and substituted three long-service payments for the former 'additional increments',[4] to accrue after 10, 15 and 22 years' employment, respectively. The Trustram Eve award added a fourth, payable after 25 years as a constable. These increments fell due automatically and could be withheld only—like the ordinary annual increases—as a punishment under the discipline code. All long-service

[1] Cmnd. 1222, op. cit., paras. 74, 76 and 80.

[2] See *post:* pp. 354–5 and 390.

[3] *Oaksey Report* I, op. cit., para. 39. To facilitate comparison, Table 38 shows the 1946 rates likewise as £ p.a.

[4] A system of 'special increments'—an acceleration by up to two points on the constable scale for those satisfying certain conditions—was also abolished in 1949.

TABLE 38

POLICE
(Men, England and Wales)

	Salary Scale[1] *as from*		
	6 *Nov.* 1946	1 *July* 1949	3 *August* 1951*
	£ p.a.	£ p.a.	£ p.a.
Constable			
On appointment	273.87	330	400
After 2 years' service	281.70	340	410
,, 3 ,, ,,	289.52	350	420
,, 4 ,, ,,	297.35	360	430
,, 5 ,, ,,	305.17	370	440
,, 6 ,, ,,	313.00	380	450
,, 7 ,, ,,	320.82	390	460
,, 8 ,, ,,	328.65		
,, 9 ,, ,,	336.47		
,, 10 ,, ,,	344.30	400	470
,, 15 ,, ,,	354.73[2]	410	480
,, 22 ,, ,,	365.17	420	490
,, 25 ,, ,,			505
Sergeant			
On promotion	391.25	445	540
After 1 year's service	399.07	455	550
,, 2 years' ,,	406.90	465	560
,, 3 ,, ,,	414.72	475	570
,, 4 ,, ,,	422.55	485	585
,, 5 ,, ,,	430.37		

	6 *Nov.* 1946	1 *July* 1949	3 *August* 1951*
	£ p.a.	£ p.a.	£ p.a.
Inspector	475 × 10 –515	530 × 15–575	645 × 15– 690
Chief inspector	550 × 10 –590	605 × 20–645	735 × 20– 775
Superintendent, class II[3]	550 × 15 –610 585 × 17½–655	700 × 25–750	850 × 25– 900
Superintendent, class I[3]	615 × 20 –695 660 × 25 –760	800 × 25–850	950 × 25–1,000
Chief superintendent	615 × 20 –695 770 × 25 –870 800 × 25 –875[4]	900 × 25–950	1,050 × 25–1,100

[1] The figures *exclude* rent and all other allowances. The rates for constables and sergeants applied both in London and the provinces, though as from 1 July 1949 an additional £10 p.a. was paid to those in the City of London and Metropolitan Police. *The salaries for inspectors and all higher ranks relate to the provinces only.*

[2] Payable after 17 (not 15) years' service.

[3] The division into class I and II dates from 1949.

[4] There were alternative scales in a few forces.

* As from 14 January 1954 these rates were increased by £45 for constables, £50 for sergeants and £55 for the higher grades; they have been further revised since.

increments were abolished in 1955—though only to make their re-appearance in 1960. As regards the two inspector grades on Table 38, incidentally, it may be noted that the 1946 figures were the first set of national standard rates.

Superintendents

For superintendents there was neither standardization of duties nor of remuneration until even later: Right up to 1949 there existed a series of scales depending on the type and size of police force.[1] A thorough-going examination of commands was instituted in 1947 by the Police Post-War Committee, who found that the system was full of anomalies; as a result of their recommendations, the following formula for grading superintendents' posts was adopted:

Divisional establishment		*Grade of post*
County forces	*Borough forces*	
40– 80	less than 150	superintendent, class II
81–150	151–300	superintendent, class I
over 150	over 300	chief superintendent

The question of remuneration was entrusted to a separate Committee, who were 'impressed . . . by the contention that superintendents' responsibilities have not been properly evaluated in terms of pay for some considerable time',[2] and that standards were inadequate in comparison with others in the police hierarchy. Their Report—published in 1948—was accepted by the Government; however, in view of the issue of the latter's White Paper on Personal Incomes, Costs and Prices,[3] actual implementation was deferred until 1949 when the Oaksey Committee—apart from some minor adjustments—endorsed the findings of the earlier body. Following the Trustram Eve proposals, the salaries of all superintendents were raised by £150 per annum, these 1951 scales remaining in operation until the beginning of 1954.

Chief Constables

Chief constables are appointed by the standing joint committee or watch committee; the Home Secretary's approval must be obtained in each case. No person without previous police experience is to be selected 'unless he possesses some exceptional qualification or experi-

[1] For details see *Report of the Committee on Superintendents' Pay* (*Home Office Memorandum*, op. cit., Appx. 'K').

[2] ibid. para. 24.

[3] Cmd. 7321 (HMSO 1948).

ence which specially fits him for the post, or there is no candidate from the police service who is considered sufficiently well qualified'.[1]

The remuneration of chief and assistant chief constables was referred to a second Home Office Committee, appointed in 1947 'to consider and submit proposals for the rationalization and reduction of the present unduly high number of scales . . .'[2] Their opinion was that some simple basis for assessing chiefs' responsibilities should be adopted; after considering possible criteria such as population or incidence of crime, they concluded that the authorized establishment of a force would be the best index. The Committee also gave some thought to whether remuneration could be regulated by reference to that in other professions, but felt that there was no occupation with which comparisons could usefully be made.

The Committee's proposals were accepted by the Government, but here again implementation was postponed on 'White Paper' grounds. They were not therefore in operation when the Oaksey Committee reported, but the latter commended the earlier Committee's figures, apart from minor points of detail. Following the Trustram Eve award, the 1949 standards were increased as shown on Table 39 opposite, and have been further revised since.

Detectives
Every police force has a criminal investigation department, employing two main types of detective. The majority—the detectives proper —are those engaged on outside work : They go about in plain clothes and more or less decide for themselves how they will set about their tasks. 'Indoor' CID men, on the other hand, perform office and administrative jobs or else are specialists in the adjuncts of criminal investigation.

At one time detectives in the Metropolitan and Liverpool City Police received higher salaries than corresponding grades in the uniform branch, and it has long been a subject for debate whether detectives, rank for rank, are 'worth' more than other policemen. In general, a detective's promotion prospects are better,[3] his work is more varied and commands more prestige; on the other hand, he has many unpleasant tasks and his hours are long and irregular. The Home Office view, as expressed to the Oaksey Committee, was that whatever additional payments were made to detectives, these should not indicate recognition of extra responsibility or a higher standard of trust: 'It might well give rise to serious difficulties if transfer to the

---

[1] SI 1952 No. 1704, s. 6.

[2] *Report of a Committee on the Pay of Chief Constables in England and Wales* (*Home Office Memorandum*, op. cit. Appx. 'M') Preamble.

[3] cf. p. 162 *ante*.

TABLE 39

POLICE

CHIEF AND ASSISTANT CHIEF CONSTABLES
(England and Wales, excluding London)

	Salary Scale as from	
	1 *July* 1949	3 *August* 1951*
Assistant chief constable	£ *p.a.*	£ *p.a.*
Strength of force		
401– 600	1,050 × 50–1,200	1,200 × 50–1,350
601– 800	1,100 × 50–1,250	1,250 × 50–1,400
801–1,200	1,200 × 50–1,350	1,350 × 50–1,500
1,201–1,600	1,350 × 50–1,500	1,500 × 50–1,650
1,601–2,500	1,450 × 50–1,600	1,600 × 50–1,750
Over 2,500	1,570 × 60–1,750	1,720 × 60–1,900
Chief constable		
Strength of force		
Under 40	700 × 50– 850	850 × 50–1,000
41– 74	850 × 50–1,000	1,000 × 50–1,150
75– 125	1,050 × 50–1,200	1,200 × 50–1,350
126– 200	1,200 × 50–1,350	1,350 × 50–1,500
201– 300	1,350 × 50–1,500	1,500 × 50–1,650
301– 400	1,450 × 50–1,600	1,600 × 50–1,750
401– 600	1,570 × 60–1,750	1,720 × 60–1,900
601– 800	1,690 × 70–1,900	1,840 × 70–2,050
801–1,200	1,890 × 70–2,100	2,040 × 70–2,250
1,201–1,600	2,300	2,450
1,601–2,500	2,500	2,650
Over 2,500	2,700	2,850

* These salaries were increased as from 14 January 1954 and have been further revised since.

uniform branch both involved a monetary loss and also implied allocation to an inferior form of duty'.[1]

The Oaksey Committee's own proposals on the subject were that outside detectives should receive a commuted overtime payment, to be known as a 'detective duty allowance'; apart from this, overtime should not be paid for. Further, outside CID men should get a 'detective expenses allowance' of 10s. a week to compensate them for their numerous incidental outgoings; they should also be entitled to a refund of any items of expenditure of 2s. 6d. or more. These recommendations were accepted, the detective duty allowance as from 31 December 1951 being £36 for constables, £43 for sergeants and £50 for inspectors and chief inspectors.[2] Superintendents do not qualify. As regards indoor personnel, these are now treated exactly

[1] *Home Office Memorandum,* op. cit. para. 129.
[2] The allowances were increased in January 1954 and since

like members of the uniform branch; neither type of detective, however, receives a 'skill differential'. We may add that the Royal Commission on the Police, in their 1960 Interim Report, stated that although they had heard little evidence in the matter, it was their impression that detective constables were inadequately rewarded for their extra tasks, and they urged a review of the detective duty allowance.[1]

Provincial Differentiation

There was no formal London weighting in the police service—although London rent allowances have been higher throughout—until July 1949; an extra £10 a year then became payable to all constables, sergeants and station sergeants in the Metropolitan and City forces. In his Report for 1952 the Commissioner of Police of the Metropolis stated that this figure was wholly inadequate to meet higher living costs in the capital;[2] the allowance was increased to £20 in January 1954.

While for grades up to (station) sergeant basic pay in London is the same as in the rest of the country, this is not true of the senior ranks. Here the two hierarchies diverge, so that similar metropolitan and provincial titles do not necessarily imply analogous duties. As to salaries, those operative at end-1951 ranged from £675–£720 a year for metropolitan inspectors to £4,500 for the Commissioner of the Metropolitan Police at the apex of the pyramid.

Quarters and Rent Allowances

Official regulations require that each member of a police force shall be provided with a free house or quarters, or be paid an allowance instead. For married men the latter is of the 'maximum limit' type, i.e. the amount actually spent on rent and rates[3] is reimbursed, subject to an upper limit. This varies according to both force and rank. In London, for example, the maximum allowance for constables was, in 1948, fixed at 35s. a week, for inspectors at 40s., and for superintendents at £120 per annum; in a large county a constable then qualified for up to 30s. weekly. Single men and policewomen get a flat-rate sum, equal to half the relevant 'limit' for their force. Any income tax due to quarters being received 'in cash' rather than in kind is refunded in the shape of a 'compensatory grant'—as is the tax on the grant itself.

The Oaksey Committee found that the then level of rent allowances permitted all but an insignificant minority of constables and sergeants

[1] Cmnd. 1222, op. cit., para. 189.
[2] Cmd. 8944 (HMSO 1953), p. 8.
[3] For unfurnished accommodation.

to recover all their outgoings in that respect. The Committee gave some thought to the question of whether these payments should be consolidated with basic salaries but, on reflection, rejected the idea, *inter alia* because it would require a very considerable degree of provincial differentiation if real incomes in the different forces were to be kept equal. However, they emphasized that the provision of free quarters was a substantial addition to emoluments—a fact which did not seem to be sufficiently appreciated by policemen or the public.[1]

Sex Differentiation

Every force has an official complement of policewomen, though the number serving at end-September 1951 was only 1,428 out of a total police strength of 62,629 in England and Wales.[2] In law they have the same powers as their male colleagues, though chiefly engaged on work connected with women and children. A permanent pay scale for women constables was not fixed by regulation until 1933; salaries for women sergeants were first so prescribed in 1945.

The pay of a woman constable introduced in August 1951 was £355–£455; that for a provincial chief inspector £625–£660. The precise relationship between the scales for the two sexes ranged from 90 to 85 per cent, the larger differential applying to the inspector grades. However, lady inspectors were given a special boost in 1953, making for a uniform 9:10 ratio throughout the service. Women detectives receive a smaller allowance than their male colleagues, but various other additions—such as for boots or 'plain clothes'—are the same as for men. No arrangements have here been made for the introduction of equal pay, and the 1960 Royal Commission—having had no complaints on the subject—gave their blessing to the continuance of the 9:10 ratio.[3]

Discipline

A policeman is a member of a disciplined force and is bound by various regulations: For example, his wife may not keep a shop in the area of her husband's employment. He is also subject to what is known as the 'discipline code',[4] among the punishments that may be imposed under the latter being a reduction in rank, an abatement of the accused's rate of pay or a fine. Where a policeman is relieved from duty pending proceedings, a 'suspension allowance' is paid. Special provisions apply to chief constables.

[1] *Oaksey Report* I, op. cit., paras. 31 and 96.
[2] *Report of HM Inspectors of Constabulary for* 1951, op. cit., p. 33. The total authorized establishment was 1,809.
[3] Cmnd. 1222, op. cit., para. 190.
[4] See the Police (Discipline) Regulations, 1952 (SI 1952 No. 1705) 1st sched.

Chapter 9

THE FIRE SERVICE

Prior to the passing of the Fire Brigades Act of 1938, there was no general enactment rendering compulsory the provision of fire services. Though local authorities had the power to provide these, they were not, except for the London County Council, compelled to do so.[1] In 1941 all brigades were unified, being merged into the National Fire Service, though local administration was restored as from 1 April 1948. Since that date—as stipulated by the Fire Services Act, 1947[2]—it is the county and county borough councils which constitute the 'fire authorities' in England and Wales, to the exclusion of county districts and the village brigade. As a result, the number of brigades is now less than one-tenth of the pre-war total of some 1,440. As in the case of the police, the Home Secretary exercises a considerable measure of central control over the service.

Staffs

The total whole-time authorized establishment of fire brigades in England and Wales on 31 December 1951 was 20,029; the additional establishment for ambulance duties—in a few areas firemen man ambulances as well as their own appliances—was 514. Those actually serving numbered 19,296 and, in addition, there were 15,297 working in a part-time capacity.[3] Excluded from these figures is the Auxiliary Fire Service, which was re-formed in 1949 as part of the country's civil defence machinery. It is now a specific duty of authorities to enrol auxiliaries, the AFS consisting of part-time volunteers, unpaid apart from the reimbursement of expenses. Likewise excluded from the statistics are brigades maintained by a number of Government departments, by British Railways and other public corporations, and by various private industrial concerns.

Regulations stipulate that every brigade shall be organized under its chief officer in ranks, and that these 'shall be such of those set out

---

[1] For a brief historical account see *Fourth Report from the Select Committee on Estimates*, Session 1953–4, 'The Fire Services' (HMSO 1954), p. 2.

[2] 10 & 11 Geo. 6. c. 41.

[3] *Report of HM Chief Inspector of Fire Services for the year* 1951, Cmd. 8622 (HMSO 1952) paras. 4–7 and pp. 14–18.

below . . . as the fire authority consider necessary in the circumstances of the brigade'.[1] We relate them to numbers at end-1951.

Fire Service:
Authorized whole-time male establishment as at 31 *December* 1951[1]

Firemen	14,887
Leading firemen	1,787
Sub-officers	1,663
Station officers	1,081
Assistant divisional officers	219
Divisional officers, grade III	97
Divisional officers, grade II	105
Divisional officers, grade I	37
Assistant chief officers	18
Chief officers	134
	20,028

[1] Data made available by courtesy of Home Office. The figures include the additional establishment (514) for ambulance work, but exclude the authorized establishment (515) for women.

The rank structure shown is the same as that obtaining in the wartime NFS, apart from changes inherent in a return to local administration such as the creation of brigade chief officer posts. Most of the grades have, however, been rechristened. Allocation to them, as far as the officer categories are concerned, is based on the number of appliances at the fire station.

Appointment and Promotion
Candidates to the basic grade must be British, of good character, between the ages of 19 (formerly 20) and 30, and meet various requirements as to health and physique: They must, for example, satisfy the brigade's chief officer of their ability 'to carry a man weighing between ten and twelve stone a distance of one hundred yards in a time not exceeding sixty seconds'. They must also have passed such examination in educational subjects as may be stipulated by the authority. Appointment to the higher ranks is invariably by promotion, though to be eligible for this, various tests have to be passed in the case of the three bottom grades. Advancement beyond station officer level is solely by selection, station officers being the source from which the whole country's senior fire staff is recruited.

[1] Fire Services (Ranks and Conditions of Service) Regulations, 1948 (SI 1948 No. 546) s. 1. The ranks are there set out in order of superiority.

Negotiating Machinery

Under section 17 of the Fire Services Act, 1947—the 1938 legislation did not deal with the subject—the Secretary of State was empowered to make regulations as to the conditions of service of members of fire brigades. The section further provided that where he was satisfied that proper arrangements were in force for the consideration of these questions, he might give effect to any recommendations so made. There were two bodies officially recognized as 'proper arrangements'. The National Joint Council for Local Authorities' Fire Brigades in Great Britain covers all members of brigades except chief officers and fire-masters, the pay of officers on the one hand, and that of the lower rank on the other, being dealt with by separate standing committees.[1] Its proposals, if approved by the Home Secretary, were promulgated by statutory instrument, differences being referred to the Minister of Labour for submission to arbitration—a clause of which ample use has been made. However, under amending legislation passed in 1959, approval by the Home Secretary and statutory sanction are no longer required. Chief officers are looked after by a separate body—the National Joint Council for Chief Officers of Local Authorities' Fire Brigades in Great Britain.[2]

Salaries

The firemen's pay history is a rather complicated affair. The position is that prior to the setting up of the National Fire Service, terms of employment were fixed independently by each brigade; there was no such thing as a national pattern of remuneration. With the formation of the NFS in 1941, a new grading system as well as a considerable standardization of service conditions were introduced. To be precise, a rate of salary was adopted which was the same as that applicable in the civil defence field (including the auxiliary police); ex-regular firemen, however, many of whom had in the past been paid on, or by analogy with, 'regular' police scales, continued to enjoy these.[3] Regular firemen i.e. continued to be remunerated on the standard of the regular police, rather than on the NFS/civil defence/auxiliary police basis.[4]

Here we must digress and add some explanation regarding the relationship between fire brigade and police pay; it is this issue which

---

[1] A third committee considers common issues, such as discipline and appeals.

[2] There is also a Central Fire Brigades Advisory Council, which advises the Home Secretary on matters such as methods of appointment, qualifications and promotion procedure.

[3] cf. Industrial Court Award No. 2076 (HMSO 1946), paras. 3 and 4.

[4] Certain limits were, however, imposed on their additional emoluments (rent allowances).

has been the *Leitmotif* in the firemen's 'financial history' in the period under review. Prior to 1938 it was not unknown for members of the police to act as firemen. Statutory authority for this was contained in the Police Act, 1893, under which boroughs could delegate their fire brigade powers to watch committees and employ constables wholly or partly as firemen; by the end of September 1939, 45 county boroughs and 19 non-county boroughs had taken advantage of these provisions.[1] The Fire Brigades Act, 1938, limited, and the 1947 Act categorically proscribed, the use of police officers on such duties, but though the species of 'police firemen' thus became extinct, in the sphere of remuneration the repercussions of their erstwhile existence took rather longer to work themselves out.

In April 1945 the basic scales and war bonus of the lower police ranks were consolidated and, at the same time, the salaries of police auxiliaries assimilated to these; the auxiliaries were also—another innovation—granted the police rent allowances. A claim for similar treatment was made on behalf of the National Fire Service—on a par with the auxiliaries throughout the war—and with effect from 30 November 1945 the standard pay of firemen and sub-officers[2] was made identical with that for police constables and sergeants. An intermediate rate was fixed for leading firemen, to which there is no corresponding police grade. The settlement did not provide for the payment of rent additions to the NFS; something akin to it—a 'supplementary allowance'—was introduced, but this was of much more modest proportions. It is this 1945 agreement which first achieved complete standardization of remuneration in the fire service.

In November 1946 the salaries of police constables and sergeants were substantially improved, whereupon the firemen promptly withdrew a more modest claim and asked for the new police rates to be applied to them.[3] The Industrial Court, who had to adjudicate the matter (December 1946), ruled that complete equality between police constables and sergeants and the analogous fire service grades should continue; this parity was to extend not only to the basic scales but also, in the case of married personnel, to the rent allowances.[4] The award became operative from 6 November 1946.

[1] cf. 26 November 1951, HC Deb. 494, *119–20*. However, the number of policemen involved was small.

[2] Then known as section leaders.

[3] cf. Fire Brigades Union, *Annual Report*, 1947, p. 229. The claim was also for increased supplementary allowances for married staff.

[4] Award No. 2076, op. cit., para. 11; leading firemen were to be dealt with in the light of this ruling. Under a supplementary award of the Industrial Court (No. 2113, HMSO 1947), firemen became likewise entitled to the 'compensatory grant' (cf. p. 172) then introduced for policemen.

TABLE 40

FIRE SERVICE
(Men, England and Wales)[1]

	Basic Scale as from	Consolidated Scale as from	
	6 November 1946	28 April 1950	27 April 1951*
	s. p.w.	s. p.w.	s. p.w.
Fireman[2]	105s. × 3s.–132s.	131s. × 3s.–152s.	138/6 × 3s.–159/6
Leading fireman	127s. × 3s.–145s.[3]	150s. × 3s.–168s.	157/6 × 3s.–175/6
Sub-officer	150s. × 3s.–165s.	173s. × 3s.–188s.	180/6 × 3s.–195/6

Officers:	5 May 1947	1 Aug. 1948	28 April 1950	1 Aug. 1951*
	£ p.a.	£ p.a.	£ p.a.	£ p.a.
Station officer	475	475 × 10–525	565 × 10–615	590 × 10–640
Assistant divisional officer	530[4]	600 × 10–650	665 × 10–715	690 × 10–740
Divisional officer, grade III	635	650 × 15–725	715 × 15–790	740 × 15–815
Divisional officer, grade II	740	725 × 15–800	790 × 15–865	815 × 15–890
Divisional officer, grade I	845	850 × 20–950	915 × 20–1,015	940 × 20–1,040

[1] For additional London allowance, payable since 28 April 1950, see text.

[2] The first increment was payable after two years on the minimum. After 10 years a long-service increment of 4s., and after 15 years a second long-service increment of 4s., could be granted. (Prior to 2 May 1947: after 17 and 22 years.)

[3] As from 4 April 1947; previously this scale was 123s. × 3s.–138s.

[4] Increased to £575 as from 1 April 1948.

* These scales were increased as from 22 February 1952 and have been further revised since.

The wage-freeze of the late forties was highly effective in the fire service; no change in basic remuneration took place for the rank-and-file between end-1946 and 1950, the NFS rates remaining in force when the brigades were returned to local control.[1] Not all was quiet, however, in the fire service world, and in April 1948—without even the pretence of a honeymoon—the new fire authorities submitted a claim to the Industrial Court for the abolition of the supplementary (rent) allowances, with a counterclaim by the employees that these—as recently improved for the police—should continue to accrue.[2] The employers contended that firemen were no longer permanently 'on call', necessitating their living on the job; whatever else they should get by way of remuneration, they should not be entitled to additional rent allowances. The men's representatives maintained that the essentially common characteristics of the fire and police services had not

[1] Officers' salaries were adjusted as shown on Table 40.

[2] Industrial Court Award No. 2156 (HMSO 1948). In the case of *single* firemen, the claim was for the police rent allowances to become payable for the first time.

altered; while the 1947 Act substituted one employing authority for another and debarred the use of police on fire duties, there had been no change as would warrant a departure from the 1946 settlement. The Court endorsed this latter view, finding against the authorities. However, they added the fatal words that 'it is not to be assumed that future increases or decreases of police pay or allowances should automatically apply to fire brigade personnel and the Court take the view that the National Joint Council when considering fire brigade remuneration should consider the advisability of consolidating pay and allowances.'[1]

Obviously, therefore, this was not the end of the matter, and late in 1949 the parties found themselves once more in the dock to have their fate decided by the Industrial Court. This time the latter ruled substantially in favour of the employers:[2] The system of rent allowances and compensatory grants was abolished, and a consolidated scale introduced, operative from 28 April 1950. A London allowance was also instituted. It will be recalled that, in the case of the police, the Oaksey Committee had advised against consolidation.

The next revision took effect from 27 April 1951, when the three lower ranks were given an increase of 7s. 6d. a week; a consequential rise of £25 per annum was granted to the higher grades as from 1 August of that year. In the meanwhile, the Trustram Eve award to the police had been announced and, as was to be expected, the firemen were not going to stomach so substantial an improvement in the remuneration of their erstwhile equals without one more attempt to make good the lost ground. Again it proved impossible to reach agreement, and after a 'spit and polish' boycott and nation-wide demonstrations, the Minister of Labour appointed a special Board of Arbitration to resolve the dispute. Their terms of reference were:

'(1) To determine whether the remuneration of Firemen in Local Authorities' Fire Brigades in England and Wales should be equivalent to the pay and allowances received by Police Constables.
(2) If this is decided in the negative, to fix the remuneration of such Firemen.'[3]

Summarizing their conclusions, the Board point out that while in pre-war days parity obviously existed in areas where local brigades were staffed by policemen, these formed only part of the fire services.

[1] Industrial Court Award No. 2156 (HMSC 1948), para. 6.
[2] See Industrial Court Award No. 2249 (HMSO 1950).
[3] National Joint Council for Local Authorities' Fire Brigades in England and Wales, *Report of a Board of Arbitration in the Matter of a Difference . . . on the Remuneration of Firemen* (January 1952). The terms of reference were confined to the basic grade.

An examination of the various awards made both between the wars and since suggested that, while there was a broad similarity between the two fields, it was recognized that they were not identical. Similarly, comparisons of relative duties were not very profitable. 'It appears to us that the proper way of deciding the remuneration of the fire service is not to relate it to police remuneration but to determine it on its own merits.'[1] The verdict was unequivocally against 'parity'.

Having got this far, the Board were unable to agree as to what positive proposals to put forward, and it fell to the chairman to make an award. Effect was given to this by regulations operative from 22 February 1952, which at the same time provided for improvements for senior staff; the increase was 16s. 6d. a week for the three bottom grades and £52 per annum for the officer ranks. There have been further revisions since.

Chief and Assistant Chief Fire Officers
Every fire brigade is headed by a chief officer—in a number of cases he serves at the same time as chief ambulance officer—who is directly responsible to the fire authority, though his appointment must be confirmed from the centre. In the largest brigades there is also an assistant chief officer; elsewhere any fireman of not below station officer rank may act as deputy chief. The business of negotiating remuneration for this—the top—sector of the service falls, as indicated, to a separate national council. Chiefs have therefore been above the din of the battle described earlier on.

A new pattern of salaries for chief officers was provisionally introduced on 1 April 1948;[2] under this fire authorities were divided into ten groups on the basis of their rateable values, with adjustments according to population. Prolonged discussions took place subsequently on the need for revision, anomalies having arisen amongst other things because of the changes in the pay of the officer ranks, unaccompanied by corresponding movements at the top. Eventually, the National Joint Council recommended seven scales in lieu of the ten, with a further 'discretionary' category for the largest authorities.[3] Neither population nor rateable value were to be the sole basis of the new scheme; these were to be considered in conjunction with factors such as fire risk and establishment. The proposals received official blessing and became operative from 1 April 1951.

[1] *Report of a Board of Arbitration in the Matter of a Difference . . . on the Remuneration of Firemen* (January 1952), paras. 33–5.

[2] The scales were drawn up by a committee appointed by the Home Secretary. Their report was enclosed with National Fire Service Circular No. 7A/1947.

[3] i.e. with populations over 600,000.

TABLE 41

FIRE SERVICE

CHIEF AND ASSISTANT CHIEF OFFICERS
(England and Wales)

	Salary Scale as from	
	1 *January* 1949	1 *April* 1951*
Assistant chief fire officer[1]	£ *p.a.*	£ *p.a.*
Grade II	950×25–1,025	$1,025 \times 25$–1,100
Grade I	$1,000 \times 25$–1,075	$1,125 \times 25$–1,200[2]

	1 *April* 1948	
	£ *p.a.*	
Chief fire officer[3]		
Grade X	600×20– 700	
Grade IX	700×20– 800	
Grade VIII	800×20– 900	
Grade VII	875×25–1,000	750×40– 875[4]
Grade VI	975×25–1,100	850×50–1,000
Grade V	$1,050 \times 30$–1,200	$1,000 \times 50$–1,200
Grade IV	$1,100 \times 40$–1,300	$1,150 \times 50$–1,350
Grade III	$1,200 \times 40$–1,400	$1,300 \times 50$–1,500
Grade II	$1,250 \times 50$–1,500	$1,450 \times 50$–1,650
Grade I[2]	$1,350 \times 50$–1,600	$1,600 \times 50$–1,800

[1] The scales shown in the last column were agreed in 1953, but a majority of brigades applied them as from 1 April 1951.

[2] There was a further discretionary grade.

[3] The figures for 1948 and 1951 are not comparable.

[4] The last increment was £45.

* Certain revisions of grading and pay took effect from 1 April 1954, and there have been further increases since.

To give some illustrations, Durham, Cheshire, Liverpool and Manchester were allocated to grade I; grade VII comprised small authorities such as Westmorland, Merioneth and Gloucester. Authorities in the discretionary category included London, Middlesex, Lancashire and Birmingham; salaries in force for these latter ranged (1951) from £1,750 × £50–£1,950 for Kent, Surrey and the West Riding of Yorkshire to £2,700 for the chief fire officer in the capital.[1] It should be pointed out that, unlike their juniors, chief and assistant chief officers continue to be entitled to free residential accommodation or an allowance in lieu.

Part-time Firemen
The nature of fire duties is such as to call for the employment or potential employment of a large number of part-time personnel,

[1] Certain grading revisions plus an increase of £75 a year became operative from 1 April 1954.

known in official jargon as 'retained' members. They may be working at other jobs during the day—including as regular firemen—or be retired, but they undertake to be available when alerted by the fire alarm. In the period under review, a retained member received (*a*) an annual 'retaining fee' and (*b*) a 'turn-out fee' for every occasion on which he was summoned. Both varied with rank: The standard 'turn-out fee' payable in 1951, for example, was 10*s*. per fire for the basic grade and 16*s*. for station officers and above.[1]

Provincial Differentiation
As a corollary of the abolition of rent allowances in 1950, a London weighting was formally introduced into the fire service. All those below assistant chief officer in the Metropolitan Police District and City of London qualify, the rates operative as from end-April 1950 being 10*s*. a week/£26 per annum. We may add that the amount has since been raised, though only for those at stations *within* the LCC area.

Sex Differentiation
Although women were employed in considerable numbers in the war-time NFS, the total in local authority brigades had shrunk to 479 by the end of 1951. The actual job of fire-fighting falls exclusively on men, women being almost entirely confined to control room duties. There are five ranks for female brigade members, viz. firewoman, leading and senior leading firewoman, and assistant group and group officer. The maximum of a firewoman's scale, introduced in February 1952, was £325, which was 68 per cent of the fireman's maximum if the latter's discretionary long-service increments are included. As for salaries above this level, there is no real correspondence between the two sexes' higher ranks; hence pay for senior women personnel is related to that of analogous local authority employees rather than to that of male firemen. No scheme for equal pay has been agreed upon[2]

---

[1] There were other detailed provisions regarding the duties of retainees, as well as for supplemental fees where attendance per fire exceeded two hours, etc.

[2] Like policemen, firemen are subject to a special discipline code.

Chapter 10

PRISONS AND BORSTALS

Under the Prison Act, 1952—under which much of the relevant law has been consolidated—all jurisdiction concerning prisons and related institutions vests in the Secretary of State for Home Affairs.[1] For purposes of administration there has existed, since 1877, a statutory Board known as the Prison Commission; it is a self-contained Government department whose responsibility, subject to the Home Secretary's overall control, now extends to all prisons, borstals and similar establishments.

The staffs of prisons and borstals—those working in Broadmoor and analogous institutions are, as we saw, now part of the National Health Service—have traditionally been divided into 'superior' and 'subordinate', though the 1952 Act no longer gives this distinction the force of statute. The superior ranks are the governors, chaplains and medical officers; every prison must have one of each of these categories. The subordinate grades—the prison officers—include the main body of 'discipline' staff, together with specialists and tradesmen. They are engaged by the Prison Commissioners direct, 'superior' ranks being appointed by the Home Secretary. With a few exceptions, all full-time personnel have the status of permanent civil servants.

Subordinate Grades

Established staff as at 30 *November* 1951[1]	
Officers	3,389
Principal officers	366
Chief officers, class II	62
Chief officers, class I	25
Works staff	115
	3,957

[1] Data made available by courtesy of Prison Commission. The numbers relate to England and Wales only and exclude auxiliary officers undergoing training.

These figures only cover those belonging to the main prison hierarchy. Not included (apart from 'superior' staff) are civilian instruc-

[1] Prison Act, 1952 (15 & 16 Geo. 6. and 1 Eliz. 2. c. 52) ss. 1 and 43.

tors; night patrols and other manual workers; a few very small categories such as industrial managers; and various headquarters personnel. The total number of employees in the Commission's service at end-1951 was about 6,500.

Salaries

Statute decrees that 'there shall be paid out of moneys provided by Parliament to the inspectors and other officers and servants of the Prison Commissioners such salaries as the Secretary of State may with the consent of the Treasury determine'.[1] Prior to April 1919 there were separate rates of pay for local and convict prisons, but in that year a uniform standard was adopted. During the 1939–45 war, prison remuneration was governed by an arbitration award of 1938, supplemented by the Civil Service war bonus; consolidated scales were introduced on 1 January 1946. In the view of the staff, however, these did not constitute that complete overhaul which they felt that war and post-war conditions called for, and eventually—improved salaries for the police had meanwhile been announced—revised rates were conceded with effect from 1 December 1946.

In June 1949, following the Oaksey recommendations for policemen, the Prison Officers' Association—who represent the subordinate grades—resubmitted an earlier request for enhanced pay. They held that since recruiting difficulties were a problem common to the police and prison services, the remedy being tried for the former should also be applied to the latter. After protracted negotiations, the claim was referred to the Civil Service Arbitration Tribunal (May 1950);[2] with the exception of some minor modifications, it was conceded in full.

It was again events in the police world—the Trustram Eve award —which were responsible for the next development; the repercussions of that settlement were, ultimately, another reference to arbitration early in 1952. The staffs maintained that post-war pay revisions in the prison service had derived—implicitly if not explicitly—from those granted to the police; the May 1950 claim, for instance, showed that the Association had satisfied the Civil Service Arbitration Tribunal that conditions in the two fields were sufficiently alike to justify similar treatment.[3]

The official side did not accept this interpretation: the Home Secretary 'had never held the view that there was any such relationship between the pay of the Police and Prison Service that increases

---

[1] Prison Act, 1952, s. 3(2).

[2] Civil Service Arbitration Tribunal Award No. 120 (HMSO 1950).

[3] cf. Civil Service Arbitration Tribunal Award No. 180 (HMSO 1952), para. 4.

granted to the Police would automatically bring the pay of the Prison Service under review'.[1] Even if there was such a relativity, it did not follow that it could never be disturbed, nor did the Commissioners agree that the prison service was equally undermanned. The award of the Tribunal is shown in the last column of Table 42; it represented a rise of about 15 per cent and became operative from 1 January 1952.[2]

As in the fire service then, 'relativity with the police' has been a central theme in prison pay history. Section 8 of the 1952 Prison Act does indeed stipulate that 'every prison officer while acting as such shall have all the powers, authority, protection and privileges of a constable', though privileges in matters of remuneration are unlikely to have been in the drafter's mind. Up to 1919 there was little difference in the scales for the two categories, but following the Desborough improvements then granted to the police, the prison officers' request for comparable treatment was explicitly turned down by the 1923 Stanhope Committee. We may add that the analogous Wynn-Parry Committee, in their Report on prison remuneration in 1958, stated that they found the formulation of concrete scales in this sphere extremely difficult, as the prison service was *sui generis*. They experienced the same trouble when considering 'to what class, organization, or index' their figures should be geared for purposes of future adjustments, the real problem being the rank and file. Mainly for want of something better, the Committee finally recommended that subsequent pay movements for prison officers should be linked to those of civil servants with salary ranges similar to those which they were now putting forward for the officer grades.[3] No proposal of any sort was made as to 'relativity with the police'.

The bulk of prison staffs are engaged on ordinary 'discipline' duties, though apart from their custodial functions they are also to exercise a good influence over inmates both by example and precept.[4] The work of a basic-grade officer varies: he may be detailed to the workshop, supervise prisoners attending evening classes or act as gatekeeper. Advancement depends both on vacancies and the passing of an examination; the Select Committee on Estimates, in the course of their 1951–2 review of the Prison Vote, pointed out in this connection that it was obviously a source of dissatisfaction that a basic-grade man had to wait an average of eighteen years before promo-

[1] Civil Service Arbitration Tribunal Award No. 180 (HMSO 1952), p. 5.
[2] Civil Service pay addition did not accrue, but several revisions have taken place since.
[3] *Report of the Committee on Remuneration and Conditions of Service of Certain Grades in the Prison Services*, Cmnd. 544 (HMSO) 1958), paras. 89, 97 and 98.
[4] cf. Civil Service Arbitration Tribunal Award No. 120, op. cit., para. 3.

tion.[1] Principal officers are frequently in charge of a defined unit of prison administration such as a 'hall' or the prison canteen; chief officers, in turn, are responsible to the governor for the daily routine of the whole institution.

TABLE 42

PRISONS AND BORSTALS

DISCIPLINE STAFF
(Men, Great Britain)

	Salary Scale[1] *as from*		
	1 *December* 1946	13 *May* 1950	1 *January* 1952*
	s. p.w.	*s. p.w.*	*s. p.w.*
Officer	98/0 × 3/0–125/0	118/0 × 4/6–149/6	135/6 × 5/0–172/0
after 15 years	128/0	154/0	177/0
,, 20 ,,	131/0	158/6	182/0
Principal officer	133/0 × 4/0–145/0	160/0 × 6/0–174/0	184/0 × 6/0–200/0
Chief officer, class II	155/0 × 5/0–170/0	180/0 × 6/0–192/0	207/0 × 7/0–221/0
Chief officer, class I	180/0 × 5/0–195/0	200/0 × 6/0–218/0	230/0 × 7/0–251/0

[1] Excluding rent, borstal and all other special allowances.

* All salaries were increased as from 1 January 1953 and have been further revised since.

There is a detailed pattern of allowances in the prison service. Thus a considerable number of discipline staff act in a specialist capacity—for example, as trade instructors, hospital officers, cook and baker officers or building trade assistants—for which varying additions are paid. In the period under review, a special weekly allowance of 4s. 6d. over and above the scales shown on Table 42 also accrued to all subordinate grades in borstal institutions. The 1958 Wynn-Parry Committee, however, felt that discrimination between prison and borstal personnel was no longer justified and recommended that the differential be abolished forthwith.[2] They similarly urged that the allowances for taking finger-prints, assisting at executions and inflicting corporal punishment should be done away with, but gave their official blessing to the continuance of certain others such as those for compounding medicines, the haircutting of inmates and assisting at post-mortems.[3]

[1] *Seventh Report from the Select Committee on Estimates*, Session 1951–2, 'Prisons' (HMSO 1952), p. xii, para. 15.

[2] Cmnd. 544, op. cit., para. 86. The allowance was then at the rate of 7s. 6d. p.w.

[3] For details see ibid. para. 76 and ff.

Governors

Governors—described as 'gaolers' in earlier legislation[1]—are the responsible heads of prison and borstal establishments. Numbers for 1951 are set out below:

Governor grades as at 30 *November* 1951[1]	
Assistant governors, class II	91
Assistant governors, class I	33
Governors, class III	37
Governors, class II	18
Governors, class I	10
	189

[1] Data made available by courtesy of Prison Commission.

As shown, there are three grades of governor, supported in all borstals and the larger prisons by assistant governors. Assistant governors I act as deputies to their chiefs or in other posts of special responsibility; those in class II may, for example, serve as house-masters in borstals—formerly a separate category. Recruitment is by open competition, by the promotion of chief officers and foremen of works, and by the advancement of other subordinate personnel who show promise and have qualified via a special staff course. All enter as assistant governors II, except for chief officer promotees who normally join the superior ranks as class I assistants. No formal professional qualifications are demanded, though it has been said that the time has long passed when governor posts were a suitable niche for the retired officer with the reputation merely of 'a good disciplinarian'.[2] Salaries are set out on Table 43 overleaf.

Chaplains

Full-time chaplains—there were twenty-four in September 1952—are to be found only at the larger prisons and borstals. They are not now established civil servants but, in consultation with the bishops concerned, are engaged for periods not usually exceeding seven years. The purpose of this arrangement is that 'chaplains should not spend so long in this highly specialized work as to lose the freshness of touch which it requires'.[3] At the smaller establishments appointment is on a part-time basis.

[1] Prison Act, 1865 (28 & 29 Vict. c. 126) s. 4 (now repealed).
[2] cf. Civil Service Arbitration Tribunal Award No. 213 (HMSO 1953), para. 8.
[3] Home Office, *Prisons and Borstals, England and Wales* (HMSO 1950), p. 70.

TABLE 43

PRISONS AND BORSTALS

GOVERNORS
(Men, London)

	Salary Scale as from	
	1 *January* 1946	1 *January* 1951*
	£ *p.a.*	£ *p.a.*
Assistant governor		
Class II	360 × 20– 580	395 × 20– 415
		× 25– 465
		× 20– 565
		× 25– 650
Class I	600 × 25– 700	650 × 25– 700
		× 30– 750
Governor		
Class III	800 × 25– 950	850 × 30–1,000
		× 40–1,050
Class II	1,000 × 30–1,150	1,100 × 40–1,220
		× 50–1,275[1]
Class I	1,250	1,400[1]

[1] Operative as from 1 September 1950.

* All salaries were increased as from 1 January 1952 and 1 April 1952, and have been further revised since.

The salary of full-time chaplains was fixed at £520 per annum in 1947;[1] a claim for a substantial improvement was referred to arbitration in September 1952. The staffs' spokesmen—the Institution of Professional Civil Servants—argued that although chaplains were one of the three 'superior' categories in the prison service, this was not reflected in their pay; though no suggestion had been made that their importance had diminished, their salary had, since 1935, increased by a mere £100.[2] The Prison Commissioners replied that chaplains should not receive remuneration so far out of proportion to that of other clergy as the scale claimed: Chaplains were recruited from parochial service and returned to it at the end of their seven years. The relativity with parochial clergy was not now less favourable than before the war, 'although admittedly former relativities with other grades in the prison service have been seriously

[1] The remuneration of those retained beyond the normal period was higher in some cases.

[2] Civil Service Arbitration Tribunal Award No. 191 (HMSO 1952), para. 6.

disturbed . . .'.[1] The Tribunal awarded that as from 1 January 1951 the salary of full-time chaplains should be £700 a year—as against the £900–£1,075 asked for and the £600 offered—to attract the centrally-agreed pay addition as from the beginning of 1952.

Medical Officers

Medical staffs in the employ of the Prison Commission are members of the general Civil Service medical class. They serve part-time at the smaller establishments, but hold full-time appointments at the larger prisons. The pay of a basic-grade medical officer as from 1 January 1952 was £1,500–£2,100; that of a senior medical officer £2,200; the Director of Medical Services then received £2,300 per annum. Thus a basic-grade medico had—except in his first year—a salary more than twice that of his chaplain colleague,[2] though unlike the latter he is not entitled to free accommodation.

Provincial Differentiation

The bulk of prison officers are, officially, on undifferentiated scales, i.e. their *basic* rates are the same in whatever part of the country they may be serving. All discipline, specialist and works staff are in this category, due to their liability to fairly frequent transfers from one centre to another. Governors and other superior ranks,[3] however, are on the normal Civil Service system of provincial differentiation.

Side by side with this formal absence of area differentiation, there is a pattern of 'inconvenience of locality' allowances—payable at some of the more out-of-the-way prisons to compensate for extra expenditure in respect of shopping and recreation. In the case of Dartmoor, this addition was introduced in 1854 owing to its 'remote and desolate situation . . . the privations of all kinds to which officers are exposed and the severity of the climate'.[4] However—and in particular since 1945—the scheme has been extended to several other institutions.[5] The size of the payment varies: For Dartmoor staff it was fixed at 16s. 6d. a week as from 1 December 1951; elsewhere, it is mostly rather smaller. The Wynn-Parry Committee, we may add —though conceding that the allowances were a hang-over from the days when remuneration in convict prisons differed from that in local institutions—decided, on balance, in favour of their retention.[6]

---

[1] Civil Service Arbitration Tribunal Award No. 191 (HMSO 1952), para. 12.

[2] Pay addition i.e. increased chaplains' salaries to £760 p.a. as from 1 Jan. 1952.

[3] As well as 'civilian instructors', whom we have not dealt with.

[4] Civil Service Arbitration Tribunal Award No. 85 (HMSO 1945), p. 2.

[5] Almost 900 staff received an inconvenience allowance at end-1951. On 1 June 1957 1,470 officers at 27 institutions in England and Wales were eligible.

[6] Cmnd. 544, op. cit., paras. 81–5.

Quarters and Rent Allowances
In addition to basic pay, all discipline staff, governors and chaplains
are provided with free quarters or else receive a rent allowance.
Medical officers, however, are not eligible for this emolument.

Sex Differentiation
Of the total of 3,957 subordinate staff at end-November 1951, 221
were women, the majority being in the bottom grade. Their duties
are similar to those of male personnel. In the period under review,
pay was differentiated at every stage, the precise ratio of women's to
men's scales ranging from 86 to 91 per cent (subordinate grades,
1950–1). The one woman class I governor's 1951 salary of £1,300 was
about 93 per cent of the comparable male figure. However, since 1955
these differentials have been progressively eliminated for, as civil
servants, women prison officers were automatically covered by the
equal pay agreement concluded for the non-industrial Civil Service.
This, as we saw in Chapter 1, provided for equal pay to be fully
operative as from January 1961. An interesting point is that like
treatment has not been accorded to policewomen; the Civil Service
bargaining umbrella does, of course, not extend to them.

Chapter 11

THE POST OFFICE

The Post Office was established in the seventeenth century as a mail-carrying organization, but is now responsible for several other major services. It is by far the largest Government department and, prior to the post-war spate of nationalization, was the biggest single commercial concern in the country. We may add that though in future the Post Office is to enjoy a much greater degree of financial independence than hitherto,[1] it will remain a department of the Crown.

For purposes of organization Great Britain and Northern Ireland are divided into a number of territorial directorates, each under the charge of a regional director. Executive control of postal and telegraph, and certain aspects of telephone, work falls on smaller units—known as Head Post Office Districts. Each of these is under a head postmaster, who is also responsible for the subordinate establishments in his area, such as branch and 'salaried' sub-offices, there being some 1,200 Crown offices in all. In addition, there are spread throughout the country some 22,000 'scale-payment' sub-offices, most conducted in conjunction with a private business. Control of most branches of telephone and engineering work is devolved on separate Telephone Areas. In London the administrative set-up is somewhat different.

Staff

Postal employees have the status of civil servants and are in the same position as the latter in such matters as security of tenure and superannuation arrangements. Their status in this respect will not be affected by the proposed reforms of the Post Office financial structure. Numbers for October 1951 are given overleaf.

Group A is largely made up of members of the ordinary Civil Service classes, including their temporary and departmental variants; their remuneration is as described in Chapter 1. Group C is composed of cleaners, doorkeepers and similar categories, and falls outside the scope of this study. D mainly consists of engineering and related grades; we deal with these briefly towards the end of the chapter. Our main concern here is with the manipulative worker—what might perhaps be termed the 'typical' Post Office employee.

[1] As proposed in a Bill published in December 1960.

Post Office staffs as at 1 October 1951[1]

A	Administrative, executive, clerical, professional, etc. grades		39,736
B	Manipulative group[2]		214,472

(a) *Postal grades:*

Postmen	84,538	
Postmen, higher grade	19,947	
Supervisors	3,849	
	108,334	

(b) *Telegraph grades:*

Telegraphists	10,184	
Supervisors	1,001	
	11,185	

(c) *Telephone grades:*

Telephonists	47,653	
Supervisors	5,689	
	53,342	

(d) *Counter and writing grades:*

Postal and telegraph officers	21,854	
Supervisors	4,334	
	26,188	

	(e) Various	15,423	
C	Cleaners and other ancillary groups		8,482
D	Industrial staff		72,476
			335,166

[1] Data made available by courtesy of Post Office. All unestablished and part-time staff are included, each part-timer being counted as $\frac{1}{2}$.

[2] The figure for 'supervisors' under (a), (b), (c) and (d) includes all levels of supervisory staff. The numbers for the telegraph grades include radio operators.

The great majority of postal staffs fall within the ambit of the Civil Service National Whitley Council. Questions of pay—insofar as they are not handled on an all-Service basis—are left to individual associations and unions who negotiate directly with the Post Office. However, ultimate control in all matters of remuneration and service conditions rests with the Treasury. The competent body for the adjudication of disputes is the Civil Service Arbitration Tribunal.

The Manipulative Grades
The manipulative group is made up of a number of distinct hier-archies, the chief of which are the postal, the telegraph, the telephone and the counter and writing grades. A major reorganization in this field took place in 1946, its principal objects being to introduce a more logical allocation of work, to align remuneration more closely to duties, and to offer postmen a better career. Another feature of the 1946 reforms was the adoption of a simpler system of provincial differentiation.

Rank-and-file Pay[1]
The first post-war revision of pay—apart from the consolidation of war bonus—went hand in hand with the reorganization of 1946: The rates then introduced are those shown in the first column of Tables 44 to 47 below. The next adjustment—effective from October 1947—was mainly designed to provide increases for those reaching age 21; the improvement of maxima was small. This 1947 settlement also involved the shortening of scales, while two juvenile categories—boy messengers and girl probationers—ceased their separate existence, emerging as junior postmen and telephonists, respectively.

In October 1948 a comprehensive claim was presented by the Union of Post Office Workers—who represent the bulk of the rank-and-file; this time the parties could not reach agreement and the matter was referred to the Civil Service Arbitration Tribunal.[2] The latter awarded a rise of 6*s.* per week on all adult male rates, though telephonists were given two additional increments—a step towards 'parity' with telegraphists, then an avowed aim of Union policy. The revised standards applied from 4 June 1949.

Another dispute—again covering the principal rank-and-file cat-egories—had to be submitted to arbitration in May 1951,[3] when the Tribunal granted 8*s.* a week to the majority of adult male grades.[4] On another part of the claim—for a shorter scale—the Tribunal did not then pronounce, though when the further negotiations which it recommended proved abortive, it had to decide the issue subse-quently (September 1951).[5] As a result, the scales fixed under the earlier settlement were shortened by two points, the last column of

[1] About 24 per cent of the manipulatives were unestablished at end-1951; generally speaking, however, all temporary personnel received the same pay as their established counterparts, though this was not necessarily true of service conditions.
[2] Civil Service Arbitration Tribunal Award No. 108 (HMSO 1949).
[3] Civil Service Arbitration Tribunal Award No. 149 (HMSO 1951).
[4] Certain classes of postmen received more. Juveniles were given 4*s.* p.w.
[5] Civil Service Arbitration Tribunal Award No. 164 (HMSO 1951).

G

Tables 44–47 showing the combined effect of the two awards. We may add that—here as elsewhere—lengths of scales have been a fluctuating variable: At the beginning of 1960, for example, the position was that postmen reached their maximum at age 25 as against 26 at end-1951; postal and telegraph officers, on the other hand, had a longer scale again, attaining their maximum at age 33 as compared with 30 under the second 1951 dispensation.

1951 also witnessed the replacement of the Post Office's separate pattern of provincial differentiation by the general Civil Service system; this involved appreciable—and in some cases substantial—increases for those in the provinces and outer London. As from 1 January 1952 non-industrial grades qualified for the Civil Service 'pay addition', which in the case of the rank-and-file amounted to 10 per cent of the relevant 1951 scale. The 1952 salaries were next improved as from January 1953 and have been further stepped up since.

Supervising Salaries

As for their juniors, the first post-war revision took effect from June 1946—apart from the 'consolidation' operation of the previous year. Here also the revised rates were related to the new allocation of duties: While previously there was a common hierarchy for 'indoor' postal, telegraph and counter and writing work, we have, since 1946, the present division on a functional basis.

Following the October 1947 adjustments for the rank-and-file, the Post Office agreed to raise the minima of all first-line supervisors, to ensure that these were better off than those of their charges in receipt of allowances. However, further problems were created by the June 1949 arbitration award; its ultimate repercussions were a Tribunal hearing[1] of the seniors' own grievances. The staffs' spokesmen maintained (*inter alia*) that the 1946 standards had not sufficiently recognized the new and heavier duties under 're-allocation'; the Post Office took the line that there had not, since 1938, been any material change in the nature of supervisors' work taken as a whole. The Tribunal ruled that the 1946 salaries be increased by £30 throughout;[2] maxima for the telephone grades were to be augmented, in addition, by from £50 to £70. The award took effect from 1 July 1950.

Following the January 1951 improvements for the rank-and-file, the staffs presented a fresh claim later that year. In the last minute it proved possible to reach agreement 'out of court', the settlement providing for a £20 a year rise as from April 1951. Subsequently, supervisors benefited from the 1951 change-over to the Civil Service

[1] Civil Service Arbitration Tribunal Award No. 139 (HMSO 1951).
[2] Minus the rise given to first-line supervisors in 1947.

system of provincial differentiation and from the all-Service pay addition in 1952. Enhanced scales were secured at arbitration as from 1 January 1953.[1]

The pay history of the higher ranks in these first post-war years has thus been one long struggle not to fall behind their manipulative juniors. At the 1951 arbitration hearing, for example, the staff representatives stated that there were rank-and-file officers receiving for a normal week's work more than the maximum of their supervisor's scale, and that this 'extraordinary and indefensible situation' had arisen because, since 1946, considerable changes in rank-and-file remuneration had not been reflected higher up the ladder.[2] The official reply was that, while the Postmaster General could not agree that differentials were sacrosanct, he regarded it as proper that there should be a gap between the maximum plus allowance of a rank-and-file worker and the minimum of the corresponding first-line supervisor; such relativity was in fact one of the two chief criteria used by him in determining the remuneration of the higher grades.[3] We may add that the Royal (Priestley) Commission on the Civil Service likewise concluded that the main factor in laying down salaries for manipulative supervisors must be internal vertical relativities.[4]

The Postal Grades

The postal grades are those directly concerned with the handling of mail. The rank-and-file here consists of two levels: Postmen, who deliver and collect mail and carry out primary sorting work; and postmen, higher grade—one of the creations of 1946—who deal with the more important rank-and-file sorting jobs and in some cases supervise their juniors.[5] A considerable number of staff receive additional allowances—for example, for motor driving or motor cycle telegram work or for duties in railway 'travelling post offices'.

From postman, higher grade there is advancement to assistant inspector; his tasks include outdoor patrol to watch over collection arrangements and so on. Inspectors—the next rung—are usually responsible for the organization of all outdoor services. Chief inspectors are to be found only in London, in 'travelling post offices'[6]

[1] Civil Service Arbitration Tribunal Award No. 236 (HMSO 1953). Further revisions have taken place since.

[2] cf. Award No. 139, op. cit., pp. 8–9.

[3] ibid. pp. 11, 12 and 14.

[4] *Royal Commission on the Civil Service* 1953–5, Cmd. 9613 (HMSO 1955), para. 675.

[5] Though postmen fall under 'wages' rather than 'salaries', we have included them here, as they are an integral part of the otherwise salaried manipulative hierarchy.

[6] Inspectors working in travelling post offices again qualify for allowances.

and at the largest provincial centres; there were only about a hundred such appointments in 1951. More generally, we may point out, promotion outlets for postmen are much inferior to those for the other manipulative hierarchies, as is indicated by relative ratios of supervising to rank-and-file posts.[1]

[1] cf. p. 192 *ante*

TABLE 44

POST OFFICE

POSTAL GRADES
(Men, London)

	Salary Scale as from			
	1 *June* 1946	1 *Oct.* 1947	4 *June* 1949	1 *Jan.* 1951*
	s. p.w.	*s. p.w.*	*s. p.w.*	*s. p.w.*
Postman				
Age 16 and under		50/0	52/0	56/0
17		56/0	58/0	62/0
18	55/6	62/0	65/0	69/0
19	62/0	68/0	71/0	75/0
20	68/6	73/6	76/6	80/6
21	79/6	92/0	98/0	106/0
22	83/0	95/0	101/0	111/0
23	86/6	98/0	104/0	116/0
24	90/0	101/6	107/6	122/0
25 and over	95/0	105/0	111/0	
	×4/0–115/0[1]	×5/0–120/0	×5/0–126/0	×6/0–134/0
Postman, higher grade				
Age 21				108/6
22				112/0
23				116/0
24[2]	95/0	106/6	112/6	128/0
	×4/6–122/0	×5/6–112/0	×5/6–118/0	×6/0–152/0
	×5/0–127/0	×5/0–132/0	×5/0–138/0	

	1 *June* 1946	1 *Oct.* 1947	1 *July* 1950	1 *April* 1951*
	£ *p.a.*	£ *p.a.*	£ *p.a.*	£ *p.a.*
Assistant inspector	375×15–450	390×15–450	405×15–480	425×15–500
Inspector	475×20–550		505×20–580	525×20–600
Chief inspector	580×25–680		610×25–710	630×25–730

[1] In sub-district offices and sub-offices, 113/0.

[2] Until 1951 '24 and under'; since 1 January 1951 '24 and over'.

* All scales were increased as from 1 January 1952 and 1 January 1953, and have been further revised since.

Telegraph Grades

TABLE 45

POST OFFICE

TELEGRAPH GRADES
(Men, London)

	Salary Scale as from			
	1 *June* 1946	1 *Oct*. 1947	4 *June* 1949	1 *Jan*. 1951*
	s. p.w.	*s. p.w.*	*s. p.w.*	*s. p.w.*
Telegraphist				
Age 16 and under	45/0	50/0	52/0	56/0
17	51/0	56/0	58/0	62/0
18	57/0	62/0	65/0	69/0
19	63/0	68/0	71/0	75/0
20	72/6	77/6	80/6	84/6
21	82/0	94/6	100/6	108/6
22	85/0	98/0	104/0	112/0
23	90/0	102/0	108/0	116/0
24	95/0	106/0	112/0	122/0
25 and over	100/0	110/0	116/0	128/0
	×4/6–109/0	×5/0–120/0	×5/0–126/0	×6/0–152/0
	×4/0–133/0	×4/6–138/0	×4/6–144/0	

	1 *June* 1946	1 *Oct*. 1947	1 *July* 1950	1 *April* 1951*
	£ *p.a.*	£ *p.a.*	£ *p.a.*	£ *p.a.*
Assistant supervisor	395×15–460	410×15–460	425×15–490	445×15–510
Supervisor	485×20–550		515×20–580	535×20–600
Supervisor, higher grade	580×25–680		610×25–710	630×25–730

* All scales were increased as from 1 January 1952 and 1 January 1953, and have been further revised since.

Telegraphists are mainly concerned with the sending and receiving of telegrams by teleprinter or telephone; they also perform various ancillary duties and a number of technical allowances are payable to certain qualified teleprinter operators. The employment of men is generally confined to offices open at night. It should be noted that there is a separate group of cable-room personnel engaged in the overseas services in the Central Telegraph Office, whose salaries were considerably higher than those of the 'ordinary' telegraphists shown on Table 45. Another small body is the wireless telegraph staff, consisting of radio operators plus supervisors; they work at wireless coast stations and on Post Office cable ships and again have their own pattern of remuneration.

The Telephone Grades

Telephonists are recruited by interview, at which candidates are tested for speech, hearing, and so on. In the period under review, men were not normally taken on under 21; girls entered at 15 or 16, establishment being subject to the passing of an examination. In addition to actual operating duties, the rank-and-file carry out minor clerical work—largely routine record-keeping—for which a regular extra payment is made. Male staff do some simple testing of equipment. A number of telephonists receive supervision allowances—up to 12s. a week in the period under review—and at one time were able to earn considerably more than their seniors.

TABLE 46

POST OFFICE

TELEPHONE GRADES
(Men, London)

	Salary Scale as from			
	1 *June* 1946	1 *Oct.* 1947	4 *June* 1949	1 *Jan.* 1951*
	s. p.w.	*s. p.w.*	*s. p.w.*	*s. p.w.*
Telephonist				
Age 21	79/6	92/0	98/0	106/0
22	83/0	95/6	101/6	111/0
23	87/0	99/0	105/0	116/0
24	91/0	102/6	108/6	121/0
25 and over	96/0	106/0	112/0	126/0
	×4/0–120/0	×5/0–116/0	×5/0–122/0	×5/0–136/0
		×4/6–125/0	×4/6–140/0	×6/0–148/0

	1 *June* 1946	1 *Oct.* 1947	1 *July* 1950	1 *April* 1951*
	£ *p.a.*	£ *p.a.*	£ *p.a.*	£ *p.a.*
Assistant supervisor	335×15–380	365×15–380	415×15–460	435×15–480
Supervisor	390×15–420		470×15–500	490×15–520
Chief supervisor	430×15–490		530×15–590	550×15–610
Senior chief supervisor	540×20–640		640×20–740	660×20–760

* All scales were increased as from 1 January 1952 and 1 January 1953, and have been further revised since.

Any of the higher ranks may be in charge of a telephone exchange, depending on its size. An assistant supervisor would be responsible for small, and supervisors for medium-sized, exchanges; the latter grade also train juniors or act as 'travelling' supervisors. The two top tiers are confined to the largest units; a senior chief supervisor, for instance, controls the Trunk Exchange in London employing several thousand staff. Both rank-and-file and senior personnel working at the International and Continental Exchanges qualify for foreign language allowances.

The Counter and Writing Grades

TABLE 47

POST OFFICE

COUNTER AND WRITING GRADES[1]
(Men, London)

	Salary Scale as from			
	1 *June* 1946	1 *Oct.* 1947	4 *June* 1949	1 *Jan.* 1951*
	s. p.w.	*s. p.w.*	*s. p.w.*	*s. p.w.*
Postal and telegraph officer				
Age 16	46/0	51/0	53/0	57/0
17	52/0	57/0	59/0	63/0
18	58/0	63/0	66/0	70/0
19	65/0	70/0	73/0	77/0
20	75/0	80/0	83/0	97/0
21	85/0	96/0	102/0	110/0
22	89/0	101/0	107/0	116/0
23	93/0	106/0	112/0	123/0
24	97/0	111/0	117/0	130/0
25[2] and over	104/0	116/0	122/0	137/0
	×6/0–110/0	×6/0–158/0	×6/0–164/0	×7/0–172/0
	×5/0–150/0			

	1 *June* 1946	1 *Oct.* 1947	1 *July* 1950	1 *April* 1951*
	£ *p.a.*	£. *p.a.*	£ *p.a*	£. *p.a.*
Overseer	450×20–550	470×20–550	480×20–580	500×20–600
Assistant superintendent	580×25–680		610×25–710	630×25–730
Superintendent	725×25–800		755×25–830	775×25–850
Chief superintendent[3]	—	—	—	875×25–950

[1] The table includes the grades of superintendent and chief superintendent as a matter of convenience; they are not confined to the counter and writing hierarchy.

[2] The highest age-pay point before 1 October 1947 was 24.

[3] The London scale in this case (effective from 1 June 1951) is purely notional, no chief superintendents being employed in the metropolis. There were no such scales for the earlier period.

* All scales were increased as from 1 January 1952 and 1 January 1953, and have been further revised since.

Postal and telegraph officers—not to be confused with telegraphists —are one of the new categories emerging from the 1946 reorganization. The majority are recruited from other postal grades; the remainder enter through open competitions, the standard of the papers approximating to that of an 'O' level pass of the General Certificate of Education. Apart from counter duties, P & TOs perform many of the behind-the-scene chores connected with the running of post offices. There are a number of supervision allowances—at the rate of 12*s*. 6*d*. a week during 1947–51—while a handful of staff in London then likewise qualified for a language addition.

Overseers constitute the first supervisory tier; they carry out some of the more important writing work or act as accountants and cashiers. For these and similar tasks they may receive special payment—£50 per annum in the period under review. Assistant superintendents are variously engaged; at the largest offices they may be in charge of the counter during peak business hours; at others they serve as accountants and some again receive an allowance over and above their basic scale. As for superintendent posts, eligibility for these is shared with the telegraph and postal hierarchies, so that at this point these three structures converge.[1] However, in 1951 there were only about a dozen such appointments.

The élite in the manipulative world are undoubtedly the counter and writing grades. In the period under review, the P & TO—on reaching his maximum—could rub shoulders with the lowest level of supervisor in the postal, telegraph and telephone fields, while the overseer was roughly on a par with the postal inspector and the telegraph supervisor—one rung higher in their respective pyramids. The position was analogous one step further up the ladder. It is from the counter and writing group, moreover, that most vacancies for higher controlling staff are filled, even though formally these posts are open to seniors from elsewhere in the service.

The Higher Controlling Staff
The grade in overall charge of a post office depends both on the type of office and its size. In the case of a branch office, it may be anything from a postal and telegraph officer with a special allowance to an assistant superintendent. As regards sub-offices, those of the 'salaried' variety are under a postmaster or postmistress,[2] but 'scale payment' sub-offices—the great majority—are run by sub-postmasters and -mistresses, mostly in the 'grocery-cum' type of establishment.

[1] The telephone hierarchy has its own senior chief supervisor grade.
[2] There were 590 postmasters and postmistresses on 1 October 1951; they are not further considered.

Responsibility for a head post office is invariably in the hands of a head postmaster.

Sub-Postmasters

There were 22,360 sub-postmasters and -mistresses in October 1951, each in charge of a 'scale payment' sub-office, i.e. one normally carried on in the same premises as the individual's private shop. These establishments—it has been estimated that they discharge about 70 per cent of all counter business—are maintained in order to make postal facilities available where the existence of a Crown office would not be justified.[1]

The employment of sub-postmasters is on an agency basis. They must provide postal facilities during certain specified hours, as well as the necessary accommodation and staff (other than postmen); in return, they receive an inclusive payment based on turnover. Sub-postmasters are not on the establishment of the Post Office, and do not qualify for Civil Service privileges in such matters as sick pay or pensions.[2] They accept full financial responsibility, but can do as much or as little of the work personally as they please. Similarly, if they employ assistants, they can—subject to complying with the Fair Wages Resolution of the House of Commons—engage them on whatever terms they choose.

The present method of remunerating sub-postmasters was introduced in 1908, though the agency system as such is of much longer standing.[3] The scheme is somewhat complex; in essence it involves paying each sub-postmaster x pence per transaction, the value of x depending both on type of operation and size of sub-office. Each of the main transactions has a 'unit value' assigned to it according to average amount of time required; the units are then converted into a cash equivalent, their value decreasing, the larger the office. Thus on the basis of 1951 unit credits and money tables, the issue of a postal draft earned the sub-postmaster up to $3\frac{1}{2}d$. apiece while a savings bank transaction was worth up to $8 \cdot 4d$., though the actual amount was considerably less in the larger sub-offices. A few items are paid for on a simple cash basis, while remuneration for any telephone exchange work is calculated separately.

This system produced, in 1951, the following gross incomes, out of which the sub-postmaster had to meet his various expenses. A minimum payment of £100 a year was then being made in all cases:

---

[1] cf. Civil Service Arbitration Tribunal Award No. 205 (HMSO 1953).
[2] Gratuities on retirement may be paid under certain conditions.
[3] cf. 27 May 1949, HC Deb. 465, 1698.

No. of sub-postmasters/ -mistresses	Pay range as at 31 December 1951 £ p.a. (gross)[1]
8,116	– 200
5,443	200– 400
3,081	400– 600
2,125	600– 800
1,518	800–1,000
965	1,000–1,200
946	Over 1,200
22,194	

[1] These figures were submitted to the Civil Service Arbitration Tribunal in November 1952; they were compiled by the staff representatives but regarded as substantially correct by the official side. There have been a number of revisions since.

The question of sub-postmasters' remuneration has been frequently raised in the House of Commons—more than that of any other grade of postal employee. On one occasion an ardent champion of their cause asked the Postmaster-General whether he was aware that, owing to the long hours and low pay in the telegraphic sub-offices, these were rapidly becoming known as sweat shops; another MP—pointing out that there were some 3,000 postmasters receiving less than £3 a week—enquired whether it was fair to expect people to act as maids of all work 'in return for this miserably inadequate remuneration'.[1] The official reply has usually been that there were no out-of-the-ordinary recruitment difficulties; that pay scales were the outcome of collective bargaining in the normal way, and that it was never intended—and this appears sometimes to be forgotten—that a sub-postmastership should be an individual's sole means of livelihood.[2]

A somewhat similar system of remuneration is in existence for several hundred *caretaker operators* in respect of telephone work. This, again, is performed on a part-time agency basis, and the scale payment in 1951 ranged from 65*s*. a week for 1,830 units of telephone work to 203*s*. for 24,085 units. The reader will no doubt be glad to know that each intervening point—at intervals of 1*s*.—was related to an intermediate number of 'telephone work units'.

Assistant and Head Postmasters

The management and higher supervision of each head post office is

[1] 24 January 1951, HC Deb. 483, 129; and 30 July 1952, HC Deb. 504, 1476–7.
[2] cf. 27 May 1949, HC Deb. 465, 1698; and HC Deb. 504, loc. cit.

vested in (end-1951) 456 head postmasters, with an equal number of assistants as their deputies. The latter as a species are the product of post-war reorganization. The head postmaster is responsible to the regional director for all aspects of postal and telegraph business in his area, and is also in charge of the recruitment, payment of wages and disciplinary oversight of the telephone operating staff. Assistants and heads are not employed in London, where a rather different set-up obtains. As for the salaries shown on Table 48, allocation to the various grades was normally determined by size of office: Only Birmingham, Glasgow, Liverpool and Manchester were in the top class in the period under review.

TABLE 48

POST OFFICE

ASSISTANT AND HEAD POSTMASTERS
(Men, Provinces)

	Salary Scale as from		
Assistant	1 *April* 1946	1 *July* 1950	1 *May* 1951*
postmaster	£ *p.a.*	£ *p.a.*	£ *p.a.*
Class			
VII	$400^1 \times 15-$ 460	$430 \times 15-$ 490	(^{2})
VI	$460 \times 20-$ 520	$490 \times 20-$ 550	$540 \times 20-$ 600
V	$520 \times 20-$ 580	$550 \times 20-$ 610	$600 \times 20-$ 660
IV	$580 \times 20-$ 650	$610 \times 20-$ 680	$660 \times 20-$ 730
III	$650 \times 25-$ 725	$680 \times 25-$ 755	$730 \times 25-$ 805
II	$725 \times 25-$ 800	$755 \times 25-$ 830	$805 \times 25-$ 880
I	$800 \times 25-$ 875	$830 \times 25-$ 905	$880 \times 25-$ 955
B	$875 \times 25-$ 950	$905 \times 25-$ 980	$955 \times 25-1,030$
A	$930 \times 30-1,020$	$960 \times 30-1,050$	$1,010 \times 30-1,100$
Head	1 *June* 1946	1 *November* 1950	1 *June* 1951*
postmaster	£ *p.a.*	£ *p.a.*	£ *p.a.*
Class			
VII	$520 \times 20-$ 580	$560 \times 25-$ 625	(^{2})
VI	$560 \times 20-$ 620	$605 \times 20-$ 645	$655 \times 20-$ 695
		$\times 25-$ 670	$\times 25-$ 720
V	$620 \times 25-$ 720	$670 \times 25-$ 745	$720 \times 25-$ 795
		$\times 30-$ 775	$\times 30-$ 825
IV	$740 \times 25-$ 840	$790 \times 30-$ 910	$830 \times 30-$ 950
III	$840 \times 25-$ 940	$890 \times 30-1,010$	$925 \times 30-1,045$
II	$950 \times 30-1,050$	$1,020 \times 40-1,130$	$1,050 \times 40-1,160$
I	$1,020 \times 30$ 1,100	$1,125 \times 40-1,200$	
B	$1,150 \times 30-1,250$	$1,265 \times 50-1,375$	
A	1,350 $-1,450^3$	$1,500 \times 75-1,650^4$	

^{1} Increased to £420 as from 1 October 1947.
^{2} Salary class VII was merged into class VI as from 1 November 1951.
^{3} Maximum reached after three years.
^{4} Operative from 1 October 1950.

* All scales were increased as from 1 January 1952 and have been further revised since.

Of the ten *regional directors* in overall control of the regions, three received (1951) £2,500, six qualified for £2,075 and one had a salary of £1,675 per annum. The two latter figures attracted pay addition as from January 1952. The permanent administrative head of the Post Office, the Director General, has the rank and income of a permanent secretary of a Government department; at the political apex of the pyramid is the Postmaster General who is—and gets the remuneration of—a Minister of the Crown.

The 1951 standards of the 56 *telephone managers*—each in charge of a Telephone Area—ranged from £1,250 per annum payable to more than half, to £1,550 for the chief of the London Centre Area. Deputy managers—employed only in the largest units—received £1,250. These rates were awarded by the Civil Service Arbitration Tribunal in September 1952, but applied retrospectively from the beginning of 1951.[1]

The Engineering Department
As on the manipulative side, a major reorganization of the engineering staff structure took place in 1946. The manual grades—the great bulk—comprise labourers, technician classes IIb, IIa and I, and technical officers; all these are regarded as 'rank-and-file'. The supervisory level begins with the next rung—inspectors and assistant engineers—though whether these are to be considered as a class of their own, or merely as separate tiers in one including both them and the manual workers, is a point on which the official and staff sides have had some differences of view.[2] Inspectors and assistant engineers overlap to some extent; broadly speaking, the former supervise external construction, subscribers' installation and maintenance work; the latter perform the internal and more technical jobs and at the same time keep an eye on inspectors.

Assistant engineers normally work under the direction of executive engineers, who constitute the basic professional grade. The latter and those above form a 'linked departmental' class, salaries being the same as for the general (Treasury) class of mechanical and electrical engineers, employed in other Government departments. The pay of these professional postal engineers thus moves in line with that of their Civil Service colleagues rather than by reference to events in the Post Office'[3]

---

[1] Civil Service Arbitration Tribunal Award No. 188 (HMSO 1952). Pay addition accrued as from 1 January 1952, and there have been further revisions since.
[2] cf. Civil Service Arbitration Tribunal Award No. 122 (HMSO 1950).
[3] The Engineering Department also employs a number of other (much smaller) categories, such as the submarine cable and motor transport grades.

The Post Office 205

TABLE 49

POST OFFICE

ENGINEERING SUPERVISING GRADES
(Men, London)

	Salary Scale as from		
	1 *August* 1946 £ *p.a.*	1 *July* 1950 £ *p.a.*	1 *June* 1951* £ *p.a.*
Inspector	375 × 15–470	405 × 20–540	440 × 20–560
Assistant engineer[1]	280 × 20–580	315 × 20–415 × 25–680	340 × 20–440 × 25–680

[1] Since 1 September 1949 the minimum has been linked to age 18–20, with age-pay up to 25.

* All scales were increased as from 1 January 1952 and have been further revised since.

Provincial Differentiation

The domain of the General Post Office is Great Britain and Northern Ireland, but here again salaries are differentiated according to location. The actual classification for this purpose has been adjusted on several occasions: Immediately prior to June 1946 there were five sets of rates for the majority of manipulative staffs, but in that month a four-tier system was instituted, hand in hand with which a number of post offices were upgraded. This four-fold classification was, in turn, abolished in June 1951, when the Civil Service three-tier scheme was extended to all Post Office manipulatives[1] and their supervisors.[2] However, as we saw in Chapter 1, the Civil Service system itself underwent radical changes in the late 'fifties,[3] and these equally affected the manipulatives. The Post Office Engineering Department, we may add, has been spared these various convolutions, having had a simple two-tier pattern throughout the post-war period.

Sex Differentiation

Of the total of 335,166 Post Office employees on 1 October 1951, 91,982 were women. Most of the categories reviewed have their female counterparts, though the two sexes' duties are not necessarily identical. Women are not eligible for established posts in the postal field, though there are auxiliary postwomen (part-time) and tem-

[1] For the majority of manipulative rank-and-file grades the end-1951 deductions were 3s. p.w. off the London rate in 'intermediate' and 6s. off that standard in 'provincial' areas. For postal and telegraph officers (21 years and over) the deductions were 4s. and 8s.
[2] Head and assistant postmasters were assimilated to these arrangements during 1953–4.　　[3] cf. p. 57 *ante*.

porary postwomen (full-time but unestablished). The Engineering Department, likewise, is almost exclusively 'male'. There is a fair proportion of female first- and second-line supervisors, and women manage almost two-fifths of the 'grocery-cum' type of establishment. However, none are to be found at the highest levels.

As regards salaries, the general principle governing sex differentiation in the Civil Service has applied equally in the Post Office; the norm has been for women's maxima to constitute 80 per cent of the comparable male standard, though the 4:5 ratio was not strictly adhered to in all cases.[1] The only category to enjoy undifferentiated remuneration were sub-postmistresses:[2] for some odd reason the authorities failed to reward them at 80 per cent of $3\frac{1}{2}d.$ for issuing a postal draft.[3] Meanwhile, however, equal pay has been extended to the Post Office via the relevant agreement covering the whole non-industrial Civil Service.

[1] Also, in parallel recruitment grades such as P & TOs and telegraphists, salaries for boys and girls were the same up to age 19.
[2] And the small analogous category of (telephone) caretaker operators.
[3] 1951 'scale payment' in the smallest type of sub-office: see p. 201.

Chapter 12

THE BRITISH BROADCASTING CORPORATION

Broadcasting—alike of sound and vision—is regulated in Britain under powers conferred on the Postmaster General by the Wireless Telegraph Acts. The first licence in 1922 was granted to a private concern, but in 1926 the latter was replaced by the British Broadcasting Corporation, charged with the duty of carrying on the new medium as a public service.[1] The conditions under which the Corporation operates are prescribed both in a Charter and in a 'Licence and Agreement': While the formal power of the Government over the BBC is extensive, it has become agreed policy that the Corporation should, in peace-time, have complete independence in the day-to-day conduct of its affairs.[2] However, the Overseas Service—which is not financed from licence revenue but by a direct parliamentary grant-in-aid—is in a special category.

Under the current Charter—granted in 1952 for a period of ten years—the BBC consists of nine Governors, including the chairman, vice-chairman and national Governors for Scotland, Wales and Northern Ireland. They serve for a limited number of years. The executive head of the Corporation is the director-general, supported by a number of directors; actual responsibility for the running of services devolves on controllers and through them to heads of departments, producers, technicians and administrative staff. For broadcasting purposes the United Kingdom is divided into seven areas: London and the Home Counties—covered from headquarters—and six regions.

BBC Personnel and Negotiating Machinery

BBC personnel can be divided into 'staff' and 'performers'. The former term embraces full-time workers responsible for planning, directing and servicing the programmes—whether remunerated by

---

[1] cf. Preamble of original Charter of Incorporation, Cmd. 2756 (HMSO 1926) and current Charter, Cmd. 8605 (HMSO 1952). See s. 3 of latter for Corporation's objects in full.

[2] cf. *Memorandum on the Report of the Broadcasting Committee*, 1949, Cmd. 8291 (HMSO 1951), para. 8.

salary or wage. The 'performers', on the other hand, are not (for the most part) employees in the ordinary sense; they are the artists and speakers, large numbers of whom are engaged on an *ad hoc* basis and paid 'by the piece'. However, the distinction is not absolute; announcers, for example, perform at the microphone as part of their staff duties. Conversely, performers include a category known as 'programme contract staff', comprising the members of the BBC's standing orchestras, choirs and repertory companies, as well as individuals such as scriptwriters: All these, like 'staff', receive regular salaries.

Article 15 of the current Charter—there was a similar clause in the 1946 but not in the earlier documents—makes it incumbent upon the BBC to conclude agreements with appropriate organizations providing for (a) the negotiation of terms and conditions of service, and (b) the discussion of matters affecting safety, health and welfare, and other items of mutual interest. As far as staff is concerned, the Corporation used to give sole recognition for these purposes to the BBC Staff Association—now known as the Association of Broadcasting Staff—membership of which is open to all except performers. This exclusiveness on the part of the BBC attracted a great deal of criticism;[1] however, following the recommendations of the 1949 Broadcasting Committee, recognition has meanwhile been extended to other unions.[2] In the case of performers, we may add, negotiations have always been conducted with outside associations.

Staff[3]

BBC staff by type of work as at 31 *March* 1951	
Programme and editorial	1,562
Secretarial and clerical	3,763
Engineering: technical	2,444
Engineering: manual	937
Other manual	1,788
Catering	432
Administration and services	1,487
	12,413

[1] cf. *Report of the Broadcasting Committee* 1949 (Chairman: Lord Beveridge). Cmd. 8116 (HMSO 1951), paras. 468–9. See also 26 May 1950, HC Deb. 475, 2470–90—one of the many occasions on which the matter was raised in Parliament.

[2] The first outside unions—the National Union of Journalists and the Electrical Trades Union—were given recognition in 1955.

[3] i.e. excluding 'performers'.

The total number of staff employed by the Corporation on 31 March 1951 was 12,413, of whom 7,450 were established and 4,963 temporary; some 150 were serving outside the British Isles.[1] They were composed of the foregoing groups.

An alternative classification—particularly relevant to the question of remuneration—is given below:

Weekly-paid clerical staff	3,763
Monthly-paid staff	4,647
Weekly-paid manual staff	4,003
	12,413

Apart from its obligation to appoint a director-general, the BBC is free to employ whomever it considers necessary for the discharge of its functions, though it must afford to the three National Broadcasting Councils the services of any staff these may require.[2] Admission to established posts is subject—apart from conditions as to age, nationality and physical fitness—to a qualifying period of two years. In filling vacancies the Corporation's policy is to advance those already in the service; though the need for 'new blood' is not overlooked, preference is given at every point to internal promotion.

Clerical Staff

TABLE 50

BRITISH BROADCASTING CORPORATION
CLERICAL STAFF
(Men and Women, UK)

*Salaries as from 30 July 1951**

Grade	DW	C2W	CW	B2W	BW	A2W	AW	AW Special
Age entry points:	*s. pw*	*s. pw*	*s. pw*	*s. pw*	*s. pw*	*s. pw*	*s. pw*	*s. pw*
Age 16 & under	63/0	75/0						
Age 17	69/0	82/6	97/6					
Age 18	75/0	90/0	105/0					
Increment	5/0	5/0	5/0	5/0	5/0	5/6	6/0	7/6
Merit entry points:								
Normal	80/0	95/0	110/0	125/0	140/0	148/0	156/0	170/0
Plus	85/0	100/0	115/0	130/0	145/0	153/6	162/0	177/6
Roof	100/0	115/0	130/0	145/0	160/0	170/0	180/0	200/0

* These salaries were increased by 10 per cent as from 1 November 1953, and have been further revised since.

[1] These and other statistics given were made available by courtesy of the Corporation.

[2] Cmd. 8605, op. cit. s. 14 and s. 12(9) and (10). The Councils themselves select such personnel, though the Corporation is their legal employer.

The 1951 salaries for clerical staff are set out on Table 50. To give some examples of grading, DW related to trainees only, C2W covered those on elementary jobs such as straightforward copy-typing, while CW applied *inter alia* to telephonists and shorthand-typists. BW was the first of the senior grades and comprised those whose work required some specific training—say, bookkeeping or cataloguing. The duties of A2W included certain executive-type functions, in some cases involving substantial contact work outside the Corporation: Most secretaries to heads of departments were in this class. AW Special was very special indeed, while some top-level secretaries were outside the 'weekly' range altogether.

As shown by the table, the 1951 recruit to the BBC's clerical establishment was paid according to age if a candidate for one of the three bottom grades, though only if 18 years old or under. In all other instances, entry was at the 'normal' or 'plus' point, depending on qualifications and experience. This pattern was introduced at end-1948; previous to that, there was a much greater degree of age-linkage which, under post-war conditions, often meant that remuneration was insufficient to attract younger workers.[1]

Monthly-paid Staff

Among the monthly-paid staff are all the Corporation's more senior employees, including engineering and administrative as well as programme and editorial personnel. To all these a common system of grading is applied, the BBC having its own system of job evaluation by means of which it equates the remuneration of the various categories.

Monthly-paid staff as at 31 *March* 1951[2]

Grade D	1,078
„ C	1,175
„ B1	1,453
„ B	616
„ A1	185
„ A2	76
„ A3	20
„ A+	44
	4,647

[1] Until 1950 also—when revised salaries were introduced—there was a further grade below DW, and as yet no AW Special.

[2] Data made available by courtesy of Corporation. The numbers against each main grade include those in the related 'minus' grade (see *post*).

In September 1948 the minima of all monthly salaries were consolidated, but there was then no rise at the maximum; in October 1950, however, very considerable improvements were granted. These standards, in turn, were superseded by those set out on Table 51, which again represented a substantial advance.

TABLE 51

BRITISH BROADCASTING CORPORATION
MONTHLY GRADES
(Editorial, Programme, Engineering, Administrative, etc.)
(Men and Women, UK)

Salaries (p.a.) as from 1 *December* 1951*

Grade	D	C−	C	B1−	B1	B−	B	A1−	A1	A2−	A2
	£	£	£	£	£	£	£	£	£	£	£
Entry points:[1]											
Normal	415	500	590	695	795	900	1,000	1,125	1,255	1,380	1,485
Plus	445	535	630	740	845	955	1,060	1,190	1,325	1,455	1,570
Top	475	570	670	785	895	1,010	1,120	1,255	1,395	1,530	1,655
Efficiency line	505	605	710	830	945	1,065	1,180	1,320	1,465	1,605	1,740
	540	645	755	880	1,005	1,130	1,255	1,400	1,550	1,695	1,840
Roof	575	685	800	930	1,065	1,195	1,330	1,480	1,635	1,785	1,940
Special	605	720	840	975	1,115	1,250	1,390	1,545	1,705	1,860	2,025
awards	635	755	880	1,020	1,165	1,305	1,450	1,610	1,775	1,935	2,110

[1] 'Top' and 'plus' entry points were not applicable above A1−.

* These salaries were increased by 10 per cent as from 1 November 1953, and have been further revised since.

Here also the commencing salary used to be linked to age, with age pay from about 23/24 to 33/34. The normal/plus/top system of entry shown on Table 51 was adopted in 1948; it meant that henceforth a candidate with special qualifications could embark upon his BBC career above the minimum. It will be seen that the 1951 scales were quite short: those joining at the 'normal' point reached the 'roof' after five years' service, subject to their passing the 'efficiency line'.[1] The 'special awards' were simply a case of giving an employee one or two further increments over and above his normal 'roof'; in exceptional circumstances a 'personal grade' could be granted, i.e. above 'special award' level. On the other hand, there were the 'minus' grades: While posts were generally allocated to the main tiers— D, C, B1 and so on—particular jobs might be assessed at an intermediate point and placed in the appropriate 'minus' category. On the whole, the BBC pay pattern in the period under review gave the

[1] Here as elsewhere, the terms used are those employed in the original agreement/document.

Corporation considerable flexibility in determining an individual's precise reward, and enabled it to weight personal qualifications both over and above and 'under and below' those normal for the post in question. We may add that, apart from the discretionary element built into the scale structures themselves, there was also a system of non-recurring bonuses, which could be conferred for work of outstanding merit, long service and so on.

A word now about the concrete application of the scheme. Grade D included English monitors and booking assistants in the programme contracts department; examples of C posts are make-up supervisors, studio managers (sound) and clerks of works (building). B1 comprised announcers, sub-editors in the news division and producers (sound); on the engineering side it covered senior control room engineers (London), and in the administrative sphere the head of the secretarial training school. In Grade B were news-readers, reporters, as well as producers in the television service.

The A categories represented only a small proportion of the Corporation's staff. In A1 were to be found the BBC's parliamentary correspondents; A2 included the head of school broadcasting and of the General Overseas Service. There were two tiers above this level—A3 and A+, the former covering (*inter alia*) the heads of news output, TV films and of the drama department. It is the programme head who is responsible for the character, compilation and presentation of each programme; his functions have been described as analogous to those of a newspaper editor.

A+ was an omnibus grade and the niche for all the top-rank officials of the Corporation. The directors, the regional, and the programme controllers were in this category; so were the BBC's solicitor, chief engineer and controller of finance. Details of remuneration are not known, being fixed individually by the Governors; *average* pay of those in A+ on 31 March 1950 was £2,773 per annum.[1] The 1949 Broadcasting Committee concluded that the desire of the Governors not to make these figures public property was justified: In filling an important post the Corporation might want to adjust remuneration downwards on making an experimental appointment, or upwards to make certain of getting some proved man; such flexibility would be difficult if the salary earned by the previous holder had been published.[2]

The 1951 figures set out on Tables 50 and 51 remained in operation until November 1953, when the BBC announced that the majority of monthly and all weekly-paid secretarial and clerical staff were to receive a rise of 10 per cent. The statement added that the effect of the

---

[1] Particulars for a later year are not available.

[2] *Report*, op. cit., para. 449.

increases would be to bring Corporation standards once again into proper relationship with those of comparable employers elsewhere, who had granted substantial improvements since 1951.

This brings us to our next point. The BBC has stated that it sets out to ensure that salaries are equitably assessed in relation both to internal responsibilities and to comparable rates of remuneration in force outside.[1] As far as internal relativities are concerned, these were given—in its evidence to the 1949 Broadcasting Committee—as the main reason why the Corporation preferred to negotiate with the Staff Association alone: 'The BBC is far better able to do justice to the various grades of its staff relative to one another by negotiating with a staff association than it could by dealing with a widening field of individual unions whose criterion would be rates and conditions in industries other than broadcasting.'[2] At the same time the BBC has declared it to be a fundamental principle that it should act as a good employer. 'In fixing its standards the Corporation has due regard to the salaries paid by the Civil Service, nationalized industries and other public organizations, and to those prevailing in professions such as teaching, journalism, the theatre, music, etc.'[3]

Insofar as the BBC has taken account of external relativities, it has done so voluntarily—with one important exception. In renewing the Charter and Licence in 1946, the then Government stated that the Corporation had been informed that, while it was not rigidly bound to relate the salaries and conditions of its permanent staff to those ruling in the Civil Service, it should 'pay proper regard to those of the Civil Service and to the greater security offered by employment in a Public Corporation, as compared with employment in most business concerns'.[4]

In its evidence to the 1949 Broadcasting Committee, the BBC made clear that 'in general terms the Corporation has adopted the policy laid down in the White Paper'.[5] However, it asked to be relieved from the obligation, feeling strongly that the requirement did not accord with official policy as laid down by the Lord President of the Council in the Commons in 1946,[6] when he said that the appointment and remuneration of the staff of the socialized Boards were functions of management, and that the Boards should have the same freedom and privacy in this respect as any other commercial undertaking. The Treasury comment on this was that the parallel drawn

[1] Report of the Broadcasting Committee 1949, *Appendix H: Memoranda Submitted to the Committee*, Cmd. 8117 (HMSO 1951), p. 113.

[2] ibid. p. 100. See also Cmd. 8116, op. cit., para. 472.

[3] *Appendix H*, op. cit., p. 113.

[4] Cmd. 8116, op. cit., para. 446.

[5] *Appendix H*, op. cit., p. 92.

[6] In point of fact, 1947; see 12 June 1947, HC Deb. 438, 1329–31.

between the socialized boards and 'any other commercial undertaking' could hardly be taken as applying automatically to the BBC;
more stringent control of salaries was applied to non-trading than to
trading bodies, and it seemed reasonable that the Corporation should
occupy an intermediate position. The White Paper policy represented
'a very suitable balance between too detailed control on the one hand
and too great a departure on the other from the conditions of employment which apply over the main field of the public service'.[1]

The 1949 Committee, however, sided with the BBC and recommended that it be freed from the White Paper requirement.[2] The first
Government Memorandum on the Committee's Report (July 1951)
accordingly declared that the Government would not wish to repeat
their ruling of 1946, 'nor, in fact, have they sought to impose a rigid
control in these matters under the existing obligation'. Nonetheless,
it was important that the Corporation should consult the Government freely on wages policy and kindred matters, and take account
of the general policy which the Government might from time to time
be pursuing.[3] The second Memorandum on the Committee's Report
—issued after the change of Government in May 1952—stated simply
that 'in fixing the salaries and conditions of the staff the BBC should
take account of the Government's general policy on wages and
kindred matters';[4] the Corporation then is still not an altogether free
agent in determining its levels of reward, even though no longer required to model these on Whitehall standards. We may add that the
Charter itself has been silent on the subject throughout: The phrase
in the current, as in the 1946, document is simply that the Corporation shall fix such rates of remuneration as it shall consider proper.[5]

The 'Performers': Standing Orchestras, etc.

The great majority of performers are engaged by the BBC *ad hoc*
and paid on a fee basis; we are here concerned only with the relatively
small group of salaried artists.

Minimum rates for the 450 or so musicians belonging to the
BBC's standing orchestras are fixed by negotiation with the Musicians' Union. For full-time rank-and-file members of the Variety,
Revue, Midland Light, Northern, Scottish and Welsh Orchestras, the
1946 minimum—not revised until 1953—was £13 a week; for principals[6] it was £15. In the Concert Orchestra the salary was £14 for the

---

[1] *Appendix H*, op. cit., p. 271.   [2] Cmd. 8116, op. cit., paras. 447–8.
[3] Cmd. 8291 (HMSO 1951), para. 45.   [4] Cmd. 8550 (HMSO 1952), para. 37.
[5] cf. Cmd. 8605, op. cit., s. 14(3) and Cmd. 6974 (HMSO 1946), s. 7.
[6] Out of 446 musicians in BBC standing orchestras at the beginning of 1953,
198 (44 per cent) were principals.

rank-and-file, £15.10.0[1] for sub-principals and £17[1] for principals. In the BBC Symphony Orchestra the rank-and-file received £15, but the remuneration of principals and sub-principals was here settled individually with each player. The standards quoted related to working hours of 144 per four-weekly period, and they applied to broadcasting in both sound and television; where the artist was required to appear in the TV picture, he was entitled to a further payment 'per appearance'. Musicians usually earned additional fees for overtime, for 'repeat' broadcasts as well as in respect of private coaching; on the other hand, they had to provide their own instruments.

A claim by the Musicians' Union that the 1946 rates should be increased by one-third was referred to the Industrial Court in 1953.[2] The Union contended that a post in one of the BBC orchestras—as in one of the outside symphony, opera or ballet orchestras—was among the highest to which musicians (other than those in the world of dance music) could aspire; the twelve or thirteen hundred serving in these were the cream of the profession in the country. If the few hundred practitioners who had climbed to the top in other fields were to be remunerated at an analogous level, there would be general agreement that they were being inadequately paid. The Corporation maintained that the existing minima were already appreciably higher than those applicable in comparable combinations: The rank-and-file rate for the Hallé, Liverpool Philharmonic, London Philharmonic and Scottish National Orchestras, for instance, awarded by the Industrial Court a few months previously, was £11.10.0.[3] The Court ruled that the then BBC salaries for full-time musicians should be increased by £2 as from the end of February 1953; hours were to be reduced from 144 to 132 per four-weekly period.[4]

The remuneration of the BBC's *Opera Chorus*, consisting of 28 artists, was raised by the Industrial Court to £11 per week as from 12 March 1951.[5] There were here no grade distinctions. As regards the actors and actresses forming the BBC *Repertory Company*, there was, at the time of writing, no salary or minimum rate agreement, pay being negotiated with each individual according to his professional status and 'market value'.

---

[1] In this case the figure includes increases subsequent to April 1946.

[2] Industrial Court Award No. 2435 (HMSO 1953).

[3] This figure related to a considerably shorter week, however, and certain supplements were payable in some cases. The Award referred to is No. 2421 (Musicians' Union and Orchestral Employers' Association, HMSO 1952).

[4] The Court found against the claim of the Union that television should be regarded as a field of employment separate from sound broadcasting; members of BBC orchestras therefore continue to be required to perform for both media.

[5] Industrial Court Award No. 2356 (HMSO 1952).

Provincial and Sex Differentiation

In the period under review, rates of pay and service conditions in the regions were the same as those in London; there was no system of area differentiation. This, however, was not always true of performers' contracts. Staff are normally liable to serve in any part of the United Kingdom and to travel abroad as necessary.

Of the 12,413 BBC employees at end-March 1951, 5,306—about 43 per cent—were women. The majority were secretaries and clerical and administrative assistants, though there was a small number of women producers, sub-editors, script writers and so on. No discrimination in salaries has here been made either for staff or performers, with the sole exception of catering workers whose remuneration is related to that laid down by the Catering Wages Councils (formerly Boards) on a national basis.

Chapter 13

THE COAL INDUSTRY

Coal was the first major industry to be brought under central ownership in the post-war period, the Coal Industry Nationalization Act[1]
being passed in 1946. It set up a National Coal Board, whose duties
have been summarized as the working and getting of the coal of
Great Britain and the efficient development of the industry in the
public interest. On 1 January 1947 it took over the assets of some
eight hundred colliery companies, with the industry thereby formally
transferred to public auspices.

While the National Board alone has overall responsibility, its
chief executive agents are the Divisional Boards. These in turn delegate a far-reaching measure of control to the Areas, which are the
main organs of business management. Each Area was originally put
in direct charge of a cluster of collieries—the basic operational units
for production—though an intermediate level, the Group, was created in 1955 between Area and colliery. There were nine Divisions,
49 Areas and 896 collieries functioning under the NCB at end-1951.
The average (standardized) number of wage-earners was then
698,600, and there were 40,400 non-industrial staff, including clerical
and administrative grades, engineers and specialists of all kinds, as
well as colliery managers and other production personnel.[2]

When the mines were taken over, the National Board became the
employer of all but a few of the former colliery companies' staff.
'They were drawn from hundreds of companies, large and small,
prosperous and unprofitable, progressive and backward, and they
were serving on hundreds of sets of conditions.' In many cases
emoluments were partly in kind in the form of perquisites; a few
participated directly in the profits of their concern or drew bonuses
when the latter had a good year's trading. There were the widest
variations in remuneration for similar jobs,[3] so that the Board had a
task of some magnitude on hand.

[1] 9 & 10 Geo. 6. c. 59. For a discussion of personnel problems (including
salaries) in some pre-war public corporations see W. A. Robson, ed., *The British
Civil Servant* (Allen & Unwin, 1937) p. 127 and ff.
[2] National Coal Board, *Report and Accounts for* 1951 (HMSO 1952), p. 189 and
para. 354.
[3] ibid. para. 326 and National Coal Board, *Annual Report and Statement o,
Accounts for the Year ended* 31 *December* 1947 (HMSO 1948), para. 112.

Clerical and Junior Administrative Staff
The clerical and junior administrative group is easily the largest sector of non-manual staff employed by the Coal Board: There were 25,877 such workers on 31 December 1951 at or below divisional level; another 1,026 were serving at London headquarters and head-quarters-controlled out-stations. The first agreement—identical documents were signed with the National Union of Mineworkers and the Clerical and Administrative Workers' Union—was concluded in February 1948, though applied with retrospective effect from 1 July 1947.

After some hard bargaining, an appeal to the industry's National Reference Tribunal and some sporadic strikes, a new scheme was introduced in August 1951, providing for both changes in the grade structure and enhanced pay. It divided clerical personnel into 'indoor' and 'outdoor', and covered all such (full-time) staff at divisional offices and below—unlike the earlier agreement which formally only related to those at and below Area level. The indoor categories comprised typists, machine operators as well as clerks proper; among the outdoor grades were wagon, truck or tub-weighmen, colliery store-keepers, outdoor landsale clerks and any others that might be agreed upon. The majority of clerical employees are at collieries and Area offices; the rates are set out on Table 52.

The 1951 agreement was designed to make the clerical structure more flexible. Under the earlier system a grade II clerk was remunerated according to age until 27 years old, at which point he also reached his maximum; under the 1951 scheme age pay, in the case of indoor workers, ceased at 21, the scale having been lengthened at the same time. As regards typists and machine operators, similarly, the 1951 document conferred a certain discretion on the Divisions, in that it enabled them to decide on the extent to which the minima prescribed in the agreement were to be exceeded—a latitude which they had not previously possessed. As for the three clerical officer grades shown on the table, though these formally belonged to the indoor hierarchy, the rates could be applied to any outdoor staff deemed to deserve such a classification.

Management Staff
Management staff in the coal industry had no trade union prior to nationalization. Initially, therefore, the Coal Board had to devise national rates single-handed, standard salaries being introduced for mining, finance, scientific, legal and administrative workers in 1947 and for marketing, labour and welfare personnel in 1948. Since then the British Association of Colliery Management (BACM) has been formed and become recognized as representing most managerial and

professional employees from colliery undermanager upwards; the earlier figures have therefore been mostly superseded by formal agreements with BACM.[1]

[1] In a few cases other unions are also parties to the agreements.

TABLE 52
COAL INDUSTRY
CLERICAL AND JUNIOR ADMINISTRATIVE STAFF
(Men, Great Britain: Divisional[1] level and below)

Salary Scale as from 1 July 1947		*Salary Scale as from* 24 August 1951*			
		Indoor Clerical Staff		*Outdoor Clerical Staff*	
	s. p.w.		s. p.w.		s. p.w.
Clerk grade II		Clerk grade 2		Clerk grade D	
Age 15	38/6	Age 15	45/0	Age 15	45/0
16	46/0	16	53/0	16	53/0
17	56/6	17	63/0	17	63/0
18	67/0	18	75/0	18	75/0
19	77/0	19	84/0	19	84/0
20	82/6	20	90/0	20	90/0
21	100/0	21	108/0	21	108/0
22	106/0		114/0	22	114/0
23	112/0		120/0	23	120/0
24	118/0		126/0	24	126/0
25	125/0		132/0	25	132/0
27 and over	130/0		136/0	26	136/0
			140/0	27	
			145/0[2]	and over	140/0
			150/0[3]		
				Grade C	
				140/0 × 5/0 –	150/0
				Grade B	
				150/0 × 5/0 –	160/0
Clerk grade I		Clerk grade 1		Grade A	
115/6 × 6/0–157/6		124/6 × 6/0–172/6[4]		160/0 × 5/0 –	170/0
				× 2/6 –	172/6

	£ p.a.		£ p.a.
		Clerical officer	
Finance de-		Grade 3	440 × 20–540
partment,			× 10–550
grade 12	400 × 20–500		
Assistant			
staff officer	410 × 20–590	Grade 2	500 × 20–640
Finance de-			
partment,			
grade 11	500 × 20–660	Grade 1	590 × 20–710

[1] Formally, the 1947 scales applied only at and below Area level.
[2] Granted two years after reaching 140/0.
[3] Granted five years after reaching 140/0.
[4] Exceptionally, the maximum could be increased by up to 10/0 per week.

* All scales were increased as from 26 March 1952 and have been further revised since.

Finance officials: The first bilateral settlement here was concluded in August 1951, applying retrospectively as from 1st July 1950. It related to staff engaged in finance departments at headquarters, Division or Area level, though the most senior appointments were outside its province.

TABLE 53

COAL INDUSTRY
MANAGEMENT STAFF
(Men, Great Britain)[1]

Finance Officials:

Range/Scale as from 29 April 1947		Range/Scale as from 1 July 1950*	
Grade	£ p.a.	Grade	£ p.a.
j	400 × 20– 500	10A	670 × 25 – 870
i	500 × 20– 660	10	720 × 25– 970
h	675 × 25– 875	9A	795 × 25–1,070
g	900 × 25–1,150	9	995 × 35–1,295
f	1,000 × 25–1,250	8	1,045 –1,345
e	1,200 × 25–1,450	7	1,245 –1,545
d	1,250 × 40–1,650	6	1,345 –1,745
c	1,500 × 45–1,950	5	1,595 –2,095
b	1,700 –2,150		
a	2,000 –2,400		

Administrative Officials:

Salary Scale as from 28 June 1947		Range/Scale as from 1 January 1951*	
	£ p.a.		£ p.a.
Assistant staff officer	410 × 20– 590	Grade 6	660 × 25– 835
Staff officer	600 × 25– 750	Grade 5	820 × 30–1,060
Administrative assistant	375 × 25– 625	Grade 4	945 × 35–1,320
Deputy administrative officer	750 × 25– 950	Grade 3	1,195 –1,545
Administrative officer	850 × 35–1,200	Grade 2	1,545 –2,095
Assistant secretary	1,400 × 50–1,900		

[1] For additional allowance payable in London see text.

* All salaries have been increased since.

For purposes of grading various rules were laid down in the schedule to the 1951 document. At national headquarters, for instance, the chief financial and the chief cost accountant were to be in grade 5, a senior accountant in grade 7, an accountant in 9 and his deputy in grade 10. The only other personnel qualifying for the top classification were senior finance officers, though some of these received larger salaries than were provided for in the agreement. As for staff at the lower levels of organization, all Divisions and Areas were ranked by the Board, allocation varying accordingly: For example, a divisional financial or cost accountant was in grade 7 in rank I Divisions, in grade 8 in rank II, but in grade 10 in rank III Divisions. 10A posts were confined to Area offices. We may add that a somewhat different scheme was in operation in 1947. Ten tiers—j to a—then covered appointments from £400 to £2,400; it will be seen that the 1951 pattern stopped well below this level of seniority.

The first formal agreement relating to *administrative officials* came into force on 1 January 1951; the rates are set out on Table 53. Secretaries of Divisional Boards were expressly excluded from the scope of the document; their deputies were to be placed in grade 3. An Area secretary was normally, though not in all cases, in grade 4 or 3. Where no ruling was laid down, the National Board decided on the appropriate classification subject to conciliation at the request of BACM. An agreement for *marketing staff*, likewise effective from 1 January 1951, contained scales and ranges almost identical with those for administrative officials.

Production Staff

Before dealing with production staff proper—beginning with the colliery undermanager—we must refer to the category of *under-officials*, this term comprising shotfirers, deputies (who supervise operations at the coal-face), and overmen (in charge of a mine or seam or part of a mine/seam during particular shifts). At the time of nationalization, their wages and conditions of employment varied from district to district and in some instances from pit to pit; shotfirers and deputies were—like miners—paid on a shift basis. After 1947 these three grades continued to be treated as 'industrial' as far as conciliation, negotiating machinery and pensions were concerned, but in 1952—when new statutory regulations governing their qualifications and responsibilities had come into force—they were established as weekly-paid officials with a modified form of staff status. A national grade and wage structure were also introduced, the new levels being backdated to 1951. Actual rates were to be fixed by Divisions according to local circumstances. The range for deputies grade I, operative from 1 November 1951, was £14 to £16. 10. 0. a week[1] and this set the standard: Overmen received 20s.–40s. a week above, and deputies II and shotfirers 30s.–40s. below, the figure laid down in the same wages district for grade I deputies.

Immediately senior to overmen are *colliery undermanagers*, whose remuneration has always been regulated by reference to that of overmen; after the latter's pay had been settled early in 1948, it was possible for the Board and BACM to conclude a first agreement opera-

[1] Shown as £ p.a. on Table 54, to facilitate comparison.

222 **Salaries in the Public Services**

tive from 1 October 1947.[1] There was no change until July 1952, when undermanagers claimed an increase based largely on the need for maintaining a 'proper relativity' between their standards and those of their juniors. New ranges were eventually awarded by the industry's National Reference Tribunal.

TABLE 54

COAL INDUSTRY

UNDEROFFICIALS AND PRODUCTION STAFF
(Men, Great Britain)

| | Salary Range[1] as from | |
| | 1 *February* 1948 | 1951/1952* |
	£ p.a.	£ p.a.
Underofficials:		
Shotfirer	(²)	624– 780
Deputy grade II		
Deputy grade I	(²)	728– 858
Overman	(²)	780– 962
Production Staff:		
Colliery undermanager	700/800³–1,100⁴	900–1,200
Colliery manager		
(a) at collieries producing under 300 tons a day	800–1,200	950–1,250
(b) at other collieries	1,000/1,100³–1,650	1,150–1,650
Agent[5]		
(a) not directly answerable to Area production manager	1,325/1,425–2,125	1,450/1,550–2,250
(b) directly answerable to Area production manager	1,425/1,625–2,625	1,550/1,750–2,750

[1] The precise scale/rate was fixed divisionally for underofficials and at national level for the higher grades. In a number of cases the salary shown accrued subject to its exceeding that of the next lower grade by a stated amount.

[2] See text.

[3] Depending on Division.

[4] This range became operative from 1 October 1947, and in certain cases from 1 July 1947.

[5] The minimum varied with the total output of the collieries supervised.

* The rates for underofficials became operative from 1 November 1951, those for undermanagers and managers from 1 July 1952, and those for agents from 1 January 1952. All salaries have been increased since.

To *colliery managers* falls the day-to-day control and direction of the coalfields; they are responsible in law for the safety of men and mine. The first collective bargain for managers was struck in July 1951, though applied retrospectively as from February 1948: It fixed their minimum remuneration in the larger coalfields at £300 above that for undermanagers; their maximum became £1,650 per annum.

[1] In certain cases from 1 July 1947.

For smaller collieries a lower range was laid down, though with the proviso that the manager's minimum must be at least £100 in excess of that of any of his subordinates. The agreement stipulated that the position of each individual should be reviewed having regard to age, skill, experience, the size and conditions in the colliery and other relevant considerations. Salaries were revised as from 1 July 1952 —following the improvements granted lower down the hierarchy— and have been further increased since.

Overall responsibility for output at Area level lies with the Area production manager, though in the period under review one or more tiers with differing degrees of authority could be interposed between him and the colliery manager.[1] In a large Area the production department was then usually divided between a number of mining agents, who were put in charge of a group of collieries, but between agent and colliery manager there might be one or more 'sub-agent' grades. Similarly, the mining agent himself in some cases was, and in others was not, directly answerable to the Area production manager.

Salaries for *agents* ranging from £1,200 to £2,000 per annum had been promulgated by the Board in 1947, but as soon as those of colliery managers had been settled on a collective basis, similar joint discussions on those of agents began. Negotiations were protracted and the agreement eventually reached fixed standards both as from 1952 and for the period February 1948 to end-1951. For agents directly responsible to the Area production manager, the minimum— until end-1951—was £1,425, £1,525 or £1,625 a year according to the total output of the collieries supervised; maximum possible pay was £2,625. For those not directly answerable to Area headquarters, the maximum was considerably lower. These figures were augmented by £125 a year as from 1 January 1952.

The remuneration of *Area production managers* themselves is determined on a personal basis, nor was it contemplated, at the time of writing, that they would be covered by more formal arrangements. As for the *Area general manager*, this post used to be combined with that of Area production manager but, as a consequence of changes instituted in 1947, he emerged as a separate—and superior—being. Area general managers are key men in the Coal Board's organization, having sole responsibility for everything that happens in their Area. Their salaries in 1947 were up to £4,000 per annum; those of Area production managers were then up to £3,000, particulars of subsequent adjustments not being available.

---

[1] Certain changes in the grading structure have taken place since, following the establishment in 1955 of the Group as a level of management intermediate between Area and colliery. These include the creation of posts of Group manager and the abolition of those of agents. See also p. 224 *post*.

Other Staff

Several further settlements had been negotiated by end-1951 by when, indeed, a salary and grading structure had been evolved for most NCB personnel. For example, there were agreements relating to various types of engineer, of whom the mechanical and electrical group were the largest; special documents covered categories such as safety, coal preparation and HQ specialist engineers, as well as draughtsmen and tracers. There were agreements also for mining surveyors, estates staff, scientists and so on.

During 1957 the Board embarked on a review of the whole scene. They found that, as their organization had developed during the previous ten years, different groups had sprung into existence; as a result there were, by end-1956, about fifty categories of staff whose salaries were dealt with separately, although those concerned often held similar qualifications and carried analogous responsibilities. This made for unnecessary labour and much negotiation, and the Board therefore decided—with the concurrence of the British Association of Colliery Management—that there should henceforth be four main grade structures above the clerical level, each catering for a major sector of the Board's non-industrial employees.[1]

We may add that there are one or two categories for whom there are no formal bilateral arrangements, the main ones being legal, medical and nursing personnel. The remuneration for nurses, for instance, is fixed by the Board after consultation with the Royal College of Nursing; similar discussions take place with the British Medical Association. The pay of legal staff is based largely on that obtaining in the Civil Service. There are also a few grades whose rates are determined directly by Divisional Boards.

Top-level Appointments

Of the agreements for management staffs referred to, none reached to the apex of the *de facto* pyramid. Those for finance and administrative officials, as shown on Table 53, stopped at grades 5 and 2, though for the Board's own purposes both structures went up to grade 1. Similarly, there were at least three tiers above scientist I, the highest included (1951) in the relevant document. A number of top-level employees—including the various chief officers at the Board's headquarters—are, here as elsewhere, in any case remunerated on a personal basis.

The normal ceiling for senior production appointments adopted in 1947 was £4,000 to £5,000 per annum, the latter figure also being the ceiling for HQ personnel. In the case of production staff, how-

---

[1] For further details see National Coal Board, *Annual Report and Accounts for the Year ended* 28 *December* 1957 (HMSO 1958) vol. I, paras. 224–6.

ever, some of the private companies had paid a selected few of their officials very large salaries, so large that the Board felt unable to offer them in the future.[1] The majority of these pre-vesting contracts were therefore brought to an end, but in a few instances the Board was obliged to continue to grant amounts in excess of £5,000 a year, the highest of these being £7,500 plus perquisites. On the whole, the Board took the line that while with its public responsibilities it had to be 'in the first flight of good employers' and was therefore precluded from paying its employees too little, it was 'equally prevented from favouring individuals to the detriment of their fellows or at the public's expense'.[2] Particulars of post-1947 standards for top-level personnel were not available at the time of writing.

Provincial Differentiation
The agreements outlined earlier were applied on a national basis, though subject to a London 'location allowance' payable to all those employed in the metropolis. In the period under review, the addition varied from £32.10.0 to £100 per annum; where remuneration was up to £449 a year, the amount was £32.10.0, while a figure of £1,430 and over attracted £100. In between these limits the allowance was carefully graduated: On a salary of £1,000, for example, the weighting was £70.

Clerical workers in the capital were not formally covered by the national agreement, though in effect paid under the latter plus London allowance. As for senior headquarters personnel, these for the most part received inclusive sums. This was because such staff usually enjoyed a personal salary; in fixing the latter their locale was taken into account, obviating the need for a special addition.

Sex Differentiation
In the matter of sex differentiation the Coal Board used to follow Civil Service practice in several respects; the general rule was a 4:5 ratio. This, however, was not rigidly adhered to: the clerical agreement, for instance, laid down salaries for women which might constitute a strict 80 per cent, but at many points were a slightly higher proportion, of the comparable male scale. There were no special female rates for outdoor clerks; the latter are almost invariably men. Typing and machine operator posts, on the other hand, are practically always held by women. As in the Civil Service, there were certain exceptions to 'unequal pay' in the case of juveniles and other recruitment grades.

[1] cf. *Annual Report for* 1947, op. cit., paras. 115 and 108.
[2] ibid. para. 107.

H

As regards production appointments, the question of separate scales for women did not arise, as the latter are barred by statute from working underground. The finance and administrative (and equally the estates and scientist) agreements in the period under review specifically applied to men only, not enough women being employed to warrant the inclusion of special standards. One or two of the management agreements, however, such as that for architects, contained lower rates for junior female staff. Meanwhile, in the light of the 1955 Treasury arrangements for the introduction of equal pay into the Civil Service, the Coal Board resolved to adopt a parallel scheme of gradual emancipation.

Emoluments

Perquisites, such as free or concessionary coal or a free or cheap house, were an important element in the remuneration of many salaried personnel prior to nationalization—one of the factors which complicated the settlement of terms of employment after that event. The position now is that where staff continue to live in accommodation provided by the Board, an appropriate charge is made to the individual concerned, the main surviving exception to the 'no extra emoluments' rule being the supply of free or concessionary coal.

Chapter 14

ELECTRICITY SUPPLY

Under the Electricity Act, 1947,[1] the British Electricity Authority and fourteen Area Boards took over, on 1 April 1948, the country's electricity supply industry, with the exception of the territory[2] of the North of Scotland Hydro-Electric Board, and of some small non-statutory supplies amounting to a fraction of one per cent of the total. The central authority assumed the ownership of the power stations and of the network of main transmission lines known as the Grid; it was made responsible for the generation of electricity and its supply in bulk to the Area Boards. The latter—unlike the Divisional Coal Boards—are statutory corporations which, though subject to central control in matters of general policy, are otherwise auto-nomous. They carry out the sale of electricity to consumers, operating the distribution systems formerly run by some 540 separate concerns. Each Area has been divided into a number of Sub-Areas, in turn made up of Districts. For the local management of the power stations and the Grid fourteen Generation Divisions were origin-ally set up, the latter, however, being merely an administrative arrangement.

Meanwhile, the industry has undergone several bouts of re-organization. As from 1 April 1955, all British Electricity's under-takings north of the border vested in an independent South of Scot-land Electricity Board, and the title of the central body—henceforth supreme in England and Wales only—was changed to Central Elec-tricity Authority. There were consequential adjustments to twelve in the number of Area Boards, while the Generation Divisions were reduced to eleven, two of the latter having been merged in the pre-vious year. A further overhaul was effected by the Electricity Act, 1957, the main feature of which was the replacement—as from 1 January 1958—of the Central Authority by two new organs: These are the Central Electricity Generating Board—now entrusted with the power stations and the Grid—and the Electricity Council, which has been assigned 'policy' and other tasks relating to the

---

[1] 10 & 11 Geo. 6. c. 54.
[2] As extended by the 1947 Act.

industry as a whole. Some additional powers and duties have also been devolved to Area level.[1]

On 31 March 1951 the total number of employees in the industry was 176,200; of these 119,771 were manual and the remaining 56,429 salaried.[2] In accordance with section 53 of the 1947 Act, a complete network of joint negotiating machinery has been set up; the Area Boards, though they engage their own staffs and are consulted in the first place, must comply with any agreements concluded at the centre. Apart from those dealing with manual workers, there are three bodies operating in the field of the salariat; all but a small handful of top-level officials now come within the scope of one or other of these. We may add that the machinery for negotiation and consultation has not been affected by reorganization; it is now administered by the Electricity Council but continues to apply throughout Great Britain.

Clerical and Administrative Grades

In the period under review, this group comprised administrative officers with secretarial, accounting, commercial, etc. functions; show-room staff and housecraft advisers; all types of clerical personnel as well as those with technical qualifications but engaged on non-technical work. All these, in 1951, numbered approximately 39,000, of whom some 27,000 were in clerical and analogous grades; 12,000 were classed as 'higher clerical, administrative and commercial'.[3] Prior to vesting day no national negotiating arrangements existed in this sector of the industry, although some 60 per cent were then employed in municipal electricity undertakings, and as such came under local government Whitley machinery; some of the remainder were covered by agreements made with company undertakings.[4] There is now a National Joint Council for the Electricity Supply Industry (Administrative and Clerical Grades), which during 1948 laid down a number of pay scales. These were issued on an interim basis, being replaced by a more comprehensive agreement as from 1 April 1950.

The Lower Clerical Grades

As shown on Table 55, the 1950 standards were revised in mid-1951,

[1] For further details see Central Electricity Authority, *Report and Accounts 1 April–31 December 1957* (HMSO 1958), pp. 1–4.

[2] British Electricity Authority, *Third Report and Accounts 1950–1* (HMSO 1951), para. 251 and Appx. 41.

[3] Industrial Court Award No. 2339 (HMSO 1951), para. 2. The bulk of the remainder of salaried staff were in the technical engineering grades.

[4] cf. British Electricity Authority, *First Report and Statement of Accounts* (HMSO 1949), para. 584.

when the general clerical grade was divided into two classes. These were to cater for the lower and upper reaches of routine work, promotion from A to B being fairly automatic. The agreement also dealt with certain other categories such as tracers and telephone operators, whose salaries were defined, respectively, in terms of the male and female clerical scale. There were two separate grades for private secretaries, the maximum of the higher being fixed at £500 per annum as from June 1951.[1]

TABLE 55

ELECTRICITY SUPPLY
CLERICAL STAFF
(Men, Great Britain)[1]

Interim General Clerical Scale		*General Clerical Grade*		
Salaries as from		*Salaries as from*		
1 *April* 1948		1 *April* 1950		1 *June* 1951*
Age	£ p.a.	£ p.a.	*Age*	£ p.a.
				Class A
16	135	135	16	150
17	152	154	17	165
18	169	173	18	180
19	186	192	19	200
20	203	210	20	220
21	220	228	21	250
22	237	245	22	270
23	254	262	23	290
24	271	279	24	310
25	288	295	25	330
26	305	310	26	355
				Class B
27	318	325		375
28	332	340		395
29	345	355		410
30	358	365		430
31	372	375		
32	385	385		

[1] For additional allowance payable in London see text.

* These salaries were increased—by from £10 to £20 p.a.—as from 1 August 1952, and have been further revised since.

Higher Clerical, Administrative and Commercial Staff
The interim clerical scheme was broadened in August 1948 to provide —as a temporary measure—a series of ranges for more senior personnel. In 1950 these provisional figures were superseded by a neat

[1] Various revisions of both grading and pay have taken place since.

set of nine grades[1] with salaries up to £1,020 per annum—an extension in coverage in line with that then recently introduced in local government. Neither the 1948 nor the 1950 agreement was specifically designed to grant improvements in pay, although they gave incidental benefits to former local authority staff, and an appreciable rise to ex-company employees whose standards of reward had been lower than in municipal undertakings.[2] There were increases also for those shouldering new responsibilities following the reorganization of the industry.

A dispute over the remuneration of the senior categories was submitted to the Industrial Court in 1951, when the latter awarded a flat-rate addition of £50 per annum to all in grades 1 to 9.[3] These revised standards became operative in June 1951. They were further raised by the Industrial Court[4]—which on that occasion also dealt with the lower clericals—with effect from 1 August 1952.

TABLE 56

ELECTRICITY SUPPLY

HIGHER CLERICAL, ADMINISTRATIVE AND COMMERCIAL STAFF

(Men and Women, Great Britain)[1]

Salary Range[2] *as from* 1 *April* 1948		1 *April* 1950	*Salary Scale as from*	1 *June* 1951*
	£ p.a.	£ p.a.		£ p.a.
Grade A	270–450	310 × 20–390	Grade 1	360 × 20–440
Grade B	450–550			× 10–450
Grade C	350–450	390 × 20–450	Grade 2	440 × 20–500
Grade D	450–600	450 × 20–510	Grade 3	500 × 20–560
Grade E	600–760	510 × 20–570	Grade 4	560 × 20–620
		570 × 20–630	Grade 5	620 × 20–680
		630 × 25–705	Grade 6	680 × 25–755
		705 × 30–795	Grade 7	755 × 30–845
		795 × 35–900	Grade 8	845 × 35–950
		900 × 40–1,020	Grade 9	950 × 40–1,070

[1] For additional allowance payable in London see text.

[2] On 19 July 1949 the National Joint Council approved increments of from £15 to £25. Grades A-B and C-E related to different types of staff.

* All salaries were increased by £20 as from 1 August 1952, and have been further revised since.

[1] A further grade was added in 1957 at the upper end of the salary structure, to cover exceptional cases.

[2] cf. Industrial Court Award No. 2339, op. cit., p. 5.

[3] Award No. 2339. To remove anomalies, it was subsequently agreed to increase grade 1 by a further £10.

[4] Award No. 2414 (HMSO 1952).

The application of the scales set out on Table 56 was a matter for the Electricity Boards and Generation Divisions, subject to the usual right of appeal. In the case of commercial staff at District level, for example, a demonstrator of cooking and apparatus was in grade 1,[1] a senior demonstrator and/or housecraft adviser in 2, a service centre supervisor in grade 4 or 5 according to the total of juniors in his care, while district commercial officers—in charge of all commercial affairs in a District—were allocated to grades 6–9. At generating stations a station clerk was classified according to the number of workers and the precise records for which he was responsible. At units employing up to 100 personnel he was placed in grade 1 or 2; in those with over 500 staff, in 4–6.

Promotion from one tier to the next was not automatic, a higher ranking being achieved by securing a better post. In the framing of the scales all overlapping was deliberately avoided[2]—a departure from the local government APT scheme, with which there is otherwise a strong affinity. However, while electricity's former close municipal ties have had an important bearing on its post-nationalization pay standards, the latter have since asserted their independence in several respects. As it has been put, 'the Local Authorities have now . . . become only a part of the general salary picture as seen from the electricity standpoint'.[3]

Technical Engineering Staff

This group largely consists of various types of engineer directly employed as such; those with partly non-technical duties and draughtsmen-in-training were treated as administrative or clerical in the period under review.[4] Collective bargaining machinery in this instance is of long standing, the pre-vesting agreement being taken over by the National Joint Board now responsible for this sector of the industry. General revision was necessary, however, because of the changes in the industry's organization, while the absorption of employees of the former Central Electricity Board was a further complicating factor.

After lengthy negotiations, a new agreement was introduced in July 1949, the rates being further amended as from 1 July 1951: For what might be termed production staff,[5] remuneration depended

---

[1] Progression beyond £400 (1951) was subject to obtaining an 'efficiency certificate'.

[2] With one exception, i.e. between grades 1 and 2.

[3] Industrial Court Award No. 2414, op. cit., p. 3.

[4] Qualified engineering draughtsmen, however, and chemists belonged to 'technical engineering'.

[5] i.e. those at Authority HQ, Generation Divisions and power stations.

on both the megawatt capacity of generating plant and actual duties and responsibilities, this basis of classification being a feature already of the pre-nationalization pay pattern. An alternative criterion then in use—maximum demand—was, however, abandoned. In the case of distribution staff,[1] standards varied with the total number of units sold to consumers as well as, again, 'duties and responsibilities'. The agreement contained a set of salary schedules which are literally too complex to reproduce. Schedule A, for example, had thirteen classes, in each of which there were from twelve to twenty-two grades, each of the latter having a three-point scale, with varying increments granted biennially. It must suffice to say that the span covered (Schedule A, 1951) was from £375 to £1,703 per annum. A power station superintendent, for instance, was in grade 1 (the highest), and his salary might range from £757–£819 a year in a small station to £1,650–£1,703 in a very large one. These 1951 figures were revised as from August 1952 and since, while what must have been one of the most elaborate pay patterns ever devised by collective ingenuity was at any rate modified during 1954, and in 1959–60 was again in the melting pot.[2]

Managerial and Higher Executive Grades
Following protracted negotiations, an agreement establishing a National Joint Managerial and Higher Executive Grades Committee was signed in August 1951; it covers senior staff beyond the competence of the technical engineering National Joint Board on the one hand, and of the National Joint Council for clerico-administrative personnel on the other. Chief officers and their deputies, and certain others whose duties are primarily concerned with questions of establishment and negotiating machinery, are excluded. The first set of salary scales—ranging from £1,150 to £2,200 per annum and applicable retrospectively from 1 April 1952—were laid down during 1953–4. There have been various increases since, while as from November 1956 a new pay structure was introduced, linked to the organizational units of the Generation Divisions and Area Boards.

Provincial Differentiation
The standards quoted in the preceding sections related to employees throughout Great Britain, though here again an additional allowance is payable in the capital. For clerico-administrative grades under 21

[1] Those at Area, Sub-Area or District level.
[2] See British Electricity Authority, *Seventh Report and Statement of Accounts for the Year ended* 31 *March* 1955 (HMSO 1955), para. 269. During 1959–60 discussions were set in train as to the possibility of replacing the existing four schedules by one set of scales.

this amounted (1950–1) to £15 a year; for those 21 and over it was 5 per cent of salary, subject to a minimum of £30 and a maximum of £40 per annum. Under the interim schemes the London weighting was identical with that then current under the local government Charter and exclusively based on age. We may add that the allowance has meanwhile been stepped up, and there has also been a change as regards the boundaries within which it accrues. Thus under the first post-war agreements, 'London' was co-terminous with the Metropolitan Police District, but it was subsequently very considerably extended in order to bring it into line with the 'Londons' of the industry's National Joint Industrial Council for manual workers and technical engineering National Joint Board.[1]

Sex Differentiation
At end-March 1951 women constituted about 11·5 per cent of the total electricity labour force, though in the salaried sphere they are relatively more numerous. In the general clerical grades women's rates used to be fixed at an exact 80 per cent of the comparable male figure, but for telephone operators and tracers identical standards applied to the two sexes—in the former case the female, and in the latter the male, clerical scale.[2] There has not at any time been any differentiation for higher clerical, administrative and commercial staff, while the technical engineering agreement was silent on the subject, practically all those within its purview being men. Equal pay for those on equal work has since been sanctioned—in this instance via a five-year plan, to be fully operative by 1 January 1960.

Bonus Payments
A number of staff have continued to receive co-partnership and similar bonuses, to which they were entitled prior to nationalization. For all newly-engaged personnel, however, all such payments have been abolished—with one exception. This is a gift in kind to the value of, at the time of writing, £10 after 25 years' and £20 after 35 years' service, for which all workers in the industry have remained eligible.

[1] Both of which were based on the former 'District Joint Board No. 10', in the whole of which metropolitan rates were paid under pre-nationalization agreements for manual workers. The London area has since been further extended to include the borough of Slough.

[2] However, women tracers—on the male clerical scale only since 1952—did not normally progress beyond class A.

Chapter 15

THE GAS INDUSTRY

The gas industry passed into public ownership on 1 May 1949, when 1,037 separate undertakings vested in twelve Area Gas Boards into which Great Britain has been divided. In addition to the Area Boards which are individually answerable to the Minister, the Gas Act, 1948[1] established a Gas Council: It is the central organ for the industry, its task being to assist the regional bodies and to deal with matters that cannot be confined to a single locality. Among this category are labour relations, so that—despite the relatively large dose of decentralization injected into the 1948 statute—it is again the national body which is charged with the negotiation of the terms of employment. Area Boards must comply with any agreement concluded by the Council, although questions of joint consultation are the responsibility of both.[2]

The number of persons employed by the Gas Council and Area Boards on 31 March 1951 was 143,506; of this total 110,196 were operatives while the remaining 33,310 were classed as administrative, technical and clerical.[3] In contradistinction to electricity supply there were, prior to nationalization, no country-wide standards of remuneration for any section of the industry's non-manual labour force;[4] now the majority of salaried personnel are catered for by the National Joint Council for Gas Staffs. The latter's first collective agreement was signed in June 1950, to take effect from 1 April of that year. It covered all clerical, administrative, professional and technical workers with pay not exceeding £755–£800 per annum.[5]

Clerical Staff
As Table 57 shows, the post-nationalization salary structure pro-

---

[1] 11 & 12 Geo. 6. c. 67.

[2] ibid. s. 57 and Gas Council, *First Report and Accounts* (HMSO 1951), paras. 1 and 9–20.

[3] Gas Council, *Second Reports and Accounts*, 1950–1 (HMSO 1951), para. 63 and pp. 148–9.

[4] A Joint Industrial Council for manual workers has been in existence since 1919.

[5] The precise limit was £800 in the metropolitan area, £770 in provincial 'A' and £755 in provincial 'B' undertakings.

vided for four clerical tiers. Grade 'A'—linked to age-points through-out—was reserved for those on work mostly checked or closely supervised. Scale 'D', on the other hand, applied to staff on non-routine clerical and minor administrative tasks or to those who, say, themselves had a measure of control over juniors. Advancement from one

TABLE 57

GAS INDUSTRY
CLERICAL STAFF
(Men, Great Britain: Provincial 'A' Scale)[1]

	Salary Scale as from	
	1 *April* 1950	1 *June* 1951*
	£ p.a.	£ p.a.
Grade 'A'		
Age 16	135	155
17	140	160
18	160	180
19	180	200
20	200	220
21	220	245
22	245	270
23	260	290
24	275	310
25	290	325
Grade 'B'	305 × 15–365	345 × 15–405
	× 20–385	× 20–425
Grade 'C'	370 × 15–430	410 × 15–470
	× 10–440	× 10–480
Grade 'D'	425 × 15–500	465 × 15–540

[1] Provincial 'A' scales were paid in all the larger units in industrial areas, other than the 'metropolitan' area.

* All scales were increased—by from £5 to £20 p.a.—as from 1 January 1952, and have been further revised since.

rung to the next was not automatic except between 'A' and 'B'; here, as far as men were concerned, promotion normally took place at age 25, subject to obtaining an efficiency certificate. The responsibility for fitting individuals into the scheme ultimately rested with Area Boards, although recommendations from the lower levels of administration were accorded due weight.

Administrative, Professional and Technical Staff
In the case of administrative, professional and technical personnel, the agreement contained a twelve-tier pattern, the management again deciding on the appropriate scale. However, in this instance little

guidance was given as to the principles on which such allocation was to proceed. Grade 1 was for junior technical trainees only, remuneration being identical with that for clerical workers of the same age. At this stage promotion occurred as a matter of course, but this was not so as regards advancement higher up. We may add that in special circumstances—this applied equally at the clerical level—the management had discretion to exceed the standard rates.

TABLE 58

GAS INDUSTRY

ADMINISTRATIVE, PROFESSIONAL AND TECHNICAL STAFF
(Men, Great Britain: Provincial 'A' Scale)[1]

	Salary Scale as from	
	1 *April* 1950 £ p.a.	1 *June* 1951* £ p.a.
Grade 1		
Age 16	135	155
17	140	160
18	160	180
19	180	200
20	200	220
Grade 2	250 × 15–370	275 × 15[2]–410
Grade 3	250 × 15–400	275 × 15[2]–440
Grade 4	250 × 15–340	275 × 15[2]–380
	× 20–420	× 20 –460
Grade 5	385 × 20–465	425 × 20 –505
Grade 6	415 × 20–495	455 × 20 –535
Grade 7	450 × 20–530	500 × 20 –580
Grade 8	490 × 20–570	540 × 20 –620
Grade 9	520 × 20–620	570 × 20 –670
Grade 10	570 × 25–670	620 × 25 –720
Grade 11	595 × 25–720	645 × 25 –770
Grade 12	645 × 25–770	695 × 25 –820

[1] Provincial 'A' scales were paid in all the larger units in industrial areas, other than the 'metropolitan' area.

[2] At £290 the increment was £20; at £340 it was £25.

* All scales were increased—by from £5 to £25 p.a.—as from 1 January 1952, and have been further revised since.

As Table 58 shows, there was a considerable degree of overlap between the scales. Grades 2 to 4, in particular, might be called variations on a theme, and were parallel promotion outlets rather than different rungs in a vertical hierarchy. This is in strict contrast to electricity's 'higher clerical, administrative and commercial' pattern, where all overlapping was studiously avoided. There is also much less similarity here with the local government Charter than there is for clerical staff in the two spheres: It may, for example, be noted that the 1951 APT ceiling in gas was well below the £1,000 level, then the APT zenith in local government. This, of course, is not to pass judgment on relative standards of remuneration in the two fields, which are a function largely of the way in which posts were respectively fitted into the schemes.

Senior Staffs

A Senior Gas Officers' Joint Council was set up in 1951 and covers, with a few exceptions, all the higher managerial staff above the level of the main agreement. At the time of writing, no salaries had been laid down.

Intermediate Grades

There is a special National Joint Standing Committee for Intermediate Grades to deal with employees midway between manual and salaried, such as meter readers and collectors and foremen. Prior to nationalization, some of these were treated as manual, while others— particularly in municipally-owned undertakings—had staff status; it was to absorb these various categories with their different terms of service that an 'intermediate' agreement was concluded in 1950. It was left to Area Boards to whom to apply this; there was no strict uniformity in the matter.

Provincial Differentiation

In the period under review, there was a system of three-tier area differentiation, of which the provincial 'A' scale can perhaps be considered the norm. The latter was in force at all the larger works in industrial localities with the exception of the 'metropolitan' region. Staff in the smaller units in rural areas were generally assigned to provincial 'B' rates; these were £15 below provincial 'A'. We may add that 'metropolitan', as defined in the 1950 agreement, was much more extensive than the Metropolitan Police District—mainly for historical reasons—and comprised the territory of the old Gas, Light and Coke Company in its entirety. As for 'metropolitan' scales, these were a straight £30 above provincial 'A' standards.

This three-tier differential contrasts with the two-tier pattern adopted by other nationalized industries for their salaried personnel. One explanation is that pre-nationalization pay levels for clerical and administrative staff at some of the smaller gas works were relatively low: Special arrangements were therefore necessary to prevent the new regime from proving unduly costly to these units.

Sex Differentiation

In the period under review, women received less than men not only at the clerical level but also throughout the twelve administrative, professional and technical grades. The ratio was a strict 4:5, though here again equal pay has since become the rule.[1]

[1] Prior to nationalization, various co-partnership schemes were in force in the industry; however, these ceased to operate as from 1 April 1951.

Chapter 16

RAIL TRANSPORT

The Transport Act—the original instrument of nationalization—received the Royal Assent on 6 August 1947; under its terms there was set up the British Transport Commission with the general duty to secure the provision of an efficient, adequate, economical and properly integrated system of public inland transport in Great Britain.[1] The Commission's wide scope and powers were materially curtailed by the Transport Act, 1953,[2] under which, *inter alia*, the greater part of its road haulage organization was returned to private enterprise, while radical changes announced by the Government in late 1960 included the disbanding of the Commission itself.[3] Rail transport, however—though variously affected by the 1953 statute, and though to be overhauled financially and further decentralized administratively under the 1960 proposals—remains under public auspices.

Vesting day for the railways was 1 January 1948, when they passed under the control of what was then the Railway Executive. This was the giant among the Executives established under the 1947 legislation;[4] at end-December 1951 it accounted for 599,890[5] of the 888,073 employees of British Transport as a whole. The bulk of railway personnel are manual, and include categories such as locomotive and permanent way staff, the traffic grades and various types of maintenance workers. The salaried sector, at end-1951, comprised 76,978 described as 'administrative, technical and clerical'; 5,373 stationmasters, yardmasters, goods agents etc.; 2,284 traffic control staff; and 14,048 inspectors, foremen and supervisors em-

[1] cf. Transport Act, 1947 (10 & 11 Geo. 6. c. 49), s. 3.

[2] 1 & 2 Eliz. 2. c. 13.

[3] See Ministry of Transport, *Reorganization of the Nationalized Transport Undertakings*, Cmnd. 1248 (HMSO 1960). Major legislation was to be introduced to make the changes effective.

[4] Under the 1947 Act, the BTC was primarily concerned with questions of policy, day-to-day management being in the hands of a number of Executives: see also *post*.

[5] British Transport Commission, *Financial and Statistical Accounts* 1951, Cmd. 8572 (HMSO 1952), p. 173. The figure includes those engaged on collection and delivery services, but excludes marine, docks and canal staff then under the Executive's control.

ployed at headquarters, on operating or on maintenance duties.[1]
There were also three thousand odd railway police.

The machinery of negotiation in the railway industry is of long
standing, having its roots in the early years of the century, though
non-manual workers were not brought in until 1921. The present
structure—for the great majority—in essence goes back to the inter-
war period and covers both the 'conciliation'[2] and salaried grades.
Separate bodies exist for, amongst others, those engaged in railway
workshops, professional and technical personnel and the railway
police.

Salaries

It is not possible here to enter in any detail into the tangled and
stormy history of railway remuneration in which—due to the special
features of railway trade unionism—the salaried categories have
also been involved; the financial fate of the latter i.e. has been
closely bound up with that of their 'conciliation' colleagues ever
since the 1920s. The first post-nationalization settlement took effect
from 1 February 1948 when—following the recommendations of a
Court of Inquiry[3]—agreement was reached both on certain revisions
of inter-grade differentials and enhanced pay. Except for minor
adjustments for junior clerks, these standards remained in force
until 1 January 1951. Lest this give a mistaken impression of industrial calm, let it be said that the intervening period witnessed
constant claims by one or other of the unions, rejected *inter alia*
by the Railway Staff National Tribunal and a special Board of
Conciliation.[4] The 1951 settlement was itself the result of protracted
negotiations which both preceded and ensued upon the report of
yet another Court of Inquiry,[5] whose findings the staffs had found
unacceptable. The January 1951 figures constituted increases of

[1] ibid. pp. 174–5.

[2] This term is commonly used to denote all railway *manual* workers whose pay
is determined under the 1935 machinery.

[3] *Report of a Court of Inquiry* (Chairman: C. W. Guillebaud) *into Application
... for Improvement in Wages and Reductions in Weekly Hours of Work*, Cmd.
7161 (HMSO 1947). The 1948 adjustment was the second revision arising out of the
Court's recommendations, interim increases of 7s. 6d. p.w. (conciliation grades)
and £19.10.0 p.a. (salaried staff) as well as a shorter working week having been
granted from 30 June 1947.

[4] British Railways, Railway Staff National Tribunal Decision No. 11
(18 March 1949) and *Railways Conciliation and Salaried Grades: Report of Board
of Conciliation ...* (Chairman: Sir J. Forster) (HMSO 1949). Though no increases
were awarded by the Board, its report led to certain improvements in service
conditions and allowances.

[5] *Report of a Court of Inquiry* (Chairman: C. W. Guillebaud) *into Applications
for an Improvement in Wages and Salaries ...*, Cmd. 8154 (HMSO 1951).

TABLE 59

BRITISH RAILWAYS

CLERICAL STAFF
(Men, Great Britain)[1]

	Salary Scale as from		
	1 *February* 1948	1 *January* 1951	3 *Sept.* 1951*
	£ p.a.	£ p.a.	£ p.a.
Junior Clerks:			
Age 16 and under	120	130	140.10.0
,, 17	130[2]	145	156.10.0
Senior Clerks:			
Class 5			
Age 18	192.10.0	205	221.10.0
19	202.10.0	215	232. 0.0
20	212.10.0[3]	235	254. 0.0
21	222.10.0[4]	245	264.10.0
22	232.10.0	255	275.10.0
23	245. 0.0[2]	265	286. 0.0
24	260. 0.0	280	302.10.0
25	275. 0.0	295	318.10.0
26	290. 0.0	310	335. 0.0
27	305. 0.0	325	351. 0.0
28	320. 0.0	345	372.10.0
Class 4[5]	340×15–355	365×15–380	394–410.10.0[6]
Class 3	370×10–390	400×10–420	432–453.10.0
Class 2	410×15–440	440×15–455 ×20–475	475–513. 0.0
Class 1	460×15–490	495×15–525	534.10.0–567
Special Class Staff:[7]			
Category 'A'	510×20–530	550×20–570	594–615.10.0
Category 'B'	550×25 575	595×25–620	642.10.0– 669.10.0
Category 'C'	600×30–630	645×35–680	696.10.0– 734.10.0

[1] For additional allowance payable in London see text.
[2] Increased by £5 as from 1 September 1950.
[3] Increased by £9 as from 1 September 1950.
[4] Increased by £7.10.0 as from 1 September 1950.
[5] The increments shown in the two adjoining columns for classes 4, 3, 2 and 1 and 'special class' staff were paid after two years on the previous rate.
[6] The maximum of class 4 and of the 'special class' categories in this column was reached after two years on the minimum. The maximum of classes 3, 2 and 1 was reached by two increments after two and four years' service, respectively. The increments were irregular and are not, therefore, set out.
[7] Minimum scales.

* These rates were increased as from 2 November 1952 and have been further revised since.

broadly 7½ per cent, and again applied to both the manual and non-manual wings of the industry.

After a lapse of little more than six months, fresh demands were submitted by the three railway unions. Again it proved impossible to strike a bargain without third-party intervention, and the matter was referred to the Railway Staff National Tribunal. Its ruling was, among other things, that an 8 per cent rise should accrue as from 3 September 1951.[1]

In the period under review, the salary structure for male clerical staff consisted of eight classes/grades, plus age rates for juniors of 17 and under. At 18 a clerk normally moved to class 5 as a matter of course, whence progression was again by age up to a maximum attained at 28. Class 5 was designed for the more routine type of work, the higher tiers covering those with supervisory duties. A chief clerk in a goods office with five juniors under him, for example, was in class 4; a special class 'B' goods clerk, on the other hand, may have been responsible for more than 100 personnel. In the allocation of particular posts the management had the final word, though an individual could appeal under agreed procedure. It should be noted that the special class scales were minima; all other figures on Table 59 had the more usual status of 'standard rates'.

Advancement from class 5 was not automatic, though vacancies in the higher ranges were—with the exception of a limited entry of university graduates—filled from within the industry. Promotion prospects have been a sore point. Thus at the time of the hearing of the second 1951 claim, the Transport Salaried Staffs' Association drew attention—as they had done on previous occasions—to the limited opportunities for advancement, indicated by the fact that 41·9 per cent of all male clerks' posts were found in the age-scale groups, i.e. class 5 and below.[2] The Railway Executive on its part countered that, as against 1939, there had been a general improvement in the level of classification. We may add that, in the meanwhile, the clerical structure has been streamlined to some extent, the number of grades—excluding juniors—being reduced from eight to six in January 1955.

Stationmasters, Controllers, Supervisors, etc.
The 1951 pay pattern for stationmasters, goods, passenger and parcels agents, yard masters and their assistants, and for dock and railway supervisory personnel was the same as that for their clerical cousins, except that there were here no age scales: Class 5 consisted

---

[1] Railway Staff National Tribunal Decision No. 13 (7 November 1951), pp. 6–7. There were further increases in November 1952 and since.

[2] Railway Staff National Tribunal Decision No. 13, op. cit., p. 11.

of a flat rate, equivalent to the maximum of clerical 5. For traffic control officials the hierarchy formally commenced with class 3, with a proviso that assistant controllers were to be fitted into the 4th and 5th clerical grades. Stationmasters—the local representatives of British Railways—were mostly responsible for both passenger and goods work and might also be in charge of more than one station. At a busy terminus, on the other hand, remuneration was beyond the limits of Table 59: The stationmaster at the London end of one of the principal lines to the north had a 1951 salary of £950 per annum. We may add that the various types of supervisory staff are currently no longer precisely hitched to the clerical wagon, but enjoy rather higher standards. Differentials have been stepped up in particular as from January 1960, following the Report of the (Guillebaud) Railway Pay Committee of Inquiry. Differential rates *within* the group have also been introduced.

The problem of inter-grade differentials has indeed been the cause of much trouble in the post-war history of railway remunera- ation, although the far more numerous cadres of manual staffs have been the worst afflicted. The 1947 Court of Inquiry had come to the con- clusion that there was 'an urgent need for detailed and exhaustive reconsideration of the whole grading of the various classes, scales and categories which make up the complicated structure of the railway service';[1] in addition to awarding an immediate interim pay increase and a reduction of working hours, the Court pressed—as a matter of urgency—for a thoroughgoing investigation of the subject. Hence the further adjustments which took effect in 1948. However, as far as the unions were concerned, the 1948 settlement did not satisfactorily dispose of the question, with the result that 'differ- entials became the stock-in-trade of subsequent negotiations.

One aspect of the problem is the size of the gap between the wage and salaried sectors as such. In their evidence to the 1951 Court of Inquiry—as again on later occasions—the Transport Salaried Staffs' Association stated[2] that, while they did not grudge the in- creases granted to the conciliation staff, they felt that differentials had been reduced too much: Compared with the 130 per cent rise over 1939 for the lowest-paid 'conciliation man', the grade 2 porter, the improvement for the bottom man in the salaried structure on the maximum of class 5 was only 72½ per cent.[3] By-passing such comparison between the two pyramids' basic rungs, the manage-

[1] Cmd. 7161, op. cit., para. 100.
[2] Cmd. 8154, op. cit., paras. 112–16 and Railway Staff National Tribunal Decision No. 13, op. cit., p. 13.
[3] The percentage increases for the lower age-points of class 5 were considerably greater.

ment pointed out that the proportional advance of salaried and conciliation grades whose pre-war rate had been approximately the same showed that this relationship had not been upset; undue preference had not been given to either.[1] We may add that the two hierarchies—for those who reach this far—actually coalesce at the supervisory level, stationmasters, inspectors and so on being re- cruited from both clerks and senior wages personnel. Whether, in the case of the latter, such promotion is a paying proposition is another matter. A (conciliation) yard foreman, for instance, had an end-1951 wage of 142/6d a week, which was only about 9d below the salary of a yard inspector allocated to class 5.[2] However, trans- lation from 'wages' to inspectorial rank was not necessarily to that— i.e. the most junior salaried—class.

Professional and Technical Staffs
Professional and technical personnel have their own negotiating machinery—of comparatively recent origin—pay being first laid down on a national basis in June 1947.[3] It relates to grades such as draughtsmen, engineers, surveyors and chemists at the technical, rather than the fully professional, level. In the period under review, there were three sets of scales; group 'A' was remunerated according to age all the way up to 36, the salary at that point being fixed at £545 10s 0d a year in September 1951.[4] Group 'B' covered a span analogous to that of 'special class' categories 'A' and 'B', while professional group 'C' was identical with special class 'C'. There were separate standards for tracers as well as for certain staff in chief mechanical engineers' and other departments: These applied mainly to men who had come out of the workshops after completing a crafts- man's apprenticeship. All rates here were *minima*, British Railways insisting—as did the Companies previously—on the necessity of evaluating each technical appointment on its merits.

Senior Staff
In October 1950 agreement was reached for the establishment of negotiating machinery for higher administrative and technical officers with salaries above £630 but below £1,600 per annum. No definite scales were laid down, each individual having his position assessed

[1] Railway Staff National Tribunal Decision No. 14, op. cit., p. 14; Cmd. 8154, op. cit., para. 39; and Railway Staff National Tribunal Decision No. 13, op. cit., p. 35.
[2] The comparison is based on provincial standards and on rates—not earnings.
[3] Following a reference to the Railway Staff National Tribunal: see Decision No. 10 (28 May 1947).
[4] Increased as from 2 November 1952 and since.

by the management—with the unions entitled to make representations. Progression towards the maxima thus determined was by a series of merit advances. Increases of up to £75 became payable in September 1951, and further improvements were secured in 1952 and since. Meanwhile, it has also been decided that the salary ceiling should be raised beyond its original (1950) level.

Provincial Differentiation
The scales set out on Table 59 applied throughout Great Britain; in London an extra £10 per annum was payable. This accrued to staff within a 10-mile radius of Charing Cross, but those with 'special class' status—including analogous professional groups—did not qualify for the addition until 1960. In that year the weighting was extended to them, and at the same time raised to £20 for all except juniors aged 19 and under.

Sex Differentiation
The number of women in the clerical and administrative ranks of British Railways at end-December 1951 was 20,367—out of the total of 76,978 then in that category.[1] This proportion would have been higher but for the fact that British Railways—unlike London Transport—have continued to employ men for much of their clerical work. In the supervisory, stationmaster and similar grades no women were to be found apart from a few stragglers.

The female clerical hierarchy in the period under review was simpler than for men; there were only two classes—apart from the rates for juveniles—plus the three 'special' categories. Class 2 had an age-scale covering the span 18 to 28, and was regarded by the management as the equivalent of the male class 5. It applied equally to typing personnel, though these received something extra in some of the other sections of British Transport. The great bulk of women were in class 2 or below; the proportion was said to be more than 85 per cent at end-1951.[2] The sex differential was not uniform, being somewhat narrower at the base than higher up: At age 16, for example, the girl clerk's 46s 6d per week (September 1951) represented approximately 86 per cent of her male colleague's pay; at age 28 the ratio was about 4:5. Further up the ladder, there was some difference of opinion as to which female and male grades were parallel. Meanwhile—following a decision of the Railway Staff National Tribunal[3] —a scheme for equal pay has been agreed upon, to be fully operative as from December 1961.

[1] Cmd. 8572, op. cit., p. 175.
[2] cf. Railway Staff National Tribunal Decision No. 13, op. cit., p. 11.
[3] Decision No. 18 (7 November 1956).

Travel Concessions

Railway employees have for a long time enjoyed special emoluments in the way of travel facilities—on the lines of the free/concessionary coal privileges we have come across before. Thus all staff may journey to work on British Railways without charge up to a defined radius—and at reduced rates beyond. They are also entitled to a number of free tickets for holiday purposes, depending on rank and/ or length of service, and may travel at any time on payment of a fraction of the ordinary fare.

Other Sections of 'British Transport'

A few remarks only about the employees engaged in the other sections of nationalized transport. Under the 1947 Act the British Transport Commission was primarily a policy-making body, the daily conduct of affairs being entrusted to a number of statutory authorities known as Executives. In addition to the Railway Executive, those in being prior to the passing of the 1953 Act were the London Transport Executive, The Road Haulage Executive, the Docks and Inland Waterways Executive and the Hotels Executive; a year previously there was also a Road Passenger Executive. While the Commission had to satisfy itself as to the existence of adequate machinery for the settlement of terms and conditions of service, it was the Executives who were the actual employers of staff and who conducted negotiations on rates of pay and kindred matters.[1]

Though each Executive was formally independent in its personnel policy, it had to obtain the Commission's approval before the conclusion of major agreements; appointments and salaries in the higher reaches had likewise to be confirmed from the centre. The Commission did not, however, try to impose a rigid uniformity, and *de facto* there was no precise identity between the grading patterns and pay rates adopted by the different Executives. Thus some of the latter granted their salaried staffs a more generous London allowance than the £10 then operative for railway clerks. However, having determined their own wage and salary structures, there was a tendency for the Executives to march in unison. The two 1951 railway pay awards, for instance, were applied to the employees of a number of the other Executives; similarly, the improvement in railway service conditions resulting from the 1949 Board of Conciliation Report was extended to other sections of British Transport. Again, all the Executives negotiated agreements up to the same level of seniority.

---

[1] For a detailed account of the negotiating machinery established in this period see F. Gilbert, *Transport Staff Relations* (Pitman, 1951). The only instance of Commission-wide machinery was the British Transport Police Force Conference.

Only the London Transport Executive survived the Act of 1953, the functions of the remainder—including those of collective bargaining—becoming directly exercizable by the Transport Commission as from October 1953. Under the changes outlined in the 1960 White Paper[1] under which, as indicated, the Commission itself is to be axed, a series of new statutory bodies—which may strike the unsophisticated as not altogether unlike the old Executives—are to be created. These—including the proposed British Railways Board—will again assume national responsibility for the negotiation of standards of remuneration.

[1] Cmnd. 1248, op. cit.

Chapter 17

CIVIL AIR TRANSPORT

Civil air transport has not at any time come within the sphere of responsibilities of the British Transport Commission—even in the latter's heyday prior to 1953. The British Overseas Airways Corporation (BOAC) was set up in 1940, though functioning under special war-time arrangements until 1945. The Civil Aviation Act, 1946, in turn gave birth to the British European Airways Corporation (BEA) and the British South American Airways Corporation (BSAA)—to operate in Europe and Latin America, respectively. However, BSAA was subsequently merged into BOAC. We may add that, from the start, the public airways corporations have shared the field with a number of privately-owned undertakings.

Numbers and Negotiating Machinery
Staff in the service of the two nationalized concerns on 31 March 1951 totalled 23,279.[1] This figure includes pilots, stewards and other flying personnel, all types of engineering, maintenance and manual workers, as well as clerical and administrative employees.

As BEA began as a division of BOAC, the conditions of service established at its inception were based on those in the parent organization; BSAA similarly acted in close consultation with the two other corporations, Though in some instances following an independent wages policy. In November 1946 a National Joint Council for Civil Air Transport was set up, and in 1948 it admitted to membership the British Air Charter Association—now the British Independent Air Transport Association—to which many of the private companies are affiliated. Thus both public and private enterprise became part of the same national negotiating machinery, though in some cases separate bargains have been struck in respect of 'public' and 'private' employees. The National Council is responsible for all levels of the industry's staff; it has formed a number of sectional panels, each empowered to regulate the remuneration and other terms specific to those within its purview. There are also various agreements dealing with the broader aspects of service conditions; these are concluded by the National Council itself and of industry-wide application.

[1] British Overseas Airways Corporation, *Report and Accounts for* 1950–51 (HMSO 1951), para. 109, and British European Airways Corporation, *Report and Accounts for* 1950–51 (HMSO 1951), p. 53.

Pilots

In the period under review, the Pilot Officers' National Sectional Panel issued separate agreements to cover, on the one hand, those engaged by the two public corporations and, on the other, those serving the various independent operators in membership of the National Council. The major document related to all pilots in the employ of BOAC and BEA on airline duties; special categories such as test pilots were outside its scope. There were five ranks, allocation to which was at the discretion of the corporations—with promotion depending both on the possession of prescribed qualifications and establishment vacancies. The majority of staffs attained senior captain, 2nd class level, which might be regarded as the career grade. As senior captain, 1st class they reached the zenith of their flying career, though there were possibilities of advancement to top administrative appointments.

TABLE 60

CIVIL AIR TRANSPORT

PILOTS

(Employed by the Public Airways Corporations)

	Basic Salary Scale as from	
	1 *June* 1947	15 *February* 1951*
	£ p.a.	£ p.a.
Second officer	600 × 25– 700	815 × 30– 935
First officer	750 × 25– 900	1,035 × 30–1,305
Captain	1,000 × 45–1,180	1,335 × 50–1,535
Senior captain—2nd class	1,200 × 50–1,480	1,585 × 55–19,15
Senior captain—1st class	1,500 × 50–1,650	2,150
Additional cash allowances[1] *payable to UK-based staff:*		
(a) *Daily travelling allowance*[2]		
All ranks	6/0 per night[3]	7/6 per night[3]
(b) *Daily overseas allowance*[4]		
First and second officer	11/0 per day[5]	13/6 per day[5]
Captain	15/0 per day	18/0 per day
(c) *North Atlantic pay*	£ p.a.	
Second officer	225	
First officer	250	([6])
Captain	275	
Senior captain	300	

[1] For emoluments in kind and London allowance for BEA pilots, see text.
[2] Payable on services to/from Europe, Mediterranean Islands or Tangier.
[3] Away from base outside the UK.
[4] Applicable to all overseas flights not covered by (a).
[5] Away from UK, including day of departure but not of return.
[6] North Atlantic pay accrued at the rates shown in the preceding column until end-July 1951.

* In July 1953 the pilots' pension scheme became contributory, and an amount approximately equivalent to the contribution was added to salaries. A general increase took effect from 26 March 1954, and there have been further revisions since.

The remuneration of pilots, as shown on Table 60, consisted of a basic scale, in addition to which there were various allowances in cash and kind. As for the basic rates, those operatives from June 1947 were the result of an Industrial Court award,[1] and represented the first major settlement of pay and pension structure following the post-war reorganization of the industry. They superseded the interim standards[2] which had been provisionally adopted by BOAC and BEA since April 1946, as well as the rather different regime of BSAA which the latter had inherited from its brief spell of private enterprise—and the continued existence of which it defended before the Court.[3] However, the award was made to apply uniformly to the three national corporations.

In December 1950 the employees' side of the Pilot Officers' Panel lodged a claim for an increase, on which agreement was eventually reached[4] with retrospective effect from mid-February 1951. These 1951 figures constituted a substantial improvement as compared with those previously in force, especially for the upper ranks; a 1st class senior captain, for instance, 'jumped' from £1,500–£1,650 to a new flat rate of £2,150 per annum. The reason for this sizeable rise was that much higher qualifications were being required of pilots to operate the new post-war planes, while radical changes—such as the advent of the jet engine—were making fresh demands on them to keep abreast of technical developments. Another factor favouring the pilot was the enhanced earning capacity of his craft.[5]

As indicated, a pilot's basic salary was supplemented by various additions. The first of these was a non-taxable *daily travelling/overseas allowance*, paid to all United Kingdom-based personnel in respect of each day of flying duty. This emolument was intended to cover incidental expenditure incurred abroad—such as for extra drinks and laundry bills—and varied in accordance with whether or not the pilot was engaged on European schedules or farther afield. In the latter case, the amount also depended on rank.

Until end-July 1951 there was also a system of *North Atlantic pay*, under which pilots received sums ranging from £225 to £300 per annum over and above their basic income. This emolument originated in pre-war days when Imperial Airways—a predecessor of BOAC —started experimental North Atlantic flights, and introduced a

---

[1] No. 2114 (HMSO 1947).

[2] Though in effect mainly consolidating them.

[3] cf. Industrial Court Award No. 2114, op. cit., paras. 5, 10 and 14.

[4] On all points except the London allowance for BEA pilots: see *post*.

[5] The salaries of pilots were adjusted in July 1953 to compensate them for the pension contribution—5 per cent of pay—to which they then became liable. Increased remuneration was awarded by the Industrial Court (Award No. 2500, HMSO 1954) as from 26 March 1954, and there have been further revisions since.

special payment in recognition of the then abnormal nature of these services.[1] The allowance was later extended to all trans-oceanic routes; however, in 1946 it re-emerged as 'North Atlantic pay', subsequent efforts by the staff to have it restored to trans-oceanic proportions proving abortive. Meanwhile, with flights across the Atlantic becoming routine, BOAC increasingly took the view that the payment was altogether unjustified, and agreement was finally reached for its abolition as from August 1951.

Owing to what may be described as an administrative *faux pas*, BEA pilots based on the capital were granted a *London allowance* by the newly-formed British European Airways Corporation in 1946, and have enjoyed it throughout the period under review. BOAC pilots, however, have received no such bounty, and though the employers have made strenuous attempts to get the BEA addition eliminated, an independent arbitrator in 1948 having ruled in favour of its continuation, the Industrial Court in 1952 felt constrained to award likewise.[2] The weighting was graduated according to salary, ranging from £39 to £104 per annum;[3] it tapered off where pay was above £1,580, no allowance accruing when basic remuneration reached £1,684. We may point out that apart from these and other cash additions,[4] a pilot was supplied with food and accommodation whilst away from base, and he was also entitled to free passages for his wife and children on being posted overseas for periods of a year and upwards.

Independent pilots: At the time of writing, there was no precise equality between pilots' remuneration in the public and private sector—nor in some other service conditions—though, in the main, emoluments for like types of operation were analogous. Even this rough parity did not come about automatically, but was the result of a reference to the Industrial Court, necessitated by the breakdown of negotiations following the admission of the British Air Charter Association to the National Joint Council in 1948. The Court then found[5] that the standards maintained by the various private firms were in certain respects inferior to those in force in the national corporations, and were not in compliance with section 41 of the Civil Aviation Act, 1946, which required that—in the absence of

[1] cf. Industrial Court Award No. 2363 (HMSO 1952), para. 2.

[2] Industrial Court Award No. 2366 (HMSO 1952).

[3] For those under 21 the allowance varied according to age only, and ranged from 10s. to 14s. per week.

[4] Allowances were payable e.g. to pilot instructors, and to flight captains engaged on special administrative tasks.

[5] Industrial Court Award No. 2232 (HMSO 1949), paras. 4–5.

mutual agreement by the parties concerned—the terms and conditions of persons employed by any independent air transport undertaking shall not be less favourable than those observed by the three
corporations.

Other Aircrew Personnel

There are three other groups of operational flying personnel—
navigating, engineer, and radio officers; in the period under review,
they enjoyed the same service conditions as pilots and qualified for
the same allowances. In each case the 1951 agreement provided for
two levels of staff, navigating and engineer officers being dealt with
in a joint document. Basic scales for navigating officers, operative
from 1 August 1951, ranged from £800–£900 a year for grade 'B'
and from £930–£1,140 for 'A'; the two engineer officers between
them covered a somewhat wider span—i.e. £725–£1,245. Radio
officers[1] had basic salaries—again as from August 1951—between
the limits of £725 and £1,140 per annum.

As for pilots, the Industrial Court had to adjudicate on the post-
war pay and pensions structure, the terms and conditions of the three
groups forming the subject of a joint remit[2] in 1948. The award was
again back-dated to mid-1947, and here also basic standards remained unchanged until substantially augmented in 1951. Radio,
engineer and navigating officers, one may add, are very conscious
of the relationship of their remuneration to that of pilots'; one of
their spokesmen's contentions at the 1948 arbitration hearing was
that the responsibilities of the three categories had so increased in
recent years as to justify a very considerable reduction in the pilots'
former differential.[3]

Stewards

Stewards and stewardesses—the cabin services flying staff—are
looked after by the Catering Panel of the National Joint Council.
The first agreement dealing with their terms of employment dates
back to October 1948, though the all-important schedule 'A'—
containing the salary scales—has of course not remained static. All
rates here have applied alike to men and women, 'equal pay' having
been the rule in civil air transport throughout.

Turning to Table 61, we may note that all staff were treated as
trainees until age 20; grade III stewards were those receiving advanced training. Class II had to be 'competent to undertake without
supervision all duties attached to Line operations'. As for the two

---

[1] Employed by the two public corporations.
[2] Industrial Court Award No. 2169 (HMSO 1948).
[3] ibid. para. 7, p. 7.

top tiers, their task was to keep a watchful eye on their juniors, but they also had various administrative functions. Promotion depended primarily upon merit and efficiency, though class III personnel normally qualified for advancement after one year's service.

TABLE 61

CIVIL AIR TRANSPORT
STEWARDS AND STEWARDESSES

	Salary *(including Flying Pay)*[1] *as from*	
	1 *October* 1948	19 *August* 1951*
	s. p.w.	s. p.w.
Steward trainee		
Age 17	70/0	82/6
18	82/6	95/0
19	95/0	107/6
20	107/6	120/0
Steward class III	140/0	157/6
Steward class II	150/0 × 5/0–170/0	167/6 × 5/0–187/6
Steward class I	175/0 × 5/0–190/0	192/6 × 5/0–207/6
Head or senior steward	205/0 × 7/6–220/0	222/6 × 7/6–237/6

Additional cash allowances[2] *payable to UK-based staff:*

(a) *Night-stop allowance*[3]		
All ranks	6/0 per night[4]	7/6 per night[4]
(b) *Daily overseas allowance*[5]		
All ranks	11/0 per day[6]	13/6 per day[6]
(c) *North Atlantic pay*	p.w.	
Steward class III	20/0	—
All higher grades	50/0	—

[1] £1 in the case of trainees, £2 for stewards class III, II and I, and £2.10.0 for the top grade. Flying pay did not accrue if not allocated to a flying roster.

[2] For emoluments in kind and London allowance for BEA stewards, see text.

[3] Payable on services to/from Europe, Mediterranean Islands or Tangier.

[4] Away from base outside the UK.

[5] Applicable to all overseas flights not covered by (a).

[6] Away from UK, including day of departure but not of return.

* The salaries of the three top grades were increased as from 19 October 1952, and those of all staffs as from 1 October 1954. They have been further revised since.

Stewards' basic salaries were again supplemented by certain allowances, and there was also a system of *flying pay*. In the period under review, this varied between £1 and £2 10d 0d a week according to rank; all staff were eligible for this while allocated to a flying roster—normally throughout the year unless 'grounded' for some reason. As for the night-stop etc. allowances, these were identical in all but name with those for pilots, while BEA stewards received a London weighting—again on the same terms as the former. Stewards were likewise provided with free meals and accommodation whilst away from base, though in this instance not necessarily at a pilot's standard.

The introduction of the 1951 scales—constituting, in the case of adults, a rise of 17/6d a week—was coupled with the cessation of North Atlantic pay; here again this had been an additional emolument, accruing to all except trainees while employed on North Atlantic operations. Negotiations for its termination proved more difficult in this case, necessitating intervention by the Industrial Court, the stewards insisting that the other sections of flying staff had been far more generously treated by way of compensatory salary increases.[1] The Court's verdict was that North Atlantic pay be abolished as from the date of the 1951 settlement. The latter, we may add, remained in force until October 1952, when improvements of up to 22/6d a week were secured, though the rates for trainees and class III stewards then remained unchanged. All ranks benefited from the next adjustment—operative from October 1954—and there have been further revisions since.

Clerical and Junior Administrative Staff
The agreements of the Clerical and Clerical Administrative Panel in the period under review covered all 'weekly-rated clerical staff' employed in the United Kingdom;[2] also included were categories such as traffic booking grades and supplies, technical records and signals personnel. The figures on Table 62 below are those from London, where the great majority are to be found;[3] they again applied equally to men and women. The salaries operative from 1 January 1950, incidentally, were the first set of bilaterally negotiated standards for clerical workers in the industry.

The post-war pay structure, as shown, provided for five clerical grades; so far as practicable, initial engagement was to junior ranks, vacancies higher up being filled by promotion. 'General job descriptions'—in very broad terms—formed part of the official agreement; the actual allocation of posts, however, was entrusted to a special sub-committee, who issued a number of agreed 'decisions' in the matter. A traffic booking official, for example, required to have detailed knowledge of fares, timetables, health and currency regulations and to handle enquiries from the public regarding reservations

---

[1] See Industrial Court Award No. 2363, op. cit., paras. 4, 6 and 8.

[2] Including N. Ireland and Isle of Man, but excluding Channel Islands for which there was a separate agreement.

[3] In the provinces weekly rates were 7s. 6d. below the London standard for those under 21, and 12s. 6d. below for all others.

and ticket issues, was on scale 'B' or 'A'.[1] An officer engaged on transmitting and receiving signals by teleprinter was in 'D'—or in 'C' if also called upon to record, route and distribute signals and to be conversant with international and domestic signals procedures. A supervisor of a typing pool was normally in 'B'; typists themselves, however, were not covered by the scales on Table 62, having their own pattern of grading. We may add that a separate Panel of the National Council dealt with staff—administrative and technical— above the level of the clerical agreement. In the period under review its competence was restricted to 'middle management', all senior posts being filled on the authority of the Board of Directors, remuneration being fixed on a personal basis.

[1] A difference over the correct interpretation of the 'descriptions'—whether 'A' or 'B' was appropriate to ten cashiers at Kensington Air Station—resulted in an Industrial Court Award (No. 2394, HMSO 1952) that the claim for 'A' grading had not been established.

TABLE 62

CIVIL AIR TRANSPORT

CLERICAL AND CLERICAL ADMINISTRATIVE STAFF
(Men and Women, London)

	Salary Scale as from	
	1 *January* 1950	15 *July* 1951*
	s. p.w.	s. p.w.
Scale 'E'		
Age 15	47/6	57/6
16	55/0	65/0
17	62/6	72/6
18	70/0	80/0
19	77/6	87/6
20	85/0	95/0
21 and over	$97/6 \times 5/0$–112/6	$112/6 \times 5/0$–127/6
Scale 'D'		
Age 18	75/0	85/0
19	82/6	92/6
20	90/0	100/0
21 and over	$102/6 \times 5/0$–132/6[1]	$117/6 \times 5/0$–147/6[1]
Scale 'C'[2]	$122/6 \times 5/0$–152/6[1]	$137/6 \times 5/0$–167/6[1]
Scale 'B'[2]	$142/6 \times 5/0$–152/6	$157/6 \times 5/0$–167/6
	$\times 7/6$–182/6[3]	$\times 7/6$–197/6[3]
Scale 'A'[2]	$165/0 \times 7/6$–210/0[3]	$180/0 \times 7/6$–225/0[3]

[1] There was a proficiency bar after the fifth (adult) year; increments beyond the bar were not necessarily awarded at annual intervals.

[2] The minimum of the scale was linked to age 21.

[3] A proficiency bar operated after the fourth year. The final increment was payable after five years on the previous rate.

* As from 27 April 1952 all rates of those under 21 were increased by 5s. and those of adults by 9s. Further revisions have taken place since.

PART II

Chapter 18

SALARY STRUCTURE

In this section we examine various facets of the structure of salary patterns, the contents of the preceding chapters providing the raw material for our analysis. Though much of what follows is of a more general nature, the reader is reminded that, as regards most of the detailed figures, the ensuing review is linked to the same time-span as Part I.

We may begin with the question of the division into, and basis of, classes and grades. Before doing so, it might be emphasized that this matter is closely bound up with that of pay levels in general but, though from some points of view it would have been preferable to discuss the two separately, this is not really practicable. Thus a factor such as educational attainments may be of the essence of a service's class structure; alternatively, it may give rise to individual grades within a class, be in a general way weighted in the salary of the post, lead to an additional allowance, a one-time grant or, finally, it may be ignored. The same is roughly true of the function of supervision. By and large, the more concrete a characteristic, the more is it likely to influence structure as well as pay, while the more elusive attributes of jobs tend to be reflected in remuneration only.

The Division into Classes and Grades
In the Civil Service the clerico-administrative hierarchy—which is the backbone of the Civil Service pyramid—was originally built on the basis of the educational requirements expected of candidates: The clerical assistant, the clerical, the executive and the administrative classes were meant to be staffed by those leaving school at 14, at matriculation, 'Higher Schools' and university level. Though this pattern has since been modified in that recruits are now drawn from a considerably wider field, these four educational standards— or their current equivalents—are still mirrored in the class structure of Whitehall. Such a four-tier foundation has no precise parallel in any of the other public services; the executive category, in particular, is unique. Its existence has been justified on the ground that in the Civil Service the function of administration includes not only the execution of policy as laid down by the legislature, but participa-

tion in the shaping thereof to a greater extent than, say, in local government; a distinction between those formulating and those executing policy was therefore felt to be necessary.

The factor of *academic or professional qualifications* is of course an important one in many spheres. The prerequisite for belonging to a profession is to hold such qualifications, though once these have been secured, grading is largely decided by other criteria. In teaching, at the time of writing, the obtaining of a professional qualification is not as yet an absolute essential; the status of 'qualified teacher' can still be gained *either* by a professional training *or* the possession of a university degree (or equivalent), the former not being insisted upon in view of the supply position. The holding of a degree, in turn, merely makes one into a higher-paid teacher; education is not formally divided on this basis.

Though the acquiring of prescribed qualifications is a precondition for entry to certain grades, it does not, mostly, entitle one to automatic transfer to these. In local government, for instance, one is not placed in the APT division unless one is appointed to a post enjoying an APT classification. Similarly, a senior registrar does not become a consultant merely because he has the necessary training or performs analogous duties. On the other hand, grade 2 Civil Service (shorthand) typists move into grade 1 as soon as specific tests are passed, as do student nurses and student and junior medical laboratory technicians. On the whole, however, the principle adopted is that the job rather than the man is to be rated.

The function of *supervision* may determine or co-determine the shape of pay structures; in some cases, for example, it is possible to align grades to an administrative or organizational unit. Thus in the Civil Service administrative class a permanent secretary is the official head of one of the major departments, assistant secretaries are usually in charge of divisions, and principals of a branch or section of a division. Similarly, provincial police establishments are under the overall control of chief constables, under whom each force is grouped into divisions under superintendents, sub-divisions under inspectors and sections under sergeants. Ward sisters—as indicated by their title—are responsible for a defined segment of hospital organization.

Where there is no convenient administrative unit or where a further elaboration of a grade is considered necessary, this is frequently on the basis of numbers of staff supervised. Thus police superintendents have been split into class II, I or 'chief' according to the size of their divisional establishment; chief constables are allocated to one of a series of scales according to the strength of their force. Numbers supervised has likewise been one of the main criteria for stratifying senior medical auxiliaries and Civil Service supervisors of typists.

A somewhat different method of defining responsibility in terms of persons is the system operative for higher local government personnel, such as town clerks and certain chief officers. Here remuneration varies not according to staff complements, but in the light of the population of the local authority. We may add that the fact that town clerks' and chief officers' pay primarily depends on the authority's population, while that of more junior local government officials does not, is illustrative of a common feature of public service salary patterns—i.e. they frequently rest on different principles at different levels of seniority.

Equipment—rated on a cash or on a numerical basis—provides an alternative means of classification. Clerks of work in the Civil Service technical classes, for instance, have been graded according to the value of the building schemes of which they have the oversight, while fire service personnel have been ranked according to the number of appliances at their fire station. Again, the salaries of those manning the local valuation panels, set up under the Local Government Act, 1948, were primarily related to 'number of hereditaments', though it was recognized that the value of the latter was also a factor.

The above are examples of grading by organizational unit, persons or things of which the worker is in charge; in some cases, so simple a criterion is not considered adequate. Thus head teachers' salaries are not linked to the staffing complement of their schools; this would be unsatisfactory, as teacher-pupil ratios are not uniform. This could be taken care of by a classification by number of pupils, but in fact a head's remuneration is determined both by the latter and their age: There is an attempt to weight quality as well as quantity of responsibility. Similarly, hospital matrons' salaries used to be a function both of the 'beddage' of their institution and of whether the latter was a full training, an assistant nurse training or a non-training hospital, though since 1959 the *type* of training provided is ignored.

Grading may be settled by a system of *interpolation*: The Civil Service administrative class comprises several levels intermediate between those in charge of the various organizational units. Similarly, the salary of a tier may be determined by reference to that of a key grade. Certain senior nursing staff, for example, have been paid as ward sisters plus an allowance, while the remuneration of overmen and shotfirers in the coal industry was (end-1951) fixed in relation to that of grade 1 deputies in the same wages district. Again, a deputy medical officer of health was in 1950 given a minimum equal to two-thirds of that of the MOH for the area.

Age frequently serves as the mainstay of grading and pay at the bottom of salary structures, particularly in the case of routine clerical and analogous workers. However, even here age is not necessarily the sole determinant of remuneration; moreover, there has been a tendency to allow it less weight. Thus in the BBC 1951 clerical pattern age-pay still existed but to a much lesser extent than previously: It was to be found only for the three lowest tiers, who at the same time had alternative merit-entry points. In local government age-pay for the general divison was up to age 32 in 1948, reduced to 30 in 1951,[1] and has since been progressively abolished; the electricity supply and coal industries have likewise reduced the extent to which staff are rewarded on this basis.

Though mainly important at the clerical level, age-pay is not confined to it; for a number of professional occupations the normal commencing salary is related to an age-point, those older or younger receiving stated amounts above or below. Taking the position as at end-1951, the Civil Service executive and professional classes were in this category; in the case of full professional (other than scientific) appointments, the standard commonly adopted was 26. Probation officers' remuneration was age-tied from 23 to 30, while for professional and technical staff in British Railways (Group 'A'), pay varied with years right up to 36. In the National Health Service there was age-linkage for a number of technical grades on the one hand, and for senior hospital medical officers and consultants on the other; the latter were exceptional in that it is unusual for there to be an age element in the salary attaching to the top tier of a profession.[2] The age factor was absent, among others, in the pay structures of the police,[3] fire and prison services, in education and nursing, as also for all local government professional appointments.[4]

On the whole, then, there is considerable divergence in the matter as between the different public services. The primary factor of whether age pay exists appears to be the amount of routine work to be done: *faute de mieux* it is assumed that an individual's usefulness is in proportion to his maturity, but where skill and responsibility are relatively more important, these are frequently regarded as a more satisfactory determinant of remuneration. Secondly, age-pay is held

[1] Though it was 30 also in 1946.

[2] The 1960 Royal Commission on Doctors' and Dentists' Remuneration recommended certain changes, however, amounting to a lessening of the age element in the salaries for young consultants.

[3] The Royal Commission on the Police, in their 1960 Interim Report, considered whether the starting pay of constables should vary according to age, but decided to recommend against it.

[4] Some of these fields prescribed age standards of *entry* for new recruits; we are here concerned only with age-based *pay* variations.

to be appropriate where staff are recruited at different levels of seniority—in particular, where they are drawn from both juveniles and adults or where they are required to have some previous outside experience.[1] As to its significance, insofar as recruitment is concerned it is clearly a more flexible instrument than a rigid uniform minimum payable to all and sundry. Equally clearly, it is less flexible than a system allowing commencing salaries to depend on all the relevant factors of the situation, and in a period of shortage of juvenile workers, a strict regime of age-pay can be a serious embarrassment.

Experience is weighted in salary structures in a variety of ways. In the medical auxiliary world the official definition of the higher levels has frequently included a provision that holders must have done a prescribed period of service in the profession. Mostly, however, the factor of experience gives rise to separate grades implicitly rather than explicitly; it is of the essence of a hierarchical pyramid that those holding senior posts have served in its humbler reaches, even where this is not stated in so many words. Experience is of course all-important *within* the grade, where it is recognized by the system of increments. We deal with this later in this chapter.

As regards experience gained prior to joining a service, practice varies. Where this is a prerequisite for entry, it is likely to be reflected in the commencing salary itself—as in the case of public health assistant medical officers. Where, on the other hand, it is optional, it may or may not be given monetary recognition. Thus the Burnham reports provide that previous outside experience may—if considered exceptionally valuable—reckon as fully equivalent to reaching service, but will in any case count as equal to one-third of such service. Similarly, where there is a system of age-pay, a person is given full credit for whatever occupation he may have followed in the past. In other fields, however, a late entrant must be content to climb the ladder from the minimum of the bottom rung.

We have reviewed various attempts to find an objective measure of 'workload' and responsibility. In some instances numerical tests are at hand, though these are of course capable of misapplication. Thus the pay of police superintendents used to vary according to the total complement of their force, but as superintendents themselves are merely in charge of divisions, this meant that those heading a small division that happened to be part of a large establishment were on a higher scale than those responsible for a large division but belonging to a small constabulary. Again, several different criteria may suggest themselves; which is the most relevant may be a matter of con-

---

[1] cf. e.g. Civil Service Arbitration Tribunal Award No. 142 (HMSO 1951), para. 4.

troversy. In the case of fire service personnel, for example, the question has been debated whether the number of appliances at a station or the work actually falling on it should determine grading. Problems arise particularly when different decisions are reached to cover parallel cases. Thus deputy medical officers of health have received two-thirds of the remuneration of their chief—the MOH— at a time when other local authority seconds-in-command have had a salary pattern quite distinct from that of their chief officers.

Objective criteria may be only partially available. As regards pre-NHS consultants, for example, it seems to be generally agreed that training and qualifications were not the whole story; recognition by colleagues—and, the irreverent are tempted to add, a Harley Street address—were crucial. Even where classification is based on some seemingly foolproof index, such as, say—taking head teachers—the number and ages of pupils, this is no guarantee that in its detailed features the scheme is perfect: In the calculation of head teacher allowances under the 1951 Burnham Report one pupil under 15 counted as one 'unit total', one aged 15 as four, one of 16 as seven, and one aged 17 and over as ten. This meant that the additions were heavily weighted in favour of grammar-school heads. Under the revised rules introduced in 1956, pupils aged 13 and 14 were made to rank as two units apiece, while 16-year-olds were devalued somewhat —to six units. Clearly, however, a case could be made out for several alternative formulae—depending on one's views as to the relative worth of different types of headships.

Moreover, where measurable criteria are at hand, there may be a temptation to base grading on these to a greater extent than is warranted. The skill required for handling certain equipment may or may not vary with its cash value. The number of subordinates controlled may likewise be only a partial guide. Grading, in short, is a matter of appraising the total weight of the responsibility involved—its quality as well as its quantity—and any one factor taken in isolation may be misleading.

The most difficult element to assess in salaried employment then is responsibility; it is usually the item for which the highest payment is made—in contrast to many manual jobs where skill is often primary. One problem in this context is whether, in evaluating a post, *de facto* or *de jure* responsibility should be rated, this question arising particularly in the public services with their long lines of command. Frequently, responsibility here is officially assigned to some fairly senior level, though for all practical purposes it is exercised by someone much lower down the hierarchy. Thus in the course of a 1949 arbitration hearing concerning the remuneration of forestry staff, the Civil Service Union claimed that the forester shouldered a great deal of responsibility; the Forestry Commission contended that this lay, ultimately, with the district officer and that the lower grade was not entitled to any increase on this score. While this is a matter where each case must be judged on its merits, it may well be that a certain amount of frustration would be avoided if, in allocating monetary reward for the responsibility factor, a somewhat larger share were made to accrue to those actually carrying the burden and a relatively smaller one to those formally in control.

Some of the problems of grading and pay determination might well be solved by a greater use of job analysis and evaluation. If we have drawn attention to possible misapplications of numerical and similar criteria—and by implication, therefore, of job analysis—this has not been in order to disparage such techniques. In fact, the view is here taken that as far as the 'intrinsic' factors in jobs are concerned—the training and qualifications demanded, the skill and responsibility involved, the arduousness of the work, etc.—some form of job analysis should be employed in order to help rid rates of remuneration of their arbitrary element. It is true that no absolute standards will be established thereby; judgment is involved at every stage of the process. As A. K. Rice put it: 'The technique described here is not a substitute for judgment, it is only a method of collecting evidence in order that the judgment can be made.'[1] This, however, is unavoidable and if—in respect of those aspects of posts that are within its competence—job evaluation manages to introduce as much objectivity as the 'human condition' will allow, this would be a real step forward.

The limitations of job evaluation are both that in practice it does not, and that it in any case cannot, tackle all facets of pay determination. We are not referring to man- as distinct from job-factors such as special proficiency and long service, which can be covered by personal merit-rating and so on. Over and above these, there are a number of wider issues which are not normally treated as amenable to its techniques. Further, there is the crucial point that the economic factor cannot be dealt with by its methods. We return to these topics in subsequent chapters.

As to the division of salary structures into classes and grades, we may sum up by saying that, while this may be expected to vary with the nature and scope of the service, it would be rather stretching a point if we were to attempt to specify a consistent set of principles on which the different public service hierarchies can be said to have evolved. It would seem more accurate to suggest that the latter are the resultant of a complex of causes—historical, the facts and accidents of collective bargaining arrangements, the genuine needs of the service, analogies with fields considered 'comparable' at the crucial

[1] A. K. Rice, *Assessing the Job* (Industrial Welfare Society, 2nd ed., 1947).

moment of birth, on all of which has been superimposed such measure of rationalization as the two sides have been able to agree to from time to time. Thus the salary pattern of the newly-nationalized gas and electricity industries showed a fairly close resemblance to that of local government, partly because many of their non-manual workers —being previously employed by municipally-owned undertakings— were covered by the local government Charter. This in turn meant that NALGO—which operates in the local government sphere— likewise became the staff association in gas and electricity. Similarly —functional explanations notwithstanding—the main reason for the survival of the Civil Service executive class may well be largely traditional: Second division clerks had somehow to be fitted into the revised staff structure by the 1920 Reorganization Committee, and *status quo* considerations have decreed that they shall continue to occupy the niche then allocated to them. By and large, there is a tendency to fewer grades and a closer alignment of different types of personnel where a service is relatively young and unencumbered by the heritage of past practice.

Allowances
The question of allowances closely hinges on that of general class and grade structure. As indicated, the holding, say, of specific qualifications may give rise to an allowance; alternatively, it may constitute the very basis of the grading pattern. What form the extra remuneration takes is partly inherent in the type of service, partly a matter of accident and terminology, though it may also reflect genuine policy differences as to the desirable size and character of differentials. No conclusion as to the weighting of a particular factor can, however, be drawn merely from the existence or otherwise of a special addition.

The term 'allowance' is of course a generic one: Superannuation payments, annual increments, area differentials, overtime payments and so forth all belong to the species; if we deal with some of these separately, this is largely a matter of convenience. One broad distinction in the type of allowance—now using the term in its narrow sense—is between those which merely compensate an individual for a particular expense, disability or personal circumstance, and those which are designed as a straightforward addition to salary. The former include subsistence, car and travelling allowances, sick leave payments, dependants' allowances and so on. They really fall under the heading of conditions of service, and a detailed investigation is beyond the scope of this study.

That the first (emolumentary) type of allowance is part and parcel of conditions of service rather than of rates of remuneration in the strict sense does not, however, mean that they can be ignored in a consideration of the latter. For they belong to the 'net advantages' of an occupation, and differences in their incidence or the terms on which they are granted are important—much more so than some minor divergences in £ *s d*. Thus policemen and prison officers receive fairly substantial rent additions over and above their cash salary, and though these are designed to compensate them for an obvious expense, the fact that they are now the only major categories of public servants to be eligible for them, clearly amounts to their enjoying a significant supplement to their remuneration. The same is true of the family allowance system operative in the universities and the dependants' benefits for student nurses : Such schemes are not found in any of the other fields reviewed. The emolumentary type of addition then must be reckoned in full in calculating the net dvantages of an occupation.[1]

As regards those allowances which are a straightforward increase of pay, by and large these exist where the factor that is being rewarded is not sufficiently important to warrant a separate grade, or where only relatively few individuals undertake the duty or hold the qualification in question. Here, again, whether or not a supplement actually accrues depends to a large extent on grade structure : In an elaborate clerical hierarchy such as that (end-1951) of the BBC, all shades of typists can be fitted into one of the numerous levels available, where in a less complex pyramid they might retain their basic rate, augmented by an allowance. A person having the oversight of cleaners in the Civil service, for instance, receives such an allowance over and above the cleaner's wage ; clearly, this is merely a less formal equivalent of a supervisory tier.

The most common factors in respect of which allowances—other than those of the emolumentary kind—are granted are

(*a*) supervisory duties
(*b*) other additional responsibilities
(*c*) special qualifications, etc.

As an example of (*a*), we may cite the various supervision allowances available to members of the Post Office manipulative group. As regards (*b*), such additions may be either in respect of duties regarded as in some way *superior* to those normal for the grade, or simply to compensate for some *extra* burden. The weekly weighting over and above the basic prison 'discipline' scale, paid until 1958 to all subordinate staff in borstal institutions, is an illustration of the former ; the fees accruing to consultants undertaking domiciliary visits, of the latter. Among payments for special qualifications, etc.,

---

[1] The problem of 'net advantages' is dealt with more fully in Chapter 20.

are those granted to medical auxiliaries holding certificates beyond those essential for their professional work, the graduate additions for teachers and the distinction awards for National Health Service consultants.

A different type of supplement is that awarded for many years—though abolished in 1960—to nursing staff engaged on TB work and formerly also to midwifery personnel. In part these belong to the 'extra burden' genus; yet they were specifically introduced because the recruitment of this class of nurse proved particularly difficult. They are therefore an interesting example of an allowance designed to meet economic scarcity, and are something of a rare bird in this respect. Here, again, we must qualify in that increases granted for analogous reasons are, more usually, merged into the overall rate of remuneration; alternatively, where the manpower shortage is primarily a local one, it may be dealt with by some form of area differential.[1]

If we have tried to distinguish between various type of allowances, this has been to isolate some of the factors which they seek to reward; many additions contain an element of more than one of these, while others—as indicated—may not necessarily fit into any of our categories. We might now, however, turn to another aspect of the subject, namely the principle on which the amount of allowances is determined. One method is to calculate this in terms of a standard sum —i.e. one which may fluctuate with the 'intensity' of the task undertaken, but which does not vary according to the rank and salary of its holder. Thus, taking the early post-war period, the size of language allowances for Post Office telephonists depended on the number of foreign languages known or used, but not on whether the individual was a rank-and-file telephonist or supervisor.[2] Similarly, the payments for specialist duties in the prison service—accruing to those acting as trade instructor, librarian, cook and so on—were identical for basic-grade, principal and chief officers. Again, the 'service' addition for TB nurses was a uniform £30 per annum, though in pre-Health Service days those above ward sister were not entitled to the benefit.

The main alternative method of computation is to vary allowances according to the grade or salary of their recipient. Thus the addition for acting as private secretary to a Minister or head of department is higher for a Civil Service principal than for an assistant principal.

---

[1] See *post.*

[2] The allowance for the use of one foreign language was (1947–51) 12s. p.w. for the rank-and-file grade, and £32 p.a. for (assistant) supervisors; the difference of 16s. p.a. can be regarded as a rounding of the weekly figure into its annual equivalent.

Rent allowances for policemen increase with rank, though their magnitude also depends on area and marital status. Overtime pay is invariably based on remuneration, while the granting of super-annuation benefits is governed by both salary and length of service. Area differentials may or may not fluctuate with pay; we deal with these in the next section.

Provincial Differentiation

We may start this section with a word about the overall scope of the various salary patterns as far as the different parts of the British Isles are concerned. In the case of the Civil Service, Post Office, BBC and civil air transport, the national structure covers the whole of the United Kingdom. National Health Service and academic rates apply in Great Britain, as do the agreements of the nationalized coal, elec-tricity supply, gas and transport[1] industries. The competence of the Burnham Committees and of the National Joint Council for Local Authorities' Administrative, Professional, Technical and Clerical Services, on the other hand, is limited to England and Wales. This, of course, is simply a reflection of the constitutional position of these different fields, though whether such constitutional frontiers need necessarily be reproduced in collective bargaining arrangements is an interesting point. Thus public health medical and nursing personnel now have standard rates of remuneration throughout Great Britain, fixed by NHS Whitley machinery; these relate equally to employees of English and Scottish local authorities. Yet for the great majority of other local government staff there are distinct salary schemes north and south of the border.

As for provincial differentiation proper—the practice of paying varying rates according to locality *within* the national pattern—three main systems can be distinguished in the post-war period. The Civil Service, for the greater part of the latter, had—subject to a number of qualifications—a three-tier scheme, consisting of a standard Lon-don scale with graded deductions in 'intermediate' and 'provincial' centres. This system was, in mid-1951, likewise extended to Post Office manipulative (though not to Post Office engineering) staffs— in place of the four-pronged pattern in force since 1946. Another field adopting a three-tier structure following its translation to the public sector was the gas industry, though in this instance grading as between provincial 'A' and 'B' has been determined by size of works rather than on a strict basis of locality. Finally, in the case of (non-resident) public health nurses, the national scales used to be augmented by a London allowance which was higher for those inside, than for those outside, the LCC boundary. However, this latter dis-

[1] Other than civil air transport.

tinction was abolished in 1954, while—as we saw in Chapter 1[1]—radical changes were introduced in the central government sphere in the late 'fifties. Under these, the difference between 'intermediate' and 'provincial' has been totally eliminated; at the same time, a higher weighting now accrues in the 'inner ring', than in the rest, of the London pay region, so that the Civil Service can be said to have emerged with a new three-tier version of area differentiation.

At the other end of the spectrum, we find a number of fields with one uniform standard applicable throughout the country. Among these are public health doctors, medical dons at universities and, hitherto, all hospital medical personnel, though the 1960 Royal Commission on Doctors' and Dentists' Remuneration recommended that 'peripheral' hospitals—i.e. those outside towns containing teaching institutions—should be allowed to pay up to an extra £100 per annum to recruits to certain hospital grades.[2] There has been one rate, likewise, for BBC staff—though not necessarily for performers—and for BOAC (but not for BEA) pilots and stewards. As far as the judiciary is concerned, remuneration is invariably one-tier in so far as salaries are laid down by Parliament.

The most common system, however, is a two-tier one, in which a national standard exists, augmented by a 'weighting' in the metropolis. This has been the operative pattern for the great majority of local government staff, for teachers and for other than medical academics. We have met it likewise in the coal industry clerico-administrative sphere, in electricity supply and in the probation service. Another example is British Railways—though until 1960 only as regards those below 'special class' level. National Health Service nurses and medical auxiliaries are now also in this category, though in the early post-war years they had mostly still a single undifferentiated scale. The fire service, on the other hand,[3] though put on a two-tier basis in 1950, currently additionally distinguishes between inner and outer London. In the case of the police, remuneration is two-tier for constables and sergeants, supplemented by—all ranks—a network of in part area-based rent allowances.

It will be seen that—now that the Civil Service has abandoned the distinction between 'intermediate' and 'provincial'—it is not usual to find a formal and permanent differential in respect of large towns other than the capital. Though the staff in a number of fields have pressed for these, their efforts have not been successful. *De facto*, however, such 'large city' weightings can be said to exist in the police

---

[1] See p. 57 *ante*.

[2] *Royal Commission on Doctors' and Dentists' Remuneration* 1957–60, Cmnd. 939 (HMSO 1960), para. 293.

[3] With the exception of chief and assistant chief officers.

and prison services, where—if quarters are not provided in kind—rent allowances are granted which *inter alia* vary elaborately and steeply according to locality. We may here also mention two spheres in which special payments are awarded to those *not* in large urban centres, but in inconvenient or otherwise unattractive ones. First, the prison 'discipline' grades have—rent additions apart and the one-tier basis of their national scales notwithstanding—a system of 'inconvenience of locality' supplements, accruing at the more out-of-the-way institutions. Secondly, there are the substantial, though temporary, 'initial practice allowances', available to general practitioners starting new practices in 'designated'—i.e. under-doctored—areas, while a handful of GPs also receive annual 'inducement payments'. We may add that the Pilkington Commission recommended a similar scheme for the purpose of encouraging dentists to settle in remote outposts,[1] while their proposals regarding the extra £100 for would-be medical recruits to peripheral hospitals are of course also in this category, except that payment here is to be permissive rather than mandatory.

The subject of provincial differentiation is, in any event, not exhausted by an account of the various formal schemes. First, the salary pattern itself may be devised in such a way as to contain an 'area' element. Local government chief officers and town clerks, whose remuneration is governed by the population of their authority, are an example; so are chief constables who have a series of scales, depending on the size of their establishment. Size of police force, for instance, clearly reflects the area factor, though owing to, among other things, the varying incidence of crime, it is not exclusively based on it. However, here the regional differential cannot be neatly isolated. This is likewise true of those staffs—say, senior National Coal Board headquarters personnel or further education principals—whose salary is determined on a personal basis, or where—as in the case of recorders and provincial stipendiary magistrates—remuneration is altogether a local affair.

Further, where any kind of discretion exists in the actual fixing of standards, the area factor may enter into the picture by the backdoor; as we saw in Chapter 2, the 1948 Survey of the Local Government Service revealed that metropolitan borough employees were being more advantageously graded than their provincial colleagues—and this was well before the National Joint Council formally authorized special arrangements for certain metropolitan borough and Birmingham Corporation staff. Again, in the police the rank

---

[1] Cmnd. 939, op .cit., para. 392. Though GPs and dentists are fee-paid rather than salaried, we shall be making occasional reference to particular features of their pay structure.

structure is uniform only in so far as constables and sergeants are concerned; above this level the metropolitan and provincial hierarchies diverge, so that it is difficult to diagnose the precise dose of London weighting allowed for in the standards prevailing in the capital.

In spite of its pivotal role in the context of area differentiation, there is no consensus of opinion as to how 'London' is to be defined for this purpose—a situation which, we may point out, is exactly paralleled on the wider wages front.[1] If, for example, we take the position at a specific point of time—such as our favourite date of end-1951—we find that British Railways' London allowance accrued within a 10-mile radius of Charing Cross, Civil Service London scales did so within 12 miles of the latter, but the London weighting in local government, probation and the fire service was payable in the whole of the City of London and Metropolitan Police District— i.e. about 15 miles from Charing Cross. In the gas industry, further, 'metropolitan' standards applied in an area of much more generous dimensions, comprising—mainly for historical reasons—the entire domain of the old Gas, Light and Coke Company. Teachers' 'London', by contrast, was then considerably smaller than the MPD —a matter which caused numerous anomalies and strong resentment.[2] However, in 1953, 'London', for purposes of Burnham salaries, was made co-terminous with the Metropolitan Police District; the other major development has been the extension of the Civil Service London pay boundary to a span comprising 16 miles from Charing Cross. As against this growing ascendance of the Metropolitan Police District—it has likewise become the operative unit for National Health Service nurses, professional and technical staffs—the electricity supply industry has departed from this—its original—post-nationalization standard for its salaried personnel, its London rates now accruing in a considerably wider region.

Area differentials are calculated on diverse principles. In a number of fields they are based exclusively on location; elsewhere, the latter together with some other factor determine their size. Thus—confining ourselves now specifically to the position as at end-1951—differentials for civil servants, National Coal Board staff and BEA pilots

---

[1] See 'Local Variations in Wage Rates', *Ministry of Labour Gazette*, November 1958.

[2] In June 1950 the Minister of Education was asked if he was aware that, in the Chislehurst and Sidcup urban district area, clerks, caretakers, laboratory assistants, secretarial staff and school inquiry officers all received the London allowance, but the teachers employed in the same establishments did not (15 June 1950, HC Deb. 476, *41*). In 1949 similar anomalies in Kingston and Surbiton and the boroughs of Wanstead and Woodford were raised in the House.

varied according to salary;[1] in local government according to age; in electricity supply they depended on both, but in teaching on age or length of service. In probation, the fire service,[2] gas and British Railways, on the other hand, the allowance was a function solely of location, though in the case of the last-named, only relatively low-paid staff were eligible for the addition.

There is a similar divergence as far as the amount of the differential is concerned. Again basing ourselves on end-1951, the figure in British Railways, for example, was a standard £10, in local government from £10-£30, in teaching £36 or £48, in the universities[3] a uniform £50, but in the Civil Service from £5 to £100.[4]

While some of the difference in the size of allowances may be ascribed to the varying scope of the services concerned—Civil Service remuneration reaches very much higher than teachers'—the position is yet rather anomalous. Thus an officer with, say, an end-1951 provincial salary of £1,000 per annum would—if transferred to the metropolis—have received no addition to his pay if an NHS medical man or a BOAC pilot. In the fire service he would have qualified for an extra £26; in the local government APT division for an additional £30; if a head teacher, for £48;[5] if in the Civil Service or Post Office,[6] his remuneration would have gone up by £23 or £54, while if a Coal Board finance official, the amount accruing to him would have been £70.

If his (1951) post had been at the £500 point, the officer—on making a like move—would have emerged with his pay-packet unaltered, if in the BBC; have got an extra £10 a year, if working for British Railways; £30, if in the probation service; but £50, if in the academic world. Lower down the ladder, a junior with, say, a salary of £160 would have been eligible for an additional £10 per annum in local government, but for another £30 or £45 in the gas industry. Again, if we switch the exercise to an occupational plane, a consultant transferring from a provincial hospital to one in the capital would have found his remuneration unaffected, while a prison doctor translated to a London institution could have looked forward to anything up to an extra £100 a year.

Another interesting topic is the number of differentials existing in the various spheres for *other than* 'area' reasons. We saw before that

[1] For BEA pilots under 21 the London allowance varied with age only.

[2] Excluding chief and assistant chief officers.

[3] Excluding medical staff.

[4] For those with annual salaries. Weekly-paid staff had a different set of differentials.

[5] £36, if under age 37 and/or with less than 16 years' service.

[6] Excluding those who were not on the Civil Service three-tier system of provincial differentiation.

as far as the latter is concerned, systems are, broadly speaking, one-, two- or three-tier, but this has gone hand in hand with widely varying degrees of refinement based on the other factors chosen for defining the allowances. Thus in local government, throughout most of the post-war period, the London weighting was either £10 or £20 or £30 according to age.[1] In the Civil Service, on the other hand—during the years 1947 to 1957—there were, for an 'intermediate' monthly-paid officer, 46 possible levels of deduction from the London standard; for one engaged in a 'provincial' office, the analogous number was 91. This was because although the deductions were formally fixed at £5- or £10-intervals according to salary-band, there was an elaborate pattern of escalator provisions to 'ease the transition to the larger deduction'.[2] These latter, we may add, will have finally disappeared by 1962, though the series of differential rates which will operate when the transition to the new regime is complete[3] will still be high compared with most other fields.

A few remarks may be added about the rationale of provincial differentiation. Area differentials may be expected to exist on two grounds: First, because the cost of living varies in different parts of the country and second, because the demand-supply situation so varies.[4] As far as the first reason is concerned, we cannot but conclude from the evidence that the attempt to equalize 'real salaries' is at best haphazard: 'Some Londoners—in a London of uncertain boundaries—get something or other' would be an irreverent, but not an inaccurate, summing up of the position, while differences in living costs outside the metropolis are, with certain exceptions, ignored.

The second *raison d'être* for provincial differentiation is the relative shortage of occupations as between localities but, as a broad generalization, area differentials in the public services do not appear to owe much to this factor. Here again there are exceptions—such as some branches of the National Health Service; further, it is no doubt the

[1] These standards prevailed from 1 April 1948 until 1 May 1960. As from the latter date, the figures are £15, £25 and £40 according to age, except that those with salaries above a certain point now receive £45.
[2] cf. p. 56 *ante* and Royal Commission on the Civil Service (1953), *Introductory Factual Memorandum on the Civil Service*, submitted by HM Treasury (HMSO 1954), p. 5, para. 14. A Birmingham civil servant e.g. had (1951) £40 deducted, if his London standard was £1,277–£1,504; £41, if £1,505–£1,512; £42, if £1,513–£1,520, etc. Weekly staff had a different set of differentials.
[3] For details see EC 12/61, *Whitley Bulletin*, May 1961, p. 75 and ff.
[4] cf. J. R. Hicks, *The Theory of Wages* (Macmillan, 1932) p. 74: 'Even in a position of equilibrium, some local differences indeed would probably persist. Some are due to differences in the cost of living, some to the indirect attractions of living in certain localities . . .'

case that the London weightings frequently accrue to those who also happen to be in short supply. However, the principles on which the additions are computed—as, by and large, their size—strongly suggest that the overcoming of occupational scarcity cannot be their main target. More important is the qualification that geographical differentiation due to market considerations may—as mentioned—be effected by certain less immediately visible means: The elimination of age-pay for clerical recruits or a given latitude in the matter of grading clearly give scope for such informal differentiation. Yet the latter is by no means feasible under all salary patterns, and on the whole the impression is gained that public services tend to shy away from economically-inspired regional pay differences. An interesting illustration is the police, where there have been striking—and persistent—variations in the degree of undermanning throughout the country. But while rent allowances fluctuate widely with the local cost of house-room, similar fluctuations linked to the local dearth of policemen have not been introduced, would be highly unpopular and have again been pronounced against in the 1960 Report of the Royal Commission.[1] Though the latter advanced several cogent reasons for its rejection of differential rates, it is a question of whether any other method can solve the problem of differential scarcity.

The Structure of Scales, Increments, etc.

Salaries may be in the form of flat rates, ranges or scales. The practice of remunerating by *flat rate* is not widespread, except at the more august levels. Examples are (1951) the highest grade of pilot, university professors, the top class of prison governor, the three highest categories of chief constable and judges. Headmasters may also be considered as on this system: They are paid as ordinary teachers plus an allowance; *qua* heads they do not qualify for increments. In the Civil Service fixed rates are found among some of the humbler ranks such as messengers, where a post is the most senior in a particular occupational group but, more generally, mainly in the upper reaches —above assistant secretary or equivalent. In local government, on the other hand, remuneration retains its incremental character all the way up,[2] as it does in the hospital medical pyramid. We may add that, in the case of medical house officers, pay is in the shape of a fixed sum simply because posts here are tenable for less than a year.

Where a *range* exists, a minimum and a maximum are laid down

[1] *Report of Sir Malcolm Trustram Eve* (1951), para. 20 and *Royal Commission on the Police* 1960, *Interim Report*, Cmnd. 1222 (HMSO 1960), para. 167.

[2] Though the position of town clerks and chief officers in the largest authorities is not defined nationally: see Tables 15 and 16.

in the national agreement; within this span, a scale is devised at some lower level of management. In the Civil Service ranges are infrequent and have been used primarily for unestablished staff; the amount of increment is specified by the Treasury, a range thus differing from a scale only in that the individual's point of entry is at departmental discretion. In local government, town clerks and chief officers—including medical officers of health—have ranges; here again the size and number of increments are standardized from the centre.

The BBC 1951 pattern of age/merit entry points, 'special awards' and personal grades was in fact—if not in name—the equivalent of a system of ranges, while in some fields either the minimum or the maximum may be optionally increased, again producing something of a hybrid between a scale and a range. In the National Coal Board the latter has been popular; as regards hospital matrons, on the other hand, the pre-NHS ranges in force under Rushcliffe for those in the larger institutions have been superseded by fixed scales.

As the tables in Part I will have demonstrated, the 'typical' method of remuneration in the public services is the *scale*, on which an individual moves from his point of entry—the minimum or appropriate age-pay point—by prescribed payments to the maximum. Increments are mostly annual, though in a few instances—such as railway salaried grades not rewarded on an age basis—they are granted biennially. A few salary structures contain arrangements for long-service increases—notably the police and fire services. In the case of teachers, a one-time demand for these has not been conceded, though currently pressure is rather for an overall shortening of the scale. Many agreements stipulate that increments may be withheld for inefficiency or disciplinary offences, while in a number of fields—for example, university lectureships—progression beyond a certain point is subject to a special efficiency bar. Provisions permitting an acceleration of increments are much less common.

As to the size of increments, as far as clerical and analogous workers are concerned these are frequently larger in the early, than in the later, stages of the officer's career, while in many spheres a sizeable boost is given at the 19 or 20 age-point. Quoting the figures for end-1951, Post Office telegraphists, for example, received 24s. at that age, postal and telegraph officers 20s., and National Coal Board clerks 18s., all other increments being substantially smaller. In British Railways a comparable 'jump' occurred on attaining 17. Similarly, in civil air transport the annual rise for those in the two bottom clerical grades was 7s. 6d. up to, but 17s. 6d. at, age 20; thereafter it was 5s. For Civil Service clerical assistants the additions were likewise more generous in the 'teens than in the twenties. For electricity, gas and local government clerks, however, increments—in this instance at 20 and 21—were only somewhat greater than for their juvenile and adult colleagues.[1]

The granting of relatively higher increases during the early part of his working life appears to be to help the young adult to provide himself with a living wage, but also—in particular as regards postal staffs —by analogy with practice in outside industrial employment. These factors are largely inapplicable in the case of the professions, and here the annual rise attaching to any one rung of the ladder tends to be uniform, though at times it is stepped up as a person travels up his scale. As far as *different* levels within any one pyramid are concerned, increments are generally greater the more senior the grade, though here again there are exceptions: As shown on Table 28, all tiers within the pharmacy hierarchy used to attract annual payments of £25.

If we compare the amount of increment awarded at identical 'cash' points in the various public services, some interesting differences come to light. Basing ourselves on a survey of *annual* salaries operative at end-1951, we find that at the lower levels these were not as yet pronounced. On an income of £250, for instance, they merely ranged from £15 to £25. At the £500 point, a senior almoner had a £12.10.0 increment,[2] local government scales and a number of postal grades attracted £15, teachers received £18, National Coal Board clerical officers and probation officers £20, pharmacists £25, and BBC monthly grade D £30/£35. Assistant lecturers in the University of London and town clerks, however, were eligible for a £50 increase.

It is at a salary level of £1,000 that the variations become marked. Fire service grade I divisional officers received an addition of £20 at this point; technical teachers, training college senior lecturers and class I police superintendents one of £25. Head postmasters and Civil Service technical staff qualified for £30, NCB administrative officials for £30 or £35, and Civil Service principals for £40. Town clerks and junior hospital medical officers enjoyed £50, and BBC monthly staff £45–£60. The £1,000 salary of a National Health Service senior registrar, finally, attracted a rise of £100.

At the £1,500 point, increments ranged from £25 for grade V technical college heads of departments to £85 for BBC monthly staff in grade A2. Civil Service assistant secretaries got £75. At the £2,000 level, the figure varied from £50 for some mecial officers of health[3] to £125 for consultants.

---

[1] In local government and gas e.g. the increment was £25 at ages 20 and 21— as against £20 immediately before and after.

[2] The annual increment for police sergeants (end-1951 salary: £540–£585) was £10, except for the final increment which was £15.

[3] Increments were higher if the population of the MOH's authority was above 150,000: see Table 23 *ante*.

The Royal (Priestley) Commission on the Civil Service stated that there did not seem to be any strict rules governing the relationship between amount of increment and scale level; the former was not a constant percentage of the maximum and some flexibility in the matter seemed appropriate.[1] While there is some substance in these remarks, and while allowance must also be made for the fact that a particular sum of cash may represent a different level of seniority in the various scales/hierarchies, the wide divergences found are nevertheless noteworthy. On any theory of scale lengths, it seems odd that a fire service divisional officer was only worthy of £20 a year on a salary of £1,000, while a National Health Service senior registrar qualified for £100. Similarly, to grant a technical college departmental head a rise of £25 at the £1,500 point—$1\frac{2}{3}$ per cent of his remuneration—could hardly have been adequate to reward him for whatever it was that the extra increment was intended to reward him. This may be contrasted with the boost given to town clerks at the £500 level, which constituted 10 per cent of income.

One trend which can be discerned is that the size of increment is influenced by the 'climate' of the general level of remuneration prevailing in the field. Thus in teaching and the medical auxiliary world the annual increases tend to be low, while the opposite is true of medicine and the BBC. It is the 'climate' of the particular hierarchy, moreover—rather than that of the service as such—which is important. Increments are high for the specialist grades in the National Health Service rather than for all medical posts, while they are actually meagre for NHS nurses.[2]

We now come to the question of the length of scales as such. It would appear that the 'theory' of the matter is made up of various elements. First, scale length reflects the increasing usefulness of a worker as he gains experience of his job[3]—though it must not be assumed that actual grading patterns are necessarily attuned to this with any very great precision. Secondly, increments are granted as an incentive.[4] Thirdly, they are paid as a reward for long service[5] or where promotion prospects are poor. Finally, long scales are a concession to the 'need' factor: A pre-war award of the Civil Service Arbitration Tribunal[6] observed that in earlier years, when expenses were going up, it was desirable that remuneration should likewise

[1] *Royal Commission on the Civil Service* 1953–5, Cmd. 9613 (HMSO 1955), para. 321.

[2] The increment (1951) at the £1,000 level was £30 for matrons—as against £100 for senior registrars.

[3] cf. e.g. Civil Service Arbitration Tribunal Award No. 142 (HMSO 1951), p. 5.

[4] cf. *Introductory Factual Memorandum on the Civil Service*, op. cit., para. 163.

[5] ibid.

[6] No. 40 (HMSO 1938).

rise. This aspect, however, has not been emphasized in recent negotiations except in a negative sense. Long structures tend to be looked upon as deferring payment of the full rate rather than as an addition compensating for mounting outlay; instead of welcoming the extra increments, staffs maintain that not reaching the maximum until the thirties is 'anti-social' and prevents the undertaking of family responsibilities. Long scales have frequently been blamed for recruitment difficulties.

Theory apart, the shape of a scale may have various unintended repercussions. Where an occupation has a long one as, for example, the teacher, this may mean that, in times of a relatively liberal supply, employing authorities will be reluctant to employ older personnel, as these will be considerably more 'expensive' than those on the bottom rungs of the ladder. Even if this will not lead to actual unemployment, it may reduce mobility among those of more mature years, who may be less able to secure transfers than their younger colleagues. While under present conditions of shortage this problem is hardly acute, it might be so were the balance of demand and supply to shift —as indeed it was a problem prior to the 1944 reorganization.

Tables 63 and 64 overleaf set out the minima and maxima for various recruitment grades in the public services, as well as the number of years' service required to progress from one to the other. The data relate to 1 December 1951, Table 63 being restricted to clerical and other more or less routine workers, while Table 64 is composed of a selection of basic grades from what might be termed Civil Service executive level and upwards. As regards scale lengths, those in local government were—with the exception of those in the general division—very short; the clerical, higher clerical and all the APT tiers each consisted of four points only.[1] In the Civil Service, by contrast, long scales were in force for many recruitment grades, as is shown by the clerical and executive officer entries. We may add that the Treasury considers medium-length structures (six to ten points) as suitable for those in the middle ranges and short scales—culminating in flat rates—at the most senior levels and for non-office personnel.[2]

Comparisons of scale lengths should not, however, be pressed, as the whole subject is again intimately bound up with that of the general pay pattern. Thus a staff nurse is the basic (fully-trained) rung of a multi-grade structure, while the teacher, in 1951, belonged to what was formally a two-tier hierarchy; clearly this has had some impact on the length of their respective scales. Comparisons that avoid these pitfalls are those between the sub-structures of a single service; we can contrast the scales of Post Office telegraphists and

[1] i.e. they provided for three increments: For details see Tables 12 and 13 *ante*.
[2] cf. *Introductory Factual Memorandum*, op. cit., para. 162.

postal and telegraph officers, or of the Civil Service administrative and scientific officer classes. In a sense, however, this exercise is teleological, for to the extent that these pyramids are purposely aligned, grade lengths tend to be similar; such differences as are found are of interest primarily in the wider context of 'parity'. The same is true of fields which are akin in character and have therefore, in part, been modelled on each other—such as the police and fire services. The main significance of the tables then—as far as comparative scale lengths are concerned—lies in indicating how high an individual will reach without promotion. We will now look more closely at this and related matters.

TABLE 63

LENGTH OF SCALE, MINIMA AND MAXIMA OF VARIOUS RECRUITMENT GRADES IN THE PUBLIC SERVICES

CLERICAL AND ANALOGOUS WORKERS
Men, London[1] as at 1 *December* 1951

	Minimum[2] £ p.a.[5]	Length of Scale[3] Years	Maximum[4] £ p.a.[5]
Civil Service: clerical assistant	143. 0.0	17	377. 0.0
„ „ : clerical officer	150. 0.0	20	500. 0.0
Local government: general division	160. 0.0	14	455. 0.0
Post Office: telegraphist	145.12.0	13	395. 4.0
„ „ : postal and telegraph officer	148. 4.0	14	447. 4.0
BBC : grade DW	163.16.0[6]	7	260. 0.0
„ : „ C2W	195. 0.0	7	299. 0.0
National Coal Board: clerk grade 2	149.10.0	17[7]	422.10.0
Electricity supply: general clerical class 'A'	165. 0.0	10	385. 0.0
Gas industry: clerical grade 'A'	185. 0.0	9	355. 0.0
British Railways: clerical class 5[8]	150.10.0	12	382.10.0
Civil air transport: clerical scale 'E'	149.10.0	9	331.10.0

[1] All figures include the relevant London allowance. Where salaries were undifferentiated, the national standard rate is shown.

[2] All minima on this table were linked to age 16 (or '16 and under'), except those for NCB and civil air transport clerks which were payable at 15. Grades linked to a higher age-point have been excluded.

[3] i.e. number of years in grade until maximum was reached. Where there was an efficiency bar, it has been assumed that this was passed without hold-up.

[4] The maximum of the recruitment grade is shown; the ease of promotion therefrom is ignored.

[5] Weekly salaries are shown as annual rates.

[6] There were alternative (higher) merit entry points. Grade DW was for trainees only.

[7] Including two long-service increments.

[8] For purposes of table, it has been assumed that junior clerks and class 5 constituted one grade.

TABLE 64

LENGTH OF SCALE, MINIMA AND MAXIMA OF VARIOUS RECRUITMENT GRADES IN THE PUBLIC SERVICES

ADMINISTRATIVE AND PROFESSIONAL ETC. WORKERS
Men, London[1] *as at* 1 *December* 1951

	Minimum £ p.a.[4]	Length of Scale[2] Years	Maximum[3] £ p.a.[4]
Civil Service: executive officer[5]	250. 0.0	19	700. 0.0
„ „ : assistant principal	400. 0.0	11	750. 0.0
Local government: clerical division	465. 0.0[6]	3	520. 0.0[7]
„ „ : APT grade I	460. 0.0[6]	3	515. 0.0[7]
Teacher :2-year trained, no degree[8]	411. 0.0	14	678. 0.0
„ : 4-year trained, with degree[8]	507. 0.0	14	774. 0.0
Training college lecturer[8]	586. 0.0	12	898. 0.0
University of London: asst. lecturer	450. 0.0	2	550. 0.0
National Health Service: house officer[9]	350. 0.0	—	450. 0.0
„ „ „ : public health asst. medical officer	850. 0.0	6	1,150. 0.0
„ „ „ : radiographer	375. 0.0[6]	4	445. 0.0[7]
„ „ „ : physiotherapist	390. 0.0	5	450. 0.0
„ „ „ : pharmacist[10]	425. 0.0	4	525. 0.0
„ „ „ : staff nurse (general hospital)	325. 0.0	8	425. 0.0
Probation officer[10]	357.10.0	16	620. 0.0
Police constable[11]	410. 0.0	25[12]	515. 0.0
Fireman[13]	386. 2.0	8	440.14.0
Prison officer[11]	306.16.0	20[12]	412. 2.0
Post Office: engineering inspector	440. 0.0	6	560. 0.0
BBC: monthly grade D[14]	415. 0.0	5	575. 0.0
Electricity supply: higher clerical, administrative and commercial grade 1	390. 0.0	5	480. 0.0
Gas industry: APT grade 2[15]	305. 0.0	8	440. 0.0
British Overseas Airways Corporation: pilot (second officer)[16]	815. 0.0	4	935. 0.0

[1] All figures include the relevant London allowance. Where salaries were undifferentiated, the national standard rate is shown.

[2] i.e. number of years in grade until maximum was reached.

[3] The maximum of the recruitment grade is shown; the ease of promotion therefrom is ignored.   [4] Weekly salaries are shown as annual rates.

[5] The minimum was linked to age 18.

[6] Including London weighting of £20, payable between ages 21–25. The allowance was £10 for those under 21, and £30 if aged 26 and over.

[7] Including London weighting of £30. The allowance was less for those under 26.

[8] The minimum includes the basic London allowance of £36; the maximum the higher London weighting of £48, payable after 16 years' service or on reaching age 37.

[9] The minimum shown applied during 1st post, tenable for six months. £400 was payable during 2nd post (six months), and £450 during 3rd and any subsequent post. Exceptionally, salary could be up to £50 higher. £100 p.a. was deducted for board and lodging.

Some 'Structural' Comparisons

The possibilities for making comparisons are numerous: They can be made—vertically—within and—horizontally—between professions; they can be made over time and over space. Or, say, the dimension may be that of training, skill, age or sex. All these and other variations on the theme are of great interest but, at the same time, are not fully adequate in that they do not take account of all the relevant factors involved. If we are presenting a number of tables in this section, we do so in the main to give a bird's eye view of the vertical pictures portrayed in Part I: Our aim is not the 'perfect comparison'; we are not i.e. seeking to establish the *overall* identity or otherwise of the true reward of the various occupations. For the sad fact is that even a reasonably detailed study such as this is not exhaustive enough to enable this latter type of comparison to be embarked upon, though we shall revert to a consideration of some of the problems of the operation in subsequent chapters.

The tables, then, must be treated with caution to see what legitimate inferences may be drawn from them. Turning to Table 63, the grades are homogeneous to the extent that their incumbents are all employed on clerical or other routine tasks, and—with two exceptions—all the minima set out are linked to age 16. Yet we cannot pass any overall judgment on these minima, for apart from the problem of allowing for divergent service conditions and other 'net advantages', there is the motley content of the term 'clerical'. The different levels of the latter even at the 16-year stage are illustrated by the inclusion of two entries for both the Civil Service and the BBC. In brief, 'equal work' cannot be established without a close knowledge of the duties of each of the occupations concerned; hence no conclusion is warranted about the 'equalness' or otherwise of pay. The only slightly more positive comment permissible is that—for the lowest type of routine work in London at end-1951—a 16-year-old male clerk in the gas industry received at least £185, in electricity supply £165, in local government £160, but in the Civil Service £143. Even here a qualification is necessary, namely that—as we saw earlier on—these figures are affected by the somewhat capricious incidence of area differentials.

---

[10] The minimum was linked to age 23.

[11] The figures exclude rent and all other allowances.

[12] Including long-service increments.

[13] The maximum and length of scale column exclude two long-service increments (of 4s. each) which could be granted after 10 and 15 years' service.

[14] Normal minimum and ordinary 'roof' are shown. There were higher (merit) entry points, and the roof could be exceeded (see Table 51).

[15] Grade 2 is given rather than grade 1, the latter covering trainees aged 16–20.

[16] The figures shown exclude all allowances.

The maxima on the table present the additional complication in that, as indicated by the length of scale column, they are reached at widely varying levels of seniority. Further, they take no account of the ease of advancement from the recruitment tier—a matter in which there is likewise a considerable measure of divergence. Thus a gas industry grade 'A' clerk was almost automatically promoted on attaining his (modest) top salary, but this was not true of some of the other categories. We know, for example, that the Civil Service clerical officer, the local government general division, the Post Office grades and British Railways' clerical class 5 were the 'career expectation' for a proportion, at any rate, of the individuals holding these posts. The figures here therefore show relative financial prospects for those un-able—for one reason or another—to climb the ladder.

It might be thought that something concerning clerks' opportuni-ties could be learnt from looking not at the maxima of specific recruitment grades, but at the ceiling of the several clerical schemes as such. In the BBC, for instance, the maximum of the clerical pyramid—as officially defined—was £520 at end-1951, in local gov-ernment £535, in civil air transport £585, in the Civil Service £700, in the National Coal Board £710 and in British Railways £734.10.0.[1] However, in view of the differing interpretations given to the terms 'clerical' and 'administrative', the peculiarities of individual pay pat-terns, and the fact that the two hierarchies frequently overlap, the zeniths of the various clerical structures have—quite apart from the general considerations previously mentioned—no particular signifi-cance in the context of inter-service comparisons.

Table 64 is composed of a series of recruitment grades above the clerical level; they are clearly a heterogeneous lot. Yet some interest-ing points emerge. First, commencing salaries in local government were relatively high: An individual in London at end-1951, beginning his career in APT I, received[2] almost £50 more than a two-year trained teacher, £60 above a Civil Service assistant principal, £70 more than a physiotherapist, £80 in excess of an almoner, and £40 above a psychiatric social worker—all similarly on the minimum of their respective scales.[3] This has caused a number of headaches, as

[1] The figures in this instance are in terms of the official standard, i.e. national, provincial or London as the case may be.

[2] On the assumption that he was aged 21–25: see note 6 to Table 64.

[3] A number of these occupations are not included on Table 64 as, in practice, they are predominantly female. Comparisons between medical auxiliary and local government APT division salaries are not, however, affected by this, as in both these cases pay was already undifferentiated at the time. It should be added that the divergence between the two groups was somewhat narrower on the basis of their respective provincial rates.

when medical auxiliaries have been appointed by local authorities—
often with administrative responsibilities—at figures considerably
below those accruing to less qualified 'pure' administrators.[1] Again,
if we take youth leaders, it was (1951) optional whether they were
paid Burnham or APT rates, but the difference in starting salary[2] was
£49 in the case of men and as much as £86 in that of women.[3]

The table brings out, further, the very low minima of staff nurses
and probation officers—particularly the former. It also indicates that
a University of London assistant lecturer embarked on his working
life at a standard more than £50 below that of a four-year trained
graduate teacher. Again, the table confirms that firemen have lost in
the race with the police, who qualified for substantial additional rent
allowances not included in the cash figures. It illustrates the superior
commencing salary of assistant medical officers, though these were
expected to have at least three years' outside experience before
joining the public health service.

Turning to the length of scale column, we see the considerable
variation in this but, as pointed out, this is in part simply a corollary
of individual patterns' idiosyncrasies. While those recruitment grades
which also constitute the 'career expectation' tend to have relatively
long scales, this is not necessarily so: Many nurses and medical
auxiliaries do not manage to secure promotion; yet as compared with
the teacher and probation officer, their scales were short and the resultant maxima low. Thus though the non-graduate male London
teacher at end-1951 was at any rate sure of attaining a salary of £678
in the course of his ministrations, a staff nurse could not be certain
of rising beyond £425—nor a physiotherapist above £450. As against
this, a Civil Service executive officer—who is not required to have a
professional training—reached a figure of at least £700. Similarly, the
maxima for police constables, firemen and prison officers give an
indication of their financial expectations at the time,[4] the recruitment
grade here again being the summit for many.

Again for the purpose of presenting a 'horizontal' picture of relative cash rewards, two other tables have been compiled.[5] Table 65

[1] cf. E. L. Younghusband, *Social Work in Britain* (Constable, 1951), p. 13.

[2] On the assumption that the individuals concerned were aged 21–25: see
note 6 to Table 64.

[3] In this instance the difference would have been greater in the provinces,
i.e. £65 instead of £49 (men). The position would have been altered, however, if
the youth leader had qualified for any of the Burnham degree/length of training
additions.

[4] In the case of police and prison officers, rent and certain other allowances
were payable in addition.

[5] Tables 65 and 66 are based on similar material originally prepared by me for
and at the suggestion of Lady Wootton, whose idea they were. Permission to make
use of them is gratefully acknowledged.

TABLE 65

OCCUPATIONS WITH SAME SALARY (± £13 p.a.)
AS QUALIFIED NON-GRADUATE TEACHER

Men, London[1] as at 1 December 1951.

	Years of Experience in Grade[2]	Salary £ p.a.[3]
Qualified assistant teacher: 2-year trained, no degree	0	411. 0.0
Civil Service: clerical officer (age 30)	14	410. 0.0
,, ,, : executive officer (age 25)	6	400. 0.0
,, ,, : assistant principal	0	400. 0.0
,, ,, : scientific officer	0	400. 0.0
,, ,, : technical works, engineering and allied classes, grade IV (age 28)	3	415. 0.0
Local government: general division (age 27)	11	410. 0.0
National Health Service: house officer[4]	½	400. 0.0
,, ,, ,, : radiographer[5]	2	405. 0.0
,, ,, ,, : physiotherapist[6]	2	415. 0.0
,, ,, ,, : staff nurse[7]	7	412.10.0
,, ,, ,, : charge nurse[7]	2	415. 0.0
Probation officer (age 27)	4	410. 0.0
Fireman	4	409.10.0
Prison officer[8]	6	414.14.0
Post Office: postal and telegraph officer (age 28)	12	410.16.0
,, ,, : assistant engineer	4	420. 0.0
BBC: clerical grade BW[9]	4	416. 0.0
,, : monthly grade D	0	415. 0.0
National Coal Board: indoor clerk grade 2[10] (age 29)	14	409.10.0
Electricity supply: general clerical grade class B	0	405. 0.0
,, ,, : higher clerical, administrative and commercial grade 1	1	410. 0.0
Gas industry: clerical grade 'B'	2	405. 0.0
,, ,, : APT grades 2–4	6	410. 0.0
British Railways: clerical class 4	0	404. 0.0
Civil air transport · steward class III (BOAC)[11]	0	409.10.0
,, ,, ,, : clerical scale 'B' (age 21)	0	409.10.0

[1] All figures include the relevant London allowance. Where salaries were undifferentiated, the national standard rate is shown.

[2] If entering at lowest age, etc. entry-point.

[3] Weekly salaries are shown as annual rates.

[4] Salary applied during a house officer's second appointment, normally tenable for six months. £100 p.a. was deducted for board and lodging.

[5] Salary includes London weighting of £20, payable if aged 21–25. If under 21, London weighting was £10; if 26 or over, £30.

[6] A physiotherapist in sole charge with one year's service would also have qualified for inclusion.

[7] The salary is that for nurses in *general* hospitals.

[8] The salary includes 14s. 6d., a single man's rent allowance in London if no quarters were provided.

[9] Clerical grades A2W and AW would also have qualified for inclusion.

[10] An indoor clerk grade 1 with 3 or 4 years' service would also have qualified for inclusion.

[11] The salary shown includes *flying pay* but excludes all other allowances.

takes as its standard a two-year trained male non-graduate teacher, setting out on his career in London at end-1951, and shows what other public service occupations were on this level[1]—in this case drawn both from the professional and clerical sphere.[2]

The table indicates that such a teacher was roughly on a par with Civil Service assistant principals and scientific officers—likewise on their minimum—whose qualifications, however, had to be rather more exacting. It also demonstrates his superiority *vis-à-vis* the nursing and probation services. At the same time, the teacher was no more than level with various not unduly senior clerical staffs, while he enjoyed an approximately similar salary as a BOAC steward still undergoing training, and BBC monthly grade D personnel—say, booking assistants joining the programme contracts department. Ahead of him—and therefore too high for inclusion—were pharmacists, policemen,[3] university assistant lecturers and the local government clerical, higher clerical and APT divisions.

The position would be altered considerably if a *higher grade* of teacher—say, one with a four-year training and a degree—were made to serve as our standard.[4] The local government clerical, higher clerical and APT divisions (up to grade III) would now be 'in'; so would the assistant lecturer, the police constable and various Post Office supervisory grades. As regards nursing, radiography, the prison and fire services, the basic tier would be left behind and replaced by more senior levels. Among those still defying inclusion would be training college lecturers, local education authority (Soulbury) inspectors and Coal Board management staff.

If instead of our London non-graduate teacher we had chosen his *provincial* colleague as our point of departure, the teacher would have appeared in a distinctly less favourable light. His 1951 minimum would have been £375: As a result, the medical house officer, all medical auxiliaries other than radiographers, all 'monthly' BBC grades as well as class III BOAC stewards would have been beyond the level of such a table. The staff nurse would have needed four only, instead of seven, years' experience. This is because in all these fields there was no area differentiation,[5] while the teacher's rate on Table 65 is boosted to the extent of £36 on account of his residing in the metropolis.

[1] Defined as within (plus or minus) 5*s*. p.w./£13 p.a. of the teacher's minimum.

[2] Like the preceding and following table(s), Table 65 is not exhaustive.

[3] If rent allowance is included—as would be appropriate for purposes of this table.

[4] The comparisons which follow are again based on male rates operative in London at end-1951.

[5] A London weighting is now in force for all medical auxiliaries and nurses, but was (mostly) not yet operative at end-1951.

TABLE 66

OCCUPATIONS WITH SALARY OF £1,000
(± £100) PER ANNUM
Men, London[1] as at 1 December 1951

	Years of Experience in Grade	Salary £ p.a.
Civil Service: senior executive officer	3	990
,, ,, : principal	0	1,000
,, ,, : legal assistant	7[2]	1,020
,, ,, : technical works, engineering and allied classes, grade A	5	1,000
Local goverment: APT grade X	2	980
,, ,, : chief officer[3]		1,000
Head teacher (qualified, with 4 years' training and degree, in charge of primary/secondary school in 'unit total' group V)[4]		994
College for further education: lecturer/head of department grade I[5]	2	998
Training college: senior lecturer[5]	6	998
University of London: lecturer	8	1,000
National Health Service: senior registrar	0	1,000
,, ,, ,, : public health asst. medical officer	3	1,000
,, ,, ,, : chief pharmacist (in category IV hospital with special allowance of £200)[6]	6	1,025
,, ,, ,, : chief male nurse, mental (training) hospital with 1,500 beds and over[7]	6	985
Principal probation officer[8]	1	1,075
Metropolitan Police: superintendent[9]	0	950
Fire service: divisional officer grade I	2	1,006
Prison service: governor class III[9]	5	1,000
District postmaster	1	1,010
BBC: newsreader, reporter, TV producer[10]	0	1,000
National Coal Board: administrative official, grade 5	6	1,070
Electricity supply: higher clerical, administrative and commercial grade 9	0	990
British Overseas Airways Corporation: pilot (first officer)[11]	0	1,035

[1] All figures include the relevant London allowance. Where salaries were undifferentiated, the national standard rate is shown.

[2] After confirmation of appointment. Age: about 37.

[3] Chief officers (other than LCC) have a system of salary ranges. Those in authorities with populations of 10,000–45,000 might have been on £1,000 in the course of their career.

[4] Assumption made that head had reached maximum of assistant teacher scale, and that he qualified for maximum London allowance of £48.

[5] Salary includes maximum London allowance of £48.

[6] Special allowances of £100–£200 were payable in certain nominated medical teaching hospitals.

[7] Received additional allowance for purchase of uniform.

Finally, if figures parallel to Table 65 were compiled for *women*, the significant difference would be that Civil Service assistant principals and scientific officers, hospital house officers and all medical auxiliaries other than radiographers would be found to have been too 'prosperous' for inclusion; so would all BBC monthly and electricity supply administrative staff, as well as class III stewards. This is because in these spheres equal pay was already in operation at end-1951 :[1] A woman teacher's differentiated salary was not able to compete with such undifferentiated standards. On the other hand, the remuneration of firewomen and postal and telegraph officers would have been too low to permit of an entry; here, that is, the sex differential was steeper than in education.[2]

Table 66 is designed to depict a cross-section of occupations with a cash salary of approximately £1,000 per annum; it again refers to men in London at end-1951. One point which may be noted is that the Civil Service legal class and the public health medical service are represented by their recruitment grade, while in the case of pharmacy, probation and the Civil Service technical hierarchy, it is the top tier of the profession which is shown. No entry appears for any of the medical auxiliaries, because the maxima attainable in these fields did not reach sufficiently high. British Railways and the gas industry, on the other hand, are excluded merely because the formally-negotiated scales stopped below the £1,000 level.

As for the loftier strata of the public services, the material does not usefully lend itself to tabular presentation; the picture can be more easily sketched in in the text. Thus if—again basing ourselves on the standards operative at end-1951—we take a salary of £2,500 a year, the Civil Service would be represented by an administrative class under secretary (London), as well as by parallel ranks in the scientific and professional sphere. Local government chief officers in authorities with populations of 150,000 and over may have touched this point in the course of their career;[3] so might town and district council clerks—in this instance, if their authority's population was between

---

[1] In the case of the Civil Service, at these particular points.

[2] There are differences also in the precise level of worker (or his seniority) that would have ranked for inclusion.

[3] A number of LCC chief officers were also in this range.

---

[8] The salary was personal to principal probation officer in London.

[9] Free quarters (or rent allowance in lieu) were granted in addition.

[10] These categories were in monthly grade B, for which £1,000 was the normal entry point. Other groups, e.g. announcers and sound producers, reached this level in the course of their career.

[11] The salary shown is exclusive of all allowances.

75,000 and 250,000. Professors on the pre-clinical and medical side then had ranges reaching or passing £2,500; non-medical professors, however, could only achieve this figure if the amount of supplementation from their university was exceptionally liberal.[1] A consultant in the National Health Service qualified for the 'said sum' after six years' service or age 38;[2] this is ignoring any additional distinction award for which he may have been eligible. A senior administrative medical officer, employed by the four metropolitan regional hospital boards and certain other large cities, likewise enjoyed £2,500—in this case on recruitment to the grade.

Other personnel in this income bracket were metropolitan magistrates,whose standard was £2,500 at the time—with £2,800 for the chief magistrate. This latter sum, similarly, was the statutory reward of a county court judge. Provincial chief constables' pay was then up to £2,850, while assistant commissioners in the Metropolitan Police had an end-1951 salary of £2,450, with £2,750 accruing to the deputy commissioner. National Coal Board agents—if directly answerable to an Area production manager—were on maxima ranging from £1,625 to £2,625 per annum. As regards the other nationalized industries dealt with in Part I, there were no *formal* agreements at this level in 1951, though this is of course not to say that salaries of the order of £2,500 were not being paid. As for the BBC, the average remuneration of those in A+—the top tier—was £2,773 a year at end-March 1950; particulars of the spread around this figure or comparable information for a later period are not available.

Definitely too low to allow of an entry on such a hypothetical £2,500-a-year table were nursing, pharmacy, all the medical auxiliaries, probation, the prison service, airline pilots and teaching. The summit in nursing at end-1951 was £1,110 for matrons in the largest training hospitals.[3] For pharmacists it was £1,025, but only if qualifying for a special allowance of £200, payment of which was confined to certain nominated teaching institutions. The top prison governor was then worth £1,400 (London), while the top airline pilot had a basic salary[4] of £2,150. As far as education is concerned, the maximum bounty within the grasp of a primary or secondary head teacher under the 1951 Burnham Report was £1,692: This amount was the reward of a London head with a degree and five-year training if working in a school with the biggest possible 'unit total', though it was feasible for local education authorities to supplement heads' stipends if they considered them as otherwise inadequate. As regards

[1] See pp. 103–4 *ante*.
[2] If he entered the grade at the normal age-point.
[3] Excluding allowance for uniform.
[4] i.e. excluding allowances.

K

other branches of teaching, the salaries of principals of further education, training and agricultural colleges are fixed on a personal basis; except in the case of a few technical college principals, incomes did not, at end-1951, touch the £2,500 mark. We may add that the top figure formally laid down for a chief fire officer was then £1,800, though there was a further discretionary grade, the highest-rated individual covered by the latter being London's fire chief with £2,700 per annum.

At a level (1951) of £5,000 and over, only the permanent secretary to the Treasury,[1] the superior judges and the National Health Service consultant with a maximum distinction award remain. There is no information for the nationalized industries. It should here be mentioned that the remuneration attaching to many political and 'public board' appointments was in this range. However, these are of a rather different kind in that tenure of post is not permanent, and they have not therefore been included in this study.[2]

While precise conclusions about the true 'net advantages' of individual occupations cannot be arrived at without applying the more stringent standards discussed in Chapter 20, some broad facts regarding relative cash rewards in the public sector emerge. First, as the preceding pages indicate, the monetary prizes to be won in many of the public services are modest; this is especially so in the case of nursing, all medical social work, probation and education. Teachers' prospects are poor—this, of course, is hardly news—compared with those in the Civil Service, dentistry, and medicine: The disparity between the income of a first-class headmaster and a first-class doctor is considerable, though to some extent this is balanced by differences in work-load in the two fields. At the same time, there are significant variations within the teaching world: The standard of technical pay is well above that of school salaries.

The terms of employment in the Civil Service, 'fiscally' speaking, seem to be very favourable. While at the minima of the various pyramids local government has the advantage, the reverse is true as far as maxima are concerned, though these remarks do not apply to the most senior levels in the two fields, precise data for local government not being available. Thus a Civil Service executive officer had, at end-1951, a scale rising to £700, while a senior executive officer—his normal career expectation unless a promotee from below—reached £1,075; this was beyond the financial horizon of all pro-

[1] The Chief Planning Officer, Central Economic Planning Staff (a division of the Treasury) then had a salary of £6,500; however, this was an appointment outside the normal class structure of the Civil Service and has since been abolished.

[2] But see H. R. Kahn, 'Payment for Political and Public Service', *Public Administration*, Summer 1954.

fessional workers in the APT division. Again, prospects in the administrative class appear to be excellent, at any rate as compared with those in the non-commercial public services. The principal's 1951 minimum of £1,000 a year was normally attained around age 30; the career grade is the assistant secretary with a 1951 ceiling of £2,000.[1] This may be contrasted with the maximum of a university lecturer—the career zenith of the average academic—which was £1,150 (London) at the time. The inferior level of reward in education is thus not unique to the schools: The remuneration of professors would seem to be low if set against that of senior administrators in both central and local government, as also by comparison with fields such as medicine and the county court bench.

The Degree of Discretion in the Payment of Salaries
As we have seen in Part I, salaries—speaking in broad terms—are now nationally determined in all the public services, which has of course meant that the discretion left to individual employing units has greatly diminished. But it is not the case that such discretion has entirely disappeared.

Room for manoeuvre is widest in those strata of the salariat where even now no standard scales have been laid down; top-level personnel in a number of spheres—notably the nationalized industries—are in this category. Again, several pay patterns provide for a discretionary grade to head an otherwise fairly closely defined pyramid; examples are the schemes for town clerks, chief officers and chief fire officers. In teaching, as pointed out, the remuneration of technical, agricultural and training college principals is—subject to ministerial approval—fixed on a personal basis; in the Civil Service, however, there are very few posts only whose reward is settled *ad hoc*.

Where—as at the 'APT' level of local government, electricity and gas—the national pay structure consists of a series of abstract tiers, a generous measure of latitude is conferred through the power of grading, though in some instances this has been circumscribed by 'decisions' as to how particular categories are to be fitted into the scheme. However, these decisions frequently only deal with specific levels within the occupation concerned, so that considerable freedom remains with individual authorities.

A certain brand of discretion may be said to flow from the fact that the observance of agreed standards of remuneration is not—constitutionally speaking—equally obligatory in all spheres. Thus many of the pre-NHS salaries for health workers were in the form of recommendations, and though widely, they were not universally,

---

[1] All the Civil Service figures are London rates. They exclude extra-duty allowance, then a regular and substantial addition to salary.

adopted. Settlements concluded by other Whitley-type bodies are, similarly, not legally binding, and though on appeal to arbitration they acquire the status of 'recognized terms and conditions of employment' which renders them fully enforceable, there may be reluctance to conform—as there was in the case of local government chief officers—until an official ruling has been secured to that effect. Again, as we saw in Chapter 5, definitive regulations have had to be issued to give the agreements of the National Health Service Whitley councils a more solid legal foundation—in this instance, to clip the wings of a number of hospitals, who had paid their staffs *in excess* of the national scales.[1] No discretion of course exists where rates are fixed by Act of Parliament—as are all senior judicial rewards—or where they are promulgated by statutory instrument as in teaching, probation and the police service. Here there is no shadow of a doubt as to the mandatory nature of the standards thus prescribed. Civil Service scales, though not published in this manner, are *de facto* equally 'compulsory' in view of the special powers vested in the Treasury by Order-in-Council in 1920.

The majority of salaries are intended as *standard* rates; exceptions (1951) were those for British Railways' 'special class' and professional grades, for local education authority inspectors and organizers, and for musicians belonging to the BBC's standing orchestras, all of which were *minima*. However, even within an overall pattern of standard rates, there may be some flexibility through the presence of ranges at certain levels or—more rarely—via the power to augment maxima. Again, the system of increments allows of some elbow-room to the extent that these may be optionally granted for long, withheld for unsatisfactory, or accelerated for meritorious, service.

These last-mentioned types of latitude, it may be noted, differ from that arising from the existence of minimum rates of pay in that the discretion is exclusively conferred on the employing authority. In local government, for example, though increments may be increased or accelerated, it has been expressly agreed[2] that the Charter scales are standard figures—not minima on which local improvement can be negotiated. We may add that the scope for stepping up the annual rise is in any case dependent on such prosaic factors as the length of scales. Where these consist of a mere three or four points, this must make it difficult to enhance the increments of a worthy employee for fear of trespassing on a higher grade.

One of the most important channels for the exercise of discretion is via the granting of allowances and other special additions. Thus professors' basic remuneration is supplemented as decided by indi-

[1] See p. 109 *ante.*
[2] Decision of National Joint Council, dated 17 January 1951.

vidual universities, the total amount available for this purpose being determined by the University Grants Committee. Consultants in the National Health Service are eligible for one of several grades of distinction award, though the discretion here—which in magnitude is without parallel in the public services—is bestowed on the profession rather than on the employing hospital. In the Civil Service, on the other hand, individuals may only very exceptionally be paid more than the normal rate—unless for defined extra duties or qualifications. It has been specifically laid down in the official handbook of staff regulations that allowances should not be contemplated for those doing their work with out-of-the-ordinary efficiency.[1]

The element of discretion in the awarding of salaries is considerably greater higher up than in the humbler reaches of the public services. Whether—particularly at the junior levels—it is all that it might be, is another matter. The old problem of whether, in assessing remuneration, the job or the man is to be rated has, as pointed out, been decided in favour of the former. This is reasonable, for it would be costly to reward each person according to qualifications he happened to possess when these are unnecessary for the performance of his tasks. At the same time, salary systems are perhaps rather too exclusively based on initial qualifications and length of service, with insufficient provision for discretionary merit additions. Yet the recognition of ability is a clear case where the demands of economics and equity go hand in hand, nor does any valid reason suggest itself why a modest payment in one public service should be deemed to smack of nepotism, while in another—equally Exchequer-financed—substantial supplements on grounds of eminence are available. A more sustained weighting of merit should be feasible in all branches of the public sector, without offending against the exacting canons of an impartial personnel policy.

We will conclude this section with a few general remarks about the significance of salary patterns. A specific appraisal of the public service salary structure itself we defer to the final chapter.

The point was made earlier that salary structures have not evolved in accordance with any clearly definable principles, and contain much which is the product of chance development and terminology. But it would be wrong to deduce from this that the whole question can be dismissed as of no consequence. Thus the method of reward for con-

---

[1] *Estacode* C e 1. We are here discussing only the question of discretionary merit *payments*—not the weighting of merit in general. As far as the latter is concerned, the subject of promotion is of course crucial, and our above remarks should not be taken to imply that the Civil Service is failing to reward merit in that sphere.

sultants is such as to make it lucrative to be a part- rather than a full-timer, which may well mean a somewhat different service from that which would obtain if the scales were weighted in the opposite direction. Similarly—as is common knowledge—the remunerating of GPs by capitation fee puts a premium on speed rather than on quality of treatment; here this effect may be said to stem from opting for a system of payment *other than* that of the formal salary. An analogous choice in the case of general dental practitioners—where the method is 'item of service'—made possible (though it did not cause) some serious budgetary complications in the early days of the National Health Service: Dentists' earnings were so substantially and persistently above the level intended that, within two years of the 'appointed day', three applications of the axe were found to be necessary —involving an overall cut of some 30 per cent on their original scale of fees.

Turning to the more narrowly structural side, it has been implicit in our earlier remarks that whether a particular sector of a hierarchy constitutes a class or a grade does not obey any 'law'. It may, however, have some significance in that promotion is frequently easier within, than between, classes. Similarly, as we saw, the length of scale is of importance in the case of recruitment grades: It shows how high an individual will reach, if there is no advancement.

Again, whether specific (circumstances or) qualifications form the nucleus of a separate, higher grade or, alternatively, give rise to some more fluid arrangement may have some interesting causes as well as effects. Here we must refer to a most intriguing feature of pay patterns—the attempt to achieve a degree of 'fairness' in salary structure, coupled with a tacit admission that the realities of the situation demand that these standards be departed from in practice. Salary structures i.e. tend to be more egalitarian than salaries. Thus in the universities there is a basic rate of professorial reward, which is supplemented according to size of student population, the number of chairs, the proportion in scientific and technological subjects, and so on: A formal set of different scales in the light of these criteria would be highly unpopular, as is shown by the resentment which has been generated by the officially laid-down higher standards for medical and pre-clinical academic staffs. Similarly, detectives must not, in so many words, be recognized as superior police officers: They must not, officially, be given a skill differential, though more generous grading and promotion prospects are not barred. Again, the pattern of remuneration for NHS consultants is formally based on the notion that there should be equality of status between the various branches of specialist practice, as also between teaching and non-teaching institutions, but as the 1960 Royal Commission has confirmed, the *de facto* distribution of distinction awards significantly favours some specialties—and overwhelmingly so the teaching hospitals.[1]

In education the ideal—first realized in 1945—of one basic scale for the whole of the profession is still (1961) being formally sub-scribed to, even though the superstructure of allowances has been permitted to become so weighty and diversified as in effect to have introduced a considerable amount of stratification. No doubt the absence of officially distinct basic grades makes it easier for the myth to be upheld that all teachers are paid the same, and to the extent that this helps to keep the (bulk of the) profession content, it may be considered a happy blend of a sense of equity and realism. However —and this is the crux of the matter—it may make it more difficult for the rate of remuneration to do its job: If a higher basic scale were known to exist for those who in any event are going to receive numerous extras—say, graduates in grammar schools—this might possibly be more effective in attracting recruits than the present system of a non-graduate base plus three or four separate sets of additions. We may add that this attempt to have the *de jure* pay structure more egalitarian than the *de facto* has its exact parallel on the wages front, where trade unions go to great lengths to achieve uniform national rates, though not objecting if these standards are not reproduced in the actual pattern of earnings.

The question of whether the recompense for an item is by way of an allowance or compounded into the salary of the grade has several other facets. Thus it may be desirable to give recognition to some feature of a post by a *distinct* weighting, for where there is no such visible reward, the conclusion is sometimes drawn that there is no reward, with a resultant sense of grievance. Secondly, allowances can be based on criteria which it is not considered appropriate or practic-able to weight in remuneration itself: The police rent supplements, for instance, take into account marital status—a factor not otherwise reflected in salary structure. Thirdly, where a contingency is covered by a separate payment, the latter can be more directly adjusted to variations in that contingency than where it is merged into the basic rate. However, as against these potential advantages of 'extras', there is the potential curse of too much proliferation and complexity—a subject to which we shall return in our final chapter. Here we may point out that, as a broad generalization, allowances are in practice *less* frequently revised than basic standards. This has not of course been true of cost-of-living bonuses, nor does it apply in the special case of teaching where the corpus of additions has to make do for what in less inhibited fields would be given expression in a series of

[1] Cmnd. 939, op. cit., p. 76 and ff. At end-1958, for example, 84·5 per cent of 'A' awards (£2,500 p.a.) were held by consultants with teaching hospital posts.

higher scales. In most other spheres, however, it is unusual for 'non-compounded' elements of remuneration to be raised each time an increase is awarded.

Finally, where payment for a factor *is* via an allowance, the precise form of the latter may be important from the psychological point of view. Thus civil servants in the provinces used to feel that they were receiving less than the full rate for the job, because area differentiation was in the shape of a deduction from the London figure. Where the metropolitan weighting is by way of an addition over and above the provincial scale, it does not seem to cause any resentment. This is of some interest, as a 'London base' has actually been of benefit to civil servants; until 1958 their percentage pay supplements have invariably been calculated on the London standard. In other services, by contrast, analogous improvements—even for those in the metropolis—have been computed on the provincial base, with the London allowance itself remaining static for prolonged periods.[1]

[1] The April 1948 standards of London weighting in local government e.g. remained unchanged until May 1960. In teaching, similarly, the London allowance introduced in 1945 was not revised until 1959.

Chapter 19

THE DISTINCTION BETWEEN
WAGES AND SALARIES

In this chapter we pause, as it were, to examine the distinction between the two categories—wages and salaries. Certain aspects of the latter, which we here dispose of rather summarily, are discussed more fully subsequently in their particular 'public service' context.

A wage, according to the *Shorter Oxford English Dictionary*, is a 'payment to a person for service rendered; now especially the amount paid periodically for the labour or service of a workman or servant'. A salary is there defined as a 'fixed payment made periodically to a person as compensation for regular work; now usually for non-manual or non-mechanical work'. Both may include remuneration in kind as well as in cash, and their recipients must be employees— i.e. they have to be in employment under a contract of service.

'Wages' appears to be used in two chief senses. First, to signify reward for personal effort; it has this connotation in *Romans*, vi, 23—'the wages of sin is death'. Leaving morals aside, wages on this wide interpretation is concerned, broadly speaking, with the financial return to the factor of production labour,[1] and comprises salaries, stipends, emoluments and fees, as well as wages in its more restricted second meaning. This latter relates only to the remuneration of manual labour. Economists have tended to employ the term in its first all-embracing sense though, as Professor Dickinson has pointed out, 'economic writings on "wage" matters bristle with other usages'.[2] Going back to Adam Smith, most economists have been led to regard wages as any and all income derived from personal services, apart from saving and risk-bearing;[3] they have not therefore found it necessary to define it in contradistinction to salaries, or to treat the latter as a separate entity.

---

[1] The fact that a proportion of labour income is received by persons outside the wage/salary categories—i.e. the self-employed—can be ignored for present purposes.

[2] Z. C. Dickinson, *Collective Wage Determination* (New York, Ronald Press, 1941) p. 11.

[3] ibid. pp. 11–12.

Where does official usage take us on these questions of demarcation and definition? To begin with, we may quote from the Wages Councils Act, 1959—under which all legislative provisions on the subject have been consolidated—for the purposes of which a worker is 'any person who has entered into or works under a contract with an employer, whether the contract be for manual labour, clerical work or otherwise . . .'.[1] Accordingly, salaries are on the agenda of several of the Councils, the Retail Food Trades Wages Council, for example, settling the pay of clerks and cashiers, while the analogous body for hairdressing undertakings lays down standards for managers and manageresses, receptionists and manicurists.[2] Similarly, the Wages Boards originally set up under the (now repealed) Catering Wages Act, 1943—and since 1959 transformed into ordinary Wages Councils—have dealt freely with supervisory and other salaried grades. It is of course true that in the majority of cases minima are fixed for manual occupations only, but this seems to be simply because the latter are the predominant element in these fields. Here then we have an illustration of 'wages' in its all-inclusive variety, and extended to those operating in a particular sphere irrespective of whether they are manual or not.

The Ministry of Labour, on the other hand—for purposes of its major series of statistics on the subject—uses 'wages' in the narrow sense. Its by now old-established six-monthly enquiries into average weekly earnings and working hours in manufacturing and a number of the principal non-manufacturing industries in the United Kingdom speak of these interchangeably as applying to 'manual workers' and 'wage-earners';[3] the figures supplied are to exclude office staffs, managers, commercial travellers, clerks and typists, and salaried persons generally.[4] Conversely, the complementary surveys—first undertaken by the Ministry in October 1959 and henceforth to be an annual event—cover, in respect of manufacturing and certain non-manufacturing industries and services, the earnings of all classes of administrative, technical and clerical personnel 'including directors (other than those paid by fee only); managers, superintendents and works foremen; research, experimental, development, technical and

---

[1] Wages Councils Act, 1959 (7 & 8 Eliz. 2. c. 69) s. 24.

[2] For details see Ministry of Labour, *Time Rates of Wages and Hours of Labour*, published annually by HMSO.

[3] See e.g. *Ministry of Labour Gazette*, February 1961, p. 50; in the *Gazette* articles those within the scope of the enquiries are generally referred to as 'manual workers'. However, the standard covering letter and form (WE 38), sent to employers requesting the information, speak of the earnings, etc. of 'wage-earners' throughout: cf. *Guides to Official Sources No. 1: Labour Statistics* (rev. ed., HMSO 1958), pp. 75–6.

[4] Shop assistants and outworkers are also excluded.

design employees (other than operatives); draughtsmen and tracers; travellers and office (including works office) employees'.[1] In respect of all these, managements are asked to state the total amount of *salaries* paid in the period in question. In addition to directors remunerated by fee only, staff serving overseas and working proprietors are omitted, though the last-named ranked as 'administrative etc.' in the pre-war Censuses of Production.

Similarly, the Ministry's current indices of weekly and hourly *rates* of wages are based on the minimum or standard rates 'for manual wage-earners, including shop assistants but excluding clerical, technical and administrative workers'; in the case of the health services, for instance, only the figures for ancillary (domestic etc.) grades are taken into account.[2] We might add that though in the Ministry's annual handbook *Time Rates of Wages and Hours of Labour*—as in the latter's monthly follow-up *Principal Changes in Rates of Wages . . .* published in the Ministry of Labour Gazette—certain non-manual categories are reported on, this seems to be because the chief aim here is to be as comprehensive as possible, the niceties of definition not perhaps being strictly relevant.

The Inland Revenue, before and during the war, distinguished between wages and salaries because—from 1928 up to the introduction of Pay-As-You-Earn in 1944—they were assessed on different bases, wages on current, and salaries on the previous year's income. In classifying employees to this end, the Revenue was guided both by the nature of the occupation—i.e. whether it was manual or not—but also by the period by which a person was paid: In brief, a manual worker had to have his remuneration either calculated or handed over at intervals of less than a month, if he was to reckon as 'wages' for tax purposes.[3] With the institution of PAYE, however, the Revenue has no longer any occasion to discriminate between the two groups, the difference in their respective methods of assessment now being entirely superseded.

The Central Statistical Office, for the benefit of the national accounts, breaks down 'total income from employment' into, *inter*

---

[1] *Ministry of Labour Gazette*, September 1960, p. 353.

[2] ibid. February 1957, p. 50. The fact that shop assistants are included for purposes of the wage-rate indices, though left out of the half-yearly wage-earnings enquiries, appears to be due to the former's wider industrial base.

[3] The definition of 'weekly wage-earner' was laid down in s. 237 of the Income Tax Act, 1918. There was no definition of salaried workers in that Act: Schedule D, Cases I and II, Rule 2—which dealt with the method of assessing wage-earners—merely stated that 'this rule . . . does not apply to persons employed as clerks, typists, draftsmen, or in any other similar capacity'. The definition of 'weekly wage-earner' was repealed by the Income Tax (Employments) Act, 1943.

alia, wages and salaries. Hence by definition the former is used in its restricted sense,[1] though the CSO's doings in this respect have undergone various modifications over the years. Thus in *National Income and Expenditure 1946-1951*[2] the classification adopted is stated to be derived from the Census of Production, the earnings enquiries of the Ministry of Labour and, with certain exceptions, the administrative practice of the Inland Revenue before the introduction of Pay-As-You-Earn. However, the following year's Blue Book pointed out that the distinction had been revised—with a view to limiting the category of salary-earners to occupations analogous to those treated as 'administrative, technical and clerical' in the Census of Production, the latter then being promoted as the CSO's main guide in the matter.[3] Among those regraded as 'wages' were policemen, firemen and shop assistants.

We may add that until the figures gathered by the post-war Censuses of Production became available, adequate information about the salariat was confined to national government service and a few other fields, while for most industries outside the scope of these censuses, little was known of the post-war proportion of wage- and salary-earners until the results of the One Per Cent Sample—carried out in connection with the 1951 Population Census—were issued. These provided material for a more accurate division of the working population as between the two groups, and were likewise drawn upon for the first time in 1953.

The main development since is that, commencing with the 1960 Blue Book, the Central Statistical Office is relying primarily on the Ministry of Labour for its data on movements in average wages and salaries. This is because the Census of Production will no longer furnish estimates of these, the Ministry of Labour now being the chief collector of both series. However, the definition of 'administrative, technical and clerical' adopted by the latter for its new salaries survey is co-terminous with that hitherto used by the Census of Production,[4] so that the change has no particular significance for the respective identities of our two categories.

Usage in the matter of the wage-salary distinction is of course not confined to 'official channels'—of which we have given a few illustrations—though we shall not attempt to deal with the content of the

[1] But see p. 315 *post.*

[2] HMSO 1952: see explanatory notes to Table 14.

[3] *National Income and Expenditure 1946-52* (HMSO 1953), p. 73 and Central Statistics Office, *National Income Statistics: Sources and Methods* (HMSO 1956), p. 73.

[4] See e.g. Board of Trade, *Report on the Census of Production for 1958, Part I, Introductory Notes* (HMSO 1960), para. 76.

two entities as reflected in the structure and practices of the numerous bodies involved in the actual business of pay negotiation. What we have seen so far, however, is that the term 'wages' has both an extended and a restricted meaning; that in its wide sense it includes salaries while, more narrowly defined, it is marked off from the latter first and foremost in being the reward of manual, rather than of non-manual, labour. Yet 'manualness' is in many ways an imprecise concept while, further, a number of additional criteria have been variously held to distinguish the two groups. We shall now turn to a consideration of these points, as well as look at certain related differences actually found between them.[1]

Manual Work
Though the performance of manual work has been recognized as the most important single characteristic of the wage-earner, the question of who is, and who is not, manually engaged is not necessarily self-evident, and has given rise to much litigation under the Workmen's Compensation Acts, the Employers' Liability Act, 1880, and the pre-war systems of national health and unemployment insurance. In all these instances, the fact of manual labour was crucial in determining whether or not an individual was within the scope of particular legislation, and on numerous occasions the High Court was called upon to resolve the issue. The line adopted by the judiciary has been that it was a person's substantial employment which was decisive—to the exclusion of manual labour which was merely incidental or accessory thereto. The test was whether work with the hands was the essence of the post, or whether it was some other power or quality which were paramount.[2] The Ministry of Health—which also acted for the Ministry of Labour in matters of pre-war unemployment insurability—elaborated this in instructions compiled for the guidance of its inspectors: These stated that if display of taste and imagination, or the exercise of any special mental or artistic faculty, or the application of scientific knowledge—as distinct from manual dexterity—were the primary quality of the post, such employment was not manual labour, although a certain amount of the latter might be involved. Similarly, in connection with the law of master and servant, the courts have ruled that where the chief duties of a

---

[1] While we shall not feel prevented from discussing relevant matter even though only marginally of 'definitional' significance, it is not our purpose to launch into a fully-fledged analysis of *all* the differences which are found between wage- and salary-earners. Though at the end of the chapter we are inevitably led to refer to the social antecedents of the distinction, no attempt is otherwise made to look at wage- and salary-earners as social animals or to delve, say, into the 'class' implications of the subject.

[2] cf. *Halsbury's Laws of England*, 2nd ed., vol. XXXIV, p. 488, and pp. 618–19.

servant were those requiring intellectual labour—with tasks of a manual character subordinate thereto—he was not a 'workman'.[1]

As for specific court verdicts, some of these are of great interest. Thus it has been held that acrobats and professional footballers are employed not by way of manual labour but as 'public performers', 'engaged as exponents for exhibition purposes and to amuse and entertain other people at playing a game'.[2] Other judicial pronouncements, however, possibly now ring somewhat strange: A Ministry of Health decision that a chief dental mechanic was 'manual' was endorsed by the High Court; a stage manager, who also acted as one of the stage hands and in that capacity had to move the theatre scenery and furniture, was similarly declared to be a 'workman'.[3] Again, for purposes of the Truck Acts, tramcar drivers and goods guards have, among others, been found to be outside the definition of 'workman'.[4] These pre-war legal judgments do not quite tally either with current notions or present practice, and this suggests that various subtle influences may be colouring our views as to the 'manualness' of an occupation.

An illustration of this are firemen whom, as mentioned, the Central Statistical Office used to allocate to the national salaries bill but who, since 1953, are treated as wage-earners. Here designation as salaried may well have been semi-traditional, for the employment of firemen —except in the total absence of emergencies—clearly makes heavy demands on physical skills. A possible explanation is that the fact of firemen being members of a public service gives them a certain dignity, which in the past effectively tipped the scales on the salaried side of the ledger. A partly similar—though rather more debatable —example of 'downgrading' by the Government statisticians is that of the police who, in the course of duty, inevitably discharge a series of non-manual functions, though the precise balance between manual and non-manual is here perhaps at the mercy of criminals' idiosyncrasies. However, 'public service' considerations are a powerful factor in this instance, so that—the CSO notwithstanding—we continue to watch the constable pacing his beat through 'salaried' spectacles.

Another noteworthy case is that of shop assistants. In the 1946–51 Blue Book—as in the earlier National Income White Papers— they were still classed as salaried, even though the Ministry of Labour had included them for purposes of computing its Wage Rates Index

---

[1] ibid. vol. XXII, p. 209.

[2] cf. *Report of the Unemployment Insurance Statutory Committee on Remuneration Limit for Insurance of Non-Manual Workers* (HMSO 1936), para. 16.

[3] ibid. Appx. B, p. 34 and *Halsbury's Laws*, loc. cit.

[4] *Halsbury's Laws*, op. cit., vol. XIV, p. 651.

ever since 1947. However, with the Blue Book published in 1953, shop assistants appear in the wages lobby. This development is of some interest in the light of a legal decision in 1892, when it was held in the Court of Appeal that an ordinary shop assistant was not 'engaged in manual labour'; even though generally a not inconsiderable part of his duties involved such labour, this was deemed to be incidental to his real and substantial employment as a salesman.[1] To what extent shopworkers' translation to 'wages' has been hastened by a diminution of this 'substance' of salesmanship—due, say, to the activities of the 'hidden persuaders', customers' enhanced purchasing power and propensity to consume, the greater standardization of many goods or the take-it-or-leave-it attitude displayed behind some counters—is an intriguing teaser.

The difficulty of distinguishing manual from non-manual occurs of course primarily in the allotting of borderline cases; these, roughly speaking, arise in two ways. First, the nature of the work may be 'mixed': As we saw in Chapter 2, the National Joint Council for Local Authorities' Administrative, Professional, Technical and Clerical Services found it necessary to institute a separate Scheme of Conditions for the 'miscellaneous' classes, problems having emerged 'in connection with employees whose work was neither wholly manual nor yet wholly clerical'.[2] The gas industry, similarly, has had recourse to a category of 'intermediate' grades—to cater for occupations such as meter readers.[3] Other examples have already been cited earlier in this chapter.

The second area of overlap is vertical in character; it is liable to be met with in hierarchical structures at the point where the line is drawn between rank-and-file and supervisors. Even where this is a reasonably straightforward exercise as far as the formal pay structure is concerned, when it comes to practice, jobs may flounder somewhat: As it has been put, 'one difficulty is that, in many occupations, the duty of supervising others, which is not manual labour, is combined in varying degrees with the duty of sharing in manual labour oneself'.[4] The foreman, one might say, so long as he only talks to, preaches at, or swears at his men ought, strictly speaking, to be classed as salaried; to the extent that he rolls up his shirt sleeves and gives them a hand, he is a wage-earner. Perhaps, therefore, it is not altogether surprising that foremen have likewise been the subject of some official

---

[1] *Bound v. Lawrence*, 1892, 1 QB 226, CA. The case had arisen under the Employers and Workmen Act, 1875.

[2] See p. 66 *ante.*

[3] See p. 237 *ante.* In the electricity supply industry, however, meter readers are graded as 'wages'.

[4] *Report of Unemployment Insurance Statutory Committee*, op. cit., para. 14.

confusion: Until April 1958, at any rate, the Ministry of Labour was asking employers to include 'foremen'—which can only be taken to mean *all* of them—in their half-yearly returns of wage-earnings,[1] though the Board of Trade, for purposes of the Census of Production, had for many years been requesting firms to record *works* foremen as 'administrative, etc.' and their incomes as salaries.[2] What employers were making of this is anybody's guess. We may add that the Central Statistical Office made clear in its 1950 White Paper that— siding with the Board of Trade—it was allocating working foremen to wages and works foremen to salaries in the national accounts.[3]

Place of Work
It is a commonplace that the nature of both manual and non-manual employment has been undergoing a significant metamorphosis—a process the momentum of which is of course very far from having spent itself. In innumerable occupations nearly everything in the way of hard physical toil is—even in the pre-automation era to which we are confining these remarks—done by machine, and it has actually been laid down in a High Court judgment that manaul labour and manual work mean the same: For an operation to be manual i.e., it no longer needs to be laborious.[4] At the same time, with the widespread adoption of all manner of office equipment, many salaried jobs have been mechanized; that the distinction between manual and non-manual has survived, seems to indicate that working a machine is not as such basic to it. Is it perhaps that the salaried machine-operator is performing some essentially different task from his wage-earning opposite number? The short answer is that it is not the fact of manning a machine, but its *locale*, which matters. The place of work is one of the main criteria which has served to mark off manual from non-manual;[5] it is this rather than the nature of the process which has determined whether a 'manual' label has been attached. Thus if a typist is salaried while a linotype

[1] *Guides to Official Sources No. 1: Labour Statistics* (1958), op. cit., p. 76, note (2); the Ministry's regular earnings articles in the *Gazette* do not make clear how foremen are to be treated. It is possible therefore that, since 1958, the instructions to employers have been revised, particularly as in the Ministry's administrative etc. surveys, begun in 1959, *works* foremen are included.

[2] See e.g. Board of Trade, *Report on the Census of Production for 1951: Introductory Notes* (HMSO 1954), p. iii. In the pre-war Censuses of Production, however, all foremen were classed as 'operatives' (wage-earners).

[3] *National Income and Expenditure of the United Kingdom 1946 to 1949*, Cmd. 7933 (HMSO 1950), p. 53.

[4] *Report of Unemployment Insurance Statutory Committee*, op. cit., para. 15.

[5] cf. *National Income and Expenditure of the United Kingdom 1946 to 1950*, Cmd. 8203 (HMSO 1951), p. 60.

operator is wage-earning, it is by and large because the former is lodged in an office and the latter in a printing shop or factory.

Skill

A related topic to which we may now turn is the extent to which the factor of skill is implicated in our theme. By common consensus, the whole of the skilled industrial labour force belongs to the wages front, while the modern army of clerks—many of whom are on the merest routine work—is salaried. We have, moreover, a specific pronouncement that 'where the employment is essentially for the exercise of craftsmanship, however skilled, it is manual labour'.[1] By contrast, there is the musician about whom the rules tell us that he is outside the latter category, on the ground that his skill is the distinguishing feature of his pursuits; that he has to use his hands in the deployment thereof is regarded as incidental. Why, the persistent may ask, is the possession of *expertize* decisive in conferring non-manual status on the musician, while it has no such effect in the case of the craftsman, where it could likewise be argued that it is this which is the premier characteristic of his endeavours? Here we reach the heart of the matter. For it appears that, at the root of it all, 'manualness' has been a function primarily of whether one's job spelt dirt or other types of havoc for one's hands. However complex one's work, if it meant a pair of rough, greasy hands, one was 'manual' and a wage-earner; where it did not, one became a recruit —however lowly—to the ranks of the salariat.

This (what for short we shall call the) 'dirty hands' criterion is still at the bottom of the distinction between wages and salaries, though clearly it will not account for many individual instances of grading, which perforce have been dealt with by a process of analogy. Similarly, where technological changes have removed the grime and sweat from formerly unclean or physically exacting operations, this does not hitherto seem to have had much effect: Jobs transformed by new methods of production, but which initially counted as 'manual', have remained in that category—provided they are carried out in the factory which has come to be looked upon as the natural habitat of the wage-earner. The 'place of work' test has thus assumed added significance in marking off manual from non-manual even though, fundamentally, it is a *derivative* of 'dirty hands'. What will be the ultimate impact of the spread of automatic techniques on this and related distinctions is as yet rather in the realm of the speculative.[2]

---

[1] *Report of Unemployment Insurance Statutory Committee*, op. cit., Appx. B.

[2] For a discussion of some broadly related topics see Department of Scientific and Industrial Research, *Automation: A Report on the Technical Trends and their Impact on Management and Labour* (HMSO 1956).

Our foregoing remarks are in line with the fact that those requiring special uniform have mostly been classed as 'wages' in the
national income accounts. They are similarly borne out by the terms
'blackcoated' or 'white-collar' worker, which are popularly applied
to members of the salariat for whom they are exclusively reserved.
The 'dirty hands' notion may also be responsible for the oscillation
in the treatment of shop assistants, in that there is a difference in this
respect between, say, grocers, fishmongers and butchers and other
kinds of distributive personnel. Thus if one approached the man-in-
the-street, one might well find that a butcher's assistant would be
considered on a par with the generality of wage-earners, while the
well-groomed saleslady in the big department store would almost
certainly rank as salaried.

Level of Income
The next question is whether the size of income is in any way an
essential ingredient of the distinction, the overall level of remuneration being of course inferior in the manual, than in the non-manual,
camp. In 1959, for example—speaking of manufacturing industries
only—the average salary was about £790 per annum, as compared
with an average wage of £546.[1] At the same time, there is a wide
field of overlap; a substantial number of factory workers are financially well ahead of the majority of salaried typists and other clerical
grades. And that there is a considerable degree of overlap even if the
sex factor is held constant, is confirmed by the data on the distribution of earnings newly made available by the Ministry of Labour
in 1961. These show that almost 12 per cent of full-time male adult
wage-earners in the industries covered[2] were making £20 a week or
more (in a particular week) in October 1960, a level which—though
we do not know what proportion achieved it on an *annual* basis—
was far beyond the aspirations of many 'blackcoated' men.[3] These

[1] *National Income and Expenditure* 1960 (HMSO 1960), p. 66 and Table 17. In the
calculation of the average salary, directors paid by fee only are excluded. Comparable information for *all* industries and services cannot be ascertained from
Blue Book data.

[2] The industrial coverage was the same as for the regular half-yearly earnings
enquiries.

[3] See 'Distribution of Earnings of Manual Workers in October, 1960', *Ministry
of Labour Gazette*, April 1961; strictly comparable data for the salariat are not
available. The Ministry's own administrative, etc. survey, for instance (p. 298
ante), gives *average* earnings only. The figures on clerks' pay in *Clerical Salaries
Analysis* 1960 (Institute of Office Management, London, 1960) are a mixture of
rates and earnings, *excluding* e.g. all overtime earnings. The details of professional
incomes collected by the Royal Commission on Doctors' and Dentists' Remuneration refer (among other things) to a different period, as do those gathered by
some other professional bodies. The existence of 'overlap' between male wage-
earnings and male salary-earnings is nevertheless not in doubt.

certainly respectable pay-packets—as those, more generally, of workers in, say, vehicle manufacture, coalmining or printing—have not made their recipients salaried.

It is of interest, therefore, that several writers have hitherto revealed a soft spot for the size-of-compensation criterion. Kuznets has listed it as one of six factors in the light of which wages and salaries might be distinguished.[1] Professor Dickinson advises us that, in order to avoid ambiguity, 'when we use this word (i.e. wages) . . . literally, and without qualification, we should use it as in business, statistical, and legal parlance—meaning the lower and most numerous payments by employers to hired workers, most of whom do manual work'. And again, 'we shall also use "salaries" in the practical sense of the higher rates of payment to higher workers'.[2] Marschak, in the *Encyclopaedia of the Social Sciences*,[3] also appears to equate 'manual' and 'poor', and seems to be of the opinion that the theory of wages should be confined to relatively low-paid employees—manual and other. Similarly, some *obiter dicta* of the 1936 Unemployment Insurance Committee suggest that they considered size of income as an important identification mark in this context.[4] One may here add that there is of course a difference between the criteria on the basis of which two categories can be isolated, and the broad characteristics which they may nevertheless possess. No doubt the man-in-the-street, thinking of a salaried person, instinctively has in mind someone rather better off than a factory worker and, as far as the averages go, he is right: Though the range of wage-earnings is in itself substantial, their 'typical' beneficiary does—owing to the very much wider spread of salaries—get less than the average non-manual employee. However, as a means of differentiating the two groups, the size-of-compensation standard is not valid.[5]

It may be pertinent to point out that the divergence between the average wage and average salary would be considerably more pronounced if the comparison were based on *hourly* earnings in the two spheres: To qualify for his annual average, the wage-earner puts in many more hours than his 'average' opposite number in the office. The disparity between the two figures would be further increased if all labour costs incurred on behalf of employees—such as, for ex-

[1] S. Kuznets, *National Income and its Composition* 1919–38 (1941), vol. I, p. 86.
[2] Dickinson, op. cit. p. 10.
[3] Vol. XV (1935) 'Wages'.
[4] *Report of Unemployment Insurance Statutory Committee*, op. cit., para. 6.
[5] cf. Cmd. 8203, loc. cit. where 'amount of money earned' is specifically rejected by the Central Statistical Office.

ample, companies' contributions to superannuation funds—were included in the reckoning.[1] For while conditions of service are far from homogeneous for either category, and while the gap between the two groups has of recent years been narrowed by the shortening of the 'manual' working week, the extension of paid holidays and new pension schemes, material differences remain in favour of the salariat.

Periodicity of Payment

Is the period by which an employee is remunerated relevant to our subject? As previously indicated, the Inland Revenue has used this test in distinguishing between wage- and salary-earners: To be paid (or rated) by the week or shorter interval was a prerequisite for placement in the wages lobby under the pre-PAYE system of tax assessment. The Central Statistical Office, however, has specifically rejected this criterion,[2] while the Ministry of Labour's 1959 administrative etc. enquiry has strikingly brought out how widespread weekly reckoning is in the salaried sphere itself.[3] Thus out of a total of 1,277,684 male administrative, technical and clerical workers covered by the figures, 54 per cent were—though with marked variations between industry groups—weekly-paid, while for the 602,574 women the proportion was as high as 84 per cent. The survey also pinpointed the considerable divergence in earnings between 'weekly' and 'monthly' personnel: As regards men, the former drew an average (all industries) of £14 2s 10d per week—62 per cent of the £22 13s 8d accruing[4] to their 'monthly' colleagues.[5] It is the level of the latter's reward, no doubt, which has led some writers to attach significance to size-of-compensation in the context of the wage-salary distinction.

To be remunerated by the week is thus a common feature of non-manual employment, so that 'weekly versus monthly' is clearly not co-terminous with 'wages versus salaries', except that anything beyond a weekly settlement is rare on the wages front. However, the periodicity of payment would appear to correspond with certain broad groupings *within* the salaried camp: Though firms' practices differ,

---

[1] For some interesting data on this subject see 'Wages and Related Elements of Labour Costs', *Ministry of Labour Gazette*, August 1957, which gives a breakdown of expenditure on holidays, pension schemes and other 'fringe benefits' for, respectively, operatives and administrative, etc. employees in seven major industries.

[2] Cmd. 8203, loc. cit.

[3] *Ministry of Labour Gazette*, September 1960, pp. 353–5. Firms with fewer than 25 employees were outside the scope of the enquiry.

[4] Per week.

[5] Weekly-paid females averaged 72½ per cent of the equivalent earnings of 'monthly' women.

as a rough generalization we can perhaps regard a weekly basis as the typical way of remunerating clerical workers, while a monthly regime is the norm for supervisory, administrative and professional staff. This latter method, it seems, is not merely adopted because of its obvious convenience in the case of the higher incomes; it is also felt to be more appropriate for professional and other non-routine personnel,[1] many of whom might consider it undignified to be handed a small envelope each Friday afternoon. This aspect of the matter would explain why *some* women are on a monthly system, for the standard of their earnings is substantially below that of the 'weekly' males.[2]

Security

There is another facet to this question of periodicity, and this is its function as a rough measure of the security of tenure to which an individual is entitled. The two do of course not precisely coincide; professional appointments—such as, say, some university lectureships—may be terminable by quarterly notice, even though salaries are credited monthly. Similarly, many categories of public servants—in particular, judges and central government employees—are not normally discharged except in very special contingencies, but we may take it that the frequency of their reward has not the same element of eternity. However, the minimum period of notice is never *less* than the interval at which remuneration is made over; hence non-manuals as a body enjoy a greater degree of security than wage-earners.

More fundamental than the institutional factor in this connection are economic circumstances, though here again the salariat is less exposed to the chill blasts of the economic wind than the generality of manual workers. This is, first, because a higher proportion of the former earns its living in fields in which the demand for labour is less volatile. Secondly, those salaried staffs who are attached to the manufacturing industries, are—occupationally speaking—not directly related to output; hence in comparatively mild recessions redundancies taking their toll of the factory population may completely by-pass the office. Thus the ratio of administrative, technical and clerical personnel to operatives in Britains' manufacturing industries has gone up each year since 1948, but what is especially noteworthy in the present context is that the largest relative increase in the

[1] cf. *Report on Police Conditions of Service* (Oaksey Report), Cmd. 7674 (HMSO 1949), para. 39: 'It would be more in keeping with the status of the police as a profession, and with sums of these dimensions (i.e. their recommendations) for constables and sergeants to be paid an annual salary rather than a weekly wage'.

[2] In October 1959 the average earnings (all industries covered) of monthly-paid women in the Ministry's survey were the equivalent of £9.17.7 a week, as compared with an average of £14.2.10 for weekly-paid men.

salaried contingent occurred in those years—1952 and 1958—in which the total of all employees *fell*.[1] Similarly, while the number of wage-earners engaged in textiles dropped by over 100,000 during 1948–58, there was a rise of 20,000 in the case of administrative etc. workers.[2] Clearly, in any major depression the salariat is bound to be affected—as it was in the inter-war period—nor can it be ruled out that future technological developments might at some stage reverse the unprecedented growth in the demand for clerical manpower witnessed in the twentieth century. But few are likely to quarrel with the proposition that redundancy and unemployment remain a greater occupational hazard on the wages, than on the salaries, front.

Fixed and Variable Labour Costs

It has been suggested that the separation of wages and salaries can be effected on the basis of, and is useful for the analysis of, the variable and fixed elements in labour costs; Kuznets is of the opinion that this and the 'manual' criterion have most weight for the distinction between the two categories.[3] Chapman has made the point that in the commodity-producing industries such as manufacturing and mining —where the productive process mainly involves manual work— fixed and variable labour costs might be fairly well represented by salaries and wages, but that even if a breakdown for costing purposes might be helpful in these instances, this was far more doubtful as regards the distributive and service sector where the majority of non-manual personnel were themselves directly related to output.[4] This of course was written at a time when shop assistants were still being officially allocated to salaries in the national accounts, though the distributive and service industries are in any event somewhat problematical in this context: In fields such as banking and insurance, for example, most salaries represent *variable* costs. As for the manufacturing industries, it must be borne in mind that there are non-productive wage-earners such as cleaners and maintenance staffs, nor can we be certain that all other incomes allotted to the wages bill constitute variable, and those to salaries fixed, outlay. Yet though wages and salaries are thus not co-terminous with these two types of expenditure as far as the whole economy is concerned, and only more or less roughly so as regards manufacturing, in the latter case the sub-division would seem to be of definite interest. Thus in the short span of ten years, salaries have increased their share of the combined wage-and-salary bill in manufacturing industry from

---

[1] *Ministry of Labour Gazette*, July 1959, p. 250.   [2] ibid.

[3] Kuznets, op. cit., p. 87.

[4] cf. A. Chapman, *Wages and Salaries in the United Kingdom* 1920–38 (Cambridge University Press, 1953), p. 14.

25·2 per cent in 1949 to 29·5 per cent in 1959—the relative rise in the number of non-manual workers, we may add, being very much greater.[1] These figures—as those showing the considerable variations in this respect as between different industry groups[2]—could have several important implications for the economy.

Method of Payment

The question of the directness of participation in the production process leads us to our next topic—the directness of the relation of reward to effort. In April 1961, 33 per cent of all manual workers covered by the Ministry of Labour's earnings enquiries—42 per cent in the case of manufacturing industries—were on systems of payment-by-results:[3] In these instances, there is an immediate connection between output and income. A salary-earner rated 'by the piece' is a comparatively rare phenomenon to be found mainly among salesmen; their contract frequently provides for a commission element. To a certain extent, however, the absence of the method in the salaried sphere is a matter merely of definition: Some non-manual personnel who are remunerated wholly according to output are—for purposes of tax assessment and the national accounts—classed as profit-earning and self-employed rather than as salaried and employed, even where their income derives from a single employing authority. Thus National Health Service general dental practitioners are recompensed solely per item of treatment— no doubt a more complete illustration of effort-linked reward than is met with in industry but, officially, they are excluded from the salariat. So are GPs who receive fees *per caput*—fees i.e. on the basis of their *average* output.

Payment-by-results, as defined by the Ministry of Labour, only refers to arrangements under which remuneration varies directly according to the output of individuals, groups or departments. Various forms of merit-additions, good time-keeping bonuses or profit-sharing—from some of which non-manual workers may also benefit—are not covered. We might also add that certain salary schemes can in a sense be said to contain an 'output' factor *indirectly*; some of the grading formulae discussed in the last chapter are in this category, in so far as these are a function of size and quantity rather than of quality. Thus to pay a chief constable according to the strength of his force might conceivably be described as a method of rewarding him for the average amount of police protection which he is expected to supply. The weighting by out-

---

[1] *National Income and Expenditure*, 1960, op. cit., Table 17.

[2] ibid. and *Ministry of Labour Gazette*, July 1959, p. 250 and January 1961, p. 9.   [3] *Ministry of Labour Gazette*, September 1961, p. 369 and ff.

patient attendances in determining the category of a chief pharmacist's hospital, similarly, includes an 'output' element, while the incomes of National Coal Board colliery managers actually depend on the productive performance of the units in their charge. In all these instances, however, output serves as a broad measuring rod of the responsibility that is being shouldered, and is used to fix *initial* grading and salary rather than give rise to actual fluctuations in the latter in the light of personal exertion.

On a strict interpretation then, payment-by-results is a feature of the wages, not of the salaried, sector. A related point is that a manual worker is normally compensated for every hour of overtime—of which, on the average, he does several a week—and, conversely, is likely to find himself with a reduced pay-packet if away from his workplace for brief spells. Such hourly accounting is less common for the salariat, though there are definite differences here between its upper and lower reaches.

Apart from many wage-earners regularly qualifying for overtime pay, output bonuses and so on, their operative basic rates may be higher than the minima laid down in collective agreements. As a result of all these and other factors—the precise causes of the 'wage-drift' are a bone of some contention[1]—wage-earnings diverge significantly from wage-rates, as is demonstrated by the gap between the Rates and Earnings indices of the Ministry of Labour,[2] as well as by a number of more specific investigations.[3] Such wide discrepancies between salary-earnings and salary scales are less frequent, though the exact degree of coincidence varies. Thus during 1947–56 the bulk of non-industrial civil servants automatically received an addition over and above their official remuneration, because a 45½-hour emergency standard week was being worked, which was in excess of the formal ('conditioned') week of forty-two or forty-four hours. Here therefore—until the Priestley changes of 1956—earnings have been consistently above scale salary.

[1] Much has been written on this subject. But see e.g. H. A. Turner, 'Wages, Productivity and the Level of Employment: More on the "Wage Drift",' *Manchester School*, January 1960.

[2] In the 4½ years April 1956 to October 1960 the average rise in weekly earnings in the industries covered by the Ministry of Labour's (wage) earnings enquiries was (all workers) 23¼ per cent, as compared with an average increase in the level of weekly wage rates (same industries) of 14¼ per cent. In the nine years April 1947 to April 1956 the average rise of weekly earnings in manufacturing industries (only) was 89 per cent, while the average level of wage rates in these industries went up by about 62 per cent. (*Ministry of Labour Gazette*, March 1961, p. 123 and September 1956, p. 328).

[3] e.g. those published in the Bulletins of the Oxford University Institute of Statistics. See also E. Devons and R. C. Ogley, 'An Index of Wage-Rates by Industries', *Manchester School*, May 1958.

An important corollary of the closer correspondence of rates and earnings in the salaried camp is that the latter suffers less from what has become a real affliction of wage structures, i.e. the blurring or even inversion—as far as actual earnings are concerned—of differentials provided for in the rate pattern. In the case of salaries, such internal differentials as are planned tend to exist *de facto* as well as *de jure*, though the other main problem in the context of vertical relativities—the compression of the *formal* concertina itself through proportionately greater or more frequent improvements lower down the hierarchy—has caused trouble in both spheres. Another interesting effect of the better alignment of salary scales and earnings is that one source of conflict met with in wage negotiations—whether current rates or current earnings are relevant when a pay increase is being sought—does not generally seem to arise in arbitration proceedings involving non-manuals.

Finally, salaried staffs—particularly in the public services and other large undertakings—are commonly on an incremental scale under which, as we have seen, they receive a series of mostly annual and more or less automatic additions *within* the grade in which they find themselves. Such a weighting of the length of service/experience factor—unrelated i.e. to any question of promotion to a higher tier in the pay structure—is not unknown in the world of wages, but is certainly rare.[1]

Some Differences in the Nature of the Pay Bargain

The first point under this head—and it is hardly a secret—is that there is a difference in the method of concluding the pay bargain: In the case of wages the collective settlement is the order of the day, but in the sphere of salaries this is so only in so far as the public sector and an as yet limited number of other fields are concerned. In the public half the growth of joint negotiation has been impressive—both as regards type of employment covered and level of blackcoat prepared to be unionized. In the private wing of salaries, on the other hand, bargaining beyond the scope of the individual enterprise is still a long way from being the norm.

While, on the wages front, it is usually possible to pinpoint 'the rate for the job', there is very often no such thing in private non-manual employment. This is not only for lack of an appropriate body stipulating 'the rate'; it is also because 'the job' may not exist.

---

[1] In a number of industries the standard rate for a particular class of manual worker is linked to a prescribed minimum period of prior employment; in other words, experience or length of service may give rise to a higher grade within the wage structure. This, however, is equally so in the case of salary structures, which are of course hierarchical as well as incremental.

While this hardly applies to the less exalted regions of the salariat, as we travel up the occupational ladder, more jobs become *sui generis*; since salaries extend to all the higher rungs of the ladder, standardization thus tends to be more difficult. For though the processes on which two labourers are engaged may differ—there are degrees of 'unskill'—comparison, the prerequisite of standardization, is much more straightforward than it is, say, for two managing directors, whose designation derives proper meaning only from the *object* of their management and direction.

To the extent that the salary bargain is personal/'domestic' rather than collective, it should be possible for it to be more finely attuned to the economic circumstances of the firm concerned than is feasible in the wage-sector, where the ability-to-pay criterion can, at best, be applied to the particular industry as a whole when an agreement is being concluded. As regards wages, whatever rate is fixed cannot bear any direct relation to the individual employer's profit-and-loss account, except through adjustments—in practice, extras—at factory level. In the case of salaries it could, were it not that —apart from the *sui generis* element—there are a number of other disabilities specifically affecting their determination. One of these is that, awkward though it may be to define a wage on the basis of its recipient's marginal net product, over much of the salaried field this concept—even as a theoretical guide—is not available. For though they have no monopoly in this, the activities of the bulk of non-manual workers do not give rise to any measurable product at all.

The greater difficulty of 'costing' salaries—the virtual absence, in fact, of the productivity test—plus the obstacles in the way of standardization have both helped to render monetary evaluation more complex than that of wages. Another important consideration is that a sizeable share of the national salaries bill is earned outside the sphere of profit-making employment—i.e. in the public services, where some of the more obviously commercial criteria of pay determination are inoperative.[1] These factors, combined with the

[1] The proportion of the national wages and salaries bills attributable to the public services (let alone, all non-profit-making employments) cannot be computed from national income data. For example, Table 16 (*Gross domestic product by industry and type of income*) in the 1960 Blue Book does not give a breakdown of 'income from employment' in all cases. Moreover, the analysis is based on the Standard Industrial Classification, under which substantial numbers of central and local government employees are allocated to other industry groups: Post Office workers e.g. are included under 'transport and communications', not 'public administration'. Even so, the three items 'Public administration: salaries', 'Public health services: salaries' and 'Local authority educational services: teachers' salaries' alone accounted for £m966 or 21 per cent of the total salaries bill (£m4,585) in 1959. (*National Income and Expenditure* 1960, op. cit., Tables 16 and 2.)

social and 'class' overtones of the subject, have provided a certain amount of scope for non-economic forces to move into the vacuum, so that the traditional element in salary structure has become more strongly entrenched than on the wages front. The very term 'salary' includes an element of 'genteelness' though, for practical purposes, the latter is an attribute of the upper, rather than of the humbler, strata of the salariat.

The upshot of our preceding discussion is that though there are a fair number of differences between wages and salaries, none of these can be applied as strict criteria on the basis of which the two groups can be isolated with any very fine degree of precision. They must, rather, be regarded as a set of features broadly characterizing the two categories, for even the manual test is not by any means foolproof. Inevitably, the question arises as to whether the distinction is altogether worth bothering about.

It has already been pointed out that economists have not found it necessary to distinguish between wages and salaries in the course of their treatises on the former;[1] there is no such thing as a theory of salaries, and within the wider theory of wages they do not even enjoy the status of a sub-species. Though, among other things, this may reflect the confusion as to the precise content of the two terms, the implication seems to be nonetheless that the profession does not regard the issue as of any great consequence for general analysis.[2] In other ways also differentiation has become less important; as we saw, it is not now required either for Inland Revenue or national insurance purposes. The Central Statistical Office, in turn, has formally declared that only a limited significance can be attached to the separation of wages from salaries in its annual figures of the nation's accounts, adding that no attempt to divide these two kinds of labour income is made in the analogous statistics of most other countries.[3]

The writer has no very strong views as to the *intrinsic* merits of the distinction; there seems little doubt that many of the differences outlined earlier have no particular economic *raison d'être*.[4] Thus the

[1] Professor Hicks, for instance, in his *Theory of Wages*, does not mention the subject of salaries.
[2] cf. Dickinson, op. cit., p. 12. Professor Dickinson himself is of the opinion that the wage-salary and allied distinctions are significant.
[3] *National Income Statistics: Sources and Methods*, op. cit., p. 72.
[4] The implied equation—in what follows—of 'economic' and 'rational' and of 'social' and 'irrational' is not being put forward as a maxim of general validity. As will presently become clear, 'social' is here being used in its status/prestige sense: As such—but only as such—this writer admits to a tendency to regard it as subjective and irrational.

fact that salaried staffs are not[1]—unlike many wage-earners—re-munerated under systems of payment-by-results, obviously stems from the character of their work. That, on the other hand, they are on incremental scales under which they qualify for financial, even if not for occupational, promotion or, again, that they have the benefit of superior service conditions, appears to derive primarily from socio-cultural factors rather than from any inherence in the nature of non-manual employment.

As for the question of manualness itself which, as we have seen, is at the root of the matter, the very emphasis placed on this—as, indeed, the manner in which 'manualness' has been defined—would seem to point to a predominantly social inspiration. There is of course a difference in the kind of labour service sold by manual as against non-manual employees, as there is in the economic conditions under which they function: The labour of the typical manual worker is performed in conjunction with a relatively large amount of plant and machinery; that of the typical salaried person is not. Yet if such considerations were paramount, the frontier between wages and salaries might be expected to coincide specifically with this criterion or, say, correspond precisely to the variable/fixed costs test; neither is the case. Similarly, that a high degree of skill leads to a non-manual ranking only if exercised outside, but not if inside, the factory, suggests that the distinction is basically social.

That there is a far-reaching difference in the realm of status and class is a pointer in the same direction, though this is a huge subject with which we are not even remotely attempting to grapple. It may, however, just be worth mentioning that non-manual workers—however modest their calling—are absolutely debarred from the Registrar General's bottom Social Class V,[2] while studies of the relative prestige of occupations have shown that salaried persons invariably gravitate to the upper, and wage-earners to the lower, end of the prestige scale.[3] Nor is this explicable simply in terms of magnitudes of income; the mere fact of receiving a salary would seem to confer status quite apart from its size. Putting it crudely, one might perhaps say that the esteem purchased per pound sterling of remuneration is decidedly greater for the blackcoated, than for the cloth-capped, employee.

Whether one is a wage- or a salary-earner is thus relevant in the context of social distinctions. That these latter contain a generous

---

[1] With certain exceptions.

[2] See General Register Office, *Classification of Occupations*, 1950 (HMSO 1951).

[3] See e.g. Hall and Jones, 'Social Grading of Occupations', *British Journal of Sociology*, March 1950 and A. F. Davies, 'Prestige of Occupations', ibid. 1952, p. 134.

admixture of 'snobbishness' can hardly be denied, though this does not necessarily make them any less real. In its origins, then, the distinction between wages and salaries would seem to partake of this 'snob' element, and can perhaps be regarded as a descendant of the old aristocratic notion that gentlemen do not work for their living: Gentlemen in this more democratic day and age do, but if they can manage the task without manual labour—without, that is, soiling their hands—they are more likely to rank as such.

We should here perhaps make clear that we are not suggesting that, were it not for our incorrigible status-seeking propensities, labour would be a unidimensional, homogeneous commodity. On the contrary: it is a commonplace that the country's occupational and industrial structure are immensely complex, and as they have become so *pari passu* with the maturation of the economy, so has the salaried sector increased in size in both absolute and relative terms. If then we show ourselves as no more than lukewarm regarding the theoretical virtues of the distinction between manual and non-manual, this is not to imply that it is meaningless. All we have in mind is that there are possibly more objective criteria for a basic grouping of the working population.

There is, however, another major consideration, and this is that the question of the antecedents of a particular distinction does, in any event, not dispose of the further question as to whether it is now obsolete. For as far as the contemporary labour scene is concerned, the salient point is that the difference between manual and non-manual is a fact: There is for example, over and above the specific items of contrast discussed, the wide gulf between 'office' and 'works' —a gulf that, according to one writer, 'is perhaps the most outstanding feature of industrial organization'.[1] Similarly, the history, strength and structure of trade unionism—and hence the set-up of collective bargaining arrangements—bear the imprint of the manual/non-manual theme, and for the present it can be said to be one of the forces that continue to shape both the machinery and content of industrial relations.

What we are saying is, quite simply, that irrespective of logic and origin, and in spite of the heterogeneous composition of both the manual and non-manual sectors, salaries as of now are a recognized and—frontier problems notwithstanding—a recognizable entity. The distinction having 'happened', one might put it, it has produced a number of differences which, in a sense, have been cumulative. Thus whether or not it is essential for the systems of remuneration of wage- and salary-earners to diverge in all the directions indicated, we cannot disregard that they do so diverge, which in turn has its

[1] D. Lockwood, *The Blackcoated Worker* (Allen & Unwin, 1958), p. 81.

repercussions in both the economic and social sphere. Methods of payment, for instance, are relevant in the context of incentives and productivity, and at the same time have a bearing on the mode of consumption: That the income of a salaried employee is more dependable than that of a manual worker and, likewise, can be expected to rise for a period of years, may enable the former to develop a different pattern of expenditure,[1] which may then make its contribution to a distinct way of life. In brief, though at some future date the labour market may rearrange itself on alternative lines, for the present students of that market must reserve some of their attention for what is its biggest minority-shareholder.

Similarly, while from a logical angle there are no doubt other bases on which labour incomes could be more usefully broken down for purposes of the national accounts, until such other bases become practicable, separate figures for wages and salaries might well continue to be reflected in these:[2] From the standpoint of social accounting, the need is for more, rather than less, knowledge about the flows of income and expenditure. Finally, while a wholly independent self-contained theory of salaries is, clearly, not called for, the determinants of pay levels in the two spheres are, at the same time, not identical. Hence a realistic theory of wages—in the sense of a both comprehensive and 'actuality-orientated' theory of remuneration—should not ignore the distinction.

[1] For a brief discussion of the influence of the method of payment on patterns of expenditure see D. J. Robertson, 'The Present Complexity of Wage Payments and its Effects', *Scottish Journal of Political Economy*, February 1955.

[2] Though one must fervently pray that some improvement will be possible in the general methods of estimation for *individual* industries/services. The description of these in *National Income Statistics: Sources and Methods* (op. cit., pp. 80–92) almost made this writer's (very long) hair stand on end.

Chapter 20

PROBLEMS OF PAY DETERMINATION

In this chapter we seek to review some of the problems of pay determination and negotiation. We are now therefore about to tread on ground belonging to that fascinating, though hazardous, territory most conveniently summed up in the term 'wages policy'.

A comprehensive investigation of that subject can of course not be divorced from that of other aspects of economic policy; let it be said from the outset that no claim to so exhaustive an analysis is made. Thus we shall not embark on a full-scale examination of what is no doubt the major question in the field—that of wages under full employment—though we shall not entirely ignore its existence. Nor is an all-pervasive probe into the rationale of reward or the determinants of salary levels attempted; our treatment here has perforce to be selective and all that our resources will stretch to is a consideration of some of the problems involved. In the main, we shall limit ourselves to the more 'internal' facets of the topic, but as such consideration cannot take place in a vacuum and so as to indicate both whence we proceed and whither we have been led, we will devote some space also to the wider issues.

The heading of this chapter may call for a brief comment. The distinction between wages and salaries was dealt with in Chapter 19; our finding was that—a number of qualifications notwithstanding—salaries are a recognized entity and as such one of the facts of the contemporary labour scene. At the same time, their autonomy must not be exaggerated; some of the questions that are now to occupy us are not confined either to salaries or to the public sector, but are common to the problems of pay determination as such. It was thought that more justice could be done to them by a somewhat broader frame of reference, though public service salaries will continue to be our particular bias.

I

From a purely economic standpoint, a wage—using the term now in its wide sense—is the price of labour determined, as other prices are, by the interplay of demand and supply. Like such other prices also it is subject to special forces which interfere with the smooth functioning of the market mechanism. As regards prices generally, the economist investigates these forces in that they restrict the free working of supply and demand; however, in so far as the latter themselves are concerned, he takes them as given. The economist is of course aware that demand and supply prices may be the product of many factors—economic and non-economic, objective and subjective: Though he will study them from various angles, *qua* economist he does not feel called upon to delve into the nature of their constituent elements.

Prima facie, therefore, there is a case for adopting the same procedure on the wages front. Just as in the sphere of other commodities the economist can ignore, say, the motivations of consumers which lie behind the £ *s. d.* that they are willing to offer for them, so as regards wages he need not concern himself with the component factors that go to make up the demand and the supply price of labour. However—and the point is as important as it is obvious—the commodity to which this particular price accrues is animate. This introduces a new and altogether different additional dimension, which renders the interplay of demand and supply very considerably more complex. Hence the question arises as to whether analysis must not be taken rather further back, if this interaction is to be fully understood.[1]

That such an understanding is vital will need little special pleading, for wages can be regarded as one of the most crucial set of prices that impinge on the economic welfare of a country. Hence it is a matter of the greatest consequence that we should get them right and—whatever the precise reasons—experience has shown that they are not right automatically. It is here believed that we shall only have them in that category if, among other things, we make a positive effort to determine rates of remuneration—both in particular and *in toto*—on a more rational basis than hitherto.

The concept of a system of rationally-determined wages is of course not tenable—or rather is merely tautologous—if the view is held that whatever price is fixed by the blind forces of the market mechanism is right. On that premise, if wages are 'wrong', this is merely due to the various interferences thwarting that mechanism.

[1] cf. J. R. Hicks, *The Theory of Wages* (Macmillan, 1932), p. 1. Professor Hicks' main thesis is, of course, that the theory of wage determination in a free market 'is simply a special case of the general theory of value'. He agrees, however, that the need for a special theory of wages arises 'because both the supply of labour, and the demand for it, and the way in which demand and supply interact on the labour market, have certain peculiar properties, which make it impossible to apply to labour the ordinary theory of commodity value without some further consideration.'

However, though the labour market certainly is plagued by 'inter-ferences' such as, say, restrictive labour practices, others—such as trade unions themselves—have come to stay, and it is one of the very purposes of a rational wage structure to make the system tick not-withstanding. Further, the postulate of a pattern of remuneration being potentially either rational or otherwise can also claim to make sense, if the line is taken that the unaided market is not—i.e. imper-fections apart—necessarily the sole test of what constitutes the economic optimum for a country as a whole.

In drawing a distinction between the spontaneous dictates of the market and the economic optimum, we have in mind a modification of, rather than a departure from, a regime of demand and supply as that phrase is normally understood. For the formula of price being the equator of these can be held to allow of different interpretations. While its simplest meaning is that (in the present context) wages are to be regulated exclusively by the indigenous workings of market forces, it could also refer to a system of demand and supply prices the magnitude of which has, where desirable, been 'treated' somewhat before determining remuneration. Thus the price offered for a grade of labour can be left entirely to employers' forecasts as to the prob-able demand for the commodity concerned; alternatively, it could be raised in line with a deliberate decision to expand that particular sector of the economy. Again—though illustrating the point now from a different angle—if in conditions of full employment the pro-cesses of collective bargaining give rise to a growth in money wages unrelated to that in productivity, then we are faced with the question of whether a definite link must not be established between these two variables. As post-war experience has shown, we cannot simply leave it to the higgling of the labour market to produce a non-inflationary wages bill, though this is not to say that the imperfections of markets, any more than their perfections, are sacrosanct.

Even if the postulate of a rational wage is conceded as being ten-able as such, it can be objected that the notion of its serving as a guide in the context of pay determination is based on the somewhat naïve assumption that we can give it content in fairly definite terms. Now it is freely admitted that—in this as in other spheres—there is no, and cannot be any, absolute definition of rationality. Here as elsewhere it must be interpreted afresh by each generation, though the test of rationality can perhaps be pinpointed as current *raison d'être* rather than historical antiquity. But while within each generation there will be legitimate differences of opinion as to what constitutes current *raison d'être*, this does not preclude the possibility of, for example, evolving wages in such a way as is 'rational' in the light of Britain's current economic circumstances. If, in post-war years, we have had

L

an annual accretion to the wages bill which has been significantly inflationary, and a pay structure which has not been conspicuously responsive to other economic needs, this would seem to be because not sufficient steps have been taken to secure something better rather than because agreement on these matters is inherently unattainable. It should, however, be added that in so far as the inflationary problem is concerned or—to quote a more precise formula—that of achieving stable prices without jeopardizing full employment or a rising standard of living, it is one which has not yet been solved by any of the advanced industrial democracies,[1] though some of these have a distinctly better record than Britain.[2]

Nor are we trying to suggest that the subject is clear-cut or non-controversial, though few would probably quarrel with the proposition that the pay structure should be of a shape and 'size' as to be capable of making its full contribution to the achievement of the country's economic objectives. And here it is interesting to reflect that, as regards these latter, there is actually a substantial consensus of view as to their identity. Indeed, it is such that, if an opinion poll were taken as to whether the following were thought to be 'a good thing', it is an almost foregone conclusion that full employment, a stable price level, a satisfactory export performance and balance of payments, growing productivity and a rising standard of living would all be 'ticked' as being in this category. This, of course, is reducing the matter to its nethermost level of crudity and ignoring—to raise it just slightly above—the differences of outlook as to which of these goals are 'more good' than others, the steps needed if they are to materialize, and the problems engendered by trying to achieve them all. But the simple-minded may nevertheless insist that where there is so much agreement on overall aims—our list is in no particular order and not necessarily complete—it should not be beyond our twentieth-century wits to devise that combination of measures most likely to lead to maximum realization. And in such a programme, clearly, wages have an important part to play.

The matching of a pay structure to a set of economic objectives is complicated *inter alia* by two major factors. The first is that, given such objectives, the shape of the appropriate wage structure is not precisely given. Indeed, many variations on the theme might produce the desired results if we were starting 'from scratch'; seeing that we are not, there may nonetheless be certain room for manoeuvre.

[1] *Council on Prices, Productivity and Incomes, Fourth Report* (HMSO 1961), para 2.
[2] This was made painfully obvious again in a recent study published by OEEC: See Fellner, Gilbert *et al., The Problem of Rising Prices* (Organization for European Economic Co-operation, 1961).

Secondly, though the evolution of the wage system occurred in response to economic needs, the determinants of wages themselves are both economic and other; while for many purposes it will suffice to treat the price of labour as a simple economic quantity, for others it becomes relevant that it is itself the product of a much more variegated motley of forces. Thus apart from economic considerations, supply prices, for example, are significantly moulded by the fact that the recipient of the wage is a human being whose material—and in many ways whose non-material—well-being depends on their magnitude. They are similarly conditioned by their involvement in the question of the distribution of the national income, which in turn has a profound impact on social relationships. Again, we are merely making the obvious point that the pay-packet has non-economic effects as well as antecedents, the importance of the former no doubt being the reason for the strength of the latter.

Now it may be held that, just as on the economic front the market is not necessarily the automatic arbiter of the economically optimal size of rewards, so when it comes to their social constituents not all the considerations that happen to enter into these are *ipso facto* rational and relevant. Thus the valuation placed on a given kind of labour, apart from being a function of the demand for the product of that labour, its scarcity, and so on, may also—notably in the salaried sphere—reflect more elusive factors such as the influence of tradition and history. It is particularly in connection with these more elusive elements of demand price that the case for scrutiny arises, and if on examination they are found wanting, the attempt at modification need not be deemed to be trespass. Likewise, the processes—implicit and explicit—by which individuals formulate their supply price are not in any way sacrosanct; traditional factors are, of course, operative also on the side of supply.

Notwithstanding the character of some of the non-economic determinants of wages, the fact remains that the pay-packet has social, etc. implications—and very important ones at that. Hence it can be posited that, as a matter of principle, issues involving rates of remuneration should take some account of these, and a corollary of this would be that in order to judge of the rationality of a wage, the test is not an economic one alone. Now to maintain that pay determination may have regard to some of the social or ethical implications of the subject—as to argue that it may weigh economic considerations other than those spontaneously thrown up by the market—is of course a straightforward value judgment. Equally so, however, is the position that the reward of labour should be a function exclusively of the natural laws of the market. Indeed, any decision as to the principles which should bear on a problem is in that category, irrespective of the nature of the principles selected. To hold that remuneration should be the outcome only of the blind interaction of supply and demand is as much a value judgment—the justification for which must be sought outside the discipline of economics—as to opt for some alternative set of criteria.

Having said this much, this writer would make clear that, according to her own scale of values, economic considerations should—though not the sole—be among the primary determinants of remuneration. For the economic system is after all merely itself a means for adding to human welfare; indeed, it is one of the most potent tools to this end—and so to opine, one does not have to be a materialist in any of the various senses of that term. And though the economic system, by very reason of its potentialities, lends itself to abuse more easily perhaps than some other social institutions, this does not detract from the proposition that its efficient functioning is a social priority of the first magnitude. And for such functioning an adequate wage pattern is one of the essential prerequisites, which we can only dispense with if we are willing to resort to the direction of the country's manpower. The latter is not, however, an acceptable stratagem in a democratic society.

As for those non-economic factors which are nevertheless relevant in this context, some of these are—and more, we believe, could be—fitted into the framework of an economically-orientated pay structure. Some conflicts, on the other hand, are inevitable, for while there is a broad consensus of opinion as to the economic functions of the wage system—for instance, that it must secure a proper distribution of labour—there is no similar agreement as to what non-economic factors should have a bearing on the matter. Thus that basic needs are a legitimate constituent of a person's supply price will command wide support; whether 'fairness' should be a criterion of reward is more controversial; whether status and prestige should be, is very much more so. We shall return to these topics anon; here we might mention that in so far as the conflicts between economic and social goals cannot be reconciled within an economically-inspired framework of remuneration, some of the relevant social objectives can in part be realized by other media of policy. Such alternative methods—the system of taxation or the network of social services—are not available for attaining the economic purposes of wages.

There is, however, another crucial point. This is that even though economic considerations must have the last word in fashioning the pattern of reward, and even though certain relevant social objectives can be dealt with by media outside the sphere of wages policy, the latter cannot, in present circumstances, escape from the obligation of assessing the role of non-economic factors in the context of pay determination. In truth, the question of whether or not all non-economic desiderata *per se* should be discounted as independent goals of wages policy has been largely settled for us by the advent of full employment

For though an employer engages workers as a factor of production, workers supply their labour so as to be able to enjoy a certain standard of life, to receive a fair reward, and so on. Now it is inherent in our present system of collective bargaining that, in the course of their mutual encounter for purposes of pay negotiation, each side should endeavour to maximize its profit, so that it is natural for a union to try and push its sectional advantage to the greatest possible extent. Under full employment, however, it can do so to the point where the result is highly undesirable for the nation as a whole—because of the inflationary character of the settlement. Yet it is unrealistic to expect labour to refrain from driving such bargains, unless we can modify the system in such a way as not only makes sense in economic terms, but likewise represents a genuine attempt to meet such of its legitimate aspirations as can in fact be accommodated within an economically-orientated pay structure. For which —as for several other cogent—reasons, we require a consistent policy in the light of which *all* types of wage problems can be resolved. These, of course, are very big questions which we shall consider more fully later; here we merely wish to give the briefest of indications for our view that, in order to get wages 'right', we must among other things be prepared to grapple with all the factors that determine the price of labour.

The upshot of our preceding remarks is that, having regard both to the exceptional characteristics and the exceptional significance of the commodity called 'labour', we should not be content with taking demand and supply prices as given, but ought to examine also the component elements which go into their making. This, first, seems desirable for a full understanding of the subject. Secondly, since demand and supply prices, the wage bargains in which they result, and the wages bill to which the bargains add up cannot automatically be subsumed to be 'rational', but that since it is of the greatest importance that they be in that category, we should, as it were, take the necessary steps to transport them thither. We are primarily prompted by the view that such an approach is called for if the *economic* functions of wages are to be fulfilled; though 'more rationality' might clearly qualify as a goal of policy in its own right, our point here is that in the sphere of wage determination it has now become an economic necessity. Our point is, further, that if more rationality is to be achieved in this field, non-economic as well as economic factors are involved owing, quite simply, to the anatomy of the price of labour. Here we will leave the matter for the moment; we shall now first look at some specific questions, returning to the wider problem at the end of the chapter.

II

It is a corollary of the foregoing that the fact of a particular wage or salary bringing the demand for a grade of labour and its supply into equilibrium, does not automatically prove that such rate is 'right': The recruitment-retention test, on the view here taken, is not the sole basis for judging of the adequacy or otherwise of our standards of remuneration. It is, however, a highly important criterion, and this it may be worthwhile to underline. For not infrequently is it assumed that an 'either-or' attitude must be struck in these matters, so that the pointing to the existence of one facet of a problem is promptly treated as a declaration of intent to ignore all else.

The recruitment-retention test should not monopolize pay determination because, among other things, it does not necessarily reflect certain non-economic factors to which it may be decided to give weight. Thus if it were held to reign supreme, it would rule out all minimum wage legislation—or, in this country, would take the ground from under the Wages Councils and analogous Acts. Similarly, the granting of equal pay to women in the public services was clearly motivated by considerations of equity—not by any scarcity of female labour at unequal standards of remuneration. There must be a large body of informed opinion that regards both these measures as desirable reforms, even though they cannot be defended by reference to the market.

We may now, however, look at one or two ways in which the recruitment criterion may be deficient quite apart from such wider social issues. We have already expressed the view that the blind market and the economic optimum do not inevitably coincide, so that the recruitment-retention test may be inapplicable because, say, it is felt to be in the national interest to expand (or contract) some sector of the economy, entailing a deliberate policy of manning up (or down) to bring this about. However, we shall not pursue this either as it is, in essence, part of the general debate as to the degree of planning appropriate to the conduct of a country's economic affairs.

Instead let us take the proposition that, though a rate of pay may equate the demand for and the supply of a particular grade of labour, the latter may not be of the quality really suitable for the work in question. Put in another way, we have here the problem of whether a post should be remunerated on the basis of the qualifications ideally required of its holders, as against those actually possessed. Thus prison officers are supposed to exercise a good influence over their charges both by example and precept; modern methods increasingly call for their active co-operation in training and treatment. Nobody would quarrel with this; for the sake of argument, let us assume that it represents the ideal rather than the actual. The question then is whether pay should be deliberately raised so as to constitute adequate reward for the few who have achieved the ideal standard—in the hope of securing a larger supply approximating thereto. Initially, this would involve a level of salary above the equilibrium necessary to equate supply—of the existing quality—and demand; if it were felt that prison staffs are below par, such a course might be decided upon. It must be added, however, that there may be quite a number of fields in which it would be desirable to improve standards in this fashion. If the policy of attracting personnel of 'superior calibre' were adopted in many spheres, is there, one must ask, a sufficient reservoir of such persons available and what, further, is the labour market to do with all the rejects? Also, if such a course were embarked upon on a large scale, it would to that extent become ineffective. Superior pay is of course a relative concept; in proportion as its benefits are extended, it ceases to be superior. Remuneration over and above the equilibrium price of labour in order to boost its quality is thus an instrument not to be used indiscriminately, though at the same time it is one which may serve a very useful purpose.

That the question can arise does, however, show that—'economic optimum' considerations apart—the absence of recruitment difficulties merely demonstrates that a given demand price is effectively eliciting a quantitatively adequate supply; it does not necessarily mean that it is adequate in the sense of attracting that grade of worker which, in all the circumstances, ought to be attracted. Of course, the distinction between quality and quantity is not absolute: Where the quality of would-be recruits is obviously below that stipulated or expected, one would not 'count' them as having presented themselves, and hence one would regard the situation as tantamount to a quantitative deficiency of candidates. Our aim here in drawing the distinction is simply to say that equilibrium between demand and supply may conceal the fact that insufficient thought has been given to—as was put above—the quality of labour that ought, in all the circumstances, to be attracted: For example, it is well-known that Co-operative societies pay their managers salaries which are inferior to those current in the business world at large, and some have ascribed the mediocrity of branches of Co-operative enterprise to the societies' not recruiting the right calibre of managerial ability.

Whether, then, the 'circumstances' are particular principles of penology that might, with advantage, inform the country's penal system, or whether they are defined accomplishments in the way of technical know-how or business acumen, is immaterial. In either case it is possible for demand prices to be at the wrong level—and therefore economically inefficient—even though there are no visible staff shortages such as would of themselves trigger off the needed correctives.

Quality apart, the recruitment test does not necessarily clinch the question of the adequacy of a particular rate of pay, because supply may fall short for reasons other than monetary ones. First, the flow of many groups of workers—be they teachers or skilled craftsmen—partly depends on existing training facilities. Secondly, any one of the numerous conditions of work or service associated with a job may contribute to manpower difficulties. In certain sectors of the Civil Service, for instance, the time a candidate has to wait between application for a post and actual commencement of duties is a well-known deterrent, while among causes adversely affecting the availability of scientists for the atomic energy programme, security restrictions and the limitation of complements on the part of the Treasury were mentioned in an official report in 1952.[1] Again, it is widely accepted that the problem of manning up the country's police forces is due to factors including, but not solely consisting of, the size of their income. Similar considerations apply to staff wastage. Labour turnover, in short, is a complex issue and may require to be dealt with by adjustments which are not of a financial nature. To the extent that such adjustments are impracticable because the particular condition is inherent in the type of employment—such as the security element in atomic energy work—a shortage of staff does, however, indicate that the reward offered is insufficient to compensate for all the disadvantages of the occupation. Strictly speaking, it does so also in the case of the 'avoidable deterrents', except that the remedy called for is a different one.

One misconception we may dispose of here. The point has frequently been made that, in a time of full or over-full employment, a dearth of candidates does not signify a poor appeal in the labour market, as all fields are likely to be understaffed. While this may be more or less true, the conclusion is sometimes drawn that the recruitment criterion has therefore become entirely meaningless, whereas the position is rather that in such a period it is relative, in place of absolute, recruitment difficulties which are significant.

[1] *Tenth Report from Select Committee on Estimates, Session* 1951–2 (HMSO 1952), Minutes of Evidence, pp. 74 and 139.

III

If the recruitment test is one of the important determinants of employers' demand prices, so is 'fairness' on the side of supply. Thus if we approached the subject from the point of view of the man-in-the-street, his attitude as to the appropriate pay for any particular grade could probably be summarized by the phrase 'the rate for the job'; there can be little doubt that this represents one of the fundamental constituents of his supply price. This rate seems to refer to one that takes into account the various intrinsic characteristics of the post such as the physical effort, skill, degree of responsibility, training and formal qualifications required, and one that takes due note also of any special features such as, say, the dirt or danger involved. The assumption appears to be that the rate for the job is both the one which *is* currently paid for analogous work elsewhere, and hence the one which *ought* to be paid; the implication is that such a standard is equitable and just absolutely as well as relatively. We have already had occasion to point to the impact of this desire for fairness on pay structures in contradistinction to actual earnings.[1]

Nor has 'fairness' as a goal of pay policy been confined to the suppliers of labour; over an important sector of the public service it became, in 1956, the main determinant of employers' demand price —to wit, of the salaries offered by the Treasury to all non-industrial civil servants. This followed from the findings of the Royal (Priestley) Commission on the Civil Service,[2] whose 1955 Report was one of the major post-war pronouncements on the subject as far as the public sector is concerned, and who stressed the element of fairness as the primary criterion for the adequacy of salaries in this field. The Commission emphasized that the State was under a categorical obligation to remunerate its employees fairly, and they rejected a definition of fairness solely in terms of recruitment and retention,[3] though they made clear that they used the word solely in the sense of Civil Service salaries being the same as those accruing to comparable outside occupations.[4] 'The primary principle of civil service pay should be fair comparison with the current remuneration of outside staffs employed on broadly comparable work, taking account of differences in other conditions of service' is how the Commission themselves summed up their conclusions in the matter.[5]

[1] See pp. 294–5 *ante*.

[2] *Royal Commission on the Civil Service* 1953–5, Cmd. 9613 (HMSO 1955).

[3] ibid. paras. 90–4. The Anderson Committee of 1923, who considered the same matter, concluded that pay should be exclusively based on the recruitment-retention test.

[4] This is also the sense in which the term has been used in the various Fair Wages Resolutions passed by Parliament.

[5] *Priestley Report*, op. cit., p. 194.

Nor was 'fair comparison' exclusively adopted by the Civil Service; it showed distinct signs of spreading and underlay, for example, the famous 1960 British Railways wage agreement based on the recommendations of the Guillebaud Railway Pay Committee of Inquiry. We shall come back to the special case of the public sector later; here we may pose the crucial question: Is there an inherent contradiction between fairness and the economist's emphasis on the requirements of the labour market as the primary determinant of remuneration? The present writer feels that there is not—or rather that there need not be, provided that two conditions are fulfilled. First, the intrinsic characteristics of jobs must be more carefully and appropriately evaluated, with the influence of history, custom and tradition 'vetted' for current relevance. Secondly, it has to be accepted as one of the facts of life that economic considerations have a legitimate bearing on fairness.

These two 'conditions' are, of course, not independent of one another. Our ideas as to what constitutes fair compensation for a particular skill are in part a function of the scarcity of such skill. Similarly, the state of recruitment to any one market will, amongst other things, reflect the extent to which potential candidates judge the incomes to be earned there as equitable. In one sense, therefore, the notion of the rate for the job is taken care of by ordinary economic concepts: If a given post calls for special attributes, etc., the supply price of its would-be incumbent will be correspondingly greater; likewise, the cash employers are prepared to offer will be more generous, so that the demand and supply curves will intersect at a higher level of remuneration. Nonetheless, as far as the actual business of pay negotiation is concerned, the ideal of the fair wage has acquired a semi-autonomous existence; various notions have taken root as to what is a just reward for certain qualifications, only partly deriving from their scarcity value and a determinant of remuneration in their own right. An arts graduate asked to accept £10 a week at, say, age 30 would regard this, along with many others, as unfair even if there were a superabundance of such graduates unable to find a niche in the labour market.

Our views as to what is a fair reward are thus to some degree independent of market considerations. While this is reasonable, it is equally reasonable that we should revise—enlarge is perhaps the more appropriate term—our concept of fairness: At present, economic realities are allowed insufficient weight in shaping our attitudes in the matter. It is frequently assumed that basic job characteristics, as modified by conditions of service and other net benefits, define what is equitable; the requirements of the economy are tolerated at best as an outside intrusion. If we could bring ourselves to regard economic scarcity as having a legitimate bearing on fairness—i.e. that it is 'fair' to pay one worker more than his colleague merely because, even though his job is no more skilled or unpleasant, he is in short supply—a differential granted on this score would cause less heart-burning. It need not really outrage anyone if those manning posts of which the community stands in greatest need command a higher income than those whose labours could more easily be dispensed with.

The fact is that if we want to have a highly complex society aiming at a maximum output of goods and services, in which consumers are to be free to buy what they choose but in which there is to be no direction of manpower, there must be some lever to induce workers to enter those industries which will produce the wished-for assortment of goods and services. The main tool we have for this purpose is a differential pay structure[1]—and this is so irrespective of whether the market is held to be sacrosanct or whether its demands for human and other resources have themselves, where necessary, been edged in some desired direction. It must be accepted, therefore, that the relative scarcity of labour is one of the major determinants of remuneration, and workers should receive a 'scarcity supplement'—we return to this in more detail subsequently—if shortages in a particular field persist. However, as Professor Florence has pointed out, before justifying too sharp a divergence between the true reward of different jobs, we must be certain that all artificial barriers to mobility—social as well as occupational—have been removed, and that it is a natural dearth that is being overcome.[2]

In a number of other ways also economic considerations will introduce a measure of unfairness into pay, as determined on the basis of intrinsic job characteristics. Thus other things being equal, increases are less likely to be conceded where labour constitutes a comparatively large element in the cost of production or—in the case of the public services—where sheer numbers make even the smallest improvement expensive. Sudden fluctuations of trade, resulting in the unforeseen contraction of an overseas market, are likewise not the 'fault' of those adversely affected, while workers finding themselves in an expanding industry are not probably—ethically speaking—specially deserving of the higher earnings which they will be able to secure. In short, as Professor Hicks put it in another context, a certain amount of unfairness is a necessary concomitant of economic change;[3] it is here suggested that—if our economic priorities are

---

[1] For a brief but excellent discussion of this point see E. H. Phelps Brown, 'Wage Policy and Wage Differences', *Economica*, November 1955, p. 353.

[2] P. Sargant Florence, *Labour* (Hutchinson's University Library, n.d.), p. 105.

[3] Hicks, op. cit., p. 82.

right in the first place and basic job content properly evaluated—
this is fair.

There are other types of injustice in this sphere which are less easy
to countenance, because they do not similarly spring from hard
economic inevitability. Thus those who are relatively vocal or mili-
tant do, within limits, 'get away' with it. Their supply price will be
higher than if they were less clamorous, and though the demand
factor will keep the matter in perspective, they may be able to command a more generous reward for their services than their more
amenable or civically-conscious colleagues. Similarly, those engaged
in occupations with a favourable 'climate of remuneration' may derive substantial profit from this; their pay may contain a concealed
bonus granted on grounds unrelated to performance or specific
economic considerations. This is one of the reasons for our placing
emphasis on the scrutiny of demand and supply prices; for though a
certain amount of unfairness is clearly inherent in the economic
system, this certain amount is not necessarily co-terminous with its
de facto magnitude. In so far as it is, we must console ourselves with
the thought that such unfairness is not confined to economic life; it
may be part of the 'cosmic order' of things, but be that as it may,
economics has no monopoly of its manifestations. In so far as it is not,
we may come to the conclusion that it is worth our while to apply
ourselves to the matter: For we might find that, if some of the pre-
ventable inequities were eliminated, there would then be a rather
greater tolerance of those which cannot be avoided.

IV

Another basic element in remuneration to which we may now turn
is the 'need' factor. The demand for a wage which will guarantee
one's essential requirements can hardly be described as other than
reasonable; hence there is the question whether reward should be
exclusively the rate for the job as determined by the characteristics of
the post and the exigencies of the labour market, or whether it should
also be in some way linked to the needs of its individual recipients.
Quite apart from what should be, what *is* is also capable of different
interpretations. The problem owes its existence, of course, to the dual
nature of the pay packet to which we have referred.

It is thus the worker who feels impelled to stress the need factor at
the bargaining table, the crux of the collective bargain to him being
the standard of life it enables him to maintain. For the employer, on
the other hand, the wage is simply an economic quantity—an element
in his costs of production—and is shaped by considerations which
are quite independent of the needs of labour *qua* human beings.

As a result of this total divergence in the significance of the wage to employers and workers, the interplay of demand and supply has produced a compromise, in that pay is not based on need in so far as this varies between individuals within any one occupation: The rate of remuneration agreed by the processes of joint negotiation does not, in this country, take account of an employee's domestic circumstances.[1] At the same time, the notion that the wage must assure a man of a certain standard of life is probably the most fundamental element making up his supply price; further, the popular conception of such a standard is that it should be adequate to cover the requirements of the 'average family'. To the extent, then, that a rate of pay is the product of the interaction of demand and supply, the need factor becomes one of its basic ingredients.

According to one legal authority the salaries of state employees, though fixed with the sanction of the Treasury, are in the eyes of the law laid down by the Sovereign and awarded by him to his servants: 'It appears that the pay of a Crown servant is not to be considered a reward for his services, but as a payment to enable him to perform his duties.' Salaries, Mr Mustoe adds, seem to be granted for the dignity of the State, and for the decent support of those engaged in its service.[2] However, notwithstanding the legal position and the different composition of the public employer's demand price, in practice the pay of public employees is also essentially recompense for services rendered rather than to meet need. This is so at any rate as far as basic standards of remuneration are concerned; as regards the various peripheral aspects of pay, there may be a difference between the public and private sectors.[3]

The term 'need' is a highly nebulous one, there being at least three possible interpretations. First, there are the physiological needs of subsistence, but though their precise definition may present difficulty, this is a question which is not really acute in advanced industrial countries. What is still a problem in the latter is what should be allowed over and above this bare subsistence level to form a generally acceptable minimum or living wage. However, there are no absolute criteria to help in the articulation of such a standard, for the luxuries of yesterday are the necessaries of today, while many a 'must' of the American worker is far beyond the reach of the peoples of other lands. In brief, such a minimum has to be fixed to suit time and place;

---

[1] A National Arbitration Tribunal Award (No. 1432, HMSO 1950) mentioned an offer by employers to pay a higher wage to married, than to single, men. However, this is most unusual, and the award provided for a uniform rate.

[2] N. E. Mustoe, *The Law and Organization of the British Civil Service* (Pitman, 1932), p. 41.

[3] See *post*.

the economic position of the country as well as the resultant attitudes
as to what are 'necessaries' can alone determine its magnitude. Such a
standard may or may not be given the sanction of law but—either
way—it is desirable that no one should be permitted to fall below
it. For if levels of remuneration are tolerated which offend the community's collective conscience, the burden of making up the difference is merely shifted from employers to taxpayers.

The problem of giving precision to an acceptable minimum standard of life can to some extent be shelved in countries where, as in
Britain, there is no minimum wage legislation. Even here, however,
the matter cannot be altogether evaded, first, because the figures laid
down by the various statutory Wages Councils—which cover about
$3\frac{1}{2}$ million workers in agriculture, distribution, catering, road transport, etc.—are supposed to provide for at least such living wages and,
secondly, because the claim that it is impossible to manage on £x a
week at times crops up in other low-paid industries. A specific difficulty in this context is the well-known one of whom such a minimum
is to cater for. As pointed out, supply prices are framed in terms of the
family—the 'typical family' of four—although this particular demo-
graphic unit is very far from being typical, the burden of dependency
varying greatly.[1] This poses the dilemma that where a minimum is
adequate for one, it cannot also be so for two, three or four; conversely, if it is fixed at a level high enough to cover the two-child
household, it will be above the essential requirements of those with
fewer offspring.

There are, however, several possible solutions. Thus one way
enabling actual, rather than hypothetical, domestic responsibilities to
be taken into account is to base the minimum wage on the individual
person, that figure being adjusted to family needs via the system of
social security. This does of course mean that a considerable part of
the cost of supporting households on minimum standards is borne by
taxpayers, and it may be felt that this is undesirable. This objection
could therefore be met by the alternative device of a system of dependants' allowances, financed by employers via a special contribution calculated as a percentage of their total payroll or similar
method. In this way, the whole of the minimum wage bill would be a
direct charge on the goods and services it helped to produce, while
the economic function of the wage would not be interfered with: No
individual employer would be penalized by reason of the number of
dependants with which his staff happened to be blessed. The latter,
at the same time, would again receive a living wage attuned to their
actual circumstances.

---

[1] So, of course, does the number of contributors to the family budget.

The drawback of both the preceding schemes is that it would be extremely difficult to single out those in receipt of minimum rates for special treatment under any plan for either a state- or an employer-financed system of family allowances. Hence unless these are in any case a built-in feature of a country's social security pattern and, further, are of the necessary dimensions, they will not be capable of making up a person's single-man-based living wage to family proportions. There is therefore a third alternative, though it is only practicable in a fairly prosperous country. As we have previously remarked, there is nothing absolute about the size of the living wage; it contains in any event a greater or lesser conventional margin above the physiological needs standard. Hence a relatively well-off country may decide that it can afford a minimum level of reward which is generous as far as the single worker is concerned but which, at the same time, will suffice for the decencies of life of the average family. It is a less logical system of minimum wages, but it may fit in more easily with the prevailing regime of social security.

Minimum standards apart, there are of course many other types of contingency. Thus in an article published some years ago, Professor R. M. Titmuss made the general point that the distribution of the national product was out of sympathy with the contemporary distribution of social need arising from the dependencies of childhood, widowhood, sickness and old age,[1] and one's spontaneous reaction might well be that somehow or other systems of remuneration ought to take greater cognisance of such needs. Yet to weight pay rates themselves by these factors is ruled out, for the wage structure cannot discharge its economic tasks if it is adjusted to the specific commitments of individuals which are entirely unrelated to the matter. Wages must, over and above the universal minimum, represent relative values to employers, and these can hardly be expected to fluctuate with their recipients' personal circumstances.

However, there is nothing particularly harsh about this. For if it is felt that the various kinds of need are not sufficiently catered for in our current distribution of resources, the way to remedy this is either to allocate a bigger share of the national income to the social security budget, or else to hive off a part of the wage-bill itself in the form of an employer-financed scheme of family allowances—on the lines briefly indicated. The amount that can be set aside in this way must clearly not be so large as to prevent the remainder of the wage-bill from fulfilling its economic function, but in spite of this overriding

---

[1] 'Social Administration in a Changing Society', *British Journal of Sociology*, September 1951. What follows is not to imply that Professor Titmuss himself suggests that needs should be met *within* the framework of wage and salary structures.

Salaries in the Public Services

proviso, there is considerable latitude in the degree of generosity that could be meted out to the several brands of need. It is a separate issue of policy, but what may perhaps be emphasized is that, while pay rates themselves are not equipped to deal with the 'domestic situation', any harshness in this sphere is not inherent in the economic system. To the extent that we chafe under this problem, therefore, we do so not because it is insoluble—but merely because we have not gone further in solving it.

In so far as need is *within* the competence of the pattern of remuneration, we have seen that it may refer, first, to a bare physiological subsistence standard and, secondly, to a minimum 'living wage' which, over and above the first, includes an additional and variable margin for conventional necessities. This second definition merges imperceptibly—the contradiction in terms notwithstanding—into its third meaning, where need is equated simply with the mode of life to which an individual has become accustomed by reason of his income. Though, as a matter of logic, need cannot be extended to cover that part of the propensity to consume which is generated merely by a more generous pattern of expenditure, the 'standard of living' factor in pay negotiation is as crucial and as staunchly-defended a constituent of supply prices as need in its strict sense. And the higher the level of wealth in a country, the more of course is it habitual, rather than actual, need which acts on supply prices.

Here we may briefly touch on the clash between basic or 'living wage' needs on the one hand, and relative or 'standard of living' needs on the other; it is a subject which closely overlaps that of vertical differentials which, in turn, are one of the standing headaches besetting the day-to-day business of wage settlement. The problem has occurred in its most acute form, perhaps, in the case of cost-of-living increases with which we have become so familiar in the post-war period. The question which has repeatedly come up is whether these should be in the shape of a uniform sum exclusively fixed by reference to the rise in the Index of Retail Prices—with a possible leaving out altogether of those in the higher income brackets—or whether the addition should be calculated as a percentage of remuneration, enabling relative standards to be maintained.[1] The chronic—though perhaps understandable—indecision on this point is evidenced by the constant oscillation between these two alternatives, although some flat-rate bonuses are no doubt due to nothing other than the supreme simplicity of the method, so that the resultant levelling or seeming concession to the need factor is quite fortuitous. We may add that though every pay award implicitly or explicitly involves

[1] We ignore the 'inflationary' aspect of the question, as it is not relevant in the present context.

vertical differentials, the tug-of-war between them and need has crystallized in particular in connection with cost-of-living bonuses, since these latter—unlike, say, improvements flowing from an industry's enhanced prosperity—contain, as it were, a prevention-of-hardship element.

The subject of need versus differentials in the context of cost-of-living bonuses brings us to our next topic. For apart from need as an ingredient of basic standards of reward, there is another channel through which it may enter into pay levels. This is via the various 'fringe' aspects of remuneration such as increments, allowances, conditions of service and so on.

The question of need in the peripheral features of reward arises particularly in the public services. This is, first, because pay patterns here are more complex than wage structures to the extent that there is a greater profusion of incidental service conditions. Secondly, the incremental nature of salaries gives scope for the recognition of need in settling the length of a scale or the amount of an increment. For example, where the size of the latter is larger in the 'teens than in the twenties, this is in deference to the need element. Further, though in one sense the Treasury can pay its servants whatever salaries it pleases, in practice the basic rate attached to public offices must bear some sort of relationship to market levels. This is much less true of the various 'fringe' aspects of remuneration, particularly as present methods of calculating the net advantages of occupations are imprecise. It follows that there is more latitude in deciding on the principles on which such fringe benefits[1] should accrue.

It is in some degree as a result of this that the inconsistencies in dealing with the structural facets of pay—to which we have referred in Chapter 18—are found among the public services; some of these, that is, may be due to a difference of approach in the matter of weighting need. Thus one reason for remunerating senior public servants on a flat rate seems to be that, from a 'needs' point of view, annual improvements are no longer called for once given levels of income have been attained, though other scales retain their incremental character right up to the top of the pyramid. Similarly, the differing lengths of scales for recruitment grades may owe something to a differential desire to ease the burden of those assuming domestic responsibilities.

Analogous reasons may in part account for the divergent criteria underlying the various public service patterns of area differentials. As pointed out in Chapter 18, the London allowance is in some cases a uniform amount: However adequately or inadequately this may

---

[1] For the sake of brevity, this term is being used to cover *all* the various peripheral aspects of remuneration.

reflect the additional expense of living in the metropolis, it may be regarded as an attempt to compensate staffs for the 'absolute' extra cost involved. Where area differentials vary, at the same time, with age, this is merely a more precise adjustment to the same factor. Where, on the other hand, the size of the differential depends on salary, this can be considered as a basis unrelated to need—in the strict sense of that term.

Here we must qualify in that, even where area differentials increase with remuneration, they do not do so all the way. For example, BEA pilots' London weighting has been graduated in this manner, but it tapered off when pay exceeded a defined figure, while no allowance accrued to the most senior personnel. In the Civil Service the deduction from the London standard—and now the addition to the national rate—has not been tapered for top-level staff, but it no longer rises beyond a given salary.[1] Similarly, in 1950 the Industrial Court upheld a management side contention—the claim was for the institution of a London allowance for medical officers of health—that in other industries and services London weighting had been applied only to the lower income groups.[2] Thus even where area differentials rise in accordance with the relative standard of living, they would appear to do so only up to a certain point of seniority.

The extent to which other conditions of employment in the public services reflect the need factor varies. As pointed out, marital status is *inter alia* taken into account in fixing the rent allowances in the police and prison services. The size of the Civil Service transfer grants depends on family responsibilities as well as salary. The system of sickness payments—widespread in the public sector—and the few instances of family allowances are also clear illustrations of the recognition of personal need. Annual leave schedules, on the other hand, depend on remuneration and, frequently, length of service; they are not normally based on, say, the hazards to health of the particular job.

Superannuation payments, likewise, are governed by salary and length of service; except for the more favourable retirement provisions for such categories as policemen and prison officers, they are unrelated to need in its strict sense. As regards hours, these sometimes vary according to this—in this instance, the arduousness of work. Thus among medical auxiliaries speech therapists have shorter hours than almoners, and though nurses' working schedules are still substantially longer than medical auxiliaries', this is no doubt a case of patients' needs for hospital care being considered paramount—

---

[1] £1,501 since January 1961. See also p. 56 *ante*.
[2] Industrial Court Award No. 2285 (HMSO 1950), Appx. A, p. 13 and para. 21.

rather than one of indifference to those of nurses for leisure.[1] When we come to overtime payments, lower salaried staffs frequently are, but higher grades are not, eligible for these, though whether overtime should or should not attract compensation on a strict hourly basis is tending to become a matter of status as much as anything.[2] It may be added that if we step beyond the confines of public salaried employment, taking the whole labour market as our canvas, hours and other conditions of service are—as a broad generalization—fixed without regard to the need factor.

V

We have, earlier on, made the point that the question of examining the elements of demand and supply prices arises especially *à propos* of their more 'elusive' constituents. These latter can be looked upon as consisting of a rich conglomeration of factors—economic, social, traditional and so on; they reflect that wider social framework within which current economic forces operate. We make no attempt at an exhaustive analysis in this study, just as we are not investigating those economic forces themselves with which the 'elusive elements' may be said to coalesce. These last-named, however, may have some considerable potency in the shaping of actual rewards—more particularly so in the sphere of salaried employment—and we shall therefore devote this section to this topic. To begin with, we will take the case of teachers to illustrate how one such 'elusive element' of demand price—in this instance, a historical factor—appears to exercise a continuing pull on remuneration which it is difficult to reconcile with current requirements.

Teachers' remuneration in England and Wales, we are told by the McNair Committee of 1944, varied in chaotic fashion, with the profession as a whole 'disgracefully exploited'.[3] This was because elementary education was conceived of primarily as a charity—an instrument for providing a minimum of schooling for the 'children of the poor'—and it would appear that, though salaries have been centrally determined since 1919, this tradition of cheapness has dogged education for so long, that it is still difficult for the powers that be fully to

[1] Whether nurses have been adequately compensated for their long hours of work is a separate question.

[2] The Royal Commission on the Police, for example, stated that it was implicit in their whole conception of the status of the police service that casual overtime should cease to be expressly remunerated, and that their aim was to lift the uniformed constable out of the 'overtime class' of worker altogether. (*Interim Report*, Cmnd. 1222 (HMSO 1960), p. 58 and para. 187.) See also p. 312 *ante*.

[3] Board of Education, *Report of the Committee on the Supply etc. of Teachers and Youth Leaders* (HMSO 1944), para. 17.

emancipate themselves from it.[1] Adam Smith already pointed out that, though the requirements in the way of time, study, knowledge and application were at least as great in the case of teachers as in that of lawyers and doctors, the reward of the former bore no relation to that of the latter, but in his days this was largely because of over-supply. The strange phenomenon is that such comparatively low levels of remuneration have been allowed to persist in the face of an acute teacher shortage. The problem is no less serious for being well-known; in the circumstances, we can hardly draw much comfort from Smith's conclusion that this inequality was possibly beneficial as, though 'it may somewhat degrade the profession of a public teacher . . . the cheapness of literary education is . . . an advantage which greatly overbalances this trifling inconveniency'.[2]

It is of course true that the reason for teachers' inferior pay is not solely attributable to this tradition of cheapness: There are a number of other factors, especially on the side of supply. First, at a time when the expense of training had to be borne by the would-be professional himself, there was some sense in, say, a medical man commanding a more generous salary than a teacher, as the former had to recoup himself for his higher 'costs of production'. Likewise, he had —and still has—to reimburse himself for the extra years spent on his education, during which the teacher has begun to earn. Length of training is also a consideration in its own right: It confers prestige, and since that of teachers has hitherto been very short, this brevity has helped to relegate education to the ranks of the lower professions. Even more so has the non-graduate status of the bulk of the teaching labour force.

Again, though teachers can be fairly vocal—as the events of 1961 have reminded us—in pressing their demands for better pay, it might nevertheless be said that their claims are cast within a more modest mould than those of some other professionals. This is partly because education draws a proportion of its manpower from the lower middle and working, rather than the middle, classes. Teaching, with its absence of 'social' qualifications, is one of the levers by which many an able working-class child has hauled himself up the ladder into the middle strata of society, but the humble origin of such recruits has meant that they are ready to supply their labour more cheaply than those with an exclusively middle-class background. These latter regard a certain pattern of consumption as constituting their minimum standard of life, for less than which they are not willing to act. Finally, the fact that the majority of teachers are women has undoubtedly made for a supply price inferior to that of predominantly

[1] cf. ibid. para. 110.
[2] *Wealth of Nations*, 5th ed. by E. Cannan (1930), p. 135.

male professions—a situation not basically affected by the system of sex differentiation in force until recently.

Thus there are a number of contributory factors—and we mention a further one in another context later[1]—which go to explain the comparatively low level of teachers' remuneration, but though these modify, they do not invalidate, our main point. This is that, alive though we now are to the fundamental importance of education, though for many years we have been uncomfortably aware of the teacher shortage, and though we have realized that his prospects in the labour market are not all they might be, the tradition of cheapness has helped to create a climate which has somehow inhibited us from making his reward correspond more fully with the intensity of our demand. It represents an irrational element—from the economic as from any other point of view—in the demand price for teachers' services.

A related trend which can be discerned in public service remuneration is that the latter is at times influenced by certain concepts which in one instance are allowed as a determinant of pay, but in others—though seemingly also applicable—are disallowed. Thus the principle that where corruption might potentially occur, this is to be guarded against by a very generous income—making the fruits of such corruption less tempting—used to be given considerable weight in fixing the salaries of the higher judiciary. In the case of JPs, on the other hand, incorruptibility has been deemed to be assured by the opposite method of putting their services on a voluntary basis.

Again, there is the notion that social and kindred workers must be content with a small financial reward—nurses are perhaps the classic example—the balance of which is to be reckoned in terms of the intrinsic satisfaction to be derived from their labours. For other professions, however, it is not considered unethical to draw a handsome income as well as the satisfaction. Thus certain standards have been evolved as to who should work for the honour of it, who for the love of it plus, say, a modest honorarium, and who, on the other hand, may enjoy a large salary over and above analogous net advantages. Why these particular value judgments have taken root is a fascinating subject, though one which we prefer to leave open—short of a more thorough immersion in its intricacies. But it is perhaps fair to say that, irrespective of the origin of these ideas and whatever the degree of their germaneness in the context of pay determination, their impact on demand prices is somewhat arbitrary.

Akin to the role of tradition is that of the status/prestige factor; a few comments on this in relation to matters of pay may now be in place. This is a complex topic, the first question being the extent

[1] See pp. 391–2 *post*.

to which status and pay go hand in hand. There are unlikely to be many who would deny all reality to the connection; equally so, there are probably few who would claim that the two invariably and completely coincide. A good example of a wide divergence between prestige and remuneration is the clergyman: His stipend, judging by the minima laid down by the various denominations, is frequently below that of many semi-skilled workers, yet the status he enjoys—though it has undoubtedly deteriorated—is still decidedly higher. The prestige of dockers likewise does not march in step with their earnings; in this case it is below what might be inferred from the size of their pay packet. Again, female nurses—though until recently on a lower salary—rank above their male colleagues in the public estimation, this being a field in which women are presumed to excel.

Though the precise relation between pay and prestige belongs to that body of facts which it is difficult clearly to establish, it would appear that the impact of the former on the latter is most pronounced where there are no other and neutralizing considerations bearing on the matter. Thus in the case of the clergyman it is agreed that, as one devoted to spiritual pursuits in general and to Christianity in particular, he is not 'out' to get what he can. That what he does get is very little, is not therefore held against him as it would be in some other spheres, where a small income is taken to signify a lack of ability to do better. Academic staffs, for partly similar reasons, enjoy a prestige over and above that to which they would be 'entitled' on grounds of salary, and so in varying degrees do others whose profession contains an element of vocation. Again, a senior post in Government service is not rated by the remuneration attaching to it in the same measure as is one in the private sector; it has been generally accepted that standards of reward here ought to be lower than elsewhere. In the business world, by contrast, individuals are more or less given a *carte blanche* to make cash. They are only marginally subject to the inhibiting influence of public service and similar considerations; hence failure to make money is failure, and in this instance operates on status in full. To come back to the docker, here the fact that his work is both dirty and semi-casual depresses the sum total of prestige for which his wages might otherwise qualify him.

There are of course numerous related, though non-monetary, factors impinging on prestige levels. Among those that have special weight are family background; education and training; freedom of action as determined by one's ranking on the employer-ee scale; the nature of one's work—such as, as we saw, whether it is manual and dirty or not; security of tenure; conditions of service such as annual leave and so on. However, we must leave it at that.

The relation between prestige and income has two dimensions. Not only does pay influence status; the opposite is likewise the case —an important though controversial point to which Lady Wootton has drawn attention.[1] Clearly, this factor is much more in evidence at some levels of the earned income ladder than at others and in many instances—if viewed in isolation—has comparatively little weight. But even in these its absence cannot be simply passed over, for in a country in which most rewards are well above subsistence requirements, it is their relative standing *vis-à-vis* the rest, as much as their actual purchasing power, which is felt to be significant.

It is the impact of status on pay—rather than vice versa—which is directly relevant in the context of pay determination, though 'vice versa' has to be considered in view of the subtle interaction between the two. From the point of view of wages policy, then, the question is whether status and prestige ought to be assessed in determining levels of reward and, if so, whether the 'correlation' should be direct or inverse. Frequently, of course, the issue does not arise overtly. In so far as prestige enters into a person's supply price— i.e. that he is not prepared to offer his services below a certain sum in the consciousness of the status that is his—and to the extent, similarly, that employers are willing to grant such a figure, the matter is quietly settled between the parties. At other times, however, it comes into the open, as when some third party is asked to make recommendations as to the appropriate income for some particular group.

Thus the three Spens Committees—set up in the 1940s to advise on the remuneration of general practitioners, dentists and consultants under the National Health Service—were *inter alia* charged to have due regard to the desirability of maintaining the proper social and economic status of the branch of the profession which constituted their remit, the implication being that a positive addition to pay might be called for on status grounds. Similarly, the 1960 Royal Commission on Doctors' and Dentists' Remuneration, when discussing possible machinery for keeping the latter under review, reject arbitration—among other things because they did not judge it to be suitable for dealing with the profession's economic and social status in the community, and they preferred 'a Standing Review Body of eminent persons of experience in various fields of national life' for the purpose.[2] Again, at a 1951 Court of Inquiry hearing, the (then) Railway Executive had to point out that it was wrong to assume that superior status should in every instance give the salaried man the

---

[1] B. Wootton, *The Social Foundations of Wage Policy* (Allen & Unwin, 1955).
[2] *Royal Commission on Doctors' and Dentists' Remuneration* 1957–60, Cmnd. 939 (HMSO 1960), paras. 421 and 428.

right to higher remuneration, who in any case enjoyed certain benefits in the matter of conditions of service.

The subject raises a question of principle. Thus since the terms of reference of the Spens Reports were drawn up by the Government and the 1960 Royal Commission findings accepted by the latter, the inference would seem to be that status is a legitimate criterion of reward. If so, then it makes sense for any other grade of worker to cite, say, the expense of keeping up expected standards as entitling to additional remuneration: For example, one of the grounds on which an increase was claimed by Post Office telephone managers in 1952 was that, apart from official responsibilities, they had semi-official ones which they could not and ought not to evade—they had to support various civic, social and welfare activities estimated at £50 to £60 a year.[1] Similarly, if status is 'in' for purposes of pay determination, then it must be entirely reasonable for unions to insist on the maintenance of outworn status differentials, even where there is no economic justification for them of any kind. And that the preservation of such differentials has been a powerful motive for seeking wage advances in post-war Britain will not be denied.

It may of course be countered that if people feel inclined to request higher pay for reasons of status, they are welcome to it. Indeed it may be held—by way of a general objection to our approach—that the precise score on which particular groups choose to demand enhanced remuneration is immaterial, and that it can be left to demand and supply to effect the necessary compromise between whatever workers fancy asking for on whatever grounds, and between what employers will be ready to concede in the light of economic realities. In practice, however, things have not quite worked out in this manner: Throughout the post-war period increases have been granted in deference to considerations of 'relativity'—which contain a greater or lesser status element—even where such increases have conflicted with the economic purposes of the wage structure and even though they have been highly inflationary into the bargain. It is one of our contentions that some of this at any rate could be avoided, if we had a clearer idea as to what factors ought to bear on pay determination and if, further, we were prepared to apply them consistently to all occupations.

Adam Smith speaks of the honourableness or dishonourableness of an employment, forming part of its agreeableness or disagreeableness; the former is the first of his five 'counterbalancing advantages' making up for differences in the cash incomes of occupations. 'Honour makes a great part of the reward of all honourable professions,' he writes,[2] the implication being that prestige, as a

---

[1] Civil Service Arbitration Tribunal Award No. 188 (HMSO 1952), para. 7.

[2] *Wealth of Nations*, op. cit., p. 102.

definite net advantage, can be expected to be correlated with a rather lower rate of remuneration than might otherwise be appropriate. In the actual world the picture is frequently reversed—as has been shown by Lady Wootton, who has provided ample illustration of the tendency for high prestige to go hand in hand with superior pay as well as with superior service conditions.[1] Men and women being what they are, this is probably inevitable, if only because a large salary—which may be necessary on economic or justified on value-of-work grounds—will have just this impact on prestige levels. But while it would not be practicable to depress the standards of those to whom we accord a generous dose of esteem, it does not follow that the latter itself requires additional monetary recognition. This writer takes the line that status and prestige—in the 'snob/class' as distinct from the 'services rendered' sense—are altogether irrelevant in the context of pay determination, however humble or exalted the occupation. For it may be held that, while there are a number of non-economic factors with a strong claim to accommodation from the pattern of reward, the maintenance of the social hierarchy is not among them.

VI

We will now turn to the question of comparisons for purposes of pay negotiation. Such comparisons may be odious but, in some form or other, they are bound to be with us; they would appear to be the main process by which individual demand and supply prices are, in the final upshot, articulated. Taking the latter, for example, it was stated previously that the concept that remuneration must assure a person of a certain standard of life is a fundamental element of supply price. So is the notion that it must be a fair rate for the job, which we tend to assume—not necessarily correctly—also represents our value to employers. While the general level of supply prices is, broadly speaking, a function of the economic conditions prevailing in the country, the mechanism by which the demand for a specific standard of life and a specific rate for the job is translated into £ s. d. is via the making of comparisons. There being no absolute value in this sphere, the actual sum for which an individual will offer his labour is determined—in part consciously and in part subconsciously—by what accrues to 'comparable occupations'. Once arrived at, though, the figure acquires a certain momentum of its own, and in a period of rising prices an effort is made to maintain its purchasing power by frequent requests for compensatory upward adjustments.

[1] Wootton, op. cit.

In the first place, then, each person or group settles what its own standard should be in the light of that enjoyed by comparable grades, as well as according to where he feels his place is in the occupational hierarchy. His supply price is calculated by an attempt to be at least as well off as his equals, command a certain differential over and above his inferiors, and to suffer no more than the customary margin as against those on the next rung of the ladder. To indulge in comparisons is also natural because—unless one adopts a completely monastic *Weltanschauung*—pay is one, even if not the sole, reward for effort. In judging whether such reward is adequate, our yardstick is again what is granted to those making a like effort.

In this and the following two sections we shall largely abstract, in two important directions, from the overall problem of making comparisons: We shall ignore, first, what has been a major cause of complication in this sphere—namely the wholesale mix-up in the comparisons figuring in pay claims between 'intrinsic job' factors on the one hand and more strictly economic ones on the other. Secondly, we are leaving on one side the related topic of the inflationary implications of the 'propensity to compare'. In the ensuing pages, that is, we mention some of the problems of contrasting posts, taking what are more specifically economic considerations as broadly given. This *ceteris paribus* precedure is being employed for the usual reasons, and we shall be filling in some of the missing links subsequently.

Even when viewed from this restricted angle, the difficulties involved in comparing jobs are substantial. Grade titles are the flimsiest of guides, nor are the formal definitions of duties very illuminating. An additional snag in the salaried sphere is the relative dearth of information;[1] a sizeable proportion of privately-employed non-manual staffs being unorganized, the necessary details of their remuneration are not to hand—and the position is worse in the case of senior personnel. As a result, comparisons for purposes of public service collective bargaining have often had to rely largely on other branches of the public sector, although the Civil Service Pay Research Unit—set up in 1956 to gather the facts on the basis of which the Priestley method of grade-by-grade 'fair comparisons' might be implemented—has, for the benefit of its own surveys, been able to overcome this difficulty.[2] In so far as the necessary data are available, by and large it is easier to find comparable occupations for scientific,

---

[1] Mention might here be made of the pioneer surveys of clerical salaries carried out biennially by the Institute of Office Management (formerly the Office Management Association). See e.g. *Clerical Salaries Analysis* 1960 (Institute of Office Management, London, 1960).

[2] See e.g. Civil Service Pay Research Unit, *First Annual Report* 1957 (HMSO 1958).

technical and professional employees than it is for administrators. The function of administration is, as it were, shot through with the very service with which it is associated; this is not true to the same extent of engineers, doctors or lawyers. Again, it is simpler to compare routine workers than those on more complex tasks.

Our outline in Part I of this study of the pay histories in the various public services confirms that comparisons are indeed universal: the basic problem is what are comparable occupations? As the Priestley Commission put it, 'work may be identical; or very similar; or it may be broadly comparable . . .; or the content of the work may not be even broadly comparable but it may be possible to make some comparison of qualities such as skill and initiative and of the type of worker required; or there may be no basis for any comparison at all'.[1] From this wide range of possible degree of identity every category picks some target with which it seeks to achieve parity: Civil Service scientists have been chasing Civil Service administrators; Scottish judges want equality with English judges; firemen have been casting envious eyes at the police.

The most common procedure is to embark on comparisons of the 'broadly comparable' variety—a highly elastic one, as it is bound to be in view of the vagueness of the term. By way of illustration, we may quote from the 1949 arbitration proceedings arising out of a comprehensive claim by the Union of Post Office Workers.[2] The notion of 'broadly comparable' was there used to cover those of similar background; for instance, postmen were compared with railwaymen because they are largely recruited from the same source, as well as because railway personnel represent an important section of the general body of manual workers. The rates of agricultural labourers were likewise cited by the Post Office, because they form a big proportion of the rural population where many postmen ply their trade. The employers, further, submitted a statement setting out the scales for five of their own grades, with maxima ranging from 125s per week (telephonists) to 158s (postal and telegraph officers). The categories to whom these were compared ranged from shop assistants in food distribution with a maximum of 96s per week to linotype and monotype operators in printing and bookbinding, whose top figure was then 147s. The Post Office, it is true, merely maintained that these were broad general comparisons, but one is still tempted to ask who is being contrasted with whom. As a pay claim such as this is a case of adjustment in terms of shillings, the question is not irrelevant.

---

[1] *Royal Commission on the Civil Service* 1953–5, Cmd. 9613 (HMSO 1955), para. 152.

[2] See oral statement of Post Office to Civil Service Arbitration Tribunal, *The Post* (organ of Union of Post Office Workers), 18 June 1949, p. 256 and ff.

A variation on the theme is a comparison between those who occupy an analogous rung in their respective pyramids: Thus, in 1951, the 130 per cent rise over 1939 of the lowest-paid 'conciliation' man, the grade 2 porter, was set against the improvement for the bottom tier in the salaried structure of British Railways (on the maximum of class 5), which was only 72½ per cent.[1]

A far more popular type of comparison, however, is that of broad wage movements: The average increase in the earnings of railway workers as a whole is quoted against that for Post Office staffs as a whole—or vice versa. This procedure suffers from the defects inherent in all comparisons based on the earnings of different groups; they disguise variations in the proportion of skilled and unskilled, divergences of age and sex structure, and they ignore the varying incidence of overtime payments. This is quite apart from the fact that they also disregard all differences in the economic circumstances in the fields concerned. Comparisons with trends in the Ministry of Labour Index of Wage Rates are beset with roughly similar disabilities, though it must be admitted that this kind of exercise—we are again abstracting from all wider issues—has one supreme virtue, namely simplicity.

One particular problem in this sphere is the spatial one of selecting the area over which comparisons are to range: Should they extend to those in the same locality or region or country? In Britain the negotiation of basic pay rates is largely conducted on a national plane, although this is supplemented by much local activity which may significantly affect actual earnings. National frontiers in any case set the boundary; the position of analogous workers abroad is not normally adduced at the bargaining table. An exception to this are pilots whose work brings them into close contact with their opposite numbers elsewhere in the globe, and where comparisons are accordingly of international dimensions. Doctors and dentists may also soon be an exception. The 1960 Royal Commission stated that, in deciding where they should stand *vis-à-vis* members of other professions, regard should *inter alia* be paid to their relative status in the occupational hierarchy of other lands.[2] No doubt these medicos promptly point to their British counterparts when their own incomes are under review.

Much more awkward in practice, however, has been the time element. While in some instances the issue has been clear, in others the question has arisen as to which wage increase is cause and which effect. A situation has frequently emerged where Y has argued that

[1] cf. p. 243 *ante*. To some extent this is akin to the 'Allen' method—used in connection with GPs' pay claims—of estimating changes in the hierarchy of salary earners over a period of time.   [2] Cmnd. 939, op. cit., para. 17.

they are entitled to a rise because X—with whom they have kept in step in the past—had one six months ago, with X retorting that that improvement was merely to compensate them for one granted to Y a year previously; if a fresh award were now to be given to Y, X will demand similar treatment. This conundrum, of course, is merely the tangible expression of the 'wage-wage' spiral or leap-frogging of pay claims which is liable to bedevil the wages front in a period of full employment—and which has been such a familiar phenomenon of the British labour scene in post-war years. We return to this topic in the final section of this chapter.

As previously pointed out, the making of comparisons is an essential part of the process of pay determination, which is what lends significance to the whole subject. At the same time, it need not occasion surprise if there is a considerable tactical element in the relativities appearing in negotiations and arbitration proceedings. For it is a built-in feature of our present system of collective bargaining that unions should seek to establish a comparability that will achieve the desired object of improving their members' living standards, while employers, conversely, must aim at securing their factors of production at the lowest possible cost. With this in view, employers will sometimes cite any grade that happens to be earning less than the category for which a rise is being demanded, while unions will quote any that happens to be receiving more; some of the equations would probably be admitted as not holding water, if spokesmen of the two sides could afford to be sufficiently frank. The tactical nature of some comparisons is further illustrated by the lack of inhibition displayed in changing the grade with which parity is being sought. While it is true that two occupations may become either more or less alike with the passage of years—clerical workers, for instance, could assert some affinity with teachers when education was the prerogative of the few—most switches of this kind are primarily governed by considerations of expendiency. And since the initiative for pay revisions now almost invariably originates from the side of labour, the latter is no doubt the bigger culprit.

Two conclusions suggest themselves. First, that it is largely idle to expect union negotiators to turn themselves into creatures of pure reason for as long as the latter is at a discount—as it in many ways is under our present pattern of wage settlement. Secondly, that while it is easy to detect flaws and while some relativities can be dismissed as part merely of the armoury of collective bargaining, it is much more difficult to find a more satisfactory basis for making comparisons. Insistence on a near-perfect identity would rule out practically all from the start; in many there will be a number of features which can be contrasted only by reducing them to a common

denominator in terms of skill or responsibility. The important point
is—if the exercise is to be meaningful—that this should be done
systematically; to this end, job analysis and the previously advocated
wider examination of the elements of demand and supply prices must
come to the rescue. This, the reader is reminded, is only one half of
the story; as indicated in Chapter 18, job analysis can only take care
of the evaluation of the intrinsic characteristics of posts. We shall
have something to say on the economic factor in this context in
later sections.

VII

Even when two occupations have been found that can be regarded as
comparable, there is the further problem of selecting the *unit of
comparison*. This matter is in some respects more intractable, and in
others less so, on the salaries than on the wages front. In the latter,
as mentioned in our last chapter, there is the question of whether
rates or earnings should be decisive—a complication which is usually
absent, or at any rate quiescent, in the non-manual area of employment. In the last-named, on the other hand, the choice of the correct
unit for purposes of comparison is more complex because of the
incremental nature of salary patterns. Thus as regards manual
workers maxima are—in the majority of instances—payable at age
21; the rates accruing at that point can be contrasted once general
job comparability has been established. In the salaried sphere, however, there is the profusion of classes and grades to which we have
drawn attention. Comparisons of particular structural features—
of the type made in Chapter 18—are of course possible, but as there
pointed out this procedure has its limitations, especially where
maxima are concerned.

First, the term 'maximum' can mean different things. In most
public services it refers to the figure to which all will progress,
provided they remain in the service long enough; in outside employment it may signify the amount which the best members of a grade
can attain, but which the average or sub-average individual cannot.
The Priestley Commission stated in this context that great care must
be taken not to equate a Civil Service maximum, which all will
reach, with special merit rates paid only to a few out of many,
though at the same time some account must be taken of the latter.[1]

Secondly, while maxima can be used for the purpose of showing
how high individuals will climb without promotion or for contrasting the cash ceilings of different services—as was done in
Chapter 18—they are unsuitable[2] if the aim of the exercise is to

[1] *Priestley Report*, op. cit., paras. 157–8.
[2] Except in those cases where the recruitment grade is also the career grade.

demonstrate the overall identity or otherwise of the true reward of two occupations. This is because of the varying lengths of scales, because of the differing number of such scales in different pyramids, and because a comparison of maxima does not give weight to the relative ease of advancement and other 'net advantages'.[1]

The prospects of promotion in a particular service are of course closely bound up with the question of the distribution of staff over its various levels; here sole reliance on the formal pay structure is quite inadequate. Thus according to the 1948 census of local government officers, only 27·4 per cent of men were in the general division, the 1951 maximum of which was £425. In the course of a pay claim in that year the Transport Salaried Staffs Association stated that, in the case of male railway salaried personnel, fully 75½ per cent were getting less than £420, and as that figure entailed two promotions—unlike the £425 in local government which all would automatically attain—not all railway workers could be sure of reaching it.[2] Clearly, this is an important point, which must be accorded its due when comparing remuneration in the two fields.

A possible method of coping with the matter is to adjust the salaries in the fields to be contrasted by a factor reflecting grade complements. For instance, an average salary for the Civil Service executive class could be computed on the basis of the means of the various executive scales, weighted in accordance with the numbers in the different tiers. This, however, presupposes that a class's opportunities for advancement are limited to that class when, in fact, it may not be easy to define what precisely its promotion potential is. Thus a Civil Service clerical officer can rise to higher clerical officer or to executive officer; from the latter he can ascend the executive ladder and ultimately step across to the administrative class. Yet it would be most unrealistic to count the establishment of the whole higher Civil Service in evaluating clerical officers' career prospects. Similarly, promotion outlets may be shared with other hierarchies. For example, senior administrative posts in British Railways are open to the conciliation grades, and though *de facto* they are largely filled by clerical personnel, it does mean that the criterion of numbers is not foolproof.

Another reason why grade complements may be an incomplete guide is that salary structures as nationally defined may be misleading; in the Civil Service technical hierarchy, for instance, grade A *or*

---

[1] This last consideration also applies, but less so, to comparisons of the maxima of manual occupations.

[2] Railway Staff National Tribunal Decision No. 13 (7 November 1951), p. 14. The figure of £420—the maximum of class 3—was raised to £453.10.0 with retrospective effect from 3 September 1951.

grade B has normally been used for any one block of work. Similarly, departmental needs differ;[1] in the scientific Civil Service opportunities vary in accordance with both type of work and the specialization of staff; one nuclear physicist may not be interchangeable with another. Further, in one field higher posts may be created for those deserving them, while in another complements are rigidly fixed; yet again, promotion may depend on the passing of specific examinations. Finally, staff complements may be an inadequate index because of the existence of temporary personnel, who do not form part of the official establishment.

An alternative method of weighting the prospects of advancement is to take the 'career grade' in two fields, and to use the average salary earned over a man's entire working life as the unit of comparison. This, first, raises the question as to the meaning of the term 'career grade': What proportion of basic-tier recruits must reach it in order for it to qualify as such? It further necessitates the possession of effective data about the timing of one or several promotions in the course of a person's progression; provided these are available, this procedure has much to commend it. Thus if it has been ascertained that a civil servant directly recruited to the assistant principal grade of the administrative class is normally made a principal at thirty, that the average age of promotion to assistant secretary is forty, and that he usually retires from the latter rank at, say, sixty, his average salary over his working life can be calculated. Such a figure would seem to form a reasonably satisfactory basis for comparison with one similarly computed in the 'comparable sphere'.

The extent to which such average salaries are practicable and helpful, however, depends not only on the availability of valid data about the timing of past promotions: It likewise depends on whether the period in question can be regarded as reasonably stable, and on whether such averages are merely statistical means or also representative of the majority of personal histories. One objection to weighting pay scales by the promotion factor is that inherent in the use of all averages: They work unfairly against him whose case is a-typical—in this instance, who does not secure advancement— though this could possibly be dealt with by an increasing adoption of long-service increments. Further, promotion will always be subject to such variables as the rate of expansion in the field concerned and the age distribution of those currently occupying senior posts; figures relating to the past can thus never be a perfect guide. But for all the difficulties involved—and these are much less in a compact

---

[1] Much, however, here depends on the mechanics of promotion procedures. The institution in 1950 of a 'promotion pool' for executive officers e.g. was an effort to equalize advancement opportunities in different departments.

service than in an elaborate one like the Civil Service, on which we have drawn for purposes of illustration—some weighting by career prospects would seem to be essential for genuine job comparisons.

VIII

Prospects of promotion are only one of a whole species which, over and above the cash rate of pay, must be taken into account in any job comparison. Adam Smith speaks of 'certain inherent circumstances' peculiar to different industries, occupations and trades. He mentions five, arising from the nature of the employments themselves—we have already had occasion to refer to one of them[1]—which 'make up for a small pecuniary gain in some employments, and counterbalance a great one in others'.[2] Marshall develops this further into the notion of net advantages and warns against a crude contrasting of money wages: 'The true reward which an occupation offers to labour has to be calculated by deducting the money value of all its disadvantages from that of all its advantages; and we may describe this true reward as the *net advantages* of the occupation.'[3]

Professor Sargant Florence thinks that Marshall's lead might be followed up by an analysis or balance sheet of a job's attractions and deterrents, its human assets and liabilities, many of which are measurable. He cites unemployment and death rates which are known for all the different industries, and sickness, disability and accident rates which are available for many. Cost of learning, the relative degrees of fatigue and boredom, sociability as against loneliness, etc. can likewise be estimated or assessed.[4] In addition, there are the various service conditions such as hours, annual leave, sick pay provisions and so on, all of which must be given due weight in the computing of net advantages.

The value of some conditions of service is easy to measure; to calculate an hourly rate of pay for different occupations—by adjusting annual income for both hours and holidays—does not present any difficulty. Superannuation benefits, similarly, lend themselves to actuarial quantification. Those of civil servants, for instance, have been estimated by the Treasury at 15 per cent of salary;[5] those

---

[1] See p. 344 *ante*.

[2] *Wealth of Nations*, 5th ed. by E. Cannan (1930) p. 102.

[3] *Principles of Economics* (1930 ed.) p. 73.

[4] P. Sargant Florence, *Labour* (Hutchinson's University Library, n.d.), p. 104.

[5] For an average new entrant to the salaried grades, subject to a number of qualifications. For categories such as Post Office manipulative and engineering workers, the figure is about 10 per cent: See letter from Treasury dated 29 March 1954, *Whitley Bulletin*, June 1954.

M

of police officers—by the Government Actuary in 1949—at about 25 per cent of their remuneration.[1] Other public servants are likewise covered by pension schemes, though the net benefit to the staff is mostly smaller than in the Civil Service, which is alone in having a non-contributory system.[2] Superannuation rights would appear to be by far the most important item—apart from actual pay and promotion prospects—in drawing up a 'balance sheet' for various jobs. They are not, in practice, treated with the respect they deserve, though there can be little doubt that they should figure in the reckoning when comparisons are embarked upon.

In this context it is pertinent to refer to the Royal Commission on the Police, who stated in their 1960 Interim Report that it was wrong to count the constable's pension as an emolument. Their view was that the fundamental requirement of a superannuation scheme was that it should fit the kind of career judged to be appropriate to the particular occupation, and that it was therefore inconsistent to regard the employee as receiving, by way of his pension, an emolument assessable in terms of weekly income during his service.[3] This conclusion, however, involved the Commission in what would appear to be a far more serious inconsistency: For in devising their formula —likewise commended for future use—for computing a suitable scale for constables, the Commission take as their starting point (factor A) the minimum or standard time rates of wages of skilled workers in a wide range of industries. To this two substantial supplements were added—factors B and C—designed to compensate the constable for all the drawbacks of his calling, as well as to reward him, as it were, for his 'value to the community'. From this total there was deducted a figure merely representing the housing provision made for policemen, but not the value of their other perquisities, the chief—though not the only one—of which is their pension.[4]

The inconsistency is to be found in the fact that, while the Commission's scheme gives full weight to the disadvantages suffered by policemen in relation to outside employment, it does not accord corresponding weight to the advantages enjoyed by them *vis-à-vis* the latter: None of the skilled industrial workers in question can, for example, retire from their jobs after thirty years' service with a

[1] *Report of the (Oaksey) Committee on Police Conditions of Service*, Part I, Cmd. 7674 (HMSO 1949), para. 116.

[2] The *widows'* pension scheme for civil servants is contributory, though not on an actuarial basis.

[3] *Royal Commission on the Police* 1960, *Interim Report*, Cmnd. 1222 (HMSO 1960) para., 124.

[4] For full details see ibid. paras. 178–9.

pension for life equal to two-thirds of remuneration. This is in no way to imply—as was made clear in Chapter 8—that the Commission have been over-generous in the standard actually recommended; misgivings arise only over the nature of the formula thought up for its calculation. Though the Government promptly made clear that, unlike the proposed scale, they did not accept all the reasoning underlying it, one might here particularly emphasize the Commission's cavalier treatment of superannuation and other emoluments, for an acceptance of their assumptions in this respect could have repercussions on a much wider front.[1]

If superannuation, hours and annual leave do allow of quantification, many other features of jobs are much more troublesome. The differing standards of welfare amenities or perquisites for senior executives will illustrate the point. Again, there are the security restrictions in force for various classes of scientists: In the case of such intangibles, clearly, the relevant entry on the 'balance sheet' is a hazardous piece of bookkeeping.

There are other complications. As Professor Stone has reminded us,[2] what is normally regarded as a net benefit is dependent on social valuations and changes as these do. He cites the case of miners' pit-head baths, which a hundred years ago would have been something quite exceptional; nowadays such amenities would hardly be reckoned as income in kind.[3] Dr Stone suggests that an expenditure by an enterprise on behalf of an employee should, in order to be considered as part of his remuneration, confer upon him a net benefit and not merely compensate him for a particular disadvantage arising out of his employment. This is clearly a valuable principle—alike for the measurement of income in which context Professor Stone is specifically discussing the matter, as in the related one of weighting net advantages—though in the latter sphere there is the problem of whether the principle can be held to apply also to what at first sight might look like parallel situations: Is it, for instance, in order to contrast teachers' hourly rate of pay with that of doctors,

---

[1] The formula is likewise unsatisfactory in a number of other respects—see e.g. leading article in *The Times*, 25 November 1960. We are here confining ourselves to the aspect relevant to 'net advantages'. But see also p. 390 *post*.

[2] Report of Sub-Committee on National Income Statistics of the League of Nations Committee of Statistical Experts, 'Measurement of National Income and the Construction of Social Accounts', *Studies and Reports on Statistical Methods No. 7* (Geneva, 1947), Appendix by Richard Stone, p. 57.

[3] A decision to demand £1 a week *inconvenience money* for men engaged in collieries not equipped with pit-head baths was in fact taken at the annual conference of the S. Wales Area of the National Union of Mineworkers in 1957. Pit-head baths i.e. are regarded as an expected amenity, the absence of which calls for monetary compensation.

in which case they would not be 'doing' so badly as on a comparison of their annual salaries? Or can teachers claim that their relative excess of leisure be looked upon—like miners' pit-head baths—as compensation simply for the handicaps of their calling, in which event a comparison of the two professions' hourly remuneration would not be warranted?

In essence, the question just posed resolves itself into the further question of whether, and to what extent, the varying characteristics of a job can be deemed to be already reflected in its rate of remuneration or, alternatively, must be given a separate weighting in the calculation of net advantages. For example, can it be assumed that the relatively high accident rate of miners or the monotony of some factory employments have been given due recognition in the wage attaching to these occupations? Can a man entering upon such work be expected to have done so in the full knowledge of all its pros and cons, so that there is no entitlement to further accommodation? Thus in a 1949 arbitration claim for an increase in the pay of foresters, the Civil Service Union argued that the isolation of the grade, the lack of social amenities etc., were special factors to be taken into account; the Forestry Commission maintained that men choosing this life were aware of these handicaps but opted for an outdoor life notwithstanding, so that there was no case for recompensing them for these disadvantages. The problem exists because it is the size of rewards—rather than the nature of what is being rewarded—which receives attention mostly at the bargaining table, as also because practice genuinely varies. Workmen in the building industry, for instance, are paid an extra 2d an hour for 'foul or dirty work', but miners merely qualify for 'wet money'; in their case the factors of foulness and dirt are presumably taken care of by the overall level of their remuneration.

Apart from net benefits changing with social attitudes, their value is of course also a function of their diffusion among the working population. A good example is security, which used to be considered an important feature of salaried occupations in general and of public service posts in particular. With the advent of full employment, this net benefit has assumed rather lesser proportions, although in absolute terms the degree of security in the public sector has in no way diminished. Another illustration is service conditions such as pension provisions and paid holidays: While these are still far more generous for the salariat as a body than they are for the bulk of manual workers, at the same time they do not possess that scarcity value that attached to them in former days.

Net benefits, then, are relative in that their worth fluctuates under the impact of both economic and social conditions. Most of those dealt with so far, however, contain a 'universal' element in the sense that there is some broad consensus as to their nature; even where they or changes in them cannot be quantified, some estimate can be made —plus or minus. A different type of problem occurs in the appraisal of those job characteristics which are partly a matter of personal circumstance and/or individual preference. The net value of sick leave arrangements, for instance, depends on whether an employee is forced by ill-health to have recourse to them, while the extent to which railway workers gain from British Railways' travel concessions varies according to both distance from work and 'Wanderlust'. As Marshall said, individual character will always assert itself in evaluating particular perquisites, but his advice—to reckon each advantage or disadvantage at the average of the money values it has for the group of people concerned[1]—may in practice be an awkward exercise. British Railways, for example, have not found it feasible to provide reliable estimates of the total cost to the industry of the travel facilities granted to their staff,[2] and the latter might well find it equally tricky to put a precise figure on it.

In a different category, again, are those net benefits of which only a completely subjective appraisal can be made. Mr Rice, for instance, wants job analysis to set out the role a post will play in a person's life, the demands and the satisfactions in the relationships involved and so on,[3] but this would appear to be far too ambitious an aim. A private secretaryship may lead to anything from neurotic frustration to a happy marriage; alternatively, it may be a neutral influence. It is hardly possible to weight such factors—though this is in no way to deny reality to the many delicate entanglements between marriage and labour markets.

The various characteristics of posts may thus be divided into those which can be quantified in monetary terms and those which cannot; those which are inherent in jobs and those which are not; and those on which there is some consensus as to whether they are an advantage or disadvantage, and those regarding which there is no such agreement. These distinctions, of course, all cut across each other. Those which are capable of quantification do not present any difficulty; in the case of those which are not, we must content ourselves with an estimate. Those which are inherent in a post must certainly be taken into account in so far, that is, as they are not already reflected in remuneration; with a more systematic approach to the evaluation of

---

[1] *Principles of Economics*, op. cit., p. 557. Marshall is here primarily concerned with estimating the influence of net benefits on the supply of labour.

[2] See 'Wages and Related Elements of Labour Costs', *Ministry of Labour Gazette*, August 1957, pp. 278–9.

[3] A. K. Rice, *Assessing the Job* (Industrial Welfare Society, 2nd ed., 1947).

intrinsic job factors, we might know this a little more clearly than at present. Net benefits which are not inherent in posts and which vary from group to group for no particular reason could in many instances be brought into line to a much greater extent; we return to this topic in our final chapter. As for those attributes of jobs the value of which depends on personal tastes and preferences, no great harm will be done if they are left out of the calculation of net advantages.

IX

We may now turn to some of the special considerations applying to remuneration in the public services by reason of such 'publicness'. We begin with a few comments on the difficult question of where the public sector stands in the matter of the ability-to-pay and profit criterion.

As mentioned in Chapter 19, even in the private sector wage *rates* are not based on individual firms' profit-and-loss accounts. The negotiation of such rates being largely transacted at national level, they can in practice merely take account of an industry's *average* profitability, though the individual employer's economic fortunes may of course enter into labour costs via the granting of above-the-line benefits at plant level. Further, in so far as the capacity to pay high wages depends on the amount of competition for the industry's product, there is a difference of degree, rather than of kind, between the commercial public services and private industry. The demand for the products of, say, electricity supply, gas, civil air transport or British Railways is not inelastic. Statutory, etc. restrictions apart, rates and charges cannot be put up indefinitely without serious loss of revenue, so that—even if to a lesser extent than in the field of private employment—there is the limiting factor of what the traffic will bear. The only publicly-owned industry with an effective monopoly is the Post Office, but for constitutional and political reasons it is not allowed to exploit its position in this respect. On this interpretation of the phrase, ability-to-pay can thus be said to be applicable in both spheres, varying with the degree of monopoly enjoyed rather than with 'publicness'.[1] As for the non-commercial public services, they can—in one sense—remunerate their employees at whatever standard they choose, though the economic limitation of what the traffic will bear is here replaced by a political equivalent: Tax- and rate-payers may at times seem like willing enough milch-cows, but there is a point beyond which it is injudicious to milk them.

In the strict sense, however, ability-to-pay presupposes that income

[1] We ignore the ability to pay high money wages arising from inflation, as this is not relevant to the distinction between the public and private sectors or, insofar as it is, is covered by the remarks just made.

or profit is the datum to which expenditure is adjusted; it is on this interpretation of the term that there is a significant difference between public and private. As far as the central government is concerned, it is expenditure, primarily, which is the datum, revenue being raised to meet such expenditure; the position clearly diverges from that obtaining in the private sector, though this is not to say that the latter is not also faced with certain more or less unavoidable costs. In the case of the local authorities, again, rates are levied of such amounts as are needed to cover local outgoings—to the extent that central grants and other sources are insufficient. This is particularly so now that local government salaries are negotiated on a national basis; up to the time of their standardization in 1946, the remuneration of clerical and administrative staff, for instance, was more dependent on individual authorities' rate income. But even currently the picture as between central and local government is not entirely similar, in that the raising of revenue is easier at the central than at the local level—a fact which has not been without its impact on the standards of reward in the two spheres.[1]

The position of the nationalized industries is altogether more complex. Officially, they are commercial or quasi-commercial undertakings, but they are required by statute to do no more than 'break even' taking one year with another; under a 1961 Government White Paper, we may add, such balancing of surpluses and deficits on revenue account must henceforth be achieved over a five-year period.[2] Here also, then, the tariffs which are fixed are largely determined by expenditure; if a nationalized industry should be in the happy situation of accumulating a big surplus, it would be under a statutory obligation to reduce its capacity to reward its employees on an extra-generous scale. Even so, however, the public corporations might find themselves with a fair degree of manoeuvrability in this respect, were it not for the various other restrictions imposed on their pricing, etc. policies.

While the nationalized industries would not be permitted to make excessive profits in order to maintain unduly high levels of remuneration, they likewise have a statutory duty not to show a persistent loss. Here the ability-to-pay test could be a crucial influence—and in a sense in which it is not, and cannot be, in the case of civil servants or local authority employees. In practice, British Railways have been allowed to incur deficits in order, *inter alia*, to meet rising wage costs —as under the Cameron Court of Inquiry Report of 1955. The latter, with its famous dictum of 'having willed the end, the Nation must

[1] cf. pp. 391–2 *post*.
[2] See *The Financial and Economic Obligations of the Nationalized Industries*, Cmnd. 1337 (HMSO 1961), para. 19,

will the means',[1] in effect absolved the Railways from their legal obligation of breaking even, under which they would have been prevented from conceding the claim. The Government similarly came to the rescue in 1958—and notably again in 1960 in order to make possible the implementation of the Guillebaud Railway Pay Committee recommendations, though how it will act in such contingencies in future is, at the time of writing, somewhat uncertain.

Though public servants do not benefit from private industry's positive ability-to-pay, at least they do not suffer from voluntary service financial impotence. Thus the Independent Committee, appointed by the Minister of Labour in 1948 to adjudicate on a dispute between the BBC and the Musicians' Union, rejected the contention of the Corporation that casual studio fees for their musicians should continue to be related to those granted by private musical societies; these private fees were inadequate, and as the BBC was not to the same extent affected by considerations of monetary stringency, they did not constitute a proper yardstick for BBC standards.[2] The representatives of prison chaplains have likewise argued that the Archbishop of Canterbury's statement of November 1951—that the remuneration of parochial clergy should be £500 net—referred not to what they ought to receive but to what fiscal resources were available to the Church; this figure should not be the criterion for fixing Government salaries.[3] Again, the representatives of pharmacists in 1949 submitted to the Industrial Court that the highly unpopular recommendations of the pre-NHS Joint Negotiating Committee were due mainly to the straitened circumstances of the voluntary hospitals who pleaded inability to pay more: 'With the inauguration of the National Health Service, Hospital Pharmacists naturally considered that the special financial position of the Voluntary Hospitals would no longer prevent the introduction of salary scales commensurate with their professional qualifications and responsibilities.'[4]

We may sum up these brief remarks by saying that, as far as 'cashing in' on high profits is concerned, this does not apply in fields such as the Civil, National Health and local government services because they are not profit-making enterprises. As regards the com-

[1] *Interim Report of a Court of Inquiry into a Dispute between the British Transport Commission and the National Union of Railwaymen* (HMSO 1955), para. 10.

[2] Ministry of Labour and National Service, *British Broadcasting Corporation and Musicians' Union: Report of the Independent Committee . . .* (HMSO 1948), paras. 50–4 and 61.

[3] Civil Service Arbitration Tribunal Award No. 191 (HMSO 1952), para. 8.

[4] Industrial Court Award No. 2231 (HMSO 1949), p. 4. In the last two examples we do of course not know the precise weight these arguments carried, but there is other evidence (e.g. the case of social workers quoted later) to bear out our remarks at the beginning of the paragraph.

mercial public corporations, it has also been largely inoperative because *de jure* they are under a statutory obligation to do no more than break even, because of the various other restrictions imposed, and because *de facto*—speaking in very broad terms—such profits have not been earned. As to the converse case of losses, the non-commercial public services are again immune, while the employees of the commercial ones have not hitherto been exposed to these in full. Current indications are, however, that ability-to-pay in the nationalized industries—both in the positive and negative sense—may be operative to a rather greater extent in the 'sixties than in the 'fifties.

Let us look at one or two other facets of 'publicness'. One direction in which a few public (and kindred) servants benefit is that, in the case of some very august offices, the salary appears to contain an element of tribute to such office as well as pecuniary reward for its holder. Thus part of the not inconsiderable differential between the pay of a High Court judge and that of a county court judge[1] may well be due not to the actual difference in knowledge and judicial capacity between the two categories, but to the exalted position of the former. A superior judgeship is somehow more conspicuously the repository of the dignity of British justice than a county court judgeship—which is more of a bread-and-butter affair. The situation is similar as regards ordinary clergy and (a number of) bishops: If we take some of the ancient bishoprics who, as it were, are the living symbols of the Church, the level of remuneration is probably in part a mark of respect for, and in homage to, the latter. That of many clergymen, on the other hand, is at the senior office worker level.

A rather different type of contrast between the public and private sectors is that pay in the latter is more flexible: Special merit rises, end-of-the-year bonuses and so on are more frequent, although there is some difference also as between the public services in this respect. Whether this is a positive or adverse factor clearly depends on the individual. The absence of the opportunity to have one's salary adjusted according to one's actual performance is a disadvantage as far as the above-the-average employee is concerned; for those below par, however, not to have to submit to personal assessment is a net benefit.

Some consequences of 'publicness' are extremely difficult to evaluate. Thus all rewards in the non-commercial public services are common property; questions about them may be, and are, freely asked in both Houses of Parliament. As such dissertations have often amounted to a complaint that remuneration is inadequate, they may

---

[1] See Table 36 *ante*; the differential has been further widened since. The fact that the post-tax differential is very much smaller is not relevant in this context.

well have helped to create a favourable climate of opinion smoothing the path of subsequent claims. But the precise result of this can only be a matter for surmise.

A related question is the impact of 'publicness' on those brought within its jurisdiction for the first time. This has, of course, been very various, though there has no doubt been a levelling effect for those at the top of the earned income ladder. Revealing in this context is a passage in the 1948 Spens Report on the remuneration of consultants and specialists. Referring to the evidence that it had been possible in the past for a small proportion of practitioners to obtain incomes of a very high order, the Committee state: 'Bearing in mind that the salaries we have recommended . . . would remove the hardships at present experienced during the period of training; that in a public service the specialist ought not at any stage of his career to require to supplement his earnings by private means; that his remuneration will be maintained at a consistent level until the age of retirement is reached; and that throughout his career the specialist will enjoy financial security in marked contrast with the uncertainties of private practice, we concluded that some reduction was justifiable not only in the ceiling figure of the incomes attainable in the past, but also in the proportion of consultants attaining to the highest levels of re-muneration.'[1] Another example of the disappearance of the most glittering prizes on nationalization is provided by the coal industry: The National Coal Board brought to an end the bulk of pre-vesting contracts involving the payment of salaries in excess of £5,000 a year.[2]

It would be misleading, however, to make too much of the levelling which 'publicness' has produced at one extreme of the occupational pyramid. Thus as the Spens Committee made clear, the clipping of the financial wings of the most successful consultants was to be offset by the more generous provision to be made for the budding specialist —as well as by the greater security available to him throughout his subsequent career. Similarly, as is well-known, dentists' relative incomes have been much enhanced under the National Health Service. Again, on the nationalization of the electricity supply industry, it was found that the standards of reward of ex-company administrative, etc. staffs had been below those of their colleagues in municipal undertakings; it was the former rather than the latter who derived an immediate gain from nationalization.[3]

---

[1] *Report of the Inter-Departmental Committee on the Remuneration of Consultants and Specialists*, Cmd. 7420 (HMSO 1948), para. 12. The Committee add, however, that there must remain for a significant minority the opportunity to earn incomes comparable with the highest which can be earned in other professions.

[2] cf. pp. 224–5 *ante*.   [3] cf. p. 230 *ante*.

Further, the extension of the public sector has meant an ameliora-
tion in the prospects of advancement; for instance, the larger field
covered by an Area Gas Board's activities provides—to quote the
Gas Council's own words—'opportunities for promotion greater
than hitherto, and less dependent on the accident of the undertaking
in which an entrant to the industry happened to begin his career'.[1]
The much expanded employment of social workers in the public services has had the same result. As it has been put, it has had 'the double
effect of lengthening the ladder of promotion and improving salary
scales'.[2] Here the translation from voluntary to public service has of
course also been a factor.

Where the 'nationalization' of a particular grade of employee is only
partial, the respective dimensions of the two sectors clearly assume
importance. Thus though the introduction of the Health Service has
involved a lowering of top specialists' pay levels, this tendency has
been kept in check by the continued existence of a substantial private
sector. The distinction awards for consultants were doubtless designed not only with a view to maintaining the profession's former
financial expectations, but also with an eye on the incomes currently
available to independent specialists. In the case of civil air transport,
on the other hand, it is the public airways corporations which have
set the standard. The 1946 Civil Aviation Act, for example, specifically required that the terms and conditions of persons employed by
independent air transport undertakings shall not be less favourable
than those observed by the national corporations, and in 1949 it
needed the intervention of the Industrial Court to ensure compliance
with this provision.[3]

Different pronouncements have been made as to the duties of the
State in its entrepreneurial capacity: It should be a 'model employer',
in the 'first flight of good employers', or at any rate a 'good employer'.
These terms are not particularly precise even if all wider considerations—such as those stemming from the Government's dual role of
both employer and guardian of the public interest—are ignored. The
Tomlin Commission of 1929–31 in fact concluded that the phrase
'model employer' lent itself to such varied and contradictory interpretations, as to afford no practical help for fixing wages or for
indicating the responsibilities of the State towards its staffs.[4]

The 1955 Priestley Commission, on the other hand, felt that guidance could now be secured from the term 'good employer'. The
latter was not necessarily the one who proffered the most generous

[1] Gas Council, *Second Report and Statement of Accounts* (HMSO 1951), para. 88.
[2] E. L. Younghusband, *Social Work in Britain* (Constable, 1951), p. 6.
[3] See pp. 251–2 *ante*.
[4] *Royal Commission on the Civil Service*, Cmd. 3909 (HMSO 1931), para. 311.

reward, but the one who sought to provide stability and continuity of employment, adequate facilities for training and advancement, and who consulted with representatives of his staff upon changes affecting their pay and working conditions. The rates of remuneration of such employers would compare well with those of the generality of employers, would move readily but not a-typically upward when the trend was in that direction, and would be rather more stable than most when the trend was downward.[1] The Commission further elaborated this when dealing with the question of what position a Civil Service scale ought to occupy in relation to outside rates, when these exhibited considerable variation among themselves. It disagreed with the Treasury that the Civil Service figure should merely be in harmony with those granted by a representative selection of firms for comparable jobs; the Government should be a good employer in the sense that, while it ought not to be among those who offered the highest remuneration, it should be among those who paid somewhat above the average.[2]

The various other public services have likewise declared it to be their duty to be 'good bosses'. Thus the principle embodied in the 1946 Charter for the local government service was that the latter should not take the lead in determining pay standards but be in the 'first flight of good employers'.[3] The National Coal Board has expressed itself in similar vein.[4] Two comments may here be apposite. First, that though the concept of the good/model employer has hitherto recognized the claims of, say, taxpayers in the case of government servants' salaries, or those of consumers in the case of NCB pay levels, the national interest as a whole has not up to now figured in it. Secondly, that while it would be wrong to dismiss the formula as merely a pious platitude—in the 1956–60 post-Priestley era, for example, steps were taken in the Civil Service conscientiously to translate it into practice—it has at the same time been sufficiently elastic to allow of considerable divergences of application.

At least as illuminating, therefore, as these rankings on the model/good employer scale are a number of other assumptions underlying our standards of reward in the public services. As regards the Civil Service, there is a general consensus of opinion that in so far as top-level staff are concerned, the highest prizes are inappropriate.[5]

---

[1] *Royal Commission on the Civil Service* 1953–5, Cmd. 9613 (HMSO 1955), para. 146.   [2] ibid. paras. 171–3.

[3] See introductory statement issued by National Joint Council for Local Authorities' Administrative, Professional, Technical and Clerical Services, *Local Government Service*, February–March 1946.

[4] cf. p. 225 *ante.*

[5] See e.g. *Report of the (Chorley) Committee on Higher Civil Service Remuneration*, Cmd. 7635 (HMSO 1949), para. 18, and *Priestley Report*, op. cit., para. 364.

Possibly the legal position, to which we have briefly referred, has contributed to this; be that as it may, 'fair comparison' has never purported to extend all the way up. As for the nationalized industries, at the time of their birth it was widely accepted that in this instance standards should be midway between those ruling in the Civil Service and the private sector; the latter i.e. has been expected to exercise its pull more fully in the sphere of commercial public enterprise. We may add that the salaries of the chairmen and members of the Boards of the nationalized industries have hitherto been fixed on this 'midway' principle, though the latter was rather seriously breached *à propos* of the reorganization of British Railways in 1961.[1]

The fact that Civil Service standards, in their upper reaches, are intended to be inferior to those in the commercial public corporations does not prevent the former from being something of a 'salary leader' within the whole area of public employment. A good example of this has been the subject of equal pay for women: Nearly all the public services not already practising this, instituted equal pay when the Government decided on this course; even in the details of implementation the Treasury model was adopted. As we saw also, there used to be a specific obligation on the BBC to have regard to Whitehall salaries in regulating those of its own employees, and though this provision was subsequently relaxed, the Corporation has continued to be required to take account of the Government's general wages policy.[2] Other public services, likewise, watch with the closest attention the ECs emanating from Great George Street. Essentially, however, it is a case of seeing what the Government does, and to use this as a base to be hewn into shape according to whatever is felt to be appropriate to the field in question.

Different aspects of 'publicness' assume different prominence in different periods. One such matter is the dilemma in which the Government may find itself when improving the remuneration of its own employees—in view of the possible or likely repercussions of such adjustments on the whole industrial front. This is especially so at a time when an active wages policy is being pursued as in the 1948–50 White Paper period,[3] or during times of inflationary pressure generally when the Government may wish to avoid even the slightest encouragement to the wage-price-wage spiral. In such circumstances, post-war administrations have conceded claims 'in principle' but deferred their implementation—as in the case of the 1947/8 pay recommendations for police superintendents and chief constables, as in

---

[1] This topic will be further considered in our final chapter.

[2] See pp. 213–4 *ante*.

[3] i.e. the period ushered in by the White Paper *Statement on Personal Incomes, Costs and Prices*, Cmd. 7321 (HMSO 1948).

that of the 1949 Chorley proposals for higher civil servants.[1] In 1957, similarly, ministerial consent was withheld from a Whitley Council agreement providing for a 3 per cent increase for National Health clerical and administrative officers.[2] But the most recent, the most thoroughgoing and by far the most dramatic example of this facet of 'publicness' in action was inaugurated by the Chancellor of the Exchequer as part of his summer budget of July 1961, when he announced a comprehensive pay-pause—except for commitments already entered into, but including the freezing of arbitration awards in excess of such commitments—for all public servants for which the Government had direct responsibility. These 1961 measures have sharply brought into focus the potential clash between the Government's responsibilities to the country *qua* Government and its duties *vis-à-vis* its staffs *qua* 'good employer'. However, they are part of a much wider complex of problems, which we must reserve for subsequent consideration.

X

In bringing this discussion to a close, the writer is aware of many gaps, some of which we shall endeavour to fill in our final chapter. There is, however, one question to which we wish to return at this stage—the broad subject of 'more rationality' in the context of pay determination.

By a rational wage system we mean one designed to make a maximum contribution to the nation's overall economic objectives—i.e. that will further, or be consistent with, such major policy goals as the growth of the economy, the maintenance of full employment and a stable price level. Secondly, we have in mind a pay structure that is as fair as is compatible with the first requirement. Thirdly, one with a bias towards simplicity—that, for instance, makes room for meaningful differentials by getting rid of incidental and fortuitous ones. Finally, it is implicit in the notion of a rational pattern of remuneration that if its aims are not realized by the *status quo*, action be taken to introduce the appropriate correctives, and that whatever policies are instituted, are applied on a non-arbitrary basis. We may add that while we regard the first objective as primary, we consider them all as closely interrelated, believing their joint achievement to be necessary if we are to have an economically viable wage system.

Our emphasis on the need for 'more rationality' flows both from our detailed study of salaries in the public services—to which we revert more specifically in the next chapter—and from what indeed is now a commonly-held view of the post-war performance of Britain's

---

[1] See p. 169, p. 170 and p. 33 *ante*.   [2] These examples are not exhaustive.

general wages front. This latter can perhaps be summed up to the effect that in return for a highly elaborate mechanism—the intricacies of which it must take a very large number of persons to negotiate, compute and apply—we have had a system of wages which has not been conspicuously successful in inducing workers to give of their best, which has only been imperfectly responsive to the requirements of the economy, and a major characteristic of which has been its contribution to the forces of inflation by virtue of the fact that the addition to money incomes has substantially outstripped the real growth of the economy. This is not to suggest that the picture is wholly black, nor is it to imply that all the country's economic ills should be attributed to the behaviour of wages: If, for example, Britain had enjoyed a higher rate of productive growth, wage advances would no doubt have been less inflationary, and the growth of productivity is hardly in the hands of labour alone.[1] Again, as has been pointed out, the United Kingdom's post-war record clearly shows that pay and profits have very generally gone up together and in much the same proportion and, as the same authors put it, 'there is no one section of the community that can be blamed for what has been going wrong'.[2] Even so, one cannot fail to accept the proposition that 'Britain cannot regain economic health so long as collectively bargained wage increases run ahead of increases in productivity by some £400 million or £500 million a year'.[3]

The reason for the persistent tendency in post-war Britain for pay and profits to rise faster than production is a very big question, and one on which widely divergent views have been expressed. We shall not here enter into the details of the argument, though one's appraisal of the causes of the problem are of course the key to the remedies favoured; it might therefore be made clear that we side with that body of opinion which seeks to effect a synthesis between the 'demand pull' and the 'cost push' school. On this view inflation is (primarily) due not only to the pull of excess demand, but is also generated by the at any rate partly independent upward push imparted to the system by negotiated pay increases—in turn passed on to consumers in the form of higher prices.[4] It is a corollary of this interpretation

---

[1] This is a shorthand way of saying that, though 'wage-push' has itself hindered economic growth, it has clearly not been the only factor. If productivity had risen faster as a result, say, of more—and the right kind of—investment, personal incomes no doubt would have increased further too. But the gap between the total rise in personal incomes and the total growth of production might well have been significantly smaller.

[2] *Council on Prices, Productivity and Incomes, Fourth Report* (HMSO 1961), paras. 34 and 36.   [3] *The Economist*, 15 July 1961, p. 218.

[4] The relative importance of these two major causes of inflation has, however, greatly varied in the post-war period—both as between countries and over time.

that in addition to monetary and fiscal measures acting on demand, and various 'efficiency' measures designed to make the economy more competitive and raise productivity, direct action on the wages/personal incomes front is called for.

These views have gained an increasing number of followers of late: 'There is now a wide measure of agreement that both "demand pull" and "cost push" have been active, that they have reinforced one another, and that policy has to tackle both',[1] and again, 'a large body of opinion now thinks that some form of wage policy other than leaving wages to free collective bargaining is necessary, if full employment and stable prices are to be combined'.[2] Particularly significant in this context are two authoritative reports both published in the summer of 1961. One is an international study of the problem of rising prices, undertaken by a group of independent experts on behalf of (what was then) OEEC;[3] the other is an evaluation by Britain's own Council on Prices, Productivity and Incomes[4]—generally known as the 'three wise men'. The reader is referred to both publications for a full and extremely lucid exposition of the whole topic; in both documents the need is accepted for, among other measures, a national wages or money income policy,[5] and that need is likewise accepted by the present writer. The United Kingdom, we may add, was one of the countries in particular, concerning which the OEEC experts found that excessive wage increases had constituted both an important and independent inflationary force in recent years.[6]

The main purpose of a national wages policy is to ensure that the accretion to the country's total wage-and-salary bill should correspond to the growth of productivity in the economy as a whole, so that 'wage-push' would be eliminated as a source of inflation. It rests on the premise that apart from a number of specific evils directly caused by the latter—such as the failure to pay our way in our international dealings, resulting in recurring balance of payments crises—rising prices are not compatible with steady growth. Hence if we could rid ourselves of inflation, we should be ridding ourselves not only of these specific evils, but also make it possible for the national product and thus our standards of living to advance more rapidly.

[1] *Council on Prices, Productivity and Incomes, Fourth Report*, op. cit., para. 29.

[2] Sir Robert Hall, *The Economist*, 16 September 1961, p. 1042.

[3] Fellner, Gilbert *et al.*, *The Problem of Rising Prices* (Organization for European Economic Co-operation, 1961).

[4] *Council on Prices, Productivity and Incomes, Fourth Report* (HMSO 1961). The Council had been reconstituted in 1960.

[5] The need for a comprehensive national wages policy is accepted by four of the six OEEC authors only.

[6] *The Problem of Rising Prices*, op. cit., p. 46.

One basic ingredient of a wages policy—as envisaged both in the two reports cited and elsewhere—is the periodic establishment of a 'projection' or 'norm' which would give precision to the expected growth of overall productivity in the country, and which would similarly define the extent to which wages and salaries can be augmented without inflationary consequences. What else a national wages policy would involve is, at the time of writing (autumn 1961), much less clear.

One fundamental question—indeed, the crux of the matter—is the nature of this projection or norm. Is it merely to be available as a guide, of which the two sides to any particular bargain can take note if they choose but which, alternatively, they are free to ignore? Or do we mean something more definite? Or is it in effect to be a ceiling, providing for a kind of 'wage-fund' that will be available for distribution in the period stipulated?[1] The 'three wise men'—though it was not of course their purpose to lay down the mechanics of their policy —simply speak of a projection which 'would be a guide for those responsible in their own particular fields for the planning of production, the fixing of prices and profit margins, and the settlement of wages and salaries'.[2] The Council reject a detailed system of state control; the projection would not be prescribed as an absolute limit, and the main sanction envisaged seems to be the understanding that 'if pay and profits did rise more than productivity the Government would take steps promptly to check spending'.[3]

The OEEC experts[4] on the other hand, though likewise opposed to a statutory system, seem to favour a 'norm' with distinctly more teeth in it. They write that its establishment 'should create a situation in which the burden of proof would be upon any group in labour or management which wants to deviate from it'.[5] They propose the setting up of central machinery in this context, and also recommended that the state should be represented at important wage negotiations —not as mediator, but as an interested party representing the general public's stake in the outcome. They considered it essential for the government to have a wages policy for employees in the public sector, and it is implicit in their comments that this should similarly

---

[1] This question will probably have been answered by the time these remarks appear in print; no doubt we have given a hostage to fortune by venturing into this topic at this particular time. In the light of current indications, however, it looks as though our ensuing discussion is unlikely to be overtaken altogether by the turn of events.

[2] *Council on Prices, Productivity and Incomes, Fourth Report*, op. cit., para. 67.

[3] ibid. paras. 9 and 68.

[4] As previously stated, only four of the six authors of the OEEC report were in favour of a specific national wages policy; subsequent reference to the 'OEEC experts' is to the findings of this majority only.

[5] *The Problem of Rising Prices*, op. cit., p. 59.

extend to the machinery of arbitration. As regards the private sector, however, they did not find it possible to draw up a blueprint that would have universal applicability for the diverse group of countries forming the subject of their review.[1]

It is here felt that unless definite, detailed and enforceable procedures are evolved for the purpose, a national wages policy is unlikely to succeed.[2] This is not because we think that trade unions are irresponsible or lacking in public spirit, nor are we suggesting that the voluntary principle has outlived its usefulness in the British system of industrial relations. We are, however, much impressed by the point made by the Prices, etc. Council that one reason for opposition to the kind of proposals outlined by them is 'the fear that self-discipline will only leave the way open to others'.[3] This, it would seem, is not merely an actual fear; it is also a very legitimate one. For it is difficult to see how any trade union can 'risk' being guided by the projection, when it knows that other unions may blandly ignore that guidance—and, moreover, would do so with impunity. Nor can the sanction of drastic fiscal or monetary measures effectively allay this fear, for these would almost inevitably punish culprits and non-culprits alike.[4] Similarly—even with the elimination of *excess* demand—under full employment it may, in many instances, continue to be worthwhile for employers to concede inflationary wage claims: It may be their best means of making sure of scarce categories of labour and, as hitherto, they may be able to recoup themselves by a corresponding adjustment of selling prices. Unless therefore a national wages policy is made foolproof, so that those willing to comply with the norm do not thereby hazard actual damage to their own economic interests, its chances of success would seem to be seriously prejudiced. It may indeed share the fate of past appeals emanating from the Government urging restraint in the national interest; except for the wage-freeze of the late 'forties, these have met with but little

[1] *The Problem of Rising Prices*, op. cit., pp. 59–60.

[2] It is because they did not wish to move in this direction that two of the OEEC authors parted company from their colleagues over some of the essentials of a national wages policy. It is not quite clear, however, how far the majority were prepared to go.

[3] *Council on Prices, Productivity and Incomes, Fourth Report*, op. cit., para. 69.

[4] *A propos* of a plan for a ceiling on increases in wages and profits in specific industries, the suggestion has been made that 'if persuasion fails, and particular firms or industries persistently and grossly disregard the State's advice, the State should not hesitate to use means such as an adjustment of profits tax, social security contributions, or PAYE to ensure that the offenders pay back—with something over—what they have gained by their selfishness': *Opportunity Knocks* (Liberal Party Publication Department, London, 1961), p. 17. It is here felt, however, that such discriminatory fiscal action would not be feasible.

response, and there is now almost universal agreement that exhortation is not good enough.

The institution of an effective national wages policy is thus a measure the radical nature of which it would be hard to exaggerate. 'The difficulties in the way of formulating the details of such a policy' writes Sir Robert Hall—the Government's top professional economist from 1947 until 1961—'are formidable, and include agreement on workable definitions of the terms, and the treatment of wage differentials. But they are not insuperable and are as nothing compared to the difficulties of getting the policy accepted at all. This would require considerable changes in the attitude of employers, who would have to become more competitive about prices and less competitive about "poaching" labour through open or concealed bidding up. On the part of organized labour, the change would be nothing less than revolutionary . . .'[1]

Let us now look at a few of the problems that, as we see it, would have to be tackled if the projection or norm is to add up to an actual policy, bringing in its train the elimination of 'wage-push' inflation. First, it is a commonplace that in a dynamic economy some industries must expand and others contract; this will mean, therefore, that in any given period some industries would be eligible for a more-than-average share of the 'wage-fund' and others for a less-than-average allocation. This, however, presupposes the existence of definite criteria as to how this is to be achieved: If, as the OEEC experts put it, the burden of proof is to be upon those who wish to deviate from the norm, then a body of rules is necessary by reference to which that burden can be discharged. For example, would industries qualify for a more-than-average bounty on the strength of expected productivity growth? Or of actual growth in the immediately preceding period? Or would those with export potential—or export performance—be favoured? Or all those who happened to want more workers? It seems an inevitable corollary of the plan that specific principles be evolved which would in effect amount both to the framing of a programme of economic priorities as well as a clear enunciation as to which of several possible economic tests—or what combination of such tests—should be decisive. We might add that the remarkable conversion of all shades of political opinion to some form of economic planning will of course make this task easier. At the same time, a comprehensive national wages policy may require the process to be taken rather farther than some of the new converts—as indeed many of the old ones—may care for.

Nor could these principles be concerned exclusively with the laying down of various economic criteria in the light of which above- and

[1] *The Economist*, 16 September 1961, p. 1042.

below-norm industries can be identified. For apart from such special treatment meted out on economic grounds, the institution of a system of controlled wage advances would entail the freezing, as between industries and services, of whatever differentials happen to exist at the time of its introduction. Now if all such differentials were merely the product of economic factors and decreed by hard economic necessity, there would be nothing much that could be done about it. It is, however, widely recognized that economic forces operate in a given social and institutional framework; the price that accrues to a particular grade of labour at a particular date, while it can be assumed to have been pushed downwards by unfavourable economic circumstances or upwards by favourable ones, at the same time revolves around a norm that is the product of many pressures—economic and other. As a result, the pay structure—quite apart from its imperfect attunement to the requirements of the economy—is endowed with both anomalies and inequities, which have been a source of some considerable friction in the past. We must expect that these will be felt to be even more irksome under a national wages policy and, much as we might like to, we shall not be able simply to wash our hands of the matter.

If we could build our pay structure *de novo*, one way of dealing with this problem would be to evaluate all occupations on the basis of the intrinsic characteristics of posts, ignoring whatever may now strike us as irrelevant accretions: This would give us the fair rate for the job, which would then have to be made unfair only in so far as was inherent in the economics of the situation. In practice, we are of course fairly seriously handicapped in this respect, though it is here felt that even within the framework of an economically-geared system of wage advances, provision must be made for the adjustment of differentials on other than strictly economic grounds.

Such questions may in any event have to be faced in deciding how the 'wage-fund' is to be distributed within industries: Lower-paid workers may favour a *per caput*, and higher-paid a percentage-of-remuneration, method; the superiority of neither is self-evident, and different considerations may well apply in different cases. And while this particular issue can be left simply to the discretion of the two sides of each industry, it must be realized that the exercise of this discretion may subsequently cause appreciable inter-industry embarrassment. Similarly controversial will be the extent of the above-norm increase for expanding industries, for there is no law in economics which decrees whether the excess is to be 5 per cent, 10 per cent or 20 per cent. As previously pointed out, the precise shape of any economically-adequate wage structure is not given; the exact width of differentials is a matter of social attitudes, custom and psychology rather than of economics. While from a purely economic standpoint the answer is whatever width of differential will do the trick, as that width is amenable to a certain amount of 'conditioning', it will to some degree be up for acceptability by the general body of workers, if they are to be willing partners in the whole enterprise.

The point we are trying to make is that a national wages policy cannot be made to rest on the assumption that the various semi- and extra-economic factors, which in practice co-determine the price of labour, are merely irrelevant. Indeed, its success may well depend on the extent to which, given its overall economic orientation, it can nevertheless accommodate some of the non-economic aspirations of the suppliers of work. Many of these centre around concepts of 'fairness' and here, first, it should be frankly stated that in one important respect a national wages policy will involve a distinct loss of fairness as that phrase is normally understood. For pay increases would be designed to guide workers into those sectors which ought to expand and away from those which ought to contract; while this would lead to a better distribution of labour—both as between occupations and skills and as between industries—it means that the maintenance of traditional differentials can no longer have that pride of place which it has hitherto enjoyed in union bargaining policy. In other words, what has been one of the characteristics of British collective bargaining since the war—'the remarkable degree of uniformity in the size of the increases negotiated during each particular wage round in different industries, despite considerable differences in the economic climate prevailing in these industries'[1]—would have to be modified; some cherished relativities are clearly going to be upset if one side of the equation—but one side only—happens to be an above- or below-norm industry.[2] One may add, though, that in any given period a good many fields may be expected to be neutral, 'norm-wise', and here inter-industry relativities could therefore remain undisturbed.

What is of some importance, however, is that—our foregoing remarks notwithstanding—a national wages policy of the type here envisaged could provide the opportunity for a pay structure which is, all in all, more equitable than the present one. For fairness is being attained in a strictly limited sense only when everyone is religiously securing the same rise as everyone else: Throughout the post-war period the uniformity of wage advances has not merely been rather

[1] *The Problem of Rising Prices*, op. cit., p. 426.
[2] Strictly speaking, a national wages policy could provide for the same average (norm-linked) increase to apply to all occupations and industries. While this would equally ensure the elimination of 'wage-push' inflation, such a policy would make very little sense in terms of other economic objectives.

poor economics; it has also done relatively little to make the pay structure more equitable structurally speaking, though this is not to say that a wholesale instalment of such structural adjustments would have been practicable. But what concerns us here is that a national wages policy would, despite its overall economic bias, allow of a gradual infusion of fairness in a more 'absolute' sense of the term. Supposing, for example, that it can be demonstrated that—skill for skill and taking into account all relevant net advantages—the services of those engaged in agriculture are currently being undervalued in the labour market. Then—unless there are specific economic grounds against it—the 'wage-fund' might well allot to such workers an above-the-norm increase such as would, over the years, rectify the position. Nor need this open the flood-gates, if such action is taken in accordance with a previously-defined programme of priorities. Similarly, the question of what is a desirable minimum living wage might be looked at. So might the problem of vertical differentials generally: Some of these may be found to be too narrow just as others may turn out to be too wide, and here there should be ample opportunity both for more economic good sense and for more equity.

The rationale of a national wages policy is that it should obviate the necessity for what have been widely described as the 'stop-go' economic measures of recent years, thereby (among other things) preparing the ground for a faster rate of productive growth than has been achieved hitherto. Once the initial hurdles have been overcome, the accretion to money incomes that ought to be feasible should, however, give some room for manoeuvre: It is for this reason that, as well as lead to a better and 'non-inflationary' distribution of labour, the plan would provide scope for the eventual emergence of a pattern of remuneration more closely related to services rendered than the current regime. The elimination of anomalies would be another step in this direction. Clearly, a pay structure which is sound economically can never be completely fair, nor—by definition—can the measure of injustice inherent in the situation be evenly spread between particular groups. Nevertheless, quite apart from its substantial economic benefits, a comprehensive wages policy would in time permit of a larger dose of overall fairness than the present system. And this is particularly so since—as we see it—its institution will entail a number of steps outside the sphere of the wage pattern itself before it can become a practical proposition.

This brings us to what is perhaps the most fundamental point of all, namely whether a national wages policy has any chance of proving acceptable to labour in the first place. For the view expressed earlier that such a policy must be watertight and given teeth—by which we mean, if necessary, statutory teeth—was not to suggest that the policy *per se* should be forced upon those affected. The good will of labour is one of the prerequisites for any viable wages policy; it is also an essential if we wish men and women to give of their best.

Here the Council on Prices, Productivity and Incomes rendered a particularly valuable service in the emphasis they placed throughout their (1961) report on the need for a *money income* rather than a *wages* policy; in other words, their projection of the economically sustainable increase in money incomes is to extend fully as much to profits as it is to pay. There can be no shadow of a doubt that a wages policy which is not part of a wider plan applying equally strictly to other forms of personal income is doomed from the start: We cannot expect one section of the community—but one section only—to abjure the canons of *laissez-faire* to which, in this sphere, we have hitherto all been equally wedded. If then the term 'wages policy' has been used in these pages, this is simply because we are confining our discussion to that part of the subject: We are not attempting to consider the thorny, though rather different, problems that will likewise attend the genesis of a 'profits policy'—such as that, while it ought to be as foolproof as that on the wages front, it must not be designed in a way as would penalize efficiency or stifle enterprise.

Though we do not propose to delve into the complexities of a profits policy, there is one related aspect which we must touch on, as it is relevant to the whole question of whether the principle of a national wages policy can hope to win its crucial adherents. One difficulty about the plan for a controlled adjustment of money incomes is that it involves a freezing of the distribution of (pre-tax) incomes as between factors of production. Now it is of course well-known that, the absolute size of post-war wage rises notwithstanding, labour has not managed to increase its share of the national income. 'After important gains during the previous decade due to the change from depression to full employment, the share of labour, apart from cyclical shifts, has remained remarkably constant in almost all countries since around 1950.'[1] But though the notion that by pushing up wages, workers gain at the expense of profits, has thus been an illusion as far as the post-war period is concerned, under a system of free collective bargaining the *possibility* remains that labour might, in the future, somehow or other be able to augment that share. As, however, the institution of a national wages policy would put an end to that possibility, it may be held that this confers entitlement to some 'compensation'.

To say this is of course to step into the very heart of political controversy, though some of the most eminent students of the sub-

---

[1] *The Problem of Rising Prices*, op. cit., p. 53. See also ibid. pp. 424–5 and *Council on Prices, Productivity and Incomes, Fourth Report*, op. cit., para. 62.

ject now freely acknowledge that wages policy cannot be purposefully tackled without coming to grips with this type of issue. Thus in the course of two articles written for the *Economist* by the former Economic Adviser to HM Government, Sir Robert Hall states that 'among other things, any government which attempts a wage and price policy will have to recognize that the national income can be redistributed to some extent by tax policy and that taxes must be seen to be fair'. He continues that 'the points where our system is most vulnerable are probably the absence of any taxes on capital gains, and the treatment of business expenses, which leads many firms to somewhat extravagant competition with one another', adding that while it was no doubt very difficult to devise suitable taxes in these fields, we ought to recognize that these were sore points with those who did not enjoy them.[1] In a special article in *The Times*, Professor Phelps Brown writes in very similar vein.[2] In brief, our argument is that since there are inequitable features in our present socio-economic structure, if we wish those at a disadvantage to allow one of the channels for redressing the balance to be closed—granted that that channel is a narrow one—we will have to be ready for some kind of a 'deal'. Thus quite apart from the fact that a wages policy must be accompanied by a profits policy, a prerequisite for its initial institution would appear to be what one might call a more 'equitable base' as a foundation on which it is to rest.

What precisely such a base implies we do not propose to go into. We would merely comment that it is certainly compatible with incentives for capital as well as for labour, though the view that whatever incentives happen to exist at a particular point of time must *ipso facto* be essential for the efficient functioning of the economic system is not borne out by the facts—in that the system has not, perhaps, been all that efficient. We would also add our belief that, in order to gain the good will of labour, revolutionary measures will not be required. Trade unions, like other institutions, have their definite weaknesses, but when it comes to the big issues, they can be remarkably sensible. Thus the need for ploughing back profits for investment and reserves is well understood; responsible union opinion is aware that the fruits of industry cannot all find their way into the pockets of wage-earners. Nor were impossible *quid pro quos* asked for at the time of the wages standstill in the late 'forties. As far as the political aspect is concerned, the co-operation of labour in this country for the necessary wage restraint can, it is felt, be secured, provided a genuine effort is made to this end.

As we see it, it is less than helpful to make out that this aspect of the

[1] *The Economist*, 23 September 1961, p. 1,132.
[2] 'Money Incomes in Full Employment', *The Times*, 21 September 1961.

subject is irrelevant to the problem of evolving a wages policy, though this is not to say that anything that any seller of labour might regard as equitable or fair is necessarily in that category and must, as it were, be appeased. Nor, more generally, are we suggesting that the degree of inflation in the economy should be made dependent on the good will of labour. There are of course several major tools of policy that impinge on the inflationary situation; as briefly indicated, such monetary and fiscal measures must be employed to curb excess demand just as—and it is a point calling for particular emphasis —the country's economic problem must be attacked in a more positive manner by action aimed at raising its productive efficiency. But if the need for a national wages policy is accepted, then labour's co-operation cannot be dispensed with, and in so far as the latter is contingent on reasonable demands, we should endeavour to meet these.

Here it must be said that the Government's first excursion in the direction of a wages policy—to wit, the Chancellor's July 1961 measures—gave little concrete evidence that this lesson had been learnt. While the wage pause was brought in as a temporary expedient only, and while these remarks must be tentative in that they are being written in its early phases, it is already abundantly clear that it has caused extreme resentment. Nor is this really surprising, for the unilateral breaking of agreements and partial paralysis of the institutions of collective bargaining is not a particularly apt way of preparing for the latter's overhaul on a long-term and enduring basis. Seeing that one of the stated purposes of the 'pause' was to give time for the bringing in of a more permanent wages policy, it was not perhaps the most propitious prologue to the main act.

Nevertheless, the need for a less one-sided approach being fairly obvious, it is unlikely that the issue will be similarly sidestepped, should any *serious* attempt be made to institute a national wages policy. Hence it may well be that, what at first sight looks like political dynamite, will be the least difficult part of the business of 'selling' such a policy. Much more awkward, in the event, may be the far-reaching measure of public re-education as to the necessity for it in the first place. And even when this has been grasped at the intellectual level, its implications will not be lightly stomached, for only a fundamental reorientation of attitudes can make the workings of the scheme palatable.

Nor can one pretend that a wages policy would not have radical implications for the functions and activities of trade unions. For free collective bargaining has manifestly come to be cherished as an activity *per se*; the conviction that it is a divine right almost—to use Lady Wootton's striking phrase[1]—has become something of an article

[1] *The Observer*, 13 July 1958.

of faith. Yet if the net effect of the system is that everyone's earnings go up by approximately the same, and if that 'same' is of a magnitude such as is, among other things, preventing a more rapid improvement of its recipients' own *real* wages, the faith in its immutability is perhaps somewhat misplaced.

While a national wages policy as here envisaged would deprive the unions of important traditional functions, it is not the case that it would rob them of their *raison d'être*. There are other vital spheres in which their services will continue to be invaluable; they would also have an important role to play in the working out of the procedures antecedent to the introduction of the policy—as, indeed, in their subsequent application. Clearly, even with an overall plan numerous details will remain to be filled in;[1] it is not being suggested that all the minutiae should be rigidly spelt out under central auspices. But the core of the matter is that the two primary objectives of trade union endeavour are to enhance their members' living standards and the maintenance of full employment. Since one of the very purposes of a national wages policy is to make possible a faster raising of these standards than is feasible under free collective bargaining, and as this is to be achieved without sacrificing full employment, there is no clash between its institution and the true aims of the trade union movement.

There is one alternative course of action which appears to find some support, and which would largely obviate the need for awkward decisions about principles and priorities of the type indicated—as also for many of the other unpopular innovations inseparable from the inauguration of a full-blooded national wages policy. This is to apply the latter rigidly where this is easily feasible, i.e. in the public services, with the greater part of the economy left free—subject to generous doses of exhortation—to treat the norm of permissible increases as it deems fit. The 1961 pay pause was conceived on these lines, and the temptation no doubt exists to model any long-term wages policy on some such pattern. We return to the subject in our final chapter.

There are of course other alternatives to a national wages policy— based on a rejection of the whole idea in any of its possible shapes or forms. First, and very briefly, there is the solution of somehow 'breaking' the unions, but even those who might favour the outcome—

---

[1] There is, for example, the vexed question of fitting in payment-by-results schemes and other plant-level arrangements into the framework of a national wages policy. We have not been able to give adequate consideration to this problem, though we do not believe it to be insuperable. We are mentioning the subject here as, subject to a number of general rules which would have to be laid down centrally, the details of such arrangements would obviously continue to be a matter for employer-union negotiation.

this writer is hardly among them[1]—are unlikely, if it came to it, to attempt to bring it about. More important, there is the (related) prescription of stopping inflation by a severe damping down of demand, but it is a remedy which, as it has been put, is worse than the disease.[2] For this medicine is incompatible alike with economic growth and full employment—which many would regard as the ultimate aims of economic policy.

In this context it is pertinent to point to one consideration in particular, which sometimes appears to be overlooked. A programme of checking rising prices via rigorous draughts of deflation—and there is impressive evidence that merely a firm control of aggregate demand is not enough[3]—commends itself among other things because the institution of a wages and profits policy would constitute too radical a departure from the canons of a free economy. But to apply curbs to spending through the medium of fiscal action is plainly making use of the legislature's powers of coercion, and though it is true that some coercion in this sphere has come to be regarded as inevitable, this does not really alter its character. Similarly, while the raising of, say, Bank Rate and the resultant higher cost of credit entails no formal compulsion, *widespread* deflation induced by such means can nevertheless be said to be *imposed*. Hence to cure the problem of mounting prices by drastic deflationary measures is— quite apart from its dubious economic wisdom—not free or voluntary in any meaningful sense of these terms.

The only acceptable alternative to a national wages policy would seem to be if we could after all, somehow or other, achieve an expansion of the national product of a size as would approximately match the money incomes which we have become accustomed to hand out to ourselves. But while a much more substantial growth of productivity should be the objective, and while such a higher growth rate would of itself greatly lighten the task of implementing a national wages policy, it is questionable whether, without the latter's help, such acceleration will be feasible in the first place. Much of course will depend on international developments such as whether or not Britain joins the European Common Market and, either way, on the behaviour of the price levels of her chief competitors relative to her own. But whatever the future may hold, it can hardly be denied that the British economy is in urgent need of vigorous and imaginative action designed to stimulate economic growth; while some of that

---

[1] This is not to say that certain reforms in this sphere—i.e. apart from those directly relevant to our subject—are not called for. In this connection, Mr Eric Wigham's *What's Wrong with the Unions?* (Penguin Books, 1961) is most timely.

[2] *Council on Prices, Productivity and Incomes, Fourth Report,* op. cit., para. 8.

[3] cf. ibid. and *The Problem of Rising Prices,* op. cit., pp. 56–7.

impetus must come from less 'featherbedding' and more competition, some of it will have to derive from direct 'growth' measures
—such as a higher rate of the right type of investment. A national
wages policy, as we see it, would certainly form an integral part of
such a wider economic plan; if we have treated this topic with neg-
lect, this is solely because it is outside the scope of this discussion.
What is relevant here, however, is that if priority is to be accorded to
a programme of modernization and economic expansion, this must
of itself be expected to impart an inflationary push to the system.
Hence if we wish to break the vicious circle and reap the fruits of
technological progress, it is doubtful whether we can get by—at any
rate in the period ahead—without the discipline of a money income
policy.

Even supposing that we could, the need for a more rational approach to problems of remuneration remains. For even in the absence
of a formal national wages policy, simply in the course of the ordinary
business of pay-fixing questions constantly arise to which there is no
automatic answer, and where some answers may therefore be more
appropriate than others, and where it might thus not be a waste of
effort to have a set of guiding principles. The most obvious example
is when a breakdown in negotiations occurs and the dispute is submitted to third parties—be they domestic tribunals, the Industrial
Court or some *ad hoc* body. In the past, the theory has been that
these bodies should receive no directives of any kind; the criteria
upon which they adjudicated on any particular issue were entirely
within their own discretion. Thus they could 'split the difference',
decide the matter by reference to ability-to-pay or other economic
tests, or with a view to 'fairness', or with an eye on the cost of living,
or against the background of an undefined national interest. At the
same time, arbitral bodies have come under fire for not having awarded less inflationary settlements, but when we have strenuously refused to recognize the need for a code in the light of which the
various types of pay problems might be determined, it is a little odd
to blame the results on those who have merely exercised their judgment in the unfettered manner wished upon them.

Nor is it, for instance, good enough virtuously to proclaim that
arbitration awards should not be inflationary. Granted they are
not in that category if matched by increases in productivity, how are
arbitral bodies to interpret this maxim in any specific instance?
If they are not to mete out identical treatment to all and sundry,
then rules are required for the purpose—whether we have a formal
wages policy or not. Again, in the case of the public services it can
hardly be maintained that all the answers have been self-evident—
as witness the various commissions and committees that have been

called upon over the years to pronounce on the basis of reward for public employees. Yet the *ad hoc* investigation of the remuneration of particular groups is only a partial solution; while individual services obviously have to contend with a number of problems peculiar to themselves, many others are not in fact *sui generis*. Thus making 'fair comparison' the chief criterion for settling the salaries of civil servants, with demand and supply more or less ousted from the scene, was in many ways an invitation to the wider wages front to do likewise.[1] Similarly, as mentioned, if social status is legitimate in the context of National Health doctors' incomes, then the much more modest—even if far more inflationary—status differentials insisted upon at a lower level must be commendable. There can be but little doubt that the absence of a body of principles and the general lack of consistency have themselves contributed to the inflationary character of pay increases and been responsible for much else that has not gone as well as it might *in re* wages and salaries.

The problem of wages under full employment provides a major illustration of how the pressure of events has made it necessary to have 'more rationality' in the sphere of pay determination. For we are unlikely ever to be very far from the inflationary threshold; indeed, the economy may well have to be balanced somewhere in that vicinity if—quite apart from such special measures as the current situation may call for—sufficient stimulus to its dynamic development is to exist. Hence even without a formal wages policy, we shall need a set of rules by reference to which wage problems can be resolved without setting up irresistible pressures for their (inflationary) rectification. Thus we are being made to take note of rationality in the course not of pursuing some abstract ideal of logic or equity—greatly desirable though these certainly are in themselves—but in the course simply of devising a viable wage system.

It is the inherent logic of the subject matter which likewise requires that we must be ready to assess the relevance of all the considerations that *de facto* impinge on the price of labour; inconvenient though this may be, they cannot be dealt with in isolation. For the economic and non-economic constituents of demand and supply prices constantly act and react on one another; for practical purposes they also of course coalesce, so that they are all equally fraught with economic consequences. Hence the onus for tackling these questions cannot be neatly split according to guiding principle involved; indeed, the latter may itself defy allocation to any one pigeon-hole. It is here believed that any pattern of reward is much

[1] The Priestley formula is further discussed in Chapter 21: see p. 399 and ff. *post*.

more likely to achieve its economic ends, if it attempts to come to terms with all the forces that bear on levels of remuneration.

One corollary of this is that if the economist would wish his voice to be heeded on these topics, he must be willing to transgress into related disciplines. For though many wage questions, clearly, can be exhaustively investigated through economic spectacles alone, it would seem that such is not feasible where pay determination is concerned. In that sphere he cannot ultimately escape from the entanglements of his subject—whether it is a case of interpreting what is or of advising what should be.

One of the basic problems of pay determination, as we see it, is to effect a compromise between the demands of the economic system and those of the suppliers of labour in more than a purely mechanical sense. And just because economic considerations must have the final say in shaping the network of rewards, it becomes necessary to make the latter as acceptable otherwise as is consonant with the primary requirement. And since the settlement of wages under full employment is liable to be inflationary—in other words, since an economically tolerable compromise is in any event not automatically reached —we accept the need for a national wages policy. For it has to be remembered that, in its absence, unions are more or less forced to push their sectional advantage as far as the labour market will allow; it is inherent in our present collective bargaining arrangements and there is currently no alternative mechanism to safeguard their legitimate interests. Moreover, much as we may now decry pushfulness, we have at the same time put a premium on it for, once successful, we treat it as a hard economic fact at the next 'annual round', while those acting responsibly are doubly penalized in that not only have they to manage on a smaller income, but they also 'count' for less in the scheme of things. Somehow or other, therefore, we shall have to break the equivalence between showing restraint and falling to the back of the queue for, until we do, it is folly to expect such restraint however much it may be in the national interest. Even more so is it folly to let the latter go by default—which, in a nutshell, is the case for a national wages policy.

Such a policy would act in conjunction with monetary and fiscal measures on the one hand, and with efficiency and growth measures on the other; it would form part of a plan comprising all types of personal income—itself superimposed on what we have previously called a more equitable base. Some such agenda seems to us to represent the best hope for attaining full employment plus a rising standard of life—enjoyed by all in an atmosphere clear of the indignities of a nation living beyond its means, and conferring important new freedoms for the one inevitably relinquished. It is a bold and difficult programme, and little is gained by pretending that it is otherwise. Nor, of course, do we claim to have resolved the many complex problems that arise. Here it must suffice to add that none of the benefits of a national wages policy are likely to be ours unless we are prepared to face the issues in a way we have not hitherto been prepared to. Further, that, difficult though the plan is, it is in no way beyond reach.

Chapter 21

SALARY POLICY

I

In this—our final—chapter we attempt to draw together some of the
conclusions to which this study has led. Salaries in the public services
will now exclusively again engage our attention.

There are probably many fields of enquiry in which one's findings
will vary according to whether or not one views the subject through
the eyes of the historian. Seen in that perspective, there can be no
doubt that great improvements have taken place in the conditions of
salaried employment in the public services. Thus the principle that
the regulation of reward is not one for unilateral imposition on the
part of employing authorities is—recent events notwithstanding—
widely recognized; such joint negotiation, further, not merely
covers a small sector of the salariat but extends high up, if not to the
top of, the pyramid. And though, as we saw in Chapter 20, we may
have now reached the stage where bilateralism may have to join with
the 'national interest' in what would accordingly become a tripartite
system, this does not detract from the achievement represented by
bilateralism itself. Moreover, in the world of salaries it is the public
sector in which collective bargaining has come to maturity.

Secondly, the remuneration which is agreed is roughly related to the
job in question; while in the working out of this equation perfection
has not been attained, some effort is made in that direction. Lest
this seem too obvious a point to deserve mention, one need only
refer to Miss Cohen's valuable survey of early Civil Service history.
In those days appointments were frequently obtained by patronage
or purchase; the holders of posts did not necessarily execute their
duties in person; the emoluments of public offices had a great
variety of origins: A salary formed a part merely of an officer's total
receipts, being supplemented—often far exceeded—by fees collected
from doubtful sources by dubious means. Nor was there any consistency between the scales of remuneration in similar offices.[1]
This of course was the position in the late eighteenth century, but
one has only to go back to the beginning of the twentieth to find a

[1] cf. E. W. Cohen, *The Growth of the British Civil Service*, 1780–1939 (Allen &
Unwin, 1941), pp. 26–8.

total absence of any kind of common system of grading or pay even within a single service. In many cases the development of national salary patterns did not materialize until after the second world war, the Civil Service itself not reaching its present degree of unification until 1943.

However, though it is tempting to lose oneself in these reflections, it is more fruitful in many ways not to; Britain after all belongs to the advanced industrial economies, and it seems more profitable to approach our topic from the vantage point of what might be appropriate to a country in these circumstances. Looked at in this light, the vista is less pleasing; there is a debit side to the account. Perhaps the main impression which this study of public service salaries has left on the investigator is that of their complexity and of the multiplicity of arrangements which are found, leading among other things to considerable inconsistencies between the different fields. Hand in hand with this devotion to detail, there is a certain reluctance to take a broad view, just as despite the richness of texture, there appears to be a lack of differentiation where this is called for.

Before going into these strictures, it may be pertinent briefly to state what the objections to complexities and anomalies are. First, there is the simple but important fact that elaboration is extremely costly in terms both of manpower and other resources. Secondly, in a society in which all forms of direction of labour are ruled out, a major responsibility rests on rates of remuneration to secure the required distribution of the working population, but the pattern of reward is impeded in this, if submerged in a complicated structure of grades, service conditions and 'extras' which blur the picture. This takes us to the question of inconsistencies between the public services, for mobility is particularly desirable perhaps within that area: As Professor Robson has put it, 'if we desire to widen the experience of our officials in order to give them a broader outlook, every effort must be made to encourage and facilitate transfer'; as the same writer has also pointed out, 'transfer is possible as a general practice only if the public service is unified'.[1]

Next, many of those covered by separate salary schemes find themselves working in close association—such as medical auxiliaries and local government administrative staff, probation officers and policemen, teachers and school doctors—and whether we like it or not, they compare every single one of the minutiae of their conditions of employment. Again, even where there is no physical contact, comparisons, as pointed out, are well-nigh universal. Finally, if a

[1] W. A. Robson, ed., *The British Civil Servant* (Allen & Unwin, 1937), pp. 22–3. This, he added, did not mean that uniform conditions must be applied throughout, but it did imply a much greater degree of consistency.

N

certain amount of 'fuss' is being made about the presence of anomalies, this is also because—in so far as the various services are trying to meet identical contingencies—it is reasonable that they should follow a similar course. If the cost of living in London is higher than in the provinces, then it is so for all those residing in the metropolis, and some unity of approach in handling the matter would seem to be called for. Thus, though membership of the public sector does not imply any inherent identity as between its constituent branches, this does not, as we see it, affect the case for consistency.

In essence, then, the exception to anomalies is twofold. First, that they offend the tidy and pedantic mind or—where some issue of substance is at stake—our sense of justice. Secondly, that they cause trouble; while they may not upset the machine, they make it cumbrous and less effective. And here one might refer to the not inconsiderable bulk of pay claims which directly or indirectly stem from the existence of anomalies; though doubtless containing also a simple tactical element, they nevertheless bear witness to the genuine grievances engendered. Further, as we saw in Chapter 20, lack of rationality in a full employment economy has rather wider implications, in that pressures are set up for adjustments which almost invariably are inflationary in character: It is a luxury which can ill be afforded. True, the incongruities do not necessarily involve substantial divergences of either pay or service conditions, but it is the small differences, those at the margin, which frequently give rise to friction—and one cannot easily complain if the 'margin' is taken seriously. In fact, where the discrepancy is such as to remove one class of employee on to another plane altogether, there may be less resentment than where there are minor inconsistencies—modest enough, that is, to leave the two categories as competing groups, as between whom parity of pay and esteem are still within the bounds of possibility. In short, our thesis is that the public service salary structure can be taken to task on both counts; those with an innate suspicion of theoretical rationalizers need not at any rate be similarly disdainful of those who would oil the wheels of the machine.

II

The complexity of salary systems cannot be fully gauged from this study: Our review in Part I is not an adequate measure of the elaboration which is to be found, as this very profusion has necessitated some drastic selection in the material included, while the equally extensive data on service conditions have had to be almost wholly omitted. Much more significant, however, is that 'drastic selection' has been necessary also in quite different quarters. Thus the Priestley Commission, commenting that their terms of reference mentioned the 'main categories of the Civil Service' and that accordingly 'we have had to decide which out of the many classes in the Service we should regard as "main" ', continue: 'While we were naturally anxious not to exclude any important class, our task would have been unmanageable had we not drawn a strict line of demarcation'.[1] Similar problems were faced by the Ministry of Health and Department of Health for Scotland in drawing up their memorandum of evidence to the Royal Commission on Doctors' and Dentists' Remuneration. In this case, the data submitted on 'connected occupations' in the Health Service were curtailed, not only because some of the information would have been of little relevance, but 'because of the sheer volume of that information'.[2]

Let us recapitulate some of the specific evidence. First, the reader is referred to Chapter 14, where mention was made of the 1951 agreement setting out the salaries of technical engineering staff in the electricity supply industry. One of the (several) schedules to that document had thirteen classes, *each* with from twelve to twenty-two grades, *each* of the latter with a three-point scale of varying increments.[3] In the Post Office there is the complex device for remunerating sub-postmasters, of which a brief outline was given in Chapter 11.[4] Again, the method of calculating the allowances currently payable under the Burnham reports to head and deputy head teachers and to those holding 'graded posts' involves what will strike some as altogether unnecessary pieces of arithmetic.[5]

Next, there is the highly complicated pay structure for National Health nurses; as the management side have themselves pointed out, any revision of remuneration affects the carefully balanced relativities between the various tiers in the hierarchy.[6] The 'central pool' from which general practitioners are rewarded—on a basis reminiscent in some ways of the pre-feudal one of sharing out the total product—

[1] *Royal Commission on the Civil Service* 1953–5, Cmd. 9613 (HMSO 1955), para. 348.

[2] Royal Commission on Doctors' and Dentists' Remuneration, *Factual Memorandum by the Ministry of Health and the Department of Health for Scotland*, Written Evidence, vol. 1 (HMSO 1957), p. 62.

[3] See p. 232 *ante*; the structure of the agreement has since been altered. However, a recent advertisement (*The Times*, 29 March 1961) offered a salary in National Joint Board 'Class BX, Grade 5, Scale 14', suggesting that the scheme has remained one of very considerable complexity.

[4] cf. p. 201 *ante*. For a more detailed account see e.g. Civil Service Arbitration Tribunal Award No. 205 (HMSO 1953).

[5] See Ministry of Education, *Report of the Burnham Committee on Scales of Salaries for Teachers in Primary and Secondary Schools, England and Wales*, 1961 (HMSO 1961), Sections J, L and N and Appx. VII.

[6] Industrial Court Award No. 2427 (HMSO 1953), p. 4. There were then some 250 separate grades.

N*

is another illustration:[1] The 1960 Royal Commission, though favouring its continuance in view of certain practical advantages and its general acceptance by the profession, nevertheless found it necessary to express the hope 'that more will be done to render the pool system intelligible to those whose living depends on it'.[2] It may also be revealing that between the inception of the National Health Service and the end of 1958, the ten Whitley Councils in the field had published no fewer than 546 formal agreements.[3]

In the Civil Service we have the departmental and linked departmental variants of the basic Treasury classes. There is also the executive class which mostly overlaps other pyramids on administrative duties, and to the undue elaboration of which the Priestley Commission drew attention.[4] Again, the Gardiner Committee on the 'works group' of government professionals concluded that, as regards the higher tiers, refinements of grading had produced an excessive number of pay levels.[5] Or to quote the admirably restrained words of the Civil Service Pay Research Unit, 'it must be recognized that as there are within the scope of our operations over 700,000 civil servants organized in some 1,400 different grades, coverage by the Unit will inevitably mean a long term programme'.[6]

A different type of intricacy is found in the upper reaches of the local government service, where the pattern of negotiating machinery established after the war was such that the remuneration of county council clerks was not within the competence of any collective bargaining body, that of town clerks within the purview of the Joint Negotiating Committee for Town and District Council Clerks, but that of their deputies within the jurisdiction of the Joint Negotiating Committee for Chief Officers. The latter, in turn, was made responsible for the salaries and conditions of certain chief officers whatever their remuneration, for all local government staffs if their pay was sufficiently high, while those chief officers whose reward was sufficiently modest came under the aegis of the National Joint Council for Local Authorities' Administrative, Professional, Technical and Clerical Services. Again, as between town and county council clerks, the position regarding additional emoluments for duties at

---

[1] For details see *Royal Commission on Doctors' and Dentists' Remuneration* 1957–60, Cmnd. 939 (HMSO 1960), p. 108 and ff.

[2] ibid. para. 337.

[3] *Report of the Ministry of Health for the year ended 31 December 1958*, Part I, Cmnd. 806 (HMSO 1959), p. 224.

[4] *Priestley Report*, op. cit., para. 461.

[5] *Report of the Committee on the Organization, Structure and Remuneration of the Works Group of Professional Civil Servants* (HMSO 1951), para. 26.

[6] Civil Service Pay Research Unit, *Annual Report* 1958 (HMSO 1959), para. 23.

parliamentary and local elections and other fees is somewhat awkward to disentangle.[1]

Yet another kind of complexity exists in the sphere of the judiciary—small though it is—through the several authorities charged with the administration of justice: As a result, some judicial stipends are the business of the Lord Chancellor, some of the Home Secretary and some of the local authority. In the probation service, on the other hand, salaries merely appear involved—thanks to their being couched in the legal parlance which custom has evidently made obligatory for all statutory instruments.

The richness of grade and scale patterns is paralleled in the matter of service conditions and other peripheral features of remuneration. Thus until 1956 civil servants had (apart from that actually put in) both a notional and an operative standard working week. There were also—not counting the technical classes and various special provisions—four different methods of dealing with overtime.[2] Again, some idea of the labour imposed on establishment officers by the Civil Service 1947–58 regime of provincial differentiation can be got from a perusal of the circulars issued when the scheme began to be modified.[3] We may add that though the new system represents a sizeable improvement, it is still much less straightforward[4] than those apparently considered satisfactory in other public services.

The effects of such elaboration, moreover, are not confined to the chores of day-to-day administration, or to the burden of petty adjustment each time a change in salaries or conditions is agreed upon. They may have rather wider repercussions, as is illustrated by the police where it seems fairly certain that a complicated structure of net advantages has contributed to the problem of undermanning. Thus the Oaksey Committee reported in 1949 that police remuneration contained a very substantial element of 'concealed emoluments' in the form of free accommodation (or a tax-free rent allowance), exemption from rates, free clothing and footwear for use on duty, and a generous pension scheme. The latter alone, it was estimated by the Government Actuary, was then worth the equivalent of about 25 per cent of pay, of which only one-fifth was borne by policemen. Oaksey's conclusion on the subject was that 'the value of these concealed emoluments tends to be underestimated by the men and is

[1] cf. pp. 74 and 76–7 *ante*.

[2] Here again—in the Treasury's factual memorandum of evidence—it was necessary to inform the Priestley Commission that it was 'not practicable to set out all the details of the overtime arrangements'.

[3] See e.g. EC 58/57, *Whitley Bulletin*, February 1958, p. 27 and ff. The circular itself is a model of clarity. See also p. 274 *ante*.

[4] See e.g. EC 12/61, *Whitley Bulletin*, May 1961, pp. 75–7.

not fully appreciated by potential recruits or the public in general'.[1]

That this is so has been confirmed *à propos* of the 1960 Royal Commission on the Police,[2] when the representatives of the junior ranks—the Police Federations—made much of the comparison between the minimum and maximum of the constable's scale and average industrial earnings, pointing to the dramatic change in favour of the latter which had occurred in this relationship in the period 1935–59. Though there is little doubt that the policeman has lost ground in this way and that his income did require a boost, this is no reason for obscuring the actual current differential between him and the average industrial worker. Yet to contrast points on the constable's *scale* with average outside *earnings* is obscuring that differential, for it leaves out of account both the various cash allowances enhancing policemen's remuneration and the advantages which they enjoy through their other concealed emoluments.[3] However, though policemen have a basic rate which constitutes a comparatively small part only of the net advantages of their occupation, this scale is bound to be quoted in preference to a more refined figure, for the evaluation of net advantages is, as we saw, a difficult matter the nature of which is liable to be misunderstood, and on which agreement is in any case not easily reached. Thus the Home Office and County Councils Association in their evidence to the 1960 Commission estimated police subsidiary emoluments at about £300, the Association of Chief Police Officers at £150–£200, while the Commission themselves held that all such emoluments other than housing—to be reckoned at £70–£80 per annum—should be ignored.[4]

It is highly probable therefore that, as the Oaksey Committee concluded and as the Treasury and local authority witnesses reiterated at the 1960 enquiry, the present balance between police basic pay and emoluments gives a misleading impression to both serving officers and potential recruits: By and large these are likely to decide in the light of the *cash* rate only—as by implication they have now been encouraged—whether to join or remain in the service. The absence of a straightforward consolidated scale may thus have aggravated the police manpower problem to a by no means negligible extent—and may well continue to do so, the Royal Commission making no recommendation for a change in this respect.[5]

---

[1] *Report of the Committee on Police Conditions of Service*, Part I, Cmd. 7674 (HMSO 1949), paras. 177 (iii) and 116.

[2] *Interim Report*, Cmnd. 1222 (HMSO 1960).

[3] See p. 166 and pp. 354–5 *ante*.

[4] Cmnd. 1222, op. cit., paras. 133 and 178–9.

[5] See ibid. paras. 135–42. Consolidation as a future possibility was not ruled out.

III

The multiplicity of arrangements within individual services inevitably leads to inconsistencies between them. Thus in Chapter 18 we came across the capricious nature of scale structures and increments.[1] We likewise examined the rather anomalous position as regards area weightings:[2] These vary from service to service—but not in accordance with relative degrees of undermanning, nor are they in any way precisely attuned to regional living costs. We may add that sex differentials in the public services used to display analogous vagaries, though the introduction of equal pay itself is clearly a move in the opposite direction.

As mentioned in our last chapter, some of the structural inconsistencies found may be due to genuine differences of view; for example, the conflict between absolute and relative need has not been without its impact.[3] But over and above what can reasonably be imputed to this cause, this writer has, in the course of this study, been repeatedly struck by the phenomenon of what for short might be called the element of 'accident' in the national salary structure— i.e. features in the latter which do not derive from market factors on the one hand, the intrinsic attributes of jobs on the other, nor from the purposive application of divergent principles just referred to. By element of 'accident' we thus simply mean the unintended—the chance repercussions on the pay pattern of some past occurrence, historical happening, constitutional or institutional development. It is not being maintained that these facts, happenings or developments are necessarily accidental in themselves—merely that, in so far as the public service salary structure is concerned, their impact has in many ways been fortuitous.

This topic deserves a closer look : We will begin with what might be described as 'constitutional accidents', arising from the country's institutional framework and the given set-up of the organs of administration. Our first illustration is borrowed from Britain's divison of functions as between central and local government. As will be clear, large numbers of public servants are direct employees of the central departments, others of the local authority; the former are paid out of the Exchequer, the latter from the local Rate Fund (itself subsidized from parliamentary sources). While there are all manner of reasons for our particular demarcation between central and local government—with the nature of these we are not here concerned— whether a public servant is remunerated by the Treasury or County Hall ought not as such to influence the size of his reward : The matter

[1] See pp. 265–6 and p. 277 ff.
[2] See p. 272 and ff.
[3] cf. pp. 337–8 *ante*.

is not akin to differences in ability-to-pay due to genuine economic factors. Yet there is evidence that pay-packets are so affected,[1] and while civil servants may feel hemmed in at times by the dead hand of the Treasury, when it comes to the subject of cash this dead hand has—pay pauses apart—been rather more forthcoming than the empty hand of the local authorities; it is the Treasury which has been the more accommodating paymaster. In so far then as the more modest level of local government remuneration is the incidental by-product of the country's constitutional arrangements, this can be viewed as an accidental feature of the national salary structure.

Again, in the case of doctors, standards seem to depend in considerable measure on where the individual happens to work, i.e. whether he is engaged in the National Health, the Civil, or the school medical, service. It is not that his income as a school doctor is lower than in the Civil Service medical class, and inferior in the latter as compared with the National Health Service by virtue of economic considerations. It would appear rather that as important as that X is a doctor and as decisive as the degree of undermanning in the field he serves, is the fact that he is a local authority/Civil Service/National Health Service man, each of which has somehow acquired an 'appropriate level' of remuneration.

One qualification is called for. Just as there are different sectors in the medical profession, so within each of these sectors are there differences of skill and *expertize*. Hence one reason why school doctors are financially worse off than their opposite numbers in general practice could be that—apart from their lighter work-load—first-class medicos are not being sought for looking after school children's health. That thus bluntly expressed such an explanation would prove distasteful, is not necessarily significant: A local authority could hardly advertise its readiness to recruit less-than-the-best to its school medical staff, but it may nevertheless be tacitly understood that such will do, and that the lower salary offered reflects this 'gentlemen's agreement'. To the extent that this is so—to verify, one would have to penetrate authorities' collective unconscious —the constitutional factor is of less weight.

The problem of delimiting with precision the sphere of individual public services again has had its side effects. Thus judges of the Supreme Court are paid out of the Consolidated Fund; their remuneration can be increased only by Act of Parliament. Judicial officers on the other hand, such as official referees to whom the trial of questions arising in civil proceedings before the High Court may be entrusted, also have definite judicial functions: They have been jocularly described as dealing with those cases that are too difficult

[1] cf. pp. 290–1 *ante*.

for the judges.[1] However, for administrative purposes they belong to Whitehall, so that their salaries are raised whenever those of senior civil servants are. Though High Court judges have been expected to display a stoic indifference to the shrinking of their incomes relative to those in the world outside, they may yet have looked askance at the narrowing of the gap between themselves and their junior partners in the same enterprise.

A further illustration may be cited from the organization of the country's educational services. As we saw, training colleges in England and Wales are the responsibility of the Minister of Education, while the universities are outside his jurisdiction. In consequence, the personnel employed in these two types of institution belong to quite separate species: A lecturer instructing would-be teachers in a university education department will, for example, qualify for occupational family allowances, but one doing so within the confines of a training college will not. The latter on the other hand—like all teachers under the Ministry of Education—has a much bigger voice in matters of salary negotiation than has been accorded to academics.

Another type of accidental effect derives from the varying strength and structure of trade unions and professional associations, and from the imprint of these factors on joint negotiating arrangements. Thus—reverting for a moment to the wider wages front—we find organizations such as those affiliated to the Confederation of Shipbuilding and Engineering Unions catering for complete crafts; they conclude bargains with employers' federations which, in broad terms, set the pace for (say) engineering workers and electricians wherever these ply their trade. Looking at other occupations common to many industries, however, there is no analogous basic standard; cleaners, it is reasonable to hope, are employed in every factory but there is no such thing as a national cleaner's rate. Similarly, clerical staffs have no nation-wide salary, there being no all-embracing clerks' union/employers' federation. While there are important bodies in this sphere such as NALGO, the Civil Service Clerical Association and the Clerical and Administrative Workers' Union, these have not—severally or jointly—acquired the necessary hegemony.

Just as the span of the bargaining umbrella differs for individual occupations, so it does for broad groups. In the gas industry, for instance, the bulk of clerico-administrative staff and of engineering technical and professional personnel have been placed under a single negotiating body and hence covered by the same collective agreement. In electricity supply, by contrast, these two categories have

[1] 14 February 1951, 170 HL Deb., 317.

been treated quite separately for purposes of salary determination. The reason for this is apparently that at the time of nationalization there already existed, in the case of electricity, the Electrical Power Engineers' Association organizing technical workers, while in gas no analogous 'technical' union had found a foothold: Following nationalization it was thus decided to set up a National Joint Council for Gas Staffs comprising both clerico-administrative and technical/professional employees (below a stipulated level of seniority). The fact, therefore, that in gas the pay of an engineer and an administrator have been assimilated and moved together, while in electricity they have been 'organically' quite unrelated,[1] may be ascribed to the peculiarities of trade union configuration having in turn become perpetuated in collective bargaining machinery.

Let it be added that our contention is not that the development of trade unionism as such is a matter of 'accident'. The strength of a trade union is clearly a function of the degree of industrial concentration, of divergent rates of technological change and of the overall prosperity of industries; it is likewise a function of, say, political and ideological factors. The point we are trying to make is merely that, irrespective of what causes have produced what unions of what strength at a given point of time, their incidence has given rise to certain alignments and non-alignments which, in terms of the pay structure, are fortuitous.

The presence of particular unions at the crucial moment when collective bargaining arrangements take shape is of course also a question of the antiquity of services. As stated in Chapter 18, there is a tendency to a closer grouping of different types of personnel where a field is relatively new. This, for instance, may explain why the BBC managed to evolve a common grading scheme covering alike 'programme', (non-manual) engineering and administrative staff, the Corporation having developed its own system of job evaluation by means of which the salaries of these very heterogeneous categories have been equated.

In addition to the occupational dimension, the span of the bargaining umbrella also has a spatial one; as we saw previously, the domain of the several public service salary patterns varies in so far as the parts of the British Isles are concerned. Thus a pay increase for clerks agreed upon by the National Joint Council for Local Authorities' Administrative, Professional, Technical and Clerical Services will affect England and Wales only; a similar deal concluded by the National Health Service Administrative and Clerical Staffs Council will extend also to Scotland, but an analogous directive from H.M.

---

[1] Though 'organically' unrelated, an increase granted to one may nonetheless have led to a 'sympathetic' rise for the other.

Treasury's Lords Commissioners will warm the hearts of Ulster, Scottish and English clerks. While in this instance the collective bargaining set-up simply mirrors the constitutional position, it is an interesting point whether such constitutional frontiers need necessarily be reproduced in negotiating structures: Thus in the case of the public health services, standard rates exist throughout Great Britain equally relating to medical, dental and nursing personnel in English and Scottish local authorities. For the great majority of other local government officers, however, there are distinct collective bargaining and salary schemes north and south of the border.

Elements of 'accident' can also be detected in some of the mechanics of the various negotiating machines. Thus—pay pauses apart—non-industrial Government servants have the Civil Service Arbitration Tribunal ready at hand, while the majority of other public employees have recourse to national arbitral bodies: In the early post-war period, we may add, arbitration played a significant role in settling remuneration in the public salaried sector.[1] In the case of teachers, however, there has hitherto been no similar body to whom disputes could be referred,[2] though if arbitration is a proper adjunct of the machinery of collective bargaining, one might possibly have expected it to be available all round. Another respect in which education has been unique is that only in that sphere has it been normal for the period of currency to be formally inscribed into the collective agreement: While the stipulating of such a fixed term has a great deal to commend it, the case for it hardly rests on the degree of formalization of the bargaining process—which appears to be one of the main reasons why the practice is met with in the world of Burnham alone. We may add that similar chance divergences are found in matters such as the measure of retrospection or the method of assimilation when new agreements are being introduced; here what are on the face of them trivial procedural discrepancies, may make quite a sizeable difference in terms of £ s. d.

The accidental impact on the public service salary structure of constitutional factors, the particular set-up of the organs of administration or of trade union and collective bargaining arrangements—of which a few examples have been given—have by and large meant that various differentials, alignments and practices have crystallized for which, as far as relative levels of remuneration are concerned, there is no very clear basis. The element of accident, moreover, is cumulative in that territories having once become delimi-

---

[1] This may be seen from the detailed references given in Part I, although the method of effecting settlements has not been indicated in each case.

[2] Although third-party assistance has on occasion been secured by roundabout means: see e.g. p. 85 *ante*.

ted, they develop their own idiosyncrasies—reinforced by the tendency to complexity discussed previously. In the absence of a policy of co-ordination, however, such proliferation is bound to lead to anomalies--rendered more irksome because the frontiers dividing the several pay patterns themselves contain a fortuitous element.

This is not to suggest that the world will come to a premature end because there are complexities, chance features and anomalies in Britain's public service salary structure. Nor are the latter altogether surprising; they are part of what Professor Sargant Florence has so aptly called the 'criss-cross interlacing of occupation and industry'.[1] Again, while we have been heavily critical of the richness of individual pay patterns, there have also been major improvements. If the Civil Service grade structure is still highly intricate, it is much less so than in 1939 when—to quote but one example— chaos reigned in the professional and technical sphere. Similarly, though we have carped at certain arrangements in the upper regions of local government, prior to 1946 national standards of remuneration were altogether non-existent, while several further illustrations were given in Part I of measures taken during the 'forties and 'fifties with a view to streamlining and simplification. However, what is important is that the trend to rationalization is not universal; while some opportunities have been taken, more have been missed. Maturity may also mean a move in the reverse direction; positive zeal in the elaboration of employment conditions is not unknown— though unmistakably this testifies also to the fund of energy and good will devoted to the subject from all sides of the bargaining table.

On the whole, then, it would be rash to assume that, given time only, all will be well—and there are a number of additional considerations. Thus even though, on a long view, there has been progress *within* individual salary schemes, there has been comparatively little as *between* the public services, and while prevailing inconsistencies may not be surprising, this does not detract from their nuisance value in the context of pay negotiation. Taking, for example, the problems of 'relativity' which loom so large, in so far as these must be with us, they should at any rate owe their presence to economic factors only. Thus where a shortage of labour makes it essential to reward a particular group at a level higher than that called for by the intrinsic characteristics of the post, the disgruntlement this may generate in 'comparable' quarters may not be wholly avoidable. But to the extent that friction is due merely to the multiplicity of arrangements and to the freezing of accidental distinctions into a

[1] P. Sargant Florence, *Labour* (Hutchinson's University Library, n.d.), p. 14.

permanent constituent of salary structure, it is an unnecessary irritant. Secondly, though in the preceding discussion we have primarily confined ourselves to the more structural aspects of remuneration, the fortuitous features found are not, basically, unrelated to the phenomenon considered in our last chapter, when we mentioned the somewhat arbitrary way in which traditional notions—the elusive elements of demand and supply prices—have secured a niche in salary determination. Again, evidence of a certain *ad hoc*ness of approach can be discerned in some of the wider matters of principle —which brings us to our next topic.

IV

The question of the criteria which ought to bear on the pay of public employees is a difficult one. This is, first, because of the existence of different kinds of public services; though one cannot avoid talking in terms of the commercial and the non-commercial ones, this is in some respects an over-simplification. Secondly, in the case of the latter, some of the factors shaping the magnitude of private employers' demand prices are lacking; in the Civil, local government and National Health services neither the productivity nor the profit yardstick of wage-determination is available. While under post-war inflationary conditions these have likewise been only semi-operative elsewhere, the total absence of these ordinary measuring rods is one of the reasons no doubt why in the public services the need has been felt for some guide by reference to which rewards might be laid down. Thirdly, when we come to the nationalized industries, the fact that the conflict between their commercial and their public character has been clearly resolved, has had its ramifications in the sphere of remuneration. Finally, there is the dilemma arising from the Government's simultaneous role of guardian of the national interest and of employer.

We shall not be able to explore these questions exhaustively; some observations, however, are called for. First, we may take the principle that public servants should not qualify for the top prizes; in other words, that they ought to be ready to make some financial sacrifice in deference to the 'public service' motive. This probably commands wide support, and this writer certainly would not wish to quarrel with it. In practice, however, its operation is somewhat arbitrary because the maxim is administered in the light of the notion that where, constitutionally speaking, a service is purveying commercial or industrial goods, we cannot expect the same sense of vocation from its employees as where it is not. Yet the duties of an accountant in the Civil Service are as 'commercial' as are those of one in the Coal Board, while a staff welfare officer in the latter is as

O

'social' as his opposite number in Whitehall. The matter would of course be different if the nationalized industries were full-blooded commercial enterprises, able to offer higher pay out of accumulated profits but, as we saw in Chapter 20, neither *de jure* nor *de facto* have they hitherto been profit-making in this sense.

The uneven weighting given to the 'public service' motive as between its two main halves must also be seen against the fact that the constitutional status of branches of the public sector is itself partly accidental.[1] Thus the Post Office, according to the nature of its functions, is of a piece with the other nationalized industries, but as for historical reasons it is (and remains despite recent legislative changes) a Department of the Crown, it is manned by civil servants whose rates in the upper reaches are supposed to be below those of their counterparts in the public corporations. Again, the personnel employed in a local authority transport department are, industrially, engaged in the same field as those working for British Railways or nationalized London Transport; the service which is being produced and the criteria of success which must be applied are essentially similar.

It is thus not altogether self-evident that the nationalized industries must, *ipso facto*, offer levels of pay superior to those in central or local government. This is not to imply that standards in the national corporations are over-generous, nor that they should be satisfied with second-class manpower because all that 'publicness' calls for is a kind of cosy inefficiency. Clearly, the public corporations must seek to attract the best men for the job—although, so also should the non-commerical public services. It is an interesting reflection, however, that if for this purpose a higher rate of remuneration is necessary in the former field than in the latter, this is not solely due—as seems frequently to be taken for granted—to the laws of supply and demand: It may also be because in the nationalized industries we have deliberately played down the value of the non-monetary rewards of public service thus, as it were, compelling recruits to raise their supply price.

That supply prices can be affected in this manner is illustrated by the bar, whose senior members willingly renounce large sums in order to accept judgeships. Such posts are regarded as promotion in spite of the pecuniary loss involved, because in this instance the dignity of office and the public service motive are powerfully operative—and, one must add, have not been undermined by the assump-

---

[1] We are mentioning the matter here rather than in the preceding section because, unlike the examples there quoted, the difference in remuneration between commercial and non-commercial public services has become something of a question of principle.

tion that they are not. In the case of the national corporations, however—where 'service' considerations had already been assigned an inferior place—they were dealt a further blow by the appointment in 1961 of a chairman for British Railways at a salary of full commercial dimensions, and thus widely out of step with all other incomes then available in the public sector. This one action may well have significantly augmented the figure for which future nationalized industry chairmen are prepared to come forward—with inevitable repercussions all down the line. If so, this should not then be automatically attributed to the lack of competent persons ready to forgo financial gain to work in a commercial public enterprise: It may be as much because the public service motive has been treated with a certain contempt, with the implication that in this sphere only lesser breeds can be expected to be actuated by it. The episode is an example of *ad hoc*ness causing problems on the public sector pay front, though it is also a symptom of that deeper conflict between the commercial and the public character of the nationalized industries. That conflict, clearly, is a very big issue—requiring attention on general grounds—but one beyond the scope of this discussion.

In so far as the more limited topic of ability-to-pay is concerned, there would seem to be no reason why this should not be one of the criteria of reward in the nationalized industries; it is not implicit in 'publicness' that economic considerations must be ignored. This is, however, subject to the qualification that financial capacity can only be a yardstick if it proves possible satisfactorily to establish it; while the public corporations do not have a free hand in their pricing and kindred policies, their ostensible ability or inability-to-pay must be somewhat artificial. How much commercial freedom they are to be accorded is part of the wider question just referred to; what is pertinent here is that if some way can be found of isolating, for accounting purposes, the nationalized industries' social etc. obligations from their commercial activities, then their economic fortunes could have a bearing on their standards of remuneration. To say that, if feasible, this would be desirable does not, however, imply any judgment on the broader problem itself—nor does it necessarily lend support to the view that a maximum detachment from the rest of the public services is a prerequisite for nationalized industries' efficiency. It might also be added that taking note of ability-to-pay does not, as we see it, require inconsistency in the rewards accruing in the highest strata of the public sector.

Let us now turn to the non-commercial public services, taking the position prior to the 1961 pay-pause; the dispensation that will supersede the latter's conclusion belongs, at the time of writing, in any case to the speculative. Here we find that civil servants' salaries have been settled under the Priestley formula of 'fair comparison', though those of local government personnel, NHS workers, probation officers and so on have not been fixed under any principle. The first question that arises is whether 'fair comparison' makes sufficient allowance for the scarcity factor. We have earlier enlarged on the importance of remuneration being equitable, and take the line that the Priestley Commission rendered a real service by their official recognition of 'fairness' as a criterion of reward. At the same time, the latter cannot monopolize pay determination and it is not clear whether, even in the Civil Service, demand and supply should be assigned quite so secondary a role. If, on the other hand, fairness is accepted as the sole test, then there is no reason for not applying that yardstick also to local government workers, National Health staffs, teachers, probation officers, firemen, etc., all of whom are similarly engaged in the non-commercial wing of the public sector.

The second major question posed by 'fair comparison' is its inflationary implications; indeed, the Priestley formula has been strongly criticized on this score. For one of its novel features was that it broke the aloofness which Civil Service salaries were formerly meant to maintain *vis-à-vis* the wages and the general economic front. Thus the Tomlin Commission of 1929–31 had proposed that rewards should reflect 'the long-term trend both in wage levels and the economic conditions of the country',[1] and they frowned, for example, on direct adjustments to the cost of living, regarding it as undesirable that the conditions of government servants should be related too closely to factors of a temporary character. *A propos* of a claim in 1955 for improved pay for National Health nursing and midwifery staff, the management side voiced similar sentiments.[2] Under the Priestley formula, however, such aloofness was no longer required. The Commission's view was definitely that remuneration should move by comparison with current outside rates rather than long-run trends, while in times of unusually marked and rapid fluctuations a central settlement would be best.[3]

This process of alignment with outside developments was given an interesting twist by an agreement concluded in December 1960 between the official and staff sides of the Civil Service National Whitley Council. This document subsequently met with considerable opposition from some of the individual staff associations, and had not been ratified when the Chancellor announced his pay-pause in mid-1961. However, it deserves mention in view of the radical proposal it contained that fluctuations in the official Index of Wage

[1] *Royal Commission on the Civil Service*, Cmd. 3909 (HMSO 1931), para. 308.

[2] Industrial Court Award No. 2560 (HMSO 1955), p. 6.

[3] *Priestley Report*, op. cit., para. 132.

Rates were to become part of the built-in machinery for fixing the remuneration of all non-industrial civil servants up to and including the level of the administrative class principal's maximum.[1] In brief, the agreement[2] provided that in the November of any year in which the Index of Weekly Wage Rates had increased by five or more points over the figure occasioning the previous central settlement, there would be a review as to whether a further central pay bargain was justified. This method was to go hand in hand with that specifically favoured by Priestley—i.e. revisions, grade by grade, in the light of the detailed findings of the Civil Service Pay Research Unit, though such surveys were only to be carried out quinquennially for each staff category. The agreement is noteworthy in that it would have forged a link between the salaries of an important group of public servants and the Index of Wages Rates based, as we saw in Chapter 19,[3] on the recognized rates of pay of 'manual wage-earners', from which trends in clerical, technical and administrative remuneration are actually excluded.

The agreement lays bare what is doubtless one of the most controversial aspects of our topic—i.e. whether, in a period in which wages have advanced much in excess of the real growth of the economy, public servants should participate in the general 'scramble'. First, it should be pointed out that the linkage to the index envisaged in the 1960 document was not a rigid one: The commitment to embark on a review was not one by the Treasury automatically to agree to a central settlement. Secondly, as previously indicated,[4] wage rates are rising less fast than total earnings; further, in the most recent years salaries in manufacturing industry have in fact increased more steeply than wages, though the opposite is true of the post-war period as a whole. Hence a broad pegging to the Index of Wage Rates could be less inflationary than sole reliance on the current incomes of the semi-jilted 'fair comparison' outside analogues postulated by the Royal Commission. Nonetheless, the 1960 agreement[5] can be seen as an attempt to take fairness even beyond the Priestley formula, the pay pause ushered in only seven months later constituting a complete *volte-face*.

As for the question itself, it is of course a truism that the Government is responsible for the soundness of the country's economic policy, and one facet of that responsibility is to prevent inflation—whether of the 'demand-pull' or 'cost-push' variety. In view of the

---

[1] £2,325 per annum in December 1960 (national rate, excluding London weighting).

[2] For full text see *Whitley Bulletin*, February 1961, pp. 21–2.

[3] See p. 299 *ante*.   [4] See p. 312 *ante*,

[5] Which, while not implemented, had full Treasury approval.

size of the public sector, it is therefore what can be regarded as either a duty or a temptation for any government to use public servants both to lessen the absolute amount of wage-induced inflation in the system, and as an instrument making for restraint on the wider industrial front. Some such course actually seems to commend itself as an answer to the general problem posed by wages under full employment, discussed in the last chapter:[1] For as there pointed out, it would obviate the need for many of the unpopular innovations inseparable from the institution of a comprehensive plan for wages and other incomes.

It is here felt that to apply a wages policy rigidly in the public services, with the remainder of the economy subject, primarily, to guidance and exhortation only, is not a satisfactory remedy for the ills it might be intended to cure. It can be objected to, first, because it would involve a measure of exploitation on the part of the state of its position *qua* employer. And since it would have to be imposed in the face of fierce opposition—as demonstrated by the 1961 'pause'—it will not be convincing to defend it as a necessity arising out of the voluntary nature of present-day industrial relations. Rather would it be a case of abrogating that principle in one particular sphere, in which compulsion happened to be convenient. If restraint is required, public employees must certainly bear their share; they cannot be exempt from whatever burden circumstances may make imperative. Equally, however, they ought not to shoulder more than that share. While there can be no doubt that remuneration in the public services should take full account of the national interest—i.e. that pay revisions ought to be geared to the growth of the country's real wealth—this must, as we see it, be part of a wider policy covering all types of income throughout the economy.

Equity apart, there is a simple economic reason why a discriminatory wages policy is unlikely to succeed in the long run. For granted that the labour market is far from perfect, at the same time the forces of supply and demand are not dead. Hence if—as cannot be ruled out[2]—the private sector were to show but little respect for the 'norm' of economically sustainable wage advances, while that norm was strictly enforced in the public services, relative rewards in the latter would in time lag seriously behind. As a result, there would ensue a gradual exodus of public employees in search of more fertile pastures, and if the Government wished to continue to man its schools and hospitals, its fire brigades and ordnance factories, its administrative departments and postal services, it would have to raise remuneration to the going rate—whether the latter was inflationary or not. There is

[1] See p. 366 and ff.
[2] cf. p. 370 *ante*.

also the point that several categories—policemen, science teachers, midwives, to name some of the more obvious—are themselves in chronically short supply, in effect necessitating 'above-norm' increases. As these would presumably have to be offset by corresponding savings from within the public sector wage-and-salary bill, this would merely hasten the day when the whole of the latter would have to be hauled back to the standards decreed by the predominant partner in the labour market.

A partial wages policy is thus not only unlikely to achieve the objective of keeping the overall advance in personal incomes in line with the growth of total production; it may not even narrow that gap except for limited periods. The extent of such temporary relief would, among other things, depend on whether the scheme comprised the entire public sector—i.e. including the nationalized industries—or its non-commercial half alone; in the latter event, some of the elements of 'accident' previously referred to may vividly come into focus. Either type of discrimination would create very grave problems and, it is here believed, could not provide an enduring basis for regulating public sector remuneration. Hence if money incomes have outstripped, and the indications are that they will continue to outstrip, the real growth of the national product, the problem must be tackled—as we tried to show in Chapter 20—by steps designed to bring the two into balance over the economy as a whole. Permanently to use public servants as a tool of policy, because more comprehensive measures are unpalatable, would seem neither equitable nor economically feasible in the long run.

By the same token, however, fairness ought not to monopolize pay determination in the public sector any more than elsewhere in the economy; considerations of demand and supply should be permitted to modify the 'fair rate for the job'. As we see it, demand would *inter alia* include an assessment of the needs of the service or industry in accordance with a programme of national priorities, while the intrinsic characteristics of posts would, in turn, be evaluated on a less hit-and-miss basis than hitherto. We shall enlarge on this presently. As for the distinction in the criteria deemed appropriate for non-commercial and commercial public servants, this is not here favoured in so far as it rests on artificial assumptions regarding the sacrifice due to the 'public service' motive. Where there are actual divergences in economic factors as between groups of public employees, these should be taken into account, but the aim might be to prevent preconceived notions from either inflating or deflating demand and supply prices.

V

In this section we venture to throw out a few (more or less) concrete suggestions bearing on salaries and employment conditions in the public services. In general terms, these spring from the quest for 'more rationality', which, as we have sought to show earlier, has become a simple necessity in the field of pay determination. More specifically, they are based on what, despite considerable divergences between its component branches, is the broad unity of the public sector—a unity of which we may be increasingly reminded in the period ahead.

First, then, the aim of policy might be that matters such as hours, superannuation arrangements, sick leave provisions, the cost-of-living element in provincial differentiation,[1] the availability of arbitration and its procedures, and so on be standardized over the whole public sector, except where some specific reason exists against this course. Thus it is not suggested that school children or university students should be exposed to the ministrations of their mentors for the full length of the official working week. Likewise, where duties are especially strenuous, hours might be less than where they are not. Again, it makes sense that policemen and prison officers retire earlier than other groups,[2] while the service conditions of pilots would of necessity require individual treatment. Complete uniformity then is neither possible nor desirable, but standardization might well be the rule where there are no clear grounds to the contrary.

That such standardization is practicable is indicated by its actually having been effected in a few instances. Thus the hours, overtime and sick leave arrangements introduced on nationalization by the (then) British Electricity Authority were identical with those operative in local government. Similarly, probation officers have been brought within the latter's schemes of superannuation, while travelling expenses and subsistence allowances accrue on Civil Service lines. If it has been feasible to assimilate probation to local government in the one respect and to central government in the other, are there any insuperable obstacles to extending the process to these two major fields themselves?

It may be held that a general policy of aligning service conditions is putting undue strain on the rate of pay, thus exaggerating the 'cash nexus': If people can be attracted to a job by means other than its pecuniary reward, why should one not thus appeal to prospective candidates? In itself this is a valid point. However, many of the dis-

---

[1] Area differentials to deal with regional labour shortages are covered by our subsequent discussion of 'scarcity supplements'.

[2] Though the resultant greater benefit derived from their pension is a net advantage, to be set against the disadvantages of their calling.

crepancies between the public services' conditions of employment, etc., are purely fortuitous; they have not been instituted with recruitment problems in mind. Moreover, it is doubtful whether staffs —the police is the most conspicuous example—reckon their perquisites at anything like their true economic cost. On balance, therefore, alignment might be of material benefit in terms both of grievances removed and effort saved,[1] while in any such synthesis the opportunity could be taken to combine the best features from the various existing versions. The avoidance of the blurring of the real net advantages of occupations should, in turn, make pay scales more effective in doing their work.

This brings us to remuneration itself and here, it seems to us, a generous measure of streamlining of salary patterns is desirable, although the precise need for this clearly varies from service to service. We are reinforced in this conclusion by the fact that a sizeable proportion of public employees receive incomes between what are not really very wide limits and that, accordingly, an unrestricted number of differentials cannot be meaningfully accommodated. In the nursing hierarchy, for instance, a large cadre of tiers is sharing a quite small 'differential potential'.

What we are thinking of, basically, is the elimination of excessive refinements of all kinds. In one respect, this would involve an extension merely of what is already happening; a considerable 'equating' of responsibility is anyhow taking place. Thus officers in the same Civil Service grade may be carrying out such dissimilar functions as audit, local office management, purchasing, staff inspection or accounting, while several quite separate professions have been merged into the Civil Service 'works group'. Yet in other instances, differences which can only strike the outsider as less substantial have solidified into distinct classes or grades, making their incumbents watch each other jealously lest the Treasury err in the allocation of its bounty to the extent of plus/minus £10 per annum. In proposing simplification, therefore, we are not unmindful of the large number of heterogeneous jobs performed by public servants; here as elsewhere the occupational structure is highly complex. But seeing that some fields have been able to align posts on a much bigger scale than others—thereby reducing the frictions over 'parity' at any rate within their own organization—our point is that it is feasible to generalize the process on the pattern, say, of the local government APT and

---

[1] It would be interesting to know the number of staff directly or indirectly engaged in the administration of the public services' superannuation systems alone. Statistics for FSSU—under which a new policy is taken out each year for each don until he has reached his career maximum—might in themselves be revealing.

'lettered grades' schemes. At least as important, however, is the
application of streamlining to the structure, and method of computing, of allowances—as indeed to all other types of complexity of
which a few examples were given earlier.

There are of course the pitfalls of an 'either-or' mentality. While
in many respects there could, with advantage, be more standardization, in others we need not be afraid of differences. This is where our
last stricture of the public service salary structure comes in: The
malaise from which it suffers—though we would emphasize that no
uniqueness is being claimed for it—can perhaps be summed up as a
profusion of arrangements based on semi-irrelevancies, with an
absence of differentials where such are called for. The most important
illustration of this is the timidity in introducing differentials for
economic ends.

In some instances the scarcity of particular types of worker may
call for, or be capable of alleviation by, non-monetary measures. The
potential contribution of married women to the teacher shortage is in
this category, and it is interesting to ponder how difficult it has proved
to tap this source at a time when the provision of part-time facilities
for hospital consultants has been a matter of course. In other cases,
action on the housing front might ease recruitment problems, as
might more vocational guidance at the school-leaving stage. But
since such measures have their limitations and may, for one reason
or another, be altogether inapplicable, we venture to moot a system
of allowances granted specifically on economic grounds.

In order that such a system can be worked in with the requirements
of equity, simplicity and consistency—here regarded as the other
essential ingredients of a rational pay pattern—it is necessary to con-
ceive of a rate of remuneration as consisting of two distinct parts.
The first would be designed as reward for the intrinsic characteristics
of posts: Each public service occupation would be analysed in the
light of a centralized system of job analysis and would, over and
above the universal minimum or 'living wage', be rated for skill,
responsibility, training and qualifications, arduousness and all other
relevant advantages and disadvantages. The only criterion for determining this part of remuneration would be the attributes of the job;
the aim would be 'fairness' and nothing but.

To the extent, however, that standards are fixed by methods of
job analysis, they reflect the demands of economics only in the indirect sense that the worth placed on individual characteristics is
itself influenced by the question of scarcity. But the evaluation of
skill, responsibility or particular qualifications is not solely a function of the latter; while it responds to its impact, the process is a
subtle and long-term one. Further, there is the crucial point that

economic circumstances must be expected to diverge from field to field; a system of standard prices, such as job evaluation would yield, cannot deal with such variation. What we have in mind, therefore, is that the second element in remuneration should be devoted exclusively to a monetary weighting of economic factors.[1] This would take the form of supplements which would be in line with overall economic priorities, with—where not in conflict with these (and where applicable)—ability-to-pay, and which would take account also of any other economic matters such as, say, particular regional shortages. Fairness would not enter into this part of reward or, as was put in our last chapter, it would have to be regarded as fair that this part of remuneration was unfair.

It is fundamental to the idea that this 'scarcity supplement' be treated as a separate entity; in other words, it must remain a distinct payment and not be merged into the general rate of remuneration. If two grades qualify for the same salary in the light of the intrinsic characteristics of their posts, but if the demand-supply situation differed, the supplement would accrue to the scarce category only. Similarly, comparisons between two otherwise comparable occupations would be confined to the basic standards; the supplement would have to be left out of the equation. Though the overall level of reward for the two groups would diverge, provided the why and the wherefore were known and the addition explicitly granted on economic grounds, no objection reasonably could—and in time, perhaps, less would—be taken to it.

One of our main motives for these proposals stems from what, in our last chapter, we referred to as a major cause of complication in the sphere of wage determination—i.e. the wholesale mix-up in the comparisons figuring in pay claims between 'intrinsic job' factors on the one hand and more strictly economic ones on the other. It is to a considerable extent because of this confusion that claims have been, first, such time-consuming affairs and, secondly, such inflationary affairs and, thirdly, only very imperfectly responsive to economic requirements. The familiar spectacle witnessed throughout the post-war period—both on the salaries and the wages front—is that grade A obtains a rise because, say, it is in short supply or because the industry is booming and wishes to expand. Whereupon B—comparable with A as regards skill or duties, or looked upon as so com-

---

[1] The question of what is and what is not an economic factor is an intricate one, and our distinction is in some ways crude. But it would seem to correspond to a *de facto* distinction in so far as pay claims are concerned. For example, increases granted for reasons of undermanning, higher productivity or an enhanced ability-to-pay would generally rank as economic in character—in contrast to those conceded on need or value-of-work grounds, unrelated to a shortage of the particular grade.

parable on grounds of status or custom, but not working under equally favourable circumstances—promptly asks and usually secures similar treatment. Whereupon remuneration has gone up all round, though grade A remains understaffed and so on.

Under the scheme here envisaged all clerks in the public services with analogous qualifications and responsibilities would enjoy the same basic rate, though this would be adjusted for such conditions of employment in the field concerned as it was not practicable or desirable to standardize. Supplements would then be paid over and above this rate to deal, say, with the dearth of clerks in London or other large cities. Similarly, all police constables would have one basic (and consolidated) standard, but supplements—of such varying amounts as was necessary—would be at the disposal of police forces to enable them to be brought up to establishment in each area. The same basic 'price' would be used for purposes of the constabularies maintained by British Railways and other public undertakings.

The supplements would also be designed to cope with the well-known conundrum of differential scarcity due to occupational rather than regional causes. The classic case here is that of teachers : Though all teachers are scarce, the problem is particularly acute in the field of science and mathematics. Under the present proposals, these latter would be eligible for a supplement over and above the basic standard applicable to their species as such—in which event schools' science and mathematics departments might get a little nearer to being adequately staffed. This is not to imply that the problem can be entirely solved via a system of financial incentives, though the question of non-monetary measures needed to increase the national supply of science, etc. graduates is outside our terms of reference. Nor is it to deny that the prospects of teachers as a whole require revision ; we have previously discussed some of the factors that have helped to keep them at a low level. But for some time to come, the shortage of science and mathematics teachers is likely to exceed that for the generality of the profession ; as there is a universal consensus that these subjects ought to be taught, it is difficult to see how a special differential can be objected to. It is here that the form of any weighting may be important. For the advantage of a separate evaluation of the economic factor is that, unlike a higher basic scale, it cannot reasonably be held to reflect on the 'intrinsic worth' of one teacher as against another. In the universities—for whom the same medicine is recommended—there is a pattern of children's allowances under which £50 per child per annum is available to help the family man meet his commitments, and no one in his senses begrudges the *paterfamilias* however many increments he may add to his income in this way. A supplement granted to a scarce grade to enable the com-

munity to meet its commitments—or simply to allow the economic
system to function—should be equally acceptable.

One of our underlying aims is thus that the effort to satisfy that
whole complex of motives compounded of value-of-work, relativity
and status considerations should cease to be at loggerheads with the
economic purposes of the pay structure. The hope is that status,
etc. would become attached to the basic rate only; the economic
supplement would be freely known to be just that. It would be
neutral 'intrinsic worth-' and prestige-wise, and would not reflect on
those enjoying it one way or the other. There is no reason why it
should not be so regarded, seeing that all manner of other additions
are already similarly neutral. One crucial addendum is, however,
called for. If there has been opposition on the part of the profession
to a formal differential for, say, teachers of science and mathematics,
this has also been due to the very legitimate fear that such differentials can be used to depress the remuneration of the generality of the
profession. This is a fundamental problem to which a solution will
have to be found : We can only expect a greater toleration of economic
unfairness, if somehow or other we manage to ensure that such
tolerance will not be exploited to the detriment of those displaying it.

Our scheme is an attempt to, as it were, marry economics and
equity which, as mentioned in our last chapter, we believe to be one
of the basic problems of wages policy. On the one hand, it clearly
entails putting up with more economic unfairness. And in so far as
it involves the elimination of excessive grading refinements, it also
necessitates taking a broad view of the 'plus/minus £10' type of issue,
the preoccupation with which—unless it be purely bureaucratic—
arises from what may perhaps be regarded as an exaggerated sense of
justice. But there would be many compensations. Thus such inequities as that university lecturers qualify for children's allowances but
teachers do not, or that civil servants have a non-contributory superannuation scheme but local government personnel a contributory
one, would disappear. The elimination of these and similar anomalies
and the review of all the incidentals and accidentals with which
patterns of remuneration are blessed would lead, on balance, to fairer
no less than to simpler pay structures.

Further, the evaluation of the intrinsic characteristics of jobs would
provide the opportunity to settle basic rates themselves in a more
consistent and equitable manner—related, ideally, to the nature of
the job and nothing else. There is of course a major difficulty here.
For to the extent that our job analysis would be concerned with posts
ranging from, say, junior clerk to judge, the operation involves
weighting the attributes of wholly different types of employment :
Here the limitations of the technique become formidable, for in such

weighting profound social judgments enter into the picture to which, as normally practised, job evaluation gives no clue.[1]

Briefly, the dilemma is whether occupations should be evaluated taking the present social framework as rigidly given, or whether we should—in so far as such is possible—abstract from the latter and assess all posts *de novo*. On the one hand, if existing relativities are not to be departed from under any circumstances, then the labour is largely superfluous. On the other—unless it is to be wildly inflationary as regards undervalued occupations, or the whole of the difference shifted on to the scarcity supplements in the case of overvalued ones —we cannot simply ignore current levels of remuneration. In practice, therefore, some compromise would be required though—unless, after all, we would rather—there is no need to be completely bound by the *status quo*. For example, if an impartial appraisal of all the relevant facts should demonstrate that the services of nurses and probation officers are, for a variety of traditional and historical reasons, at present inadequately priced, this would call for rectification, but the latter could be put through gradually. Similarly, if some grade should emerge as perhaps somewhat overrated in the light of the work performed, this could be taken into account at subsequent pay revisions. That such modifications are feasible is shown by the fact that they already occur, except that currently it primarily depends on whether some third party happens to have been asked to investigate the matter. In the public services, one might add, such readjustments are fraught with at any rate far fewer obstacles than they would be in the private sector of the economy.

The evaluation of the intrinsic characteristics of posts can, it is believed, be effected through an application of the principles of job analysis, provided its potentialities are more boldly utilized—in other words, if there is no evading of what we have previously called the scrutiny of the more elusive elements of demand and supply prices. No absolute fairness can be claimed for the results: Standards of remuneration established by this method are merely the aggregate of a series of judgments; they are not right in some transcendental sense. Nor can they aspire to that degree of objectivity which the natural scientist may hope to achieve; such detachment is not to be attained in this field. But this does not matter for what, among other things, is unsatisfactory about current pay patterns is not the absence of the scientific but the presence of the arbitrary.

Nor is it the case that, because judgment is involved, agreement is inherently beyond reach. Perhaps this can be illustrated by drawing

[1] cf. B. Wootton, *The Social Foundations of Wage Policy* (Allen & Unwin, 1955), p. 147. For an illuminating, though critical, approach to job evaluation see ibid. pp. 143–9.

an analogy from another sphere—that of consumers' choice. It is a truism that the latter differ in their tastes and preferences; even if we hold the income variable constant, this will still be so. At the same time, after some article has been submitted to an impartial test by bodies such as the Consumers' Association or the Consumer Advisory Council, the extent to which shoppers will see eye to eye as to what constitutes a good buy will almost certainly be substantially increased. Though the analogy is far from perfect in that much bigger, more controversial and less easily testable issues are at stake, nonetheless an (as) unprejudiced (as possible) job analysis may similarly hope to command a broad measure of support for its findings as to the basic 'price' for different occupations. And a genuine effort to achieve such fair base rates may be worthwhile, one might stress, because fairness is a good in itself, because of the importance attached to it in the sphere of reward, and because there might then be a greater willingness to tolerate those inequities which have to be superimposed for reasons of economics.

It may be thought that a prescription of both job analysis and simplification conflict: It is certainly true that the application of the former is a complex process, and making allowance for promotion prospects and other unstandardized service conditions will add to the task. But such a comprehensive job analysis would, in essence, be a one-time operation; occupations would of course have to be re-examined in line with changes in job content, but it is not the case that the latter is in a constant state of flux in the majority of occupations, while variations in economic circumstances would, as indicated, be dealt with separately without details as to the nature of the work, etc. having to be marshalled each time remuneration was under review. Thus though the initial establishment of the core of the pay structure would be an undertaking of some considerable intricacy, if carried out with a view to fitting posts into a simplified system of grades, and if accompanied by a large-scale alignment of other conditions of employment, it could thereafter make many of the problems of pay determination a much less onerous assignment.

As these deliberations are drawing to a close, we might say a word also about a different type of objection likely to be raised against some of our suggestions. For the very thought of any inter-Service standardization will no doubt be distasteful to many; it will be held to spell rigidity and to smack of regimentation. This stricture would have to be taken seriously if present methods were flexible in result as well as in manner of negotiation and if, similarly, staffs were content to be 'unique' even when not in their immediate interest. But it is unusual to find associations proud of the distinction of having an unfavourable system of area differentials, or of working a longer

week or of receiving a smaller reward than their 'comparable' colleagues; everyone, in fact, is absorbed in an endeavour to do at least
as well as everyone else, obtain the same perquisites, enjoy the same
benefits. It would indeed be unnatural if it were otherwise but, in the
light of this, objection to a proposed shortcut to 'sameness'—in
matters where there are no real grounds for incongruities—is, if
understandable, not altogether convincing. Not least in terms of
flexibility, one might add, can standardization be of advantage, in
that it makes room for meaningful differentials by the elimination of
incidental and fortuitous ones.

In part, the opposition to rationalization would seem to spring
from what may perhaps be described as too great an attachment to
the *status quo:* Anomalies are known to exist, efforts are made at re-
dress, but the time-honoured right to create fresh ones is at the same
time insisted upon. But fondness for the customary is not the monopoly of anyone. One can discern it, possibly, in the tendency to appoint commissions of enquiry with restricted terms of reference, preventing a complete examination of the subject of their remit. Thus
the Priestley Commission was unable to pronounce on a whole
variety of matters such as structure, grading, recruitment, training
and promotion procedures, despite their close interrelation with the
question of salaries.[1] The Royal Commission on Equal Pay—limited
to a consideration of the implications of the claim, but not authorized
to make recommendations—is an earlier illustration.

Again, the Oaksey Committee of 1949 came to the conclusion that
a disproportionate amount of policemen's remuneration was reserved for their retirement, yet decided not to propose a change.
Further, standards which somehow have become established are
treated with a reverence not always deserved—as can be seen in the
pull exercised by the climate, which the meteorology of salary determination has allowed to settle on a profession. We have referred to
the effect of tradition in holding down the reward of teachers and
nurses: Taking the latter, despite the serious staff shortage, the many
inquests into their conditions and the improvements which certainly
have occurred under the Health Service, their pay remains at a meagre
level.[2] Much of what we have found to criticize in the public service

---

[1] '. . . we have found it extraordinarily difficult to examine and advise on the
pay rates of an organization so complex as the Civil Service without the opportunity of making positive proposals on these intimately related matters, and we
feel obliged to indicate the effect which the restricted nature of our terms of
reference has had on our attempt to fulfil our task': *Priestley Report,* op. cit.,
para. 55. The Commission devoted a special section (Chapter III) to the subject.

[2] The scale for staff nurses (general hospital) payable as from 1 January 1961
(men: 1 December 1960) was £525–£656 per annum.

salary structure can, in the last resort, be traced to too soft a spot for
the *status quo*.

Here the opportunity might be taken to remind the reader that—
as made clear earlier on—it has not been feasible and hence no attempt
has been made to consider all the problems of pay determination, or
to evaluate all the complex forces that have helped to shape the
public service salary structure. Accordingly, the writer has had to
make a choice, and inevitably this has fallen on those aspects which
seemed, in particular, to merit examination. There are of course
hazards in any less-than-complete investigation, and what should
perhaps be done by way of minimum antidote is to state the fact
without ambiguity. Thus if, in this chapter, we have urged that the
problem of scarcity be tackled more boldly, this has not been to imply
that economic factors have hitherto been ignored in the fixing of
salaries. Similarly, in going into the question of complexity and inconsistency and what we have called the element of 'accident' in the
national salary structure, we have in a sense dwelt on the 'patho-
logical' facets of the topic, but the conclusion must not be drawn that
these latter reign supreme. Without wishing in the least to shy away
from the diagnosis made or the remedies commended, this writer
would be the first to agree that much else remains to be said.

Our prescription, in a nutshell—and, again, we have not dealt with
all its ramifications—is for the evolution of a streamlined pattern of
public service salaries by a combination of job evaluation and
demand-and-supply, both working through the latter. Conceivably,
this admixture could have certain wider applications—for example,
in the context of a national wages policy the case for which was discussed in Chapter 20.[1] Our suggestions should well fit into such a
plan, for they represent an effort to apply to the pay structure itself
principles which—as we see it—would ultimately have to inform any
system of controlled wage advances. However, though accepting the
need for the latter on general grounds, the ideas here put forward for
the public services do not *per se* hinge upon the institution of an incomes policy—except that in its absence radical innovations are even
less likely of a place on the relevant agendas.

The barebones of our pay structure would start with a minimum
figure, below which no rate of reward would fall. To this would be
added an amount in respect of all the various intrinsic characteristics

[1] Ignoring all complications, one could e.g. visualize the total national wages
bill—and similarly its annual/periodic productivity-geared accretion—being
divided into two parts: One—the larger and 'fair' part—would accrue to the
working population on the basis of the intrinsic characteristics of jobs. The
second would consist of 'unfair' scarcity supplements, reinforced as necessary
by 'above-norm' increases, in which all relevant economic factors—national,
regional and plant—would be weighted.

of posts; there would be room for the recognition of merit, while a
system of 'scarcity supplements' would attune the end-product to
economic needs. Such a pattern might hope to fulfil the four functions of the wage of which Professor Sargant Florence speaks, namely
of being adequate to conduce to health and working capacity, fair in
counterbalancing the disadvantages of occupations and industries,
an incentive to efficiency and, further, that of securing the requisite
distribution of labour.[1] To which we must now add the national
interest as a crucial fifth dimension—requiring that the accretion to
personal incomes be kept in balance with the real growth of the
economy. No doubt some will question the wisdom of too much
order in this field, feeling that a less logical regime is more appropriate to the world of flesh and blood. Yet the claims of reason have
long been conceded in comparable departments of life; losses though
there have been, the gains have far outweighed them. When all is
said, the aim of a rational pattern of remuneration is nothing more
grandiose than to achieve more effectively the purposes for which it
exists.

[1] cf. Florence, op. cit., p. 107.

Index

[Compiled by Mrs J. Line]

For Product Safety Concerns and Information please contact our EU
representative GPSR@taylorandfrancis.com
Taylor & Francis Verlag GmbH, Kaufingerstraße 24, 80331 München, Germany

www.ingramcontent.com/pod-product-compliance
Lightning Source LLC
Chambersburg PA
CBHW071828270326
41929CB00013B/1927